Decentralization and Popular Democracy

Decentralization and Popular Democracy

Governance from Below in Bolivia

JEAN-PAUL FAGUET

The University of Michigan Press
Ann Arbor

First paperback edition 2013
Copyright © by the University of Michigan 2012
All rights reserved

Published in the United States of America by
The University of Michigan Press
Manufactured in the United States of America
♾ Printed on acid-free paper

2016   2015   2014   2013   5   4   3   2

A CIP catalog record for this book is available from the British Library.

Library of Congress Cataloging-in-Publication Data

Faguet, Jean-Paul.
    Decentralization and popular democracy : governance from below in
    Bolivia / Jean-Paul Faguet.
        p.   cm.
    Includes bibliographical references and index.
    ISBN 978-0-472-11819-9 (cloth : alk. paper) —
    ISBN 978-0-472-02828-3 (e-book)
        1. Decentralization in government—Bolivia.   2. Local government—
    Bolivia.   3. Central-local government relations—Bolivia.   I. Title.
    JL2229.D42F34   2012
    320.80984—dc23

                                                            2012000984

ISBN 978-0-472-03544-1 (pbk. : alk. paper)

For Lisette

CONTENTS

ACKNOWLEDGMENTS

The writing of a book is far too large an enterprise, benefiting from the help and wisdom of far too many people, to permit exhaustive acknowledgments. These are thus my thanks to those foremost in my mind at the end of this process—those who gave me the most, and to whom my debt is greatest.

I wrote most of this during a wonderful sabbatical year at UC Berkeley, and hence I am grateful to the London Scool of Economics (LSE) for giving me leave earlier than I was strictly due, and to Berkeley's Center for Latin American Studies for hosting me with such warmth and good humor. But for that invitation from Sara Lamson and Harley Shaiken, this book would still not be finished.

The years that have passed have not diminished my debt to my PhD advisers, Tim Besley and Teddy Brett. I still do not understand by what stroke of luck I ended up with Tim and Teddy, but both men exemplified the ideal of mentor. Their intellectual fingerprints are still visible on these pages, and I am grateful for that.

I thank the LSE for the William Robson Memorial Prize and a STICERD New Researcher Award, which supported ongoing research during my first years on the faculty. I was very fortunate to have my earliest research financed by a grant from the World Bank Research Committee, and am grateful to Shanta Devarajan and Gunnar Eskeland for their roles in securing this, as well as for insights that helped push me forward at an early stage. An Overseas Research Students award and additional financial support were kindly provided by the Economic and Social Research Council and the Niko Vardapetyan research award. I would not have been able to do this work without these awards.

I am grateful to Paula Giovagnoli for expert research assistance converting the second round of data (a disorganized flood) into our lovely, well-ordered database with minimal guidance and amazingly good humor. Armando Godínez guided my understanding of the structure of rural village society and taught me a great deal about conducting interviews and designing qualitative research. Ivette Arias provided timely research assistance in locating public investments in space. Alberto Leytón, Piter Olmos, Javier Reyes, David Tuchschneider, and Alejandra Velasco provided me with detailed data on municipal receipts and expenditures, as well as the wonderful *censo municipal.* George Gray Molina and Gerardo Molina of the Social Policy Analysis Unit (UDAPSO) were similarly instrumental in providing social and demographic indicators for all of Bolivia's municipalities, and Fernando Medina of the Secretariat of Popular Participation provided a huge amount of additional data on municipal characteristics.

I could not have done this work without the support, intellectual and material, of Edwin Acuña, Juan Carlos Aguilar, Jesús Aguilera, Eduardo Araujo, David Borda, Marco Camacho, Juan Carlos Franco, Luis González, Fernando Hernández, Javier Jahnsen, Guido Roca, Esteban Urgell, Rolando Vaca, Ginger Yapiz, Elsie Yavita, and other colleagues connected to the (then) Social Investment Fund, whose daily routine takes them throughout the length and breadth of Bolivia. They not only allowed me to rely upon their knowledge and intuitions, but bundled me into their jeeps, airplanes, and dugout canoes and took me to see the places and people that populate this work. Without their aid and intimate knowledge of the country I would have been lost.

I also wish to thank Pranab Bardhan, Ruth Collier, Stuart Corbridge, Tyler Dickovick, James Dunkerley, Steve Fish, Ted Miguel, Dilip Mookherjee, Ken Shadlen, Nicholas Stern, two anonymous reviewers, and seminar participants at Berkeley, the LSE, Oxford, IDB, Initiative for Policy Dialogue, Institute for the Study of the Americas, World Bank, and the LACEA99 and PACDEV09 conferences for their thoughtful comments and suggestions. I thank Melody Herr of the University of Michigan Press for her enthusiasm, wisdom, and kindness in helping me navigate the labyrinth of book publishing. And I thank my LSE Development Management students for their many suggestions and elucidations (including unintentional ones) over the years. Their contributions have improved this study in many critical ways, notwithstanding any remaining errors, which are my own.

Last I must thank my mother and father, who instilled in me a love of knowledge and respect for learning from an early age. And Lisette, my beloved, who suffered my efforts for far too long. You placed a well-judged distance between this slowly developing text and our married life, and then one day snatched it from my hands, scrutinized it intensely, and returned uncounted suggestions, modifications, and an avalanche of ideas.

Invariably I have forgotten or cannot name countless others—Alberto the FIS chauffeur, with whom I spent a week in a jeep crisscrossing an area larger than Holland, who knew every municipal and civic leader we encountered; the *moto-taxista*, his eyes wide with worry, who stopped to check on me after I crashed a motorcycle on a muddy forest road returning from Cachuela Esperanza; the young man from Atocha who guided me across the frozen highlands of southern Bolivia back to Potosí; the *corregidor* of Porongo, who restrained my foolish attempt to ford a swollen, angry river Piraí, and whose wisdom was rewarded with a night in a pickup truck without food. Please forgive my inadequate memory—I am grateful to you all.

Perhaps most important of all are the people whose opinions and whose lives are reflected in these pages. Many of them live in conditions that we in the rich West find hard to imagine. And yet they gave me their time, information, and wisdom for no good reason—because I asked. It is not clear that they will ever gain anything from this. But their generosity made this book possible, and I am grateful.

LIST OF ABBREVIATIONS

Note: Norms of abbreviation and capitalization adhere to most common usage in Bolivia.

ADN	Acción Democrática Nacionalista
AGACOR	Cattle Ranchers' Association of the Cordillera
AOP	Annual Operating Plan
APG	Guaraní People's Association
Cabi	Capitanía del Alto y Bajo Isoso
CAO	Eastern Agricultural Congress
CBN	Cervecería Boliviana Nacional
CIPCA	Center for the Investigation and Promotion of the Peasantry
COB	Bolivian Confederation of Labor
Comibol	Bolivian (State) Mining Company
Condepa	Conciencia de Patria
DDE	District Director of Education
DDH	District Director of Health
FAM	Federation of Municipal Associations
FIS	Social Investment Fund
GRO	Grassroots Organization
Incerpaz	Industrias de Cerámica Paz (Viacha)
LPP	Law of Popular Participation
MBL	Movimiento Bolivia Libre
MNR	Movimiento Nacionalista Revolucionario
NGO	Nongovernmental Organization
OC	Oversight Committee
OC1	Official OC ⎫ *(distinction valid*
OC2	Opposition OC ⎭ *only for Viacha)*
PASE	Programa de Apoyo Solidario a las Escuelas
SOBOCE	Sociedad Boliviana de Cementos
UCS	Unión Cívica de Solidaridad

INTRODUCTION

The Quiet Revolution

Enthusiasm for, and experiments with, decentralization have swept the world over the past four decades. When I began studying decentralization as a graduate student in 1995, commentators were already fond of citing the remarkable growth of policy experiments (and academic studies) since the early 1980s. To many it felt like a wave that must be cresting, soon to give way to new policy enthusiasms. But we were wrong—since then both the practice and study of decentralization have grown and grown.

Ten years ago an estimated 80 percent of the world's countries were experimenting with one form or another of decentralization (Manor 1999). Since then, new or deepening reforms have been announced in nations as diverse as Japan, Mexico, Egypt, Cambodia, France, Bolivia, Indonesia, Turkey, Ethiopia, and South Korea, as well as many others. The trend does not favor poorer nations: subsidiarity, devolution, and federalism are squarely in the foreground of policy discourse in the European Union, United Kingdom, and United States. Nor does it favor richer nations: nearly every country in Africa implemented some degree of reform during the 1990s (Brosio 2000). By the early 2000s it was safe to say that decentralization had affected most, if not all, of the nations on the globe.

It is not just the number of countries decentralizing that impresses, but also the scope of authority and resources devolved to subnational governments. In Latin America, according to Campbell (2001, 2), "local governments began spending ten to 50 percent of central government revenues." Campbell calls this "the quiet revolution" and argues that it has generated a new model of governance based on innovative, capable leadership, high popular participation, and a new implicit contract governing local taxation. Rodden (2006, 1–2) makes a similar point: "Other than transitions to democracy, decentralization and the spread of federalism are perhaps the most important trends in governance around the world over the last 50 years."

Ubiquity does not imply uniformity. The word *decentralization* hides a surprising amount of variation in two dimensions. First, it encompasses reforms such as deconcentration, devolution, and delegation that in incentive terms are fundamentally different, a point to which we return in chapter 5. Comparing different reforms under a common rubric is tantamount to comparing beans and bananas; one may choose to do it, but it is probably not a good idea. Second, the word conceals great variation in the extent to which reform is effectively implemented across different countries. As we shall also see in chapter 5, there are strong reasons to expect many announced reforms to be resisted or subverted in various ways by the central authorities responsible for implementing them, leading reforms that look similar on paper to have remarkably different effects. For the student of decentralization it is difficult to overstate the importance of clear definitions. This study uses the following.

> **Decentralization** is the devolution by central (i.e., national) government of specific functions, with all of the administrative, political, and economic attributes that these entail, to democratic local (i.e., municipal) governments that are independent of the center within a legally delimited geographic and functional domain.

As a number of scholars have noted (e.g., Diaz-Cayeros 2006; Eaton 2004), the trend to decentralization coexists alongside an opposing trend toward centralization. The latter finds its most obvious expression in the ongoing construction of multicountry unions such as the European Union, the North American Free Trade Agreement, and Mercosur (Mercado Común del Sur), many of whose member states are simultaneously decentralizing power and authority to subnational levels of government. Indeed, the two trends coexist not only within multinational groupings but within individual countries as well, where authority and resources are being decentralized in some areas (e.g., education) and centralized in others (e.g., taxation). While it is important to acknowledge the existence of a strong centralizing trend as part of the larger context in which this study will operate, I do not focus on it here. This book will instead focus on decentralization, the more important of the two trends worldwide, and the local governance that results.

The Historical Context

Placed in the broader tide of human history, decentralization is also by far the more unusual phenomenon. The story of humanity's rise from the plains of Africa to the modern nation-state is a story of continuously increasing centralization as greater and greater populations and resources came under the control of governments and bureaucracies. Although it is difficult to infer social characteristics from the fossil record, evidence suggests that the earliest anatomically modern humans lived in small groups of hunter-gatherers some 200,000 years ago in Africa. It was in such groups that modern behavioral traits such as language, music, trade, and burying the dead eventually emerged about 50,000 years ago (Wade 2006). Humans continued to live in such groups for a further 35,000 years before beginning to settle down in the earliest agricultural communities some 10,000 to 15,000 years ago. Domestication of plants and animals for food generated enormous increases in food production per acre of land, typically of 10 to 100 times, and hence in the populations that could be supported (Diamond 1998). And the sedentary lifestyle of farming communities permitted both food storage and shorter birth intervals, spurring population growth further.

With farming came primitive centralization, as nomadic bands of a few dozen that were probably egalitarian and unorganized grew into settled tribes of a few hundred, acquiring primitive organization and, eventually, clear leaders (Gronn 2010). As farming improved, these villages grew into chiefdoms with populations in the thousands, centralized hereditary leaderships, and multilevel bureaucracies (Diamond 1998). In the most fertile places—river valleys in what are now Egypt, Pakistan, India, and especially Iraq—these societies eventually became the world's first cities about 6,000 years ago. Mesopotamia was the birthplace of the first states 5,700 years ago, and hence of a large advance in centralization. With populations of 50,000 or more these states encompassed many cities and villages and featured centralized decision making and control of information, far larger and more sophisticated bureaucracies and religious orders, conflict resolution through laws and judges, a sophisticated division of labor, redistributive taxation, and a capital city (Diamond 1998). In their organization and operation they inevitably gathered power and resources upward, away from the many and into the hands of the few.

The advantages that larger polities and social units had over smaller ones were significant. States and large chiefdoms could marshal far greater resources from a population that was not only more productive due to a greater division of labor but much larger as well. Second, early states were probably the first to organize education and religion in ways that motivated their soldiers to die for the polity, a sentiment that Diamond regards as unthinkable in more primitive bands and tribes. These advantages allowed states to maintain more powerful armies and so control key resources, such as water sources, fertile lands, and—later—mineral deposits and trade routes, to name a few. And it proved determinant when different types of societies clashed in war. Greater productivity, leading to greater wealth and power, and greater control over their citizens provided early states with large advantages that they used to conquer neighboring cities and chieftaincies and create empires, such as the Persian and Roman empires of more than 2,000 years ago, centralizing power further still. Although empires rose and fell through the following centuries, populations that had experienced large-scale, sophisticated forms of social organization did not revert to small, egalitarian bands. States endured as kingdoms (e.g., France, England) and cities (e.g., Florence, Venice), and—from about the seventeenth century onward—the nation-states that we have inherited. Even democracy, for over 2,000 years assumed to be the province of small political units where men could rule themselves directly, was adapted for scale and power with the invention of representative assemblies in the eighteenth century, thus removing any theoretical ceiling on democracies' maximum size (Dahl 1989).

Viewed in this context, the rise of decentralization over the past half-century represents a unexpected historical reversal. Increasing scale, complexity, and—ultimately—centralization of control has been a defining characteristic of the past 10,000 to 15,000 years of human society. Why, suddenly, do governments the world over seek to devolve power and resources to smaller populations and lower hierarchical levels? Why do they choose to reduce the scale at which government operates? Have the deep forces that gave advantages to larger, more complex social units broken down? Or has some exogenous shock changed the calculus?

Understanding Decentralization

These questions are remarkably difficult to answer. There are of course many (competing) justifications for the policy reforms that have been implemented in different countries. But to date it has not been possible to move beyond aspirations or statements of intent to identify concrete pressures for, or advantages of, decentralization comparable to the role of economies of scale and the projection of power that drive the story of centralization. Enthusiasts for reform provide plausible arguments based on theories of democracy and fiscal federalism implying that decentralization should increase citizen voice and deepen participation, resulting in a government that is more responsive and accountable to the governed. As a result, the quality and effectiveness of public services provided by the state should improve. But others deploy economic and institutional theories to argue equally plausibly that decentralization will decrease efficiency in public goods production, decrease the quality of policy-making, and increase government capture and corruption.

These arguments are explored in detail in chapter 5's review of the state of knowledge on decentralization, where it becomes clear that logic alone cannot resolve these competing claims. Inconclusive theory is a prima facie argument for empirical work, and the evidence on decentralization is nothing if not abundant. But as we shall also see, the evidence speaks with many voices. For every case of improvement following reform (in education, health, poverty, etc.) there is a countercase of deterioration. Despite four decades of policy experimentation all over the world, it is ultimately unclear what reform has or has not achieved.

Some of the broadest surveys of the literature respond with pessimism, casting doubt on whether decentralization's systematic effects can ever be identified. Perhaps if I had begun 15 years ago in a university library, I might have abandoned this research. I have seen other students do so, and it is hard to blame them. But the case for pressing forward is, I think, compelling. As a real phenomenon, decentralization is simply too important to abandon. This is not just because of the range and scope of public services and decision making being decentralized all across the world. The deeper question is of overarching importance, and one that political economists *should* be able to answer: What unit of society is best suited to govern itself? How large should the groups in which people interact to reach agreement and effect public action be? Does the relentless logic of scale in resources and power inevitably return us to the nation-state, the bigger the better?

The spring of 1994 did not find me in a library in London or anywhere else, but rather in La Paz, where I enjoyed the privileges and suffered the despairs of overseeing the World Bank's "social investment" portfolio. The most wonderful boss I will ever have allowed me to spend a week of every month in the back of a jeep bouncing across dirt roads, or flying in small airplanes to remote communities to visit schools, clinics, and training programs that were being planned or executed. Over the three previous years I had met and come to admire the hard work and perseverance of poorer Bolivians living in small villages scattered across the vast, windswept altiplano, or lost in the endless Andean valleys, or nestled in the bend of a river along the border with Brazil. These people often lacked electricity, running water, and sanitation. Their schools operated beyond capacity—young and old children jumbled into one or two classrooms, without teachers for much of the year, and often without windows, books, or roofs. Many of them lived lives less like the twentieth century and more like the first agriculturalists, plowing with animals or sowing the ground with sticks.

That spring the ambitious new government of President Gonzalo Sánchez de Lozada passed, as one of a series of major reforms, the Law of Popular Participation. I remember clearly discussions around the World Bank office in La Paz and calls from colleagues in Washington seeking information. Our attention was mostly taken up with the other three reforms: "capitalization" (a variant of privatization), education reform, and the reform of the executive branch. The draft Law of Popular Participation was mostly ignored. "They're legislating participation," we joked, in the unfunny manner of the aid world. "If only they would legislate wealth and happiness, then we could all go home!" We were wrong. We did not initially understand that this was a decentralization reform. Nor that Popular Participation, alone among the four reforms, would not only survive to the present but expand and deepen over time. Even less did we imagine the changes it would bring, serving as midwife to Evo Morales and the transformation of Bolivia's politics, and arguably changing that country forever.

My experience of that spring is not only a fond memory but also a refutation of those who see conspiracy in Bolivian reform. I have often read, even in some academic studies, that decentralization was an imposition of the World Bank or a ruse intended to distract voters from the deeper "neoliberal" reforms the government planned. Neither assertion is true. Not only did the World Bank and the rest of the aid community not oblige Bolivia to decentralize, it did not realize decentralization was imminent, and even failed to recognize it when it was announced. As for the distraction thesis, this is true only if the "distraction" in question was a deep reform implemented sincerely and rapidly, with long-lasting effects across Bolivia's government, politics, and economy. Perhaps such a reform was meant to distract the public. My own view at the time, watching huge protests against capitalization and education reform march down La Paz's main avenue, is that voters were not distracted. My view now is that the thesis is trivial.

And so by pure dumb luck I found myself working in Bolivia when one of the most remarkable decentralizations of recent times was implemented. Would it work? Would local government prove more responsive to voters, or would waste and corruption reign? How would all those villages I had traveled to react? I left the country a few months later to begin a PhD but remained intrigued by how reform would play out. Only a year later, when I had embarked on the decentralization literature, did I realize what a good natural experiment Bolivia represented.

To begin with, decentralization in Bolivia was sincerely pursued, which has probably not been the case in many countries, and represented a sharp break with the past. Since the 1952–53 revolution Bolivia had a highly centralized state apparatus in which power flowed down from the president, through ministries and state governments, to appointed officials in the farthest towns and villages. Decentralization created elected municipal governments throughout the country that were beholden to voters, not ministers. The large majority of these municipalities were rural and small. And unlike, say, Colombia, which decentralized gradually over a generation, reform in Bolivia was sudden—first announced in January 1994 and implemented that July. The change in resource flows from central ministries and agencies to municipalities was immediate and—for most municipalities—massive. Hence reform in Bolivia consisted of large changes in policy and resource flows at a discrete point in time. Last, and through yet more dumb luck, Bolivia had two years earlier carried out its first census since the 1970s, and during one of my subsequent trips it conducted a "municipal census." This data turned out to be of comparatively high quality and scope for a country of its income level, including information on the political, social and civic, economic, institutional, and administrative characteristics of all Bolivian municipalities.

And so I embarked upon what I never expected would become 15 years of research. My first task was to establish exactly how reform had happened and collect data. I returned to Bolivia in 1995, 1997, and 2007 to conduct high-level interviews with some of the architects of decentralization, influential politicians and government officials involved in the reform, and business leaders, policy experts, and academics in La Paz, Cochabamba, and

Santa Cruz who had watched the process unfold. At some point during my absence a number of my weekend football teammates had become vice ministers in the new government, and so over many coffees I obtained access to a flood of raw data on central-local resource flows, municipal budget plans, and real expenditures and investments. This data—cleaned and systematized over the following year, and subsequently updated with less coffee and far more groveling—formed the core of the database I analyze. I could now begin to ask, Why did Bolivia decentralize? What exactly did decentralization change? How did municipalities invest their newly devolved funds?

The result is chapter 1, which examines the impact of decentralization on the use of resources by sector, the allocation of resources across space, their distribution among richer and poorer municipalities, and the resulting responsiveness of local investment to objective indicators of need. Descriptive statistics from the database provide evidence on what decentralization did and did not achieve. As for any collection of descriptive statistics, I do not interpret them as more than indicative. They provide an overall picture of major trends before and after reform, but only hint at the causes of these trends. In particular, those graphs do not establish causal relationships between decentralization and the various post-1994 trends they chronicle. Such claims are made in later chapters, based on more rigorous econometric analysis presented there. But before entering into such analysis, it is instructive to lay out the large facts, survey Bolivia's fiscal topography, and become familiar with the major trends that require explanation.

And the trends, as we shall see, are stark. Local governments across Bolivia invested in systematically different sectors than central government had before, and did so in ways that were far more responsive to local needs. How did this come about? What were the political and social processes at the microlevel that led to these aggregate outcomes? To address these questions I conducted six months of fieldwork in nine municipalities in 1997, followed by an updating round of fieldwork in 2009. The research was designed as a coherent set of case studies to facilitate comparative analysis. The nine municipalities had to be broadly representative of Bolivia's economic, political, geographical, and demographic diversity. I first used the database to identify a short list of promising municipalities, then discussed these with a number of knowledgeable observers who had direct experience of those local governments and social contexts, and then selected the final list of ten cases. With the help of a close friend and professional anthropologist, Armando Godínez, I designed detailed questionnaires for different types of semistructured and unstructured interviews. After much discussion and revision, I piloted the questionnaires in Pucarani. This revealed a number of problems, mostly poor phrasing and wrong ordering of specific questions. We then revised the questionnaires again, discarded the results from the pilot, and headed into the field.

With twice the area of France, and encompassing everything from high mountain plateaus to dense tropical jungle, Bolivia is a marvelously diverse country. The research took me from the frozen mines of Atocha high up in Potosí, through Charagua, Desaguadero, Guayaramerín, Porongo, Sipe Sipe, Sucre, and Viacha, to tiny Baures on Bolivia's northern floodplain. I traveled in large and small airplanes, trucks, jeeps, motorcycles, canoes, and on foot. In Baures our Cessna landed on a soccer field after circling low several times, which successfully shooed the cows and attracted most of the children. In the relentless heat of Charagua the Guaraní need for consensus made the interviews go on forever, mostly in Guaraní, which I do not speak; I briefly took up smoking to stay awake. In Porongo my last interview one evening was finished by flashlight in a darkened schoolhouse, with most of the hamlet's curious residents squeezed inside and the rest leaning in through the door and windows. It rained that night, leaving the wise *corregidor* and me stuck on the wrong side of a swollen river, with little option the next day but to clench each other's wrists and wade into the chest-high, angry brown water. I remember this period as the most intense, exhausting, wonderful "work" I have ever done.

During three months in the spring of 1997 and three more months in the fall I interviewed over 300 people (a list is appended) in a systematic program applied to each municipality; collected maps, budgets, and other local data; and observed local life generally. The results of this research became nine case studies of different local responses to the same decentralization shock, and of the drivers of those different responses. The two case studies included in this book are the extreme cases of municipal failure and success. The extremal focus places the systematic differences in decision making that characterize each in stark relief. This, in turn, facilitates theorizing about institutional causes, effects, and necessary conditions relating to the quality of local government; hence chapters 2 and 3, which telescope in from the national level to examine how governance operates at the municipal and submunicipal level. I rely here on qualitative evidence and thick description to analyze the microlevel workings of local government in the worst and best of my case studies, Viacha and Charagua, which represent well the extremes of municipal performance in Bolivia as a whole. The other seven cases confirm the analytical insights presented here but add only modestly to them. They are written up as a bonus chapter available on the London School of Economics and University of Michigan Press websites.[1]

If decentralization led to high-quality, responsive government in one municipality and unresponsive and corrupt government in another, what can we conclude about Bolivia as a whole? Chapter 4 returns to the national database to examine whether decentralization made government more or less responsive to local needs with a set of econometric tests and an original database that includes the universe of Bolivian municipalities, territory, and people over the period 1987 through 2007. The results confirm the dramatic changes reported in chapter 1, but in more detail and with more analytical rigor.

How does the evidence from Bolivia compare to the theory of decentralization and to evidence from other countries? Can the literature help us understand Bolivia's reform better? Can Bolivia help us better understand decentralization? Chapter 5 addresses these questions via an extensive review of the state of knowledge about decentralization, beginning with theory and then moving on to the empirical literature.

In Bolivia, clear trends at the national level coincide with high variation at the local level in government quality and decision making. This leads us to a crucial question: Why are some local governments so much better than others? Chapter 6 generalizes from the experiences of Viacha and Charagua (and the other seven municipalities implicitly) to build a theoretical model in which local government performance is driven by key factors in the local economy, politics, and society. I describe a structural framework that integrates a number of well-established ideas about elections and lobbying with more recent insights about civic organizations and social linkages. I then place the economic interests, political actors, and civic organizations at the heart of this approach in a dynamic context to analyze how these actors interact over time to produce public decision making that is responsive and accountable to voters, or not.

The predictions of this model accord well with qualitative evidence from Viacha and Charagua. Do they have more general applicability? Chapter 7 returns to the database to test these ideas against data from all of Bolivia's municipalities. I focus on the determinants of local government decision making during the decentralized period, 1994–2007. The answer is strongly affirmative: the data support the theory and indeed allow us to fine-tune it further.

Thus far the theory has proven robust to microlevel qualitative evidence over the short run, and macrolevel quantitative evidence over the long run. Is it consistent with microlevel qualitative evidence over the long run? Can it explain deep changes in governance in our two case studies between 1997 and 2009? Chapter 8 returns to Viacha and Charagua 12 years later to assess the quality of local government in each and examine how local governance has changed during the intervening period. In both municipalities governance processes and policy outputs changed significantly. The factors that drove these changes are those theorized in the model, and the outcomes we observe accord well with the model's predictions. It is notable that this long-term evidence is explained so well by a model constructed before the evidence was collected.

Chapter 9 concludes this generational study of decentralization (1987–2009) in one country by summarizing the effects of reform in Bolivia and connecting these to the mixed empirical methods I employed. I argue that such blended Q^2 (qualitative and quantitative) methods combined with a large-N, one-country approach are key to understanding the complex, nuanced institutional dynamics that decentralization puts into play. I place the Bolivian experience in a broader international context and analyze what the Bolivian case tells us about decentralization more generally, including specific lessons for future reformers. The book ends with a discussion of the role decentralization played in Bolivia's political transformation, and the deep links between decentralization and democracy.

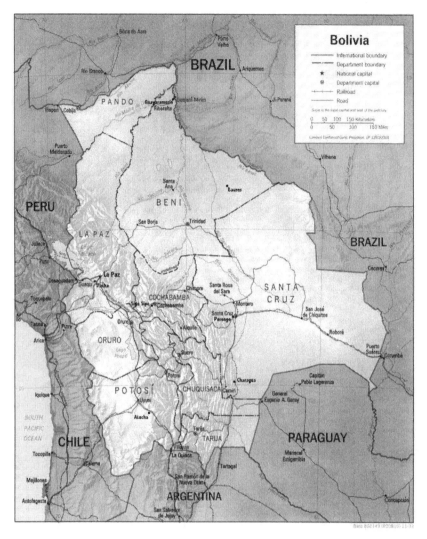

Map modified by the author to show the nine case studies. (From U.S. Central Intelligence Agency: Maps Released to the Public; downloaded from the University of Texas at Austin, Perry-Castañeda Library Map Collection [http://www.lib.utexas.edu/maps].)

CHAPTER 1

The Bolivian Decentralization Reform

Historical Background

On the eve of the 1952–53 revolution, Bolivia was a poor, backward country with extreme levels of inequality, presided over by a "typical racist state in which the non-Spanish speaking indigenous peasantry was controlled by a small, Spanish speaking white elite, [their power] based ultimately on violence more than consensus or any social pact."[1] The extent of the poverty and inequality that blighted the lives of ordinary Bolivians is hard to overstate. The country's modest GDP per capita[2] of $119 in 1952 (Dunkerley 1984) was highly unevenly distributed such that a large majority of the population lived in poor, rural agricultural communities, and a small number of mining and landowning families controlled great wealth. Only 31 percent of Bolivia's population was literate, and only 8 percent had finished secondary school in 1952. Nearly 30 percent of children died in their first year of life, and those who survived could expect to die well before 50. In a country of 2.7 million there were only 706 doctors, mostly in cities, where only 22 percent of the population lived (Dunkerley 1984).

More surprising still is the extent to which power was concentrated in the *superestado minero* (mining superstate), as Bolivia's tiny mining elite was popularly known, and above all in the hands of three men: Patiño, Aramayo, and Hochschild. These three family firms controlled 80 percent of the vital tin industry, which accounted for 80 percent of national exports and provided the government with the bulk of its revenues and foreign exchange (Dunkerley 1984). These three men's economic power was not only local—during World War II their share of world tin production reached 49 percent, and both before and immediately after the war the three companies enjoyed considerable price-setting power in international markets.

This economic power was successfully translated into an enormous influence over Bolivia's fiscal and political affairs, which the "tin barons" exercised from afar through lawyers and associates placed at the highest level in successive governments regardless of political hue. Their influence was further buttressed by the large banks that they owned, and by the country's principal newspapers, *La Razón, Ultima Hora,* and *El Diario,* in which they held large shares. The barons used their power to safeguard their commercial interests, opposing progressive taxation or labor legislation in the mining sector and repeatedly calling on the army to resolve labor disputes. An infamous example of the latter occurred in 1942, at the Catavi mine owned by Patiño. In a year when company revenues increased 84 percent, real mining wages fell by 25 percent, and workers struck to demand pay rises. After a few efforts at negotiation, the company convinced the government of Gen. Enrique Peñaranda to intervene. Despite no armed resistance by miners, the local garrison mounted a vicious attack resulting in 35 deaths including a number of the women who headed the protest in traditional fashion (Dunkerley 1984). This pattern of violent repression was played out again and again at mines large and small throughout the 1920s, 1930s, and 1940s.

The nationalist revolution of 1952 sought to change all of this. Revolutionaries' preferred tool was a strong interventionist state. Quickly the new Movimiento Nacionalista Revolucionario (National Revolutionary Movement, MNR) government expropriated the "commanding heights" of the economy—land and mines—and launched Bolivia on the road to one of the most centralized state structures in the region. The state-led modernization strategy used public corporations and regional governments to initiate a concerted drive to break down provincial fiefdoms, transform existing social relations, and create a modern, industrial, more egalitarian society. To this end the president directly appointed prefects, who in turn designated entire regional governments and associated dependencies, forming a national chain of cascading authority that emanated from the capital.

Successive governments promoted the unionization of miners, laborers, peasants, public servants, and professionals into a hierarchical labor "peak association," whose representatives negotiated national policies directly with their similars from the private sector and government. Together these three sectors planned the exploitation of Bolivia's natural resources, the development of new industries, and other sectoral and regional policies in a bid to orchestrate a rapid development process from the heights of La Paz.

The intellectual trends of the 1950s through 1970s—Dependencia theory, Import Substitution Industrialization, and Developmentalism—only contributed to this tendency, as did the military governments that overthrew elected administrations with increasing frequency from the 1960s on.[3]

With political power so little dispersed, there was little point in establishing the legal and political instruments of local governance. As a result, beyond the 9 regional capitals and an additional 25 to 30 cities, local government existed in Bolivia at best in name, as an honorary and ceremonial institution devoid of administrative capability and starved for funds. And in most of the country it did not exist at all.

Decentralization in Bolivia

The Context

Although the 1994 reform was sprung on an unsuspecting nation, the concept of decentralization was by no means new. For more than 30 years, a decentralization debate focused on Bolivia's nine departments ebbed and flowed politically—at times burning with importance, other times all but forgotten. The issue became caught up in the country's centrifugal tensions as regional elites in Santa Cruz and Tarija manipulated the threat of secession to Brazil and Argentina respectively—with which each is traditionally more integrated economically than La Paz—to extract resources from the center.[4] The Bolivian paradox of a highly centralized but weak state, and a socially diverse population with weak national identity, meant that such threats were taken seriously by the political class, which blocked all moves to devolve power and authority to Bolivia's regions.

Such opposition was overcome in large part by a reform that broke significantly with three decades of discourse among Bolivia's policy-making and regional elites. So ingrained was the regional concept of decentralization in the policy debate that, according to one close observer of the process, the first 30-odd drafts of the Law of Popular Participation (LPP) ignored municipalities entirely.[5] The idea to "go lower" originated late in the process in consultation with the president, who sought to promote accountable local government. Remaining details were finalized by a small team of technocrats with minimal consultation until the law was ready to be presented to the nation.

Bolivia represents an episode of discontinuous reform, and not—as in Colombia, for example—a process of negotiation or accommodation among competing interest groups. Although the many local contexts of decentralization are central to its success (or failure) across 315 districts, as we explore in detail below, the history and national environment are simply less significant than they are elsewhere. Thus reform is henceforth treated as a policy discontinuity, and not as a phenomenon deeply embedded in Bolivia's past.[6]

Why did Bolivia suddenly turn to decentralization? And why then? Two factors stand out. The less important one arises from Bolivia's failure to achieve sustained growth despite wrenching economic reform. Fifteen years of near-zero per capita economic growth sapped the credibility of the state and fomented social unrest. The new MNR administration of President Gonzalo Sánchez de Lozada (1993–97) saw the structure of government itself as an impediment to growth. Decentralization was an attempt to deepen structural reform in order to make the state more efficient and responsive to the population, and so regain its legitimacy in voters' eyes.

The more important factor is the rise of ethnically based, populist politics in the 1980s, which undercut the MNR's traditional dominance of the rural vote and posed a serious challenge to its (self-declared) role as the "natural party of government." This rural dominance was itself born out of the MNR's agrarian reforms of the 1952–53 revolution. Hence a party with a tradition of radical reform that found itself in secular decline sought a second, redefining moment. In a another bold move, it attempted to reorganize government, recast the relationship between citizens and the state, and so win back the loyalty of Bolivians living outside major cities. To a very important extent, decentralization was a gambit to capture rural voters for at least another generation.[7]

The Law of Popular Participation

Against this background, the Bolivian decentralization reform was announced in early 1994. When announced to the nation, the law was met with general surprise, followed by ridicule, followed by determined opposition from large parts of society.[8] It is notable that opposition to the law, which was fierce for a few months, came principally from the teachers' union, NGOs, and other social actors, and not from political parties. Judged by their public declarations, this opposition was an incoherent mix of accusations and fears that indicated a deep suspicion of the government's motives, and not a careful reading of the law. The lack of opposition from parties can largely be attributed to the sweeping reforms that were being enacted by the MNR government at the same time as decentralization. With privatization of the main state enterprises, education reform, and a comprehensive restructuring of the executive branch all being pushed at once, decentralization was relegated to the second tier of political parties' concerns. Opposition parties may also have calculated that reform would allow them to capture some local governments at a time when they were out of power nationally. Whatever the case, the opposition focused its attention elsewhere, and decentralization never became a fighting point.

First made public in January 1994, the Law of Popular Participation was promulgated by Congress in April and implemented on 1 July of that year. The scale of the change in resource flows and political power it brought about were enormous. The core of the law consists of four points (Secretaría Nacional de Participación Popular 1994).

1. **Resource Allocation.** Funds devolved to municipalities doubled to 20 percent of all national tax revenue. More important, allocation among municipalities switched from unsystematic, highly political criteria to a strict per capita basis.

2. **Responsibility for Public Services.** Ownership of local infrastructure in education, health, water & sanitation, irrigation, roads, sports, and culture was given to municipalities free of charge, with the concomitant responsibility to maintain, equip, and administer these facilities, and invest in new ones. But the staffing of this infrastructure, including responsibility for salaries, remained central attributes.

3. **Oversight Committees** (Comités de Vigilancia) were established to provide an alternative, parallel channel for representing popular demand in the policy-making process. Composed of representatives from local, grassroots groups, these bodies propose projects and oversee municipal expenditure. Their ability to suspend disbursements of Popular Participation funds if they suspect misuse or corruption can paralyze local government, and gives them real power. When suspension occurs, the center undertakes no arbitration but simply waits for the two sides to resolve their dispute, relying on economic incentives to speed agreement.

4. **Municipalization.** Existing municipalities were expanded to include

suburbs and surrounding rural areas, and 198 new municipalities (out of some 315 in all) that did not exist even in statute, let alone administration or operations of any sort, were created. For the first time, all of Bolivia's citizens and territory fell under one or another local government.

The central agencies previously charged with regional and local investment projects—the regional development corporations—were scaled back as a result. There were relatively few direct transfers of staff to municipalities, although many "quasi transfers" appear to have operated informally through the labor market. And a small, complementary program of municipal training and capacity building was established with support from international donors.

The Laws of Decentralized Administration (1995) and of Municipalities (1999) followed subsequently, further defining the municipal mandate and locating it in a broader governmental architecture. The fiscal transfer rule was also altered. Initially the strict per capita criterion was broadened to include resource transfers based on municipal poverty levels. These were joined in 2006 by municipal receipts of a quarter of the Direct Hydrocarbons Tax (IDH in Spanish), distributed preferentially to "hydrocarbons-producing areas." This last component shattered the rough horizontal equality in fiscal transfers that existed among municipalities. Since 2006, small numbers of sparsely populated municipalities in, for example, Pando and Chuquisaca receive vast per capita sums—transfers larger in absolute terms than those of far more populous and needier municipalities.

The change in local affairs that these measures catalyzed is immense. Before reform, local government was absent from the vast majority of Bolivian territory, and the broader state was present, if at all, in the form of a military garrison, schoolhouse, or health post, each reporting to its respective ministry. After reform, elected local governments sprouted throughout the land.

The first elections under the new regime were held in 1995. Parties put forward lists of candidates from which voters elected municipal councilmen in single-constituency elections. The council then elects the mayor indirectly from among those who garnered the most votes. The size of the council varies between 5 and 11 members according to municipal population. In practice, most municipal (and national) governments have historically been coalitions.

The third institution of local government is the oversight committee

(OC), in effect a nonelectoral form of representation that operates in parallel with municipal councils and mayors. These are composed of the representatives of grassroots organizations within each municipality. Municipalities are divided into four or more regions depending on size and population. Each region contains a number of grassroots organizations (GROs) that are independent and traditional, and overwhelmingly predate the 1994 reform, in many cases by centuries. They occur spontaneously and naturally throughout Bolivia, with greater density in some regions and lower density in others. Examples of such GROs include neighborhood councils in urban areas, pre-Columbian *ayllus* and *mallkus* (community self-government organizations) on the altiplano, *capitanías* (captaincies) in the Chaco, and tribal structures in Bolivia's northeastern lowlands, although there are many more. GROs have a wide variety of traditions and conventions of self-organization and leader selection that the Bolivian municipal code recognizes as legitimate, without intervention. If the LPP created a new political class of some 1,500 new councilmen and mayors, it also co-opted an already existing, much larger class of grassroots authorities and organizations that were trusted by ordinary Bolivians, and put them at the service of governance.

GRO leaders within each of a municipality's constituent regions nominate a representative to the oversight committee, using whatever system they can agree on. Committee members elect from among themselves a president, whose legal status is comparable to the mayor's. The OC's power lies in its natural moral authority, as well as its ability to suspend central government disbursements. Oversight committees thus make up a parallel, corporatist form of social representation similar to an upper house of parliament, enforcing accountability on the mayor and municipal council.

Decentralization's Effects: The Sectoral and Spatial Allocation of Funds

Central versus Local Investment by Sector

Decentralization in Bolivia began 1 July 1994. What happened next? Consider first the sectoral use of funds before and after decentralization. Bolivian national accounts categorize expenditure into 14 sectors, which I group into four broad categories as follows.

Human Capital Formation	Infrastructure	Environment	Production
Education	Communications	Environment	Agriculture
Health & Social Security	Multisectoral	Water Management	Energy
Water & Sanitation	Transport		Hydrocarbons
	Urban Development		Mining
			Industry & Tourism

Figure 1 shows how investment varied across these four categories year by year between 1987 and 2007; the dashed vertical line signals the year when decentralization began. These figures omit operating costs such as salaries or maintenance, and thus include only new investments in infrastructure, equipment, and other assets. Pre-decentralization investment was carried out almost entirely by the central government; the few municipalities with their own resources spent these on personnel and other running costs. From 1994 onward our figures omit all central government investment, in order to focus on which sectors municipalities prioritized. Doing so allows us to make a revealed preference comparison of local governments' priorities versus those of central government during the preceding period.

The difference is striking. Notice the plunge in productive investment, from as much as 53 percent of the total in 1987 to 5 percent in 1995. This is accompanied by a countervailing rise in investment in human capital formation and primary services, from a low of 6 percent in 1991 to 55 percent in 2003. Infrastructure investment—already high in the pre-decentralization period—rises further to above 60 percent of total investment in 1994–95 and remains above 50 percent through 2001. (Environmental investment, which never rises above 3 percent of the total, is essentially irrelevant and so omitted here.) These figures provide us with a first stylized fact about decentralization in Bolivia.

Stylized Fact 1: Decentralization appears to be associated with a large shift in public investment from production to human capital formation and primary services.

Because "infrastructure" covers very different types of activities, it is interesting to break this category down into individual sectors. Figure 2 does so for the same period, revealing significant internal variation. Transport dominated infrastructure investment during the period of centralized con-

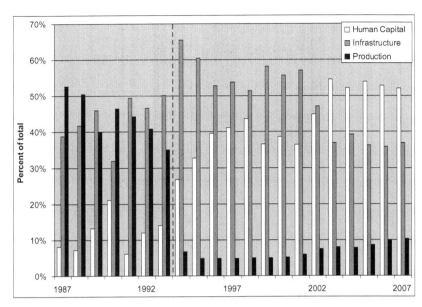

Fig. 1. Public investment by type, 1987–2007. Author's calculations. (Data from Ministry of Finance, Vice Ministry of Popular Participation, and Vice Ministry of Public Investment and External Finance.)

trol but then drops precipitously after decentralization as investment in urban development grows eight- to tenfold. After the first three years of decentralization, urban investment's share falls by about half, and transport recovers to near its previous levels, which equilibrium persists through 2002. Between 2003 and 2007 urban investment falls again to around 10 percent of the total, while transport remains at the 25–30 percent level. (Multisectoral, which is hard to characterize, and comunications, which never exceeds 2 percent, are both omitted here.) This periodicity is repeated throughout the data and mirrors larger events in Bolivia's national life.[9] Hence in the chart that follows I use the same periods to break 20 years of data into distinct periods and examine the resulting trends.

The boom in urban investment during the years immediately following decentralization can be explained in large part as one-off effects of the vast majority of Bolivia's municipalities—which existed only in name or not at all—building and equipping offices they lacked, refurbishing dilapidated central squares and municipal sports fields, and making similar investments considered essential to the identity and operation of a municipality.

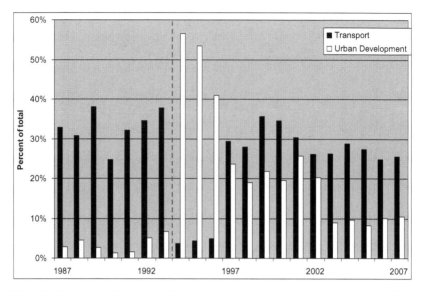

Fig. 2. Infrastructure investment by sector, 1987–2007. Author's calculations. (Data from Ministry of Finance, Vice Ministry of Popular Participation, and Vice Ministry of Public Investment and External Finance.)

Qualitative evidence (presented in the chapters that follow) indicates that such projects were widely considered a high priority in rural municipalities and enjoyed broad popular support. After three years, such investments tailed off naturally, and resources could be directed elsewhere. At least some of these freed-up resources appear to have been directed to transportation investment, which projects are often more complex and require greater technical knowledge than simple building works in a town center.

Figure 3 provides more sectoral detail of investment trends, aggregating years into the four periods described above to avoid graphical overload. The year of reform is signaled with a dark dashed line, and later periods are marked off with lighter dashed lines. Once again we see a steep fall in transportation's share of investment, which rebounds after 1996; hydrocarbons investment disappears, and energy's share falls by over 80 percent, as we would expect;[10] education leaps twentyfold after reform and increases further in the outer years; and urban investment leaps twelvefold initially but then subsides significantly. The greater detail in this graph reveals smaller but significant increases in health investment, which rises steadily fourfold over 20 years, and water & sanitation, which nearly doubles. Investment in

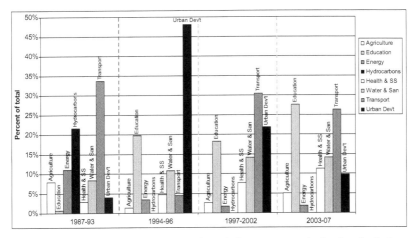

Fig. 3. Public investment by sector and period, 1987–2007. Author's calculations. (Data from Ministry of Finance, Vice Ministry of Popular Participation, and Vice Ministry of Public Investment and External Finance.)

agriculture initially plummets with decentralization but then recovers steadily to 5 percent of total investment by 2007. The graph is best viewed in color and is available on the web (see note 15).

These trends suggest a process of organizational learning in which local governments cut their teeth on comparatively simple, highly visible projects that enjoy broad support, such as education and—especially—urban development. In the process they build capacity in budgeting, bidding, technical oversight, and other skills important to public management. This allows them to progress to projects that are more complicated, expensive, and intensive in capital and technical skills, such as building roads, health clinics, and water and sewerage systems, as well as improving agricultural productivity.

Do large and small municipalities prioritize the same sectors? Might the decisions of Bolivia's few large cities distort nationwide patterns of investment? Close examination of the data reveals that the actions of a dozen (out of 315) large, urban municipalities do indeed differ from the rest. Figure 4 solves this problem by calculating the average of municipalities' sectoral shares of investment, where each municipality is equally weighted. For the sake of clarity, I compare the final three years of centralized government (1991–93) with the first three years of decentralization (1994–96); central in-

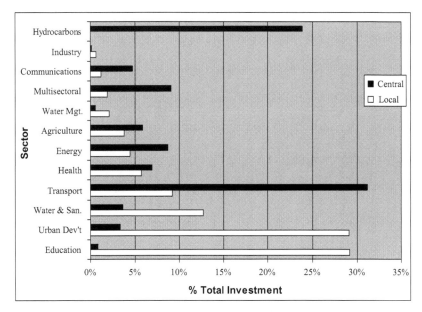

Fig. 4. Public investment by sector: central versus local government, unweighted averages. Author's calculations. (Data from Vice Ministry of Popular Participation and Vice Ministry of Public Investment and External Finance.)

vestment (dark bars) includes only resources controlled by central government agencies, while local investment (pale bars) includes only resources controlled by municipalities.

The contrasts between central and local government revealed preferences continue to be stark, but there is an important difference. When weighted equally (instead of implicitly by budget size), municipalities' top investment priority turns out to be education, followed closely by urban development. Water & sanitation is in third place, followed by transportation and then health. Municipalities' first, third, and fifth priorities are clearly human capital formation, at the expense of hydrocarbons and transport. This supports our first stylized fact, underlining the shift of resources into human capital formation. It also provides a second, allied one.

Stylized Fact 2: This national shift in investment priorities was disproportionately driven by Bolivia's smaller, poorer, more rural municipalities.

Central versus Local Investment across Space

A second telling comparison of central versus local government priorities is in their allocation of resources across space. Table 1 compares Bolivia's "co-participation"—central revenue sharing with local governments—before and after decentralization. Before decentralization 312 municipalities divided among them a mere 14 percent of all devolved funds, while the 3 main cities took 86 percent. After decentralization their shares reversed to 73 percent and 27 percent respectively. Because these three cities are Bolivia's richest and most sophisticated, a third stylized fact follows.

> **Stylized Fact 3:** Through its per capita criterion, decentralization resulted in a massive shift of resources in favor of smaller, poorer districts.

The "rest of Bolivia" saw its central transfers increase by 1,286 percent, and many municipalities enjoyed percentage increases in the tens of thousands.

This is worth exploring further. Figures 5–7 compare municipal investment per capita by central government aggregated over the last seven years before decentralization (1987–93) to that effected by local governments in three successive periods (1994–96, 1997–2002, and 2003–7). Total investment received by each municipality is represented by a dot. The most unequal distribution of resources possible would be for one municipality to receive all public investment, and all other municipalities to receive nothing. The most equal distribution of resources possible would show all the

TABLE 1. Revenue Sharing before versus after Decentralization

City	Central-to-Local Revenue Sharing (Bs'000)			% of National Total	
	1993	1995	% Change	1993	1995
La Paz	114,292	61,976	−46%	51%	10%
Santa Cruz	51,278	63,076	23%	23%	10%
Cochabamba	25,856	38,442	49%	12%	6%
3 cities subtotal	191,426	163,494	−15%	86%	27%
Rest of Bolivia	32,099	444,786	1,286%	14%	73%
Total	223,525	608,280	172%	100%	100%

Source: Ministry of Finance, Ministry of Social Communication.
Note: Average exchange rate: US$1 = Bs.5.

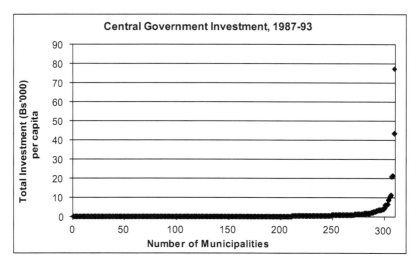

Fig. 5. Central government investment by location. Author's calculations. (Data from Ministry of Finance, Vice Ministry of Popular Participation, and Vice Ministry of Public Investment and External Finance.)

dots in a line at the same per capita value. The distribution we actually see under central government (figure 5) does not quite reach the unequal extreme but appears to be close, with one municipality receiving immense per capita sums, and five more at between 10 and 40 times the average. But our vertical axis is distorted by these few very large observations, so in figure 6 I drop the highest 12 values and examine the distribution more closely. There is indeed more variation in the 500 to 4,000 bolivianos (Bs.) range. But if we count the number of dots that lie on the horizontal axis, we find that fully 40 percent of Bolivian municipalities received no investment at all under centralized rule. With almost all national resources in its hands, plus the power to make the rules of the game, central government chose to allocate nothing to 40 percent of the municipalities in the land during each of the seven years prior to reform.

Compare this to investment under local governments during the first three years after reform (figure 7, lowest curve). This graph shows no municipality above Bs. 700/capita, none at zero (a couple are close), and 70 percent of municipalities located in a tight band between Bs. 100–300/capita. In the two periods that follow, totals rise (i.e., curves shift up the graph) as time spans lengthen, plus royalties accruing to certain municipalities surge with a worldwide natural resource boom after 2003. Nevertheless

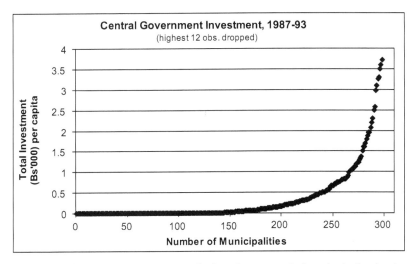

Fig. 6. Central government investment by location, expanded *y* axis. Author's calculations. (Data from Ministry of Finance, Vice Ministry of Popular Participation, and Vice Ministry of Public Investment and External Finance.)

the curves retain similar shapes as, excepting a few outliers, the distribution of investment across municipalities remains far more equal than under central government. These crude indicators provide us with a fourth stylized fact.

> **Stylized Fact 4:** Decentralized government distributed public resources much more equally across space than centralized government had done before.

Equality in per capita terms is, of course, largely a result of the design of the reform, as noted above. The ex post result is thus not as surprising as the ex ante one: central government, with a much larger budget and free rein to do as it chose, consistently chose a highly unequal distribution of investment across space.

Decentralization's Effects: Responsiveness to Need

Decentralization is thus associated with broad changes in the allocation of resources across sectors and across space. Did these changes make public

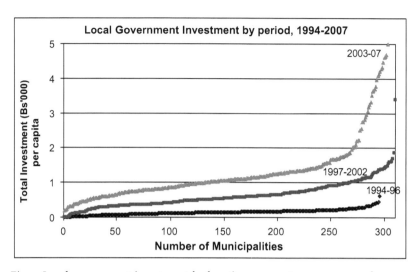

Fig. 7. Local government investment by location, 1994–96, 1997–2002, and 2003–7. Author's calculations. Highest six observations from 2003–7 omitted. Increasing transfers to municipalities over time appear as an upward shift in the curves. (Data from Ministry of Finance, Vice Ministry of Popular Participation, and Vice Ministry of Public Investment and External Finance.)

investment more or less responsive to local citizens' needs? As we shall see, improved responsiveness to local citizens is one of the central—and most disputed—arguments in favor of decentralization, and hence any evidence in this respect is of particular importance. The discussion that follows examines detailed evidence on central versus local government responsiveness sector by sector for the six most important sectors identified in figures 3 and 4 above.

The evidence is presented as scatterplots that relate public investment to objective indicators of local need under central and then local governments during the period 1987–2007. For each sector I compare public investments during the last seven years of centralized government (1987–93) to investments made by local governments during the periods identified above (1994–96, 1997–2002, and 2003–7).[11] Each graph includes a trend line summarizing the overall relationship. These scatterplots amount to a simplified, more accessible version of the econometric tests of responsiveness developed in chapter 4. The descriptive, intuitive results that follow mirror the much more rigorous analytical evidence presented there.

Education

We begin with education. Figures 8–10 show the relationship between public investment in education and two indicators of educational need: the illiteracy rate and the percentage of adults who never attended school. I interpret high illiteracy rates and high rates of nonschooling as indicators of relatively high objective need; conversely, municipalities where illiteracy is low or adults have significant levels of schooling are interpreted as having relatively less need for additional educational investment, implying the incremental investment dollar can be spent elsewhere. Investment that is responsive to need (i.e., that rises with the level of illiteracy) would result in a positively sloped trend line; investment that is regressive in terms of need (i.e., that aggravates existing disparities in illiteracy) would result in a negatively sloped trend line.

The first impression provided by figure 8 is how few dots lie above the horizontal axis. Further investigation shows that only 15 percent of Bolivian municipalities received any education investment at all from the central government during the seven years prior to reform, while the remaining 85 percent received nothing. But the lone very high observation compresses the *y* axis, obscuring possible variation at lower values. Hence figure 9 expands the vertical axis (pushing the highest values off the graph).[12] We see that there is indeed modest variation between Bs. 0–20 per capita, but the trend line clearly slopes downward. Central government chose to concentrate education resources where literacy was higher, creating a regressive pattern of investment with respect to need. This trend is echoed, although with a gentler negative slope, when we plot investment against adult nonschooling in figure 10.

Local government investment shows a very different pattern (figure 11), with 97 percent of municipal governments investing in education in 1994–96, rising steadily to 100 percent in 2003–7. The trend line has a strong positive slope in both illiteracy and nonschooling (figure 12), implying that local governments responded positively to objective local need. The trend line is similarly positive during 1997–2002 (figure 13) but turns slightly negative in 2003–7 (figure 14), implying that local investment becomes insensitive to educational need after the first decade of reform. This final switch is insufficient to revert the overall investment trend, however, which is positive in indicators of need for the entire postreform period (1994–2007).[13]

The change in trend after 2003 is an interesting and odd finding. Why

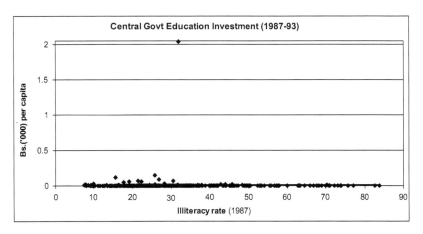

Fig. 8. Central government responsiveness to need—education. Author's calculations. (Data from Ministry of Finance, Vice Ministry of Popular Participation, Vice Ministry of Public Investment and External Finance, and National Institute of Statistics.)

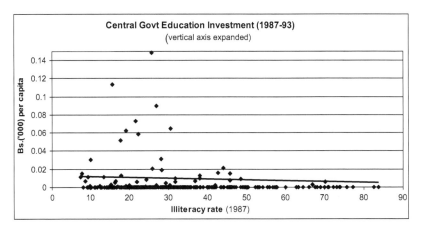

Fig. 9. Central government responsiveness to need—education (*y* axis expanded). Author's calculations. (Data from Ministry of Finance, Vice Ministry of Popular Participation, Vice Ministry of Public Investment and External Finance, and National Institute of Statistics.)

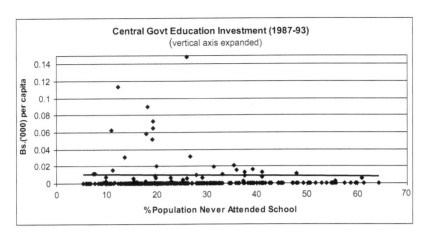

Fig. 10. Central government responsiveness to need—education (adult nonschooling). Author's calculations. (Data from Ministry of Finance, Vice Ministry of Popular Participation, Vice Ministry of Public Investment and External Finance, and National Institute of Statistics.)

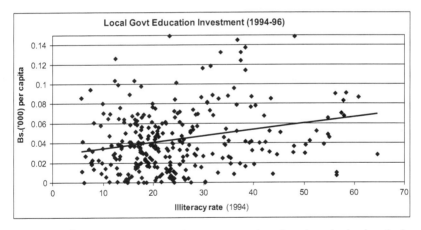

Fig. 11. Local government responsiveness to need—education. Author's calculations. (Data from Ministry of Finance, Vice Ministry of Popular Participation, Vice Ministry of Public Investment and External Finance, and National Institute of Statistics.)

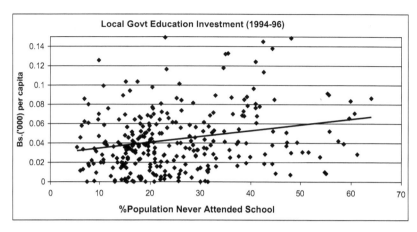

Fig. 12. Local government responsiveness to need—education (adult nonschooling). Author's calculations. (Data from Ministry of Finance, Vice Ministry of Popular Participation, Vice Ministry of Public Investment and External Finance, and National Institute of Statistics.)

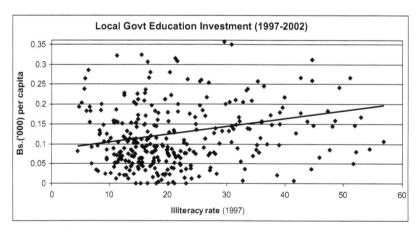

Fig. 13. Local government responsiveness to need—education, 1997–2002. Author's calculations. (Data from Ministry of Finance, Vice Ministry of Popular Participation, Vice Ministry of Public Investment and External Finance, and National Institute of Statistics.)

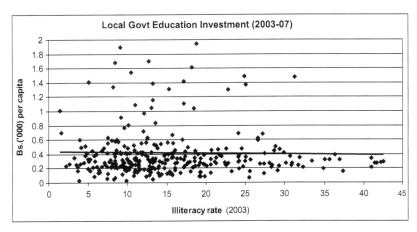

Fig. 14. Local government responsiveness to need—education, 2003–7. Author's calculations. (Data from Ministry of Finance, Vice Ministry of Popular Participation, Vice Ministry of Public Investment and External Finance, and National Institute of Statistics.)

would investment in the sector that qualitative evidence strongly suggests is the top priority of most ordinary Bolivians change from strongly responsive to local need to slightly regressive? Although we cannot answer this question definitively with the limited information and simple techniques of this chapter, two interesting explanations suggest themselves. The first is simply that the neediest municipalities invest in education first, and after some years shift resources to other sectors, leaving less needy municipalities to dominate the data for later years. A second explanation is that no such trend line can retain a strong positive slope indefinitely for the simple reason that sustained investment will tend to raise both literacy and educational attainment over time in the most deprived areas. Indeed we see this clearly in the illiteracy data, where a simple, unweighted average of municipal illiteracy rates[14] drops from 32 to 15 percent between 1987 and 2007. As illiteracy converges to the median, the trend line will tend to flatten and become more susceptible to outliers, which may drive its slope in the outer years. A more rigorous analysis must await the tools of econometrics in the chapters that follow.

Agriculture

Figures 15–18 relate agriculture investment to the rate of child malnutrition (mild) as an indicator of need. The logic is that one key cause of persistent malnutrition in Bolivia is low agricultural productivity in rural areas, especially in the altiplano and foothills regions. A responsive government might respond to high malnutrition levels with investments designed to boost agricultural productivity. Ideally I would use more direct measures of need in this sector, such as agricultural yields or irrigation capacity. But such measures do not exist for Bolivia, so I must make do with what there is.

Once again, the number of municipalities where central government invested nothing in agriculture is impressive: 76 percent. Figure 15 reveals a downward-sloping line, implying that central government invested less in agriculture where child malnutrition was higher. Thus centralized investment was regressive in terms of need.

Compare this with local investment. The number of municipalities with 0 investment falls to 33 percent immediately after reform, and continues falling to 0 in 2003–7. Figure 16 shows a strongly positive line in terms of need, a trend that continues unambiguously through the following two periods. Similar graphs using the number of slaughterhouses per capita as an indicator of need, omitted here for the sake of parsimony but available on the Internet,[15] show very similar trends. These graphs imply that local governments invested in agriculture where need was greatest.

Water & Sanitation

Figures 19–22 compare central and local government investment with the percentage of households that use public standpipes. Public standpipes are the lowest form of water service registered by Bolivian data—below that people have no access to public water service. Because most municipal water projects in Bolivia involve household connections—with plumbing that is either internal or external (i.e., private standpipes)—municipalities where a large proportion of households use public standpipes may be said to have relatively high need for water investment.

As with agriculture, central government invested nothing in water & sanitation in 76 percent of municipalities during the seven years prior to reform. During the three years after decentralization only 14 percent of local

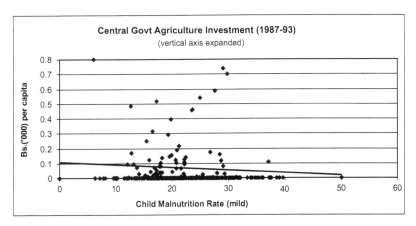

Fig. 15. Central government responsiveness to need—agriculture. Author's calculations. (Data from Ministry of Finance, Vice Ministry of Popular Participation, Vice Ministry of Public Investment and External Finance, and National Institute of Statistics.)

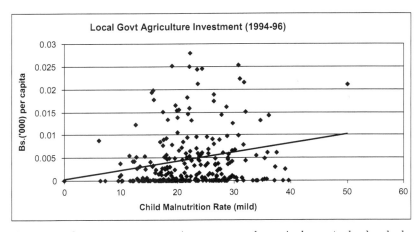

Fig. 16. Local government responsiveness to need—agriculture. Author's calculations. (Data from Ministry of Finance, Vice Ministry of Popular Participation, Vice Ministry of Public Investment and External Finance, and National Institute of Statistics.)

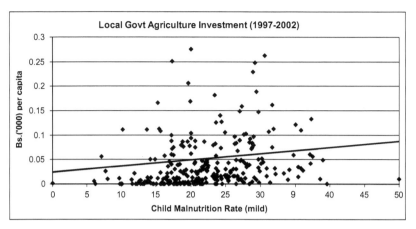

Fig. 17. Local government responsiveness to need—agriculture, 1997–2002. Author's calculations. (Data from Ministry of Finance, Vice Ministry of Popular Participation, Vice Ministry of Public Investment and External Finance, and National Institute of Statistics.)

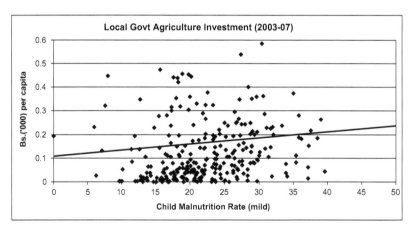

Fig. 18. Local government responsiveness to need—agriculture, 2003–7. Author's calculations. (Data from Ministry of Finance, Vice Ministry of Popular Participation, Vice Ministry of Public Investment and External Finance, and National Institute of Statistics.)

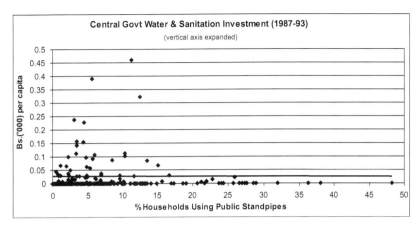

Fig. 19. Central government responsiveness to need—water and sanitation. Author's calculations. (Data from Ministry of Finance, Vice Ministry of Popular Participation, Vice Ministry of Public Investment and External Finance, and National Institute of Statistics.)

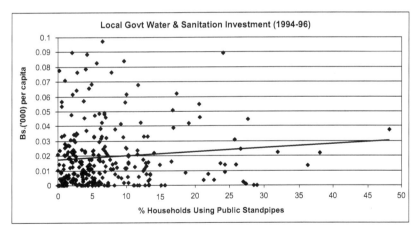

Fig. 20. Local government responsiveness to need—water and sanitation. Author's calculations. (Data from Ministry of Finance, Vice Ministry of Popular Participation, Vice Ministry of Public Investment and External Finance, and National Institute of Statistics.)

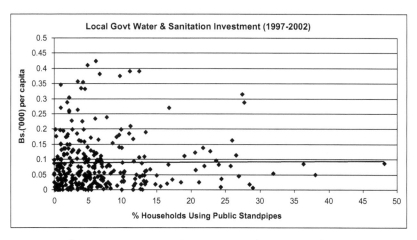

Fig. 21. Local government responsiveness to need—water and sanitation, 1997–2002. Author's calculations. (Data from Ministry of Finance, Vice Ministry of Popular Participation, Vice Ministry of Public Investment and External Finance, and National Institute of Statistics.)

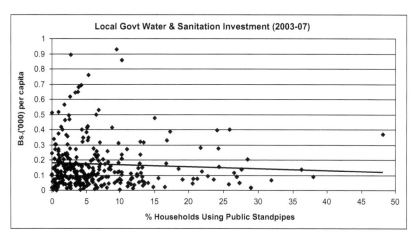

Fig. 22. Local government responsiveness to need—water and sanitation, 2003–7. Author's calculations. (Data from Ministry of Finance, Vice Ministry of Popular Participation, Vice Ministry of Public Investment and External Finance, and National Institute of Statistics.)

governments ignored the sector, falling steadily to zero by 2003–7. The trend line for centralized investment with respect to public standpipes is flat, implying no relation to local need. This line turns upward after 1994—local governments invested more in water & sanitation where fewer people have household water—implying greater responsiveness to local need. The positive trend persists for water through 2002 but turns negative during 2003–7. Similar graphs using the percentage of households that lack sewerage as the indicator of need (available on the Internet) show the same trends as for standpipes, except that the slope turns negative earlier—from 1997 instead of 2002.

The reversion of the trend is an interesting phenomenon. Unfortunately, changes in census questions relating to water service mean there is no time-variant information on access to public standpipes. But sewerage data can be compared across time and show a large drop in the simple average across municipalities of households with no sewerage, from 85 percent of households to 57 percent. This suggests two related effects, similar to the case of education, which may contribute to decreasing responsiveness: (1) needier municipalities invested first, leaving the less needy to invest in later years; and (2) convergence of sewerage access rates makes the trend line more susceptible to a few outliers, which drive its slope in outer years. A more rigorous analysis is provided in the chapters that follow.

Health

Figures 23–26 show how health investment varies with the percentage of households that use private health care. This variable is an indicator of local need for health investment in that it counts the proportion of households that require health care but lack access to public health services and hence must pay for private care. In a small minority of Bolivian municipalities, use of private health care might also signal social class or status. But extensive fieldwork plus professional knowledge of the sector indicates that this would be true in only the wealthiest, most sophisticated cities, accounting for perhaps 5 percent of the total. In the vast majority of municipalities, Bolivians resort to private care only when they have to. High usage implies an unmet need for public health services, and hence need increases with private provision.

Under central government, only 10 percent of municipalities received any investment in health during the seven years before reform. This share

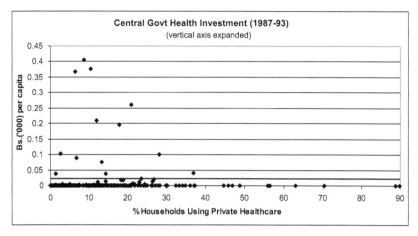

Fig. 23. Central government responsiveness to need—health. Author's calculations. (Data from Ministry of Finance, Vice Ministry of Popular Participation, Vice Ministry of Public Investment and External Finance, and National Institute of Statistics.)

rose to 85 percent after decentralization and continued rising steadily to 100 percent in the final period. Central investment shows no relation to private health care (figure 23) and hence no responsiveness to need.

Under local government, by contrast, investment becomes regressive in need initially, falling as use of private health care increases (figure 24). This trend is reversed with increasing strength in the two outer periods (figures 25 and 26), so that after 1997 local investment responds progressively to local need. This is interesting and, once again, difficult to explain at this level of analysis. One strong possibility suggested by the discussion in section 3 above (see especially figures 1 and 3) is that the neediest municipalities directed their early efforts to education and urban development, leaving the bulk of health investment to better-off localities. This created a regressive pattern in need between 1994 and 1996. Over time needier municipalities began to invest more in health, causing overall investment to become progressive in need and hence the trend line to invert between 1997 and 2007. This explanation is, of course, the mirror image of that provided for the (contrary) trend line inversion in education, providing additional evidence in its favor.

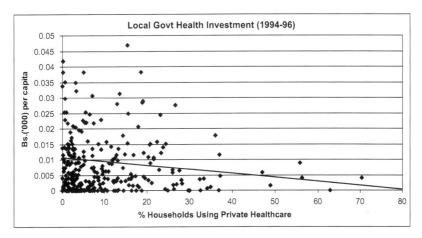

Fig. 24. Local government responsiveness to need—health. Author's calculations. (Data from Ministry of Finance, Vice Ministry of Popular Participation, Vice Ministry of Public Investment and External Finance, and National Institute of Statistics.)

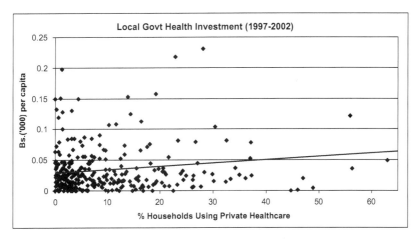

Fig. 25. Local government responsiveness to need—health, 1997–2002. Author's calculations. (Data from Ministry of Finance, Vice Ministry of Popular Participation, Vice Ministry of Public Investment and External Finance, and National Institute of Statistics.)

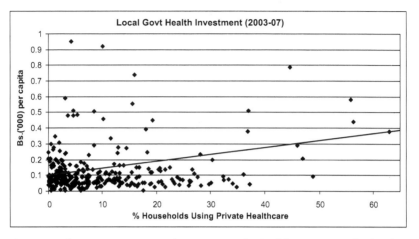

Fig. 26. Local government responsiveness to need—health, 2003–7. Author's calculations. (Data from Ministry of Finance, Vice Ministry of Popular Participation, Vice Ministry of Public Investment and External Finance, and National Institute of Statistics.)

Urban Development

Figures 27–30 show how investment in urban development varies with existing stocks of urban infrastructure. In Bolivia, where such infrastructure is generally scarce, investment in urban development almost always implies new construction. I assume that there is a greater need for urban infrastructure where such infrastructure is more scarce, and interpret low values of infrastructure stock as indicating relatively high need. For comparability with other sectors, all of the *x* axes in figures 27–30 are reversed, and so needs-responsive investment is represented by an upward-sloping line. Urban infrastructure can take on a variety of forms, including sports fields, coliseums, museums, theaters, libraries, markets, slaughterhouses, parks, zoos, cemeteries, and so forth. My database includes variables for each of these measures and more. To best investigate urban investment's responsiveness to local need, and as a robustness check, I use an aggregate indicator of the most common forms of urban infrastructure projects.

Central government invested in urban development in only 8 percent of municipalities. After reform this share zooms up to 98 percent and then quickly reaches 100 percent. Despite its low frequency, centralized investment increases as sporting and cultural infrastructure decrease, implying

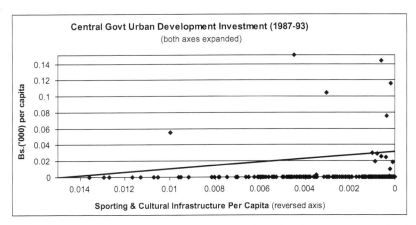

Fig. 27. Central government responsiveness to need—urban development. Author's calculations. (Data from Ministry of Finance, Vice Ministry of Popular Participation, Vice Ministry of Public Investment and External Finance, and National Institute of Statistics.)

responsiveness to local need. Under local government this pattern continues and strengthens through 2007, as municipalities choose to invest in far more urban projects, and resources devoted to this sector rise. The patterns described repeat with alternative indicators of need, such as sports fields, libraries, cultural centers, nurseries/greenhouses, and cemeteries, boosting confidence in these results.

Transport

Unfortunately a good indicator of need in this important sector, such as quality-adjusted road kilometers per capita or the local unit costs of transportation, is lacking. The only transport-related variable at our disposal is the number of parking lots per capita. This is sufficiently unsatisfactory that I do not reproduce the graphs here.[16] The story they tell, in any event, is by now familiar. Most municipalities received no transportation investment under centralization. After decentralization, municipalities receiving transportation investment rose from 30 percent to 81 percent and then on upward to 100 percent by 2003 through 2007. Centralized investment was regressive in terms of need, rising where infrastructure is more abundant and falling where it is scarce. But this line approaches the horizontal between 1994 and 1996, flattens

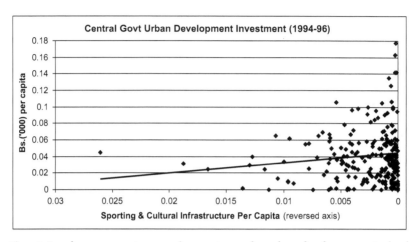

Fig. 28. Local government responsiveness to need—urban development. Author's calculations. (Data from Ministry of Finance, Vice Ministry of Popular Participation, Vice Ministry of Public Investment and External Finance, and National Institute of Statistics.)

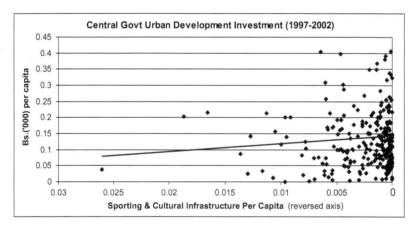

Fig. 29. Local government responsiveness to need—urban development, 1997–2002. Author's calculations. (Data from Ministry of Finance, Vice Ministry of Popular Participation, Vice Ministry of Public Investment and External Finance, and National Institute of Statistics.)

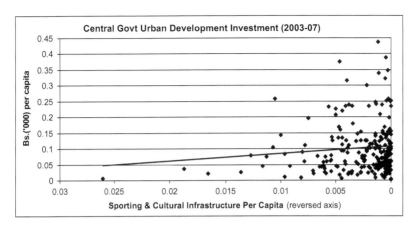

Fig. 30. Local government responsiveness to need—urban development, 2003–7. Author's calculations. (Data from Ministry of Finance, Vice Ministry of Popular Participation, Vice Ministry of Public Investment and External Finance, and National Institute of Statistics.)

completely in 1997 through 2002, and then turns positive in 2003 through 2007. Having begun with a regressive pattern in terms of need, decentralization appears to gradually shift the pattern to one that benefits underprovided municipalities and is thus responsive to local need.

Evidence from the six sectors yields one final stylized fact.

Stylized Fact 5: Local governments' investment decisions were far more responsive to local needs than central government's had been before.

Conclusions

Decentralization led to big changes in the way Bolivia is governed. Four decades after a highly centralized state was created by the nationalist revolution, its practices rooted in the verticalist traditions of the Inca and Spanish empires, decentralization created, funded, and empowered local governments throughout the land. These changes occurred very quickly, such that the switch from a centralized to decentralized regime happened literally on the evening of 30 June 1994. The shock therapy that this entailed did not permit much municipal preparation—especially in the 198 new ones—which led to problems that we shall explore in detail in the chapters that follow. But it also prevented pro-centralization interests from organizing an effective opposition to reform. As a result the decentralization implemented varied surprisingly little from that initially proposed.

The Law of Popular Participation passed by Bolivia's congress was remarkably simple and concise. It established a per capita fiscal transfer rule that was clear and comprehensible to Bolivia's large poor population. The government proceeded to advertise it throughout the country, urging citizens to hold local authorities to account for the resources they received. As we shall see, citizens did so in terms that were often emphatic and precise. More important still was the system of local governance that reform put into place. This was both simple and—with the inclusion of oversight committees—multiply redundant. It explicitly incorporated Bolivia's abundant traditions and organizations of community self-government into the municipal governance system, and thence into the state. As we shall see below, this contributed powerfully to achieving high levels of accountability in many (not all) municipalities and thus to the changes in investment flows and government responsiveness chronicled here.

The nationwide changes that followed decentralization are striking and lend credence to some of the central claims made in favor of reform. There were broad shifts in public investment flows from production to human capital formation and primary social services. This national shift was disproportionately driven by Bolivia's smaller, poorer, more rural municipalities. The change in the uses of public investment was accompanied by a change in its geographic distribution, away from a few large cities toward the large majority of smaller, poorer, more rural districts. This resulted in a far more equitable distribution of resources across municipalities than central government had previously achieved. Indeed, the change in the number of municipalities receiving public investment—total and by sector—is enormous, increasing by as much as 90 percent in some sectors.

Local governments proved consistently more responsive than central government to local needs. In the six sectors examined, public investment became more responsive to objective indicators of need after decentralization than it had been before. In four of these sectors, central government had invested regressively in terms of need, concentrating resources in districts well endowed with services and infrastructure; in one sector it invested neutrally; and in one more it invested progressively. After reform, local governments invested progressively in terms of need in all six sectors, concentrating resources where need was greatest. In four of these the change was immediate, and in two more progressivity emerged during subsequent periods. In two sectors local investment initially responsive to local need became regressive during the later periods.

This curiosity may be due to the combined effects of timing, as needier districts invest larger amounts at the outset and later redirect resources to other sectors, and progress in needs indicators, as sustained investments begin to have real effects. Indeed, there is evidence of large improvements in illiteracy and sewerage connection rates, with the former falling by more than half over the period. Unfortunately a lack of time-series data for needs-type variables hampers our ability both to relate need to investment patterns in later periods and to explain why the "curiosity"—if it is indeed real—occurs.

Finally, the broad trends described provide evidence of organizational learning by municipal governments and perhaps an increasing sophistication of their electorates. Municipalities begin the decentralization era investing large amounts in urban development and education, and much smaller amounts elsewhere. The former are sectors where projects are relatively simple and easy to understand, require fewer engineering and architectural skills to design, and need less public management capacity to execute and oversee. They tend to be concentrated in space (unlike, say, roads or irrigation systems) and highly visible in town and village centers. This makes them easy for citizens to criticize, contribute to, and learn from. They become focal points for voter assessments of politicians' performance and for community learning about the workings of public policy. They teach governments budgeting, bidding, design, evaluation, and implementation skills, and they help citizens discover the limits of policy for solving collective problems.

The evidence implies that local governments (and citizens) learn these lessons and over time apply them to investments in other sectors, such as water & sanitation, health, and agriculture, that require greater technical and organization skills. In doing so, municipalities learn to handle more complex kinds of investments and to manage a larger number and variety of projects simultaneously. The pattern of investments that emerges by 2003–7 (see figures 4 and 7)—all municipalities investing increasing amounts across a complex range of sectors—requires significant organizational skills in even poorer districts. The pattern of investment over time implies that these skills have been acquired.

CHAPTER 2

Local Government at the Extremes: Viacha

The dramatic changes in investment patterns described in the previous chapter must originate in the decisions and actions undertaken by local governments all over Bolivia. This chapter and the next examine the institutional and social underpinnings of governance in two extreme cases of low and high performance in order to understand what drives public decision making in each.

Introduction: 1997

Wilting under the afternoon sun, Viacha squats on the altiplano like a dusty *cholita* at market, tired after a long day selling pantyhose and cigarettes smuggled from Peru. Approaching along the old southern road from La Paz, the outer edges of El Alto lap like wavelets at the limits of Viacha, the two cities bridged by a thin line of nameless eateries and roadside mechanics that never quite peter out. One may be forgiven for considering Viacha a suburb of the La Paz–El Alto conurbation. Urban *viacheños* would take exception. They clearly think of their home as a city, and the surrounding countryside—when they think of it at all—as a catchment area of little importance. But to believe this is a mistake, as Viacha is in fact a large rural municipality with a medium-sized city in one corner. Of the seven districts that make it up, four are rural. Of its 54,761 inhabitants, two-thirds are dispersed among 300 rural communities that reach all the way to the border with Peru, with the remaining third living in the city.[1]

By Bolivian standards Viacha is a wealthy industrial town. It is home to the main cement plant of the Sociedad Boliviana de Cementos (SOBOCE), Bolivia's largest cement company, as well as a large bottling plant belonging to the Cervecería Boliviana Nacional (CBN), Bolivia's largest brewery. Both companies contribute directly and significantly to Viacha's municipal coffers through property taxes, business licenses, electricity bills, and—in the case of the CBN—generous in-kind lending of trucks and other heavy machinery, as well as large donations of beer, all placed at the mayor's disposal. Strung along the main road out of Viacha are numerous medium-sized and small textile, brick and tile, and other construction-related businesses, all of which contribute to local incomes and tax receipts. Municipal income includes receipts from property and vehicle taxes, licenses and place-rents for businesses and street commerce, planning and zoning approval fees, and a number of other items—more than most other cities in Bolivia. But the city is curiously free of the signs of wealth, and hence of inequality, with neighborhoods ranging in appearance from poor peri-urban to middle class, but no higher. This is probably because the most successful Viachans take up residence in La Paz, underlining the city's status as a dormitory town. Viacha's index of Unsatisfied Basic Needs[2] (0.852 on a scale where 0 is best and 1 worst) places it in the best-off 25 percent of Bolivian municipalities; its proximity to the cities of La Paz and El Alto ensures a higher level of economic activity than other cities of comparable size.

Yet by the middle of 1997 Viacha was a troubled town. After three consecutive electoral victories, the populist Unión Cívica de Solidaridad (UCS) party had lost its sheen in a hail of corruption accusations and was increasingly seen as ineffective. Two million bolivianos went unspent from the 1996 budget despite the mayor's pleas that he lacked resources to satisfy communities' needs. A rival oversight committee (OC2) was established demanding the mayor's resignation and disbandment of the official oversight committee (OC1—sanctioned by the municipal government). With two competing OCs (and two sets of neighborhood councils), the participative planning process broke down as the city became polarized between groups supporting the mayor and those demanding his resignation. In the midst of this poisonous climate, thieves broke into the municipal garage, killed the elderly guard, and stole two vehicles. This gave rise to further accusations and counteraccusations. "There are cars parked on the street all over La Paz and El Alto," the president of OC1 said, explaining that one of the stolen vehicles had been located in El Alto. "If you want to steal a car, why would you come to Viacha and steal it from a guarded garage?"[3] In his opinion, the crime was the work of the opposition seeking to sully the mayor's reputation. Others saw the hand of the mayor, ordering a robbery to blame on the opposition in advance of the upcoming elections. In interviews in March of that year, however, municipal councilmen seemed not to appreciate the severity of their problems: "Not everything is going badly, nor is all well—we have our imperfections,"[4] and then they blamed the crisis on the opposition's "exaggerations."

The eruptions of Viachan politics occur within a broader tide of urban migration that flows around and through the city, giving Viacha its character. Perched on the edge of La Paz–El Alto, Viacha is the first stop for many peasants fleeing the hardships of subsistence agriculture on the altiplano. Some move directly on to El Alto, but others stay and complete the transition to urban life in Viacha. They fill the streets with their Aymara dress, speech, and rural customs, and are the objects of ridicule by city folk who wear shoes and use electricity to cook.[5] Supporting themselves at first through menial labor or selling in the markets, and then through better-paid jobs in La Paz–El Alto to which they make the hour-long commute, they build the adobe neighborhoods of the city further and further outward. They take little pride in the history of a city that has traditionally defined itself in opposition to the countryside; they stay because the living is cheap.[6] The battle against prejudice to improve their livelihoods gives many Viachans a disconcerting blend of aggressive opportunism and rural tastes. "*Viacheños* are the New Yorkers of the region—they have vices that others don't. There's too much alcohol about and everyone shows off their money drinking,"[7] according to Carlos Núñez, financial director of SOBOCE. The city's northward expansion along the road to La Paz is in effect fusing it with El Alto,[8] leading to numerous problems of delimitation, land registration, and taxation, which the two municipalities struggle to resolve.

The rest of this chapter considers the quality of local government that Viacha achieved and the organizations most directly implicated in producing the same—the mayor, municipal council, oversight committee, and departmental and national governments—in the immediate aftermath of reform (1994–97). We then turn to deeper determinants of the quality of local governance, organized in three categories: the private sector, political parties and elections, and community and grassroots organizations. We focus on municipal performance during the first few years after decentralization in Viacha (and then Charagua in chapter 3) in order to study the different effects that the same institutional shock produced in different sociopolitical and economic environments. Later, in chapter 8, we return to both municipalities 13 years later to see how governance changed over time.

Finally, a stylistic note: when referring to village-level testimony in this chapter and the one that follows, I will often use the construction "Village X said" to mean "the leaders of Village X said" in the interest of brevity.

Local Government Institutions

The Mayor and the Local Executive Branch

The mayor of Viacha in early 1997 was Edwin Callisaya, from the Aymara community of Tilata-Santa Trinidad in rural Viacha. Before entering politics Callisaya had taken courses in business administration at the university and then gone to work in the public sector in La Paz. He was first elected to the local council for the UCS in 1993 and became mayor shortly thereafter when the (reelected) mayor resigned to become an MP. He governed in coalition with the MNR through the 1995 election, which the UCS won easily with a large electoral surge attributed by many observers to the death of its leader, Max Fernandez, in an airplane crash.[9] From 1995 to 1999 the UCS governed Viacha alone.[10]

As a son of the poor countryside, Callisaya set out to ensure that resources reached rural villages. "He argues that rural areas never received anything, and so he must invest there," said Oscar Magnani Meyta, the district director of education in Viacha.[11] Callisaya visited rural communities more often than the previous mayor and met with their inhabitants, whose concerns and desires he was well-placed to understand. He invited rural leaders to Viacha and hosted them at municipal events, including a prominent one where the yearly investment plan was agreed upon and cosigned by 56 local community leaders.[12]

Callisaya also expressed the desire to make Viacha a "model municipality," with a modern, rational administration that was transparent and a beacon to Viacha's less fortunate neighbors.[13] To this end he sought to use resources from the World Bank, the Social Investment Fund (FIS), and others—who he claimed recognized Viacha's natural importance—to increase both the size and quality of the municipal workforce. The municipal payroll rose accordingly from 70 to 150 during his mayoralty, and in the second year of his term he called a public competition to fill the posts of chief financial and technical officers. Seventy applicants with professional qualifications applied for the two positions, marking the first important step in the technification of Viachan government. Despite this, Viacha's government still seemed lost on fairly basic issues. The newly hired chief financial officer admitted to me that "SOBOCE and the CBN are our great problems—we don't know what taxes we are allowed to charge them, nor for what amount. And it's worse if they obtain legal advice. We don't know which way is north."[14]

From the outside, Callisaya's administration was seen as somewhat successful in some quarters. In an interview after the 1997 elections, the district director of education (DDE) reported that the municipality complied with minimum legal requirements by providing funds for maintenance (e.g., desks, paper, classroom supplies) as well as investment (e.g., building classrooms, fixing buildings, equipping schools).[15] But even this praise was balanced by complaints that the municipal government refused to coordinate with the DDE, planning, designing, and building educational infrastructure with no DDE input. Because the municipality has more resources than the DDE, communities solicit projects directly. The DDE is thus excluded at every stage of the project cycle, and as a result "municipal projects do not conform to the standards of the education sector,"[16] including especially those set out by the Bolivian Education Reform Program.[17] This problem is compounded by the municipality's "constructionist" mentality, which prefers building infrastructure to running programs and providing services. "The municipality thinks the money should be used for urban development projects anyway," said the DDE, complaining that what educational investment it does carry out is almost entirely restricted to building and refurbishing simple schoolhouses dotted across the countryside. "And were it not for the PASE [a central government matching-grants scheme] they would not do even that."[18]

Even this investment is unequally allocated across Viacha, with a small community like Titik'ana Takaka receiving three classrooms in addition to its existing three while many others receive nothing. The DDE estimated that some 40 percent of Viachan villages are forgotten by the municipal government. He attributed this to an ad hoc planning system that depends fundamentally on pressure politics and makes no effort to objectively assess local needs or equitably allocate investment resources. Thus, in his words, "the communities that demand the most get the most," implying a bias in favor of villages that lie closer to the city, or those with the resources to fund travel and lodging for grassroots leaders to lobby the mayor's office. The mayor effectively agreed with this analysis, admitting that communities whose leaders were most "political" were most successful at getting their projects approved and obtaining municipal funds.[19] And the chief financial officer conceded that he did not know how many projects the municipality had financed, nor how the Annual Operating Plan (AOP) had been drawn up, though he understood that the criteria used were not technical.[20]

That the municipality ran such a "system" instead of making a serious attempt at investment programming was at least partly due to the poor quality of municipal personnel, "who are mostly UCS hacks instead of professionals."[21] "The cultural level of the local authorities isn't optimal," agrees Mr. Núñez of SOBOCE. "The first things the municipal government bought when Popular Participation funds arrived were cars, TVs, and so on," he added with disdain.[22] Even some municipal councilmen agreed with this view, arguing that the increase in the municipal payroll was "all numbers and no quality, or even with decreasing quality."[23] The head of Incerpaz, the largest of Viacha's brick and tile firms, extended this judgment to the municipal council itself, asserting that "the main problem this municipality faces is a lack of qualifications and ability on the part of the municipal council and administration" and noting that qualified people tend to migrate to La Paz. "This municipality isn't sufficiently technical to devise a master plan of development for the municipality—something that the private sector in Viacha has directly requested."[24]

On the other side of Viacha, the DDE's colleague Dr. Reynaldo Aguilar, district director of health (DDH), agreed with his diagnosis, while reporting a situation that was significantly worse. "The municipal government refuses to pay its share of the Maternal & Infant Health Insurance, as the law demands"[25] he said, explaining that the municipality seized on incomplete documentation to declare the DDH's payment requests invalid and refuse disbursement. "In health the municipality is hypocritical," he sighed. "They talk a lot but invest nothing." Like the DDE, Dr. Aguilar was never invited to review Viacha's Annual Operating Plan despite requests for coordination. He detailed how the DDH lost the only hospital in the city and all of the equipment that they and others had bought for it, due to a mixture of incompetence, bad luck, and sheer lack of interest on the part of the municipality. "The mayor is terribly bad," he concluded, a sentiment shared by Subprefect Gladys Lozano, the local representative of the departmental government.[26] It is notable that the mayor managed to alienate the representatives of the Ministries of Education and Health and the prefect, arguably the three most important agents of central government in the city, during a relatively short period of time.[27] In the case of Lozano the distrust became active and angry opposition.[28]

Among Viacha's private firms, the most important politically is the CBN bottling plant. The man who formed the CBN was an unschooled laborer, Max Fernández, whose fabled ascent began at the wheel of a delivery truck and ended with him dominating the industry. Turning his populist attentions to politics, he founded the UCS party and integrated it tightly into his beer empire, distributing pamphlets out of CBN delivery trucks and selling beer at political rallies. Thus, to interview a spokesman for the CBN is to speak to the largest employer in the region, but it is also to see the other face of the Fernández family enterprise. The opinion of the mayor offered by José Luis Claros, production supervisor at the CBN bottling plant, is accordingly benign: "Our relations with the HAM are obviously good because we're from the same party," he said, explaining how the CBN provides the municipality with "trucks, machinery, beer—*everything*. And all free of charge. We give them beer in small quantities, say twenty cases at a time, for their meetings, events, celebrations. We support them too much," and his smile implied a professional impatience with this open drain on his accounts.[29] "All the same, the municipality doesn't prioritize us with any of its expenditures—it only takes."

At SOBOCE, Claros's counterpart, Núñez, was less generous in his assessment, arguing that the municipality is largely dedicated to a symbolic equality, wasting its resources on cosmetic and essentially pointless investments like "government houses" and plazas in rural areas that make locals feel they are not ignored, but that do little to improve their quality of life— a point that the local priest echoed.[30] "There's no civil leader here who gives guidance on good, significant projects" that respond to local needs, he said.[31] Luis González of the FIS agreed, adding, "Many *viacheños* want to rid themselves of Callisaya . . . but he's proven good at managing relations with the brewery, and manipulating [public opinion] through the parties and local festivals they sponsor."[32]

In addition to a showman, the mayor was a shrewd tactician, conspiring to neutralize the opposition and short-circuit municipal accountability mechanisms. "The original oversight committee used to cut his financing and give him all sorts of trouble," according to Lt. Col. Dávila, "but he wanted to be the 'little king' and considered them the enemy. When the OC was being renewed, he divided the nominating congress of grassroots leaders—divided and conquered them."[33] With no effective oversight, Callisaya was able to do as he pleased and impose his will freely. In everything from the petty to the scandalous, the executive branch was not held to account. "He buys the peasants off with stupidities, and other times he sends them away, telling them 'Come back tomorrow.'"[34] The community leaders of Santa Ana de Machaqa, to name just one example, provided details.

> The mayor comes along brightly to ask us what projects we want, but then does nothing about it. . . . The municipality isn't like the Plan Internacional [an NGO active in the area], which does come through for us. . . . We spend money making trips to Viacha to make formal requests for projects but nothing comes of it.[35]

The municipality did build a schoolhouse and public urinals in Santa Ana, but local residents were not consulted about the project design and were not told the amount of the counterpart contribution that they were expected to make. The community's request to change the urinals to an additional classroom was rejected. Then they were overcharged for their lime supplies and discovered that the wood the municipality provided was rotten.[36] But the mayor's high-handed rule proved even worse in Sombrapata. According to Subprefect Lozano, this community was excluded entirely from the municipal participative planning exercise because of the UCS's low vote tally.[37] Project quality suffered as well. "The [city's] sewerage extension was badly done with pipes that were too small," explained Dávila. "They exploded and inundated the city with waste. . . . Even today water and sewerage service does not extend beyond four blocks from the main square," leaving his military base unattended.[38] The mayor himself admits that municipal performance has been "bad" in health, garbage collection, sewerage, roads, and irrigation.[39]

The picture that emerges is of a municipal executive who makes some effort to spread resources throughout the municipality but who lacks the personnel, technical criteria, quality control, beneficiary participation, budgetary controls, and ultimately the leadership to articulate a clear investment strategy and use resources effectively. With a municipal staff awash in people but lacking skills, and an institutional structure undermined and incapable of carrying out oversight, the mayor's impulses in favor of the rural poor were drowned in a sea of mismanagement and demagoguery. Political imperatives were allowed to override all others, and the municipality ignored community needs and the requirements of the education and health networks in a crude attempt to maximize votes.

Such a situation would seem destined to lead to corruption, and in Viacha it did. Paz asserts that municipal employees stole municipal property as a matter of course.[40] According to Lozano, the mayor authorized the purchase of cement at twice the market price in a transparent kickback scheme.[41] According to Dávila the mayor bought a large piece of land alongside the main road to La Paz in a clear conflict of interest. SOBOCE's Núñez places corruption in the larger context of the municipality's overall performance.

> The municipality plans roads and related works badly. First they tear up the roads to lay down sewerage, and then a few months later they tear them up again for water works. Our cement trucks take the blame for poor state of roads, but it's also the municipality's fault with their poor-quality repairs. We have serious suspicions of corruption in all of this. It seems to be all about payments to certain firms for construction and equipment rental. Imagine—they're paying more for pavement here than in La Paz![42]

Even councilman Ticona stated simply, "Edwin Callisaya is corrupt," referring to the regular overpricing of projects during his tenure. "One cemetery was budgeted at Bs. 50,000 but then built for only Bs. 28,000. But the municipality poured Bs. 50,000 or more into it anyway. Callisaya and his officers conspired to do this."[43] But the most impressive evidence of the effects of the mayor's near-impunity concerns the checks and computer records of community counterpart contributions for the sewerage projects mentioned above.

> The account, earmarked for the purchase and laying of pipes, reached Bs. 6 million, but nothing happened. When the neighborhood councils began asking what was going on, the computer was stolen along with the checks. Shortly afterwards, the checks reappeared, having been cashed in Argentina.[44]

Both Dávila and Lozano claimed that the mayor and Edgar Robles, then-president of the municipal council, were involved, and Lozano went so far as to accuse the two of going on a vacation-cum-spending spree in Argentina with the sewerage funds.

It is not surprising, then, that by the end of his tenure Callisaya was deeply unpopular. The national auditing agency informed the municipality that it had found evidence of administrative charges against him.[45] Newspaper articles appeared documenting allegations of corruption, and the rival OC2 called repeatedly and loudly for his resignation. "The mayor acts in a 'verticalist' way like a dictator," the president of OC2 declaimed. "He is a peasant who wouldn't know how to speak to a donkey."[46] "The CBN gives the city equipment, money, and beer. But they don't give them brains, or at least not the mayor," added Dávila.[47] As *viacheños* seemed to awaken out of their torpor and political tensions mounted, the impression dawned in Viacha that the municipality was actually worse off than before the Law of Popular Participation. Local government was now larger, less efficient, and more corrupt. Voters were demoralized by the municipality's ineffectiveness in the countryside and scandalized by its corruption in the city.

Municipal Council

The UCS's electoral surge of 15 percent in Viacha's 1995 municipal election had the net effect of wresting one council seat away from Condepa. Hence the balance of councilmen in early 1997 was UCS four, Condepa two, and MNR one. Although the UCS now held a majority of seats on its own, in practice the MNR continued to cooperate with it, mirroring the parties' coalition at the national level. The president of the municipal council was Edgar Robles, a former schoolteacher from Sucre and Potosí whose family lived in La Paz. Despite having no family or community ties to Viacha, he had been elected to public office three times there—as mayor in 1991 and again in 1993 (succeeded by Callisaya when Robles became a substitute MP in La Paz), and as a councilman in 1995. Robles's fellow party-members on the council were farmers and local leaders from the Aymara communities of the Machaqas region toward Peru. Unskilled in the practice of urban politics, both they and the city seemed slightly stunned by their presence in city hall as late as 1997. The two Condepa councilmen were both city *viacheños* and former employees of public enterprises, one of them in La Paz, who entered politics by becoming party activists. And the lone MNR representative, also from Viacha, was the recently elected head of his party *comando* and a public employee who worked for the central government in La Paz.

When asked about Popular Participation, councilmen universally opined that it was a very good law and beneficial to their constituency. But they also seemed somewhat intimidated by the process and worried about the expectations it was generating in rural communities.[48] Unfortunately their worries did not spur them to action. They admitted to ignorance about the 1994 Municipal Development Plan, which maps local needs and preferences for public investment throughout Viacha,[49] implying that they were not using it as part of the budgeting and investment planning process in the municipality. And while noting that Viacha's needs in health and waste disposal were considerable, they acknowledged that the municipality's performance in these areas so far was poor, and that in electricity, roads, irrigation, and water little or nothing had been achieved.[50]

Box 1: The Cure

Esteban Ticona wheezes and sneezes his way through our second interview. His nose is bright red and his gaze floats toward me through a sea of misery. As we finish, his secretary arrives with a dark potion she has just bought from a street vendor. Elated, Ticona leaps into the Council chamber and drops his pants. She jabs him with a huge syringe and decants the murky liquid into his bottom. "Guaranteed to cure a sore throat," she says, beaming. Ticona emerges shortly, smiling, wincing, and clutching his rear.

This peculiar combination of concern with inaction may be partly explained by the municipal council's view of its role in local government, which is that of a tail wagged by the executive (i.e., mayoral) dog. "We have one secretary and one adviser," the councilmen complained. "How are we supposed to cope? They [the executive] have 140 people there."[51] When asked about the organization of the local administration, salary levels, and hiring criteria, they responded that they had made similar queries formally to the mayor but had received no response. "We do not have access to that information," they pleaded.[52] They went on to float a proposal for more training of municipal staff and more resources generally to improve the municipal administration. They seemed not to appreciate the irony that it is the municipal council that approves the local budget, and it is thus within their power to increase funding for any item that they choose.

Regarding its external role in the municipality, the council claimed to set policy and priorities according to their voters' wishes. But on this point they were directly contradicted by the voters themselves. Community leaders in Santa Ana de Machaqa testified that "councilmen obey their parties—

they're elected as representatives of the local people here, but then they go to Viacha and get absorbed by the political parties there and forget their home."[53] In Titik'ana Takaka, the leaders said that "councilmen respond mainly to the parties and the municipal government's own interests, not ours."[54] Judgments were virtually identical in the communities of District Five, District Six, Chama, and the city of Viacha.[55] Even the mayor testified that councilmen ignore their voters, explaining that "there is a party discipline that has to be obeyed."[56] As if to underline the point, Quintela and Ticona admitted to knowing nothing about how a large and controversial project to rebuild a school in Viacha was designed and tendered. "The Social Investment Fund did it all—we weren't involved."[57]

Given this panorama, it is not surprising that outsiders' views of the municipal council were unflattering. "The one who thinks on the municipal council is Edgar Robles," said Lt. Col. Dávila. "The mayor is also clever. The rest are a brotherhood of imbeciles." Luis Paz agreed, calling the councilmen "ignorant and imperceptive."[58] Some, including the subprefect and the local leader of Condepa, singled out the UCS rural councilmen for scorn as unsophisticated and easily manipulable. "They're ignorant peasants—they don't know where they're standing," elaborated the latter.[59] I had the good fortune to travel with two of these UCS rural councilmen for a long day across the Viachan hinterland to the border with Peru and back. Both men were very kind and helpful, and kept high spirits throughout a tiring ride in a crowded jeep. But neither showed much interest in the opinions and priorities of the communities we visited, all of which lay in their constituencies. I spent hours that day speaking to local leaders about their concerns and needs for municipal investment, but the two men were largely absent. Unfortunately, the criticism went deeper still. Ms. Lozano also accused some councilmen of corruption and political treachery. "The *Condepistas* used to complain and give the mayor trouble. But then the UCS found them jobs and now they're silent."[60] The district director of health asserted that the problem was more widespread—"The [entire] municipal council has been bought off—bought off by the UCS."[61]

All of the evidence points to a municipal council in Viacha that failed to operate as an independent deliberative and policy-setting body, and thus as a counterweight to the significant power of the mayor and local executive branch. Council members were of poor quality, untrained in the legal and procedural details of the post to which they had been elected and uninterested in learning the same. This was compounded by their perception of themselves as the residual in the local political equation, systematically uninformed about municipal business and powerless to affect the mayor's decisions; powerless, in fact, to learn what these decisions were until well after they had been made. This is difficult to understand given the broad authority granted to the council by Bolivia's constitutional and legal framework, as well as the system of countervailing approvals and oversight specified in the Law of Popular Participation. Indeed, Bolivian mayors emanate from municipal councils through indirect elections, and council members then have the prerogative to oust the mayor after his first, trial year via a "constructive vote of censure."[62] This option was exercised in over 100 municipalities in 1995–96 by councils that refused to tolerate the mayors they had elected. But in Viacha, councilmen sat idly by, complaining occasionally, while their municipality sank into a morass of waste and corruption.

Why did Viachan councilmen behave in this way when the legal and institutional context was identical to that of scores of municipalities with very different governing dynamics? A key piece of evidence is that the man chosen to be president of the municipal council was Edgar Robles, previous mayor and close associate of Callisaya who handed power over to him when the party elevated him to Congress. Combine him with three rural representatives who, though initially popular, were thoroughly unprepared and uninterested in exercising their responsibilities, and we have a council majority that serves as the right arm of the mayor, rubber-stamping his decisions and helping to obscure his dishonesty. Such a majority is completely unsuited for municipal oversight and control, and most unlikely to engage in it. Eventually opposition councilmen did cause trouble for the mayor, attempting to scrutinize his accounts and call him to order. When this happened, the opposition was simply bought off by the UCS wielding the huge economic power of the Cervecería Boliviana Nacional.

The trail leads directly to the door of the CBN/UCS, which would appear to have constructed a deliberate strategy of neutralizing the municipal council via candidate selection and bribery. Rural UCS candidates were thus picked with the twin aims of maximizing the rural vote and minimizing their functional independence, and not because of any personal qualities they might bring to office. The ultimate institutional effect was to short-circuit the governance process and free the mayor's hand in his conduct of official business, allowing him to do whatever he chose. The evidence suggests that it worked. The larger question of how the CBN was able to achieve this and why must await completion of our survey.

Oversight Committee(s)

Viacha is divided into five rural and two urban districts. Within each of these, communities are represented by *mallkus, ayllus,* peasants' unions, neighborhood councils, or any other natural form that civil society chooses to express itself. The organizations within each district elect a *junta,* which represents communities' interests at the district level. The president of each junta is a member of the municipal oversight committee, which elects its own president from among its seven members.

Of the nine municipalities studied during this research,[63] Viacha is distinguished by having two oversight committees. But far from increasing scrutiny, this peculiarity undermined the oversight that municipal business received. Mayor Callisaya was the enemy of the OC he inherited, which opposed his policies and caused fiscal flows from central government to Viacha to be suspended.[64] At a congress called by the Federation of Juntas to renew the OC and attended by grassroots organizations from throughout the municipality, the mayor saw his chance. Accounts of the precise events at this conference differ in the details but agree on the following facts. The congress elected Hipólito Tovar and Teddy Montalvo, both known opponents of the mayor, as representatives to the OC for the two urban districts. Tovar was also chairing the assembly, and a dispute broke out over conflict of interest and his eligibility to stand. The assembly divided on this point and the situation became tense. Then the congress was invaded by "UCS activists, many of them employees of the municipalities, who had been drinking and were drunk. They caused disturbances and broke up the congress. They also used ladies from ADRA [a food-for-work scheme active in the area] armed with clubs," who threatened the delegates and barred their exit from the meeting hall.[65] The congress recessed early before completing its agenda.

One month later, the part of the congress supporting Tovar and Montalvo reconvened and finalized its nominations. Its action was recognized by the Federation of Juntas of La Paz, which validated the election of the two men. But during the interim, another "assembly of the people" was called, in which Remigio Quispe and Walter Patzi were named representatives to the OC and the Viachan Federation of Juntas respectively. The OC formed by the five previously elected rural representatives—about whom there was no controversy—and the two new urban ones duly elected Remigio Quispe as their president; a meeting of the juntas did likewise to Walter Patzi. The municipality recognized this result and installed both Quispe and Patzi in offices in city hall. Tovar and Montalvo were thereby excluded from the acting OC. During my time in Viacha Teddy Montalvo had faded into the background, and Hipólito Tovar had assumed the role of spokesman for the rival oversight committee and for community organizations opposed to the mayor's rule.

Remigio Quispe, representative for the first (urban) district and an ex-cooperative miner from the southern mining region of Bolivia recently arrived in Viacha, reported that the previous OC had done "nothing during the past two years—there's no documentation, nothing. Now *we're* going to comply with the law and scrutinize the municipality."[66] But there was little sign of this in his actions. When asked about specific investment projects that Viacha was undertaking in the city, Quispe admitted ignorance. He knew none of the financial details of a large school project a few blocks from his office and surmised that they must have been worked out in private between municipal technicians and those of the FIS. He knew nothing of the projects completed before his tenure. Among more general issues, he did not know how many people worked in the municipality nor what their salary levels were; he did not know which IT and accounting systems had been implemented in the municipality since 1994; and he didn't know the voting details of the last election. He nonetheless claimed that Viacha had done comparatively well after decentralization and called it a "model municipality." He attributed this in part to a mayor who responded more to the people than his party. "Here in Viacha things aren't so polarized," he added, numb to the public mood. He conceded that the OC did not receive requests for projects directly from communities, as in other municipalities, and that politics played a role in the allocation of funds, with UCS representatives leveraging resources out of the municipality more successfully than others. And yet his opinion of local government's performance in Viacha was higher than that of the mayor and municipal council, with higher performance ratings across five sectors.[67]

Not surprisingly, Hipólito Tovar and his associates from the opposition district junta disagreed with this assessment of municipal success. Tovar, a retired railway mechanic and longtime resident of Viacha, was categorical—even emotional—in denouncing the mayor as a corrupt demagogue, and his administration as a disaster for the city. His associates, Alejandro

Yujra[68] and Rony Morales,[69] vice president of the opposition Viachan Federation of Juntas and secretary of the San José neighborhood council, respectively, agreed with the substance of his position, though at times taking exception to his florid language. Accusing the municipality of consulting no one in the planning of its investment, the three qualified all of the municipality's projects as "very bad" and accused it of ignoring garbage disposal and irrigation entirely. "The municipality has drawn up several Annual Operating Plans in any given year—they keep changing their mind," Morales said, explaining how the mayor manipulated the planning process to obfuscate municipal goals and the uses of funds, thereby subverting effective oversight. In this confusion, "the municipal architect set up his own construction firm and built the [Evaristo Valle] school" with 100 percent cost overruns. That architect was also the construction supervisor for the project—an obvious conflict of interest.[70]

As one might expect, these three critics found themselves frozen out of all municipal business, with no access to records, investment plans, local resolutions, or any of the other information they requested. They nevertheless toured me around a number of recent or ongoing investment projects in Viacha to substantiate their many claims. At the Evaristo Valle school they pointed out obvious cases of poor construction, including a new wall that was cracked, sinking foundations, and a sunken roof, among others. The Ballivián school showed similar problems, with cracked walls and a new section built with bricks standing instead of lying flat.[71] Montes Avenue near the central square was in a terrible state, with large sunken sections where the ground had settled and new holes opening at one end despite being repaired five times. The "Toboggan," a long, high slide located in a children's playground that seems to have particularly captured the mayor's attention, had fallen apart after only a few months, with a large central section missing. The M. Pinilla Avenue was literally an unusable ruin despite three reconstructions, occasioned in part by the exploding sewerage project described above. But of these and other projects we saw in various states of decomposition, nothing compares to the Park of the Americas. This was a large, overgrown area cordoned off by a low wire fence, with a high rubbish dump in the middle and a sewage-contaminated lake[72] off to one side. According to Morales, Viacha had invested Bs. 200,000 in this park the previous year.[73]

Outside of the city no one I spoke to knew of the existence of rival OCs.

Because there had been no controversy surrounding the nomination of rural OC members, rural leaders referred to OC1 as "the" OC. Disappointment with its performance was widespread. Local leaders from Santa Ana de Machaqa accused the OC of doing no work with them and ignoring them completely.[74] Leaders from Titik'ana Takaka asserted that the OC did not work well, but that they knew few details and were seeking information in order to sanction or overturn it. Even in the city, people as prominent as the CEO of Incerpaz doubted its existence.[75]

All of the evidence points to an official OC1 that was beholden to the mayor, completely uninformed and operationally inert, not only failing to provide any sort of counterbalance to his power but actively endorsing his manipulations. Thus we have the approval of the 1997 Annual Operating Plan, in which the mayor summoned community leaders to a "planning seminar" in the city. Having paid and fed them, he invited them all to endorse a plan that his technicians had drawn up earlier. "The communities didn't propose a single project in that plan. Each of the 56 leaders who signed was given a can of beer," said Tovar. "And Remigio Quispe approved it all" in the name of the OC. That night they celebrated at the health post with a big party. Things got out of control and a guard was killed and two vehicles stolen.[76] Quispe and the mayor both publicly blamed the opposition. So extreme was the situation that even councilman Ticona admitted that the OC did not function in Viacha, and that Quispe received a municipal salary in direct violation of the law.[77]

Meanwhile, the opposition OC2 was considerably more active, better informed, and intent on providing active oversight of municipal policies. But having been sidelined by the mayor, it was unrecognized by the state and thus powerless to oppose his actions. When representatives of OC2 and the opposition Viachan Federation of Juntas approached the departmental secretary of popular participation to request that municipal funds be frozen due to corruption, he ignored their pleas. Already liberated by his party from the political oversight of a functioning municipal council, the mayor was also able to block social oversight by dividing civil society against itself, neutralizing its mechanism for accountability, and hiring his own. And the ensuing circus of accusation and counteraccusation between OC1 and OC2 served, if anything, to divert popular attention and shield him further from public scrutiny. The result was the squandering of resources and opportunity described above.

National and Departmental Government

Until 2005, departmental governments were not elected in Bolivia. Rather, the president directly named prefects, who in turn named their subprefects and other departmental officials. Thus departmental and national government are regarded here as a continuum, as they were by most Bolivians. The highest departmental representative in Viacha was the subprefect, an honor accorded the city on account of its status as the first municipality of the Ingavi province.[78] The holder of this post in 1997 was Gladys Lozano, a local resident and former nurse who holds a university degree—probably the only person active in local politics at the time so qualified. With almost no budget or staff, and few operational responsibilities, she threw herself wholeheartedly into the political battle against the mayor, whom she despised. She clearly regarded her job as primarily, or even exclusively, political, and in a daylong journey through the countryside did not hesitate to point out the many party slogans that she had proudly painted herself on hillsides, boulders, and cliffs. But her power was limited to exhortation and public complaint. She had neither the resources nor the authority to challenge the mayor. Despite an intense desire to oust him, she was able to do little more than conspire with the local opposition.

The two other important central government authorities in Viacha were the district directors of education and health, already encountered above. Each reports to his respective departmental secretary, who in turn reports to sectoral ministries in La Paz. As we saw above, neither the DDE nor the DDH, despite strong criticisms of the mayor's policies, was able to affect local policy in significant ways. In both education and health, the municipality ignored or actively flouted sectoral policies without fear of reprisal from local authorities or their superiors in La Paz.

The mayor and municipal councilmen confirmed their own supremacy locally. "The prefecture doesn't get in the way of the municipal council," reported Ticona, adding that "the change of government has had no effect on Viacha so far—the National Fund for Regional Development [an executive agency] treats us the same as before,"[79] two sentiments with which Quintela agreed.[80] The mayor confirmed on several occasions that central and departmental government officials cooperated with the municipality, or at least kept out of its way, and that he was fully satisfied with his relationship with the authorities in La Paz.[81] Local leaders from the communities of Villa Santiago de Chacoma, Rosapata, Názacara, and the city of Viacha confirmed independently that little or nothing had changed when the national government changed hands in 1997, and that central government thus appeared to have little leverage over local policies. Both OCs supported this view. Perhaps the main reason for this was provided by Quintela, who pointed out that "the mayor's and municipal council's authority emanate from popular elections, whereas the prefect is designated. Hence in any conflict between the two the municipal authorities must prevail" because of their democratic legitimacy.[82]

The evidence from Viacha supports the argument that central government regulations on local government behavior did not constitute a binding constraint on the latter. This was not, it is important to note, for lack of wanting or even trying. The DDE and DDH were strongly opposed to different aspects of municipal policy in their respective sectors, and the subprefect on several occasions declared her heartfelt intent to topple the mayor. But central government authorities in Viacha proved too weak institutionally, and too lacking in resources and democratic legitimacy, to mount a serious challenge to the ruling administration. Once the mayor had cleared local obstacles along the path to his own impunity, he was able to travel it in comfort, secure in the knowledge that his authority would not be contradicted by the government in La Paz.

Deeper Determinants of Local Governance

Private Sector

Of the large private firms in Viacha, the most typical of local industry is Industrias de Cerámica Paz, or Incerpaz. The most successful of the tile and brick firms that line the highway between Viacha and El Alto, Incerpaz has factories in several departments and sales throughout the country. Its CEO in 1997 was Luis Paz, an engineer by training and descendant of the company's founder. He boasted of excellent, though limited, relations with the municipality. Despite the firm's size, Incerpaz paid only some US$2,000[83] per year in property tax to Viacha, and the remainder of his tax bill to the city of La Paz, where the company is legally registered. Paz asserted that that sum would rise to $13,000 to $15,000 per year if he were to change Incerpaz's legal domicile to Viacha. Sitting in his factory office from which he runs the firm, he professed a willingness to do this. He cited the case of Warnes, a similar satellite city just outside Bolivia's second city of Santa Cruz, that tempted companies to relocate there with a five-year tax holiday. "If the municipality offered to improve the main road, street lighting, and other local installations, this property would rise in value and I could borrow more," he explained. "Then it would be worthwhile for me to register in Viacha. But they don't propose anything," he added with exasperation.[84]

Incerpaz had essentially no other dealings with the municipality; neither approached the other, and Paz was content to watch municipal affairs from the sidelines. He reported that "the principal mechanism of power" in Viacha was money, and that the CBN bought power through its financial support of municipal activities. "They support all folkloric activity here," he said, in order to support the mayor and simultaneously increase beer sales. In his opinion, corruption was rampant in Viacha. "But the money from the CBN washes away corruption, and the people vote for them anyway."[85]

Paz explained the high degree of social conflict in Viacha as an endemic problem based on *viacheño* culture and even geography.

> The altiplano is very poor, with only one crop per year. In Cochabamba and Santa Cruz nature is abundant and no one lacks food. But not here—on the altiplano they're on a knife's edge of hunger and poverty. Here when they find a vein of gold they never ever let go because it's the only one they'll ever get. This is typical of the altiplano. In the valleys and tropics people are more generous. Here people work longer hours and are more productive but still they have less. We have factories in La Paz, Oruro, Cochabamba, and Santa Cruz. Our best personnel are here—much harder working. In Santa Cruz they won't work more than eight hours. Here they put in fourteen hours and charge overtime down to the penny. And they know—Bs.125.25, and they charge you the 25 cents. In Santa Cruz they don't worry about pennies.[86]

According to this interpretation, deprivation leads people of the altiplano to fight over resources in a way that is more desperate and raw than elsewhere. And the presence of a few large sources of patronage leads society to polarize around competing political-industrial poles of influence. In Paz's view, traditional forms of community government, where elected leaders are expected to serve as advocates for local interests before municipal and regional government, only exacerbate this. "The moment someone declares himself a social representative, he starts demanding donations and favors" to pay for his activities. Thus people fight over these positions and create even more social divisions at the grassroots level. Community representatives from the villages of District Five, District Six, and Chama as well as from the city agreed with Paz about the presence of industrial patronage and were not afraid to name the interests involved. "Beer and cement call the shots in Viacha."[87]

With its huge factory on the dusty outer edge of the city, SOBOCE's physical presence in Viacha is certainly large. The plant generated $30 million/year in sales and $2,340,000/year in value-added tax, which was paid in La Paz where the firm was legally based. Owned by the prominent politician and ex-minister of planning from the Movimiento de la Izquierda Revolucionaria (MIR), Samuel Doria Medina, the company had in recent years given up its previously activist stance in local politics. "We don't want to be too involved in local politics," Núñez said. "We have no intention of installing a MIR mayor."[88] The company provided regular support for the municipality's sporting and cultural events, but otherwise kept its distance from local politics. This stemmed at least in part from the political beating SOBOCE had suffered four years earlier. Núñez explained that a decade before the plant had been highly inefficient, operating at a fraction of its capacity. Then a new management team took over and increased output considerably, with a resulting increase in pollution. The local population protested vociferously, spurred on by environmental groups from La Paz. After at first holding firm, SOBOCE eventually capitulated and installed filters when it was made clear that the plant was losing potential revenue up the chimney. The fight was intense, according to those who opposed the firm. "I'm the one who pushed and pushed for them to get filters," said Robles, who was mayor at the time. "So they tried to oust me."[89] In 1993 SOBOCE invested $3 million in electric filters that dramatically reduced pollution, and thereafter it maintained a low public profile in Viacha.

This did not imply, however, that the plant's managers approved of their municipal administration. Claros and Núñez reported that local government had not involved SOBOCE in its participative planning exercises nor informed it of its municipal development plan. The mayor and municipal council had repeatedly condemned SOBOCE for damaging local roads with its large cement trucks. Yet when the firm offered to build a ring road specially for the factory, the proposal became bogged down in the municipal council, and no decision was ever made. But it was SOBOCE's electricity payments that seemed to gall the two men most. "We pay the municipality $15,000 per month for our electricity supply," Núñez said, explaining that this was set by official municipal resolution and not metered in any way. "It must be enough to light up the whole town." The plant's management had in fact offered to light the entire municipality free of charge, but local government rejected the offer. So where did the money go? "It goes directly into the municipal coffers."[90] It was thus not surprising that local officials were completely unprepared for the plant's planned growth. "We are going to invest $45 million in this place, expanding the factory and machinery to make Viacha definitively the national center of cement production," Núñez explained. The plant's local taxes and user fees would double, but so would the strain it imposed on local services. "Even so the municipal government ignores this—they have no position at all regarding this."

With regard to broader issues of local society, Núñez seemed to agree with Paz, complaining that relations with local organizations and institutions were not very productive. "The altiplano mentality is too closed, too difficult," he said. Like Incerpaz, SOBOCE also had a plant in Santa Cruz, where Núñez found the atmosphere completely different. "There it's easy to reach agreement—agree compromises that make the city grow." If SOBOCE's relations with the municipality were problematic, that was not the case for the Cervecería Boliviana Nacional. Both Núñez and Claros pointed to the dominant role of the bottling plant in Viachan local affairs. "[The plant's director] Blanco owns this town," testified the former, adding that relations between the two companies had been difficult in the past but were now quite friendly. In Núñez's view the CBN did not recognize a distinction between business and politics. These opinions were widely shared among observers of Viachan affairs. "Blanco runs the show here," declared Dávila. "He lifts an eyebrow and heads roll. He plays politics from the CBN."[91] Luis Paz and the OC2 agreed, with the former calling Blanco "the éminence grise behind the curtain."[92]

Box 2: Who's the Boss?

"They say I'm the boss in Viacha?" Blanco mocks my question and his roar echoes around the large office. "Call him," he barks at an aide. "Call him! I want him now!" A few minutes later Callisaya wanders meekly into the meeting. Dressed in blue jeans and tired cowboy boots, this CBN worker is a shadow of the proud, besuited mayor I'd met that autumn. "Sit down," Blanco commands. Callisaya gazes around in confusion. "There, next to him!" And he takes the empty seat at my side. The altiplano sun blazes in through the huge window behind Blanco's desk. He leans back in his office chair, almost horizontal, his head enveloped in a blinding halo. "They've told him that I'm the boss in Viacha," he bellows at both of us. "What do you think? Do I run the show?" Callisaya's eyes are wide open, a slight tremor in one hand. He is deeply confused. "No," he says, swallowing. He looks first at me, then at Blanco, then back at me. "No, he doesn't run the show."

After many insistent requests, I met Blanco in his office at the CBN bottling plant; despite high expectations, he did not disappoint. At well over six feet Juan Carlos Blanco is a bear of a man, with larger-than-life expressions and a booming voice that spews a stream of obscenities. When I met him he was director of the bottling plant, leader of the local UCS and a prominent figure in the national party, director of Integration Radio and host of his own radio show, and a director of the National Fund for Regional Development. He told me he worked very hard and earned $8,000/month.[93] He defended himself against the accusations noted above. "The councilmen say 'Juan Carlos Blanco said so' to shield themselves, but I don't know what's happening!" he insisted, with an enormous smile. "It's true that I have influence, but I don't use it."[94] When the interview turned to Viacha's many problems, especially accusations of official corruption, his tone changed. "There are 50 or 60 people here who bitch about the party and the municipality in order to be bought off," he explained. "We bought off Rafael Rodríguez by hiring him, and he shut up." Still, local complaints about the UCS administration had only grown, and this annoyed him.

"My problem is that I have to manage rural councilmen," he explained, referring to three of the four UCS representatives. "The pie is too small and the necessities are very large. And the people think it's all a torrent of money. . . . The town wants all of the money for itself, and then Jesús de Machaqa [a community] brings 1000 peasants marching on Viacha demanding money and projects. But I'm lacking projects!" he bellowed in frustration. The Popular Participation Law had raised local expectations significantly, and the municipality had proven unequal to the task. "The municipality's employees are bad—they can't distinguish between good and bad materials." As a result his party's popularity had decreased dramatically. "I lost the elections horribly here," he moaned, referring to the recent national poll. "The UCS used to own this town because of the money Max[95] spent. But the opposition was very agile here. Now they're making me throw out this corrupt guy," he said, referring to Callisaya. And with that Blanco admitted that Viacha's problems went deeper than implementational weakness. "There is corruption in my municipality. Everything involves a percentage, everything is cooked." Local government was corrupt from the mayor down, and municipal employees had grown used to abusing their positions for personal gain. The graft and venality extended into civil society as well. "The peasant congresses run on money. He who pays out the most money reaps the most representatives." Blanco explained that the CBN had sent beer and cash to the previous congress and won significant support among rural leaders.

The irony, in Blanco's view, was that decentralization had made his job not easier but more difficult. "Before Popular Participation the municipalities were nothing. Max gave Viacha everything," he said nostalgically. The party's authority was unquestioned. But the devolution of large sums of money to local governments had raised local expectations and increased opportunities for graft, both problematic issues for someone in Blanco's position. Worse still, the price of the electorate's gratitude had risen significantly. The projects with which the UCS was previously able to win over the city were now lost in a sea of public investment. Unable to buy the UCS's electoral share with the usual ease, Blanco turned to more explicitly political action, sponsoring cultural and sporting events and providing beer for public occasions of all varieties. This strategy gradually lost effectiveness, however, as Viachans—newly empowered—grew dissatisfied with the politics of gesture. And UCS/CBN largesse became tainted by association with the officials who dispensed it, and entwined in the public's mind with the scandal of public drunkenness and violence that led to the killing at the municipal garage.

Political Parties and Elections

Bolivian politics in 1997 was broadly centered on the MNR, the party of land reform, the 1952–53 revolution, and the 1985 economic stabilization. This is true in two senses: (1) the MNR was a multiclass coalition with strong elements on both the left and right wings of Bolivian politics in addition to its large central element, placing it at the core of many coalition governments of varying ideological complexions; and (2) many Bolivian political parties formed as reactions to the MNR, either to the right or left of it, during and after the revolution. Hence the ADN, led by former dictator Gen. Hugo Banzer, consolidated much right-wing opposition to the MNR, while the MBL and MIR opposed it from the left. The newer UCS and Condepa parties, both formed by wealthy, charismatic businessmen, were harder to place on a left-right spectrum, not least because they behaved with even more opportunism than the other parties; it is probably fair to place them slightly left of center.

The advent of decentralization in Bolivia brought a new political dynamic to Viacha, as elections that had previously been fought only in the city now extended through a large rural area. Seeing their opportunity, rural leaders from the Machaqa region took the initiative in the run-up to these elections and chose two respected local men with a history of service to their communities as candidates for the municipal council. As the LPP recognizes only candidates from legally registered parties, rural leaders needed to come to agreement with the political establishment in order to include their candidates on the ballot, and they decided that the UCS offered them the best chance. The mayor, who comanaged the campaign with Blanco, agreed to include the names on the UCS electoral list in exchange for the massive UCS vote that the Machaqa leaders promised in their region. In doing so he opened his party to the countryside for the first time. He also effectively co-opted forms of social organization and representation that were deeply rooted in the community structure of the Machaqa region, with all of their attendant legitimacy and capacity to mobilize public opinion. But then the mayor betrayed them. During the campaign he attempted to renege on his promise by changing the list to favor his own political allies, causing great consternation among *machaqueños*. In the end the original names were included, but lower down the list than had been promised. The UCS vote was sufficient to elect both to the council anyway,[96] but the goodwill Callisaya had begun to build with rural voters was tainted by the cavalier way he treated their representatives.

Such a lack of political commitment on the part of the UCS should not be surprising. The previous section documents that where the Viachan UCS was concerned, the party was the business, and the business was the party. The two concepts were intimately conflated in their means and their ends. The party availed itself of the brewery's delivery trucks, sales agents, and retailers to disseminate political literature and mobilize supporters. And political campaigns served as traveling beer rallies and brand-building exercises, the ubiquitous logo emblazoned behind every podium, campaign workers clad in blue CBN uniforms, and the famous froth gracing the lips of candidates as they communed with their voters. A number of times, as the sun set behind the mountains, I found uniformed workers from the brewery enthusiastically unloading UCS materials from their delivery trucks, working to capture the vote and earning overtime. With impeccable entrepreneurial logic, the twin imperatives "Drink *Paceña*" and "Vote UCS" were seductively paired in a seamless operation that never really shut down, a sort of permanent campaign enjoining consumers to enjoy life but also do their civic duty. Once the UCS was firmly in control of city hall, the concept of boundary-less enterprise was extended to include municipal business. "The UCS inaugurates projects, donates materials, and gives away beer as if it all came from the party, and not from the municipality's popular participation funds," Subprefect Lozano complained.

In the heated political atmosphere of Viacha, only the fellow populists of Condepa were able to challenge the UCS's dominance. The party was founded by a charismatic radio and television host who specialized in airing the grievances of La Paz's recent indigenous and mestizo migrants from the countryside. Condepa was adept at manipulating the symbols of race and oppression into an emotionally charged discourse of liberation that at times strayed toward vengeance. Without the economic power of the largest private business in Bolivia behind it, Condepa relied on its media outlets to generate a politics of identity that mobilized voters and nourished its constituency. Its position was illustrated by councilman Ticona's response when questioned about the support he received from the national party. "The party's support depends on me getting the *condepistas* jobs. But I can't because we're a minority in Viacha, and so the support of the national party has ebbed away."[97] With few links to the local business community, the party was dependent upon placing its activists in municipal jobs in order to sustain itself. The leader of the local party was an ex-railway worker named Tomás Palacios. He claimed that the party's electoral lists were set by an assembly of all local Condepa members from short lists drawn up by the party leadership. "But in effect urban members decide because rural members don't want to come to Viacha to participate."[98] The pragmatic Ticona, himself a product of this selection system, contradicted him.

Candidate lists are mostly set in La Paz by party or departmental leaders. Local people don't participate. This is true of all the parties except for the UCS, which is run out of the bottling plant. When someone ambitious isn't popular locally, he goes to La Paz to lobby [the party leadership], and often the order comes down to name him candidate.[99]

The third most important party in Viacha was the MNR, architect of the 1952–53 "nationalist revolution" in which the traditional *criollo*[100] landowning and mining upper class was overthrown in favor of an ascendant, educated middle class that nationalized the mines and redistributed land to dispossessed peasant farmers. Although the MNR was traditionally strong among rural voters, during the previous decade it had lost supporters throughout the altiplano to the potent appeal of Condepa and the UCS; between the 1993 and 1995 elections its vote tally fell by half. The local MNR leader in 1997 was councilman Quintela, who worked as a public employee in La Paz. He had been elected leader during the internal democratization of the party that had occurred a short time previously. "The MNR is the most democratic party in Bolivia," he averred. In electoral terms, this amounted to a strategy for winning over the educated professional and middle classes more concerned about good governance than government patronage—a group largely absent in Viacha. But this democratization, he then added, "only goes so far. For the *uninominal* [a local congressional seat] the local party preferred one person, but the big men in La Paz preferred another, and the other was chosen. The MNR has party discipline, and I lost."[101] Unlike the UCS, the MNR had few business links locally and resorted to selling seals and letters of approval to people looking for jobs in local, regional, or national government in order to finance itself. The MNR in Viacha was clearly a party in decline, unused to being marginalized and unsure how to stem the rapid erosion of its support.

The last party of any importance in Viacha, more by association than its electoral weight, was the MIR. Despite its association with SOBOCE and its owner, the prominent politician and vice presidential candidate Samuel Doria Medina, the MIR's fortunes were at a low ebb in 1997. Its vote had fallen by more than half in the last election, an abrupt recent change in party leadership had left much confusion locally, and some prominent observers doubted whether the Viachan MIR even continued to exist. Quintela, for one, could not name its leader. He was Antonio Soto, an unemployed former railway worker elected in April of that year. Soto explained that Doria Medina had thrown out the former leadership due to personal dislike, following a struggle for power among them. In previous years, he said, party leaders had nominated electoral lists among themselves and their wives, and had manipulated party assemblies to maintain themselves in power. Now all this had changed. "Now we're ordered by Jaime Paz or Oscar Eid [the MIR's national leaders] to keep the current leadership or re-organize it. And I'm happy to let Jaime Paz decide these things."[102] The national party required nothing of him, and Soto—who had only joined the MIR a few months earlier after many invisible years in the MNR—re-mained obediently quiet.

The deeper dynamic in Viachan politics was a long-term shift away from the traditional parties arrayed left to right along a fairly typical policy spectrum, in favor of the politics of identity, race, and redress in the form of two new, populist, highly personalized parties: Condepa and the UCS. These two competed for the support of a common electoral group with two distinct elements: (1) a large and growing constituency of rural migrants to peri-urban areas—largely uneducated people uprooted from their tight communities who were thrust into the confusion and anonymity of a pre-carious existence in the La Paz–El Alto–Viacha conurbation, and (2) the rel-atives they left behind in rural villages who were as a result increasingly connected to the urban economy. Popular opinion held that truckers and other transport workers were in the camp of the UCS, while small mer-chants voted Condepa. The larger truth was that among urbanizing indige-nous and mestizo groups political identity was weak, and the fortunes of the two parties competing for their votes ebbed and flowed unpredictably. Condepa's Palacios admitted as much when he ascribed his party's victory in the previous election to having captured all of its target voter groups, "peasants, factory workers, small businessmen, and railroad workers."[103] In recent years each party had seen its vote surge in waves of sympathy follow-ing the untimely deaths of their respective leaders; the UCS's vote surged in Viacha by two-fifths in 1995, only to be reversed in favor of Condepa in 1997. With similar populist and charismatic appeals aimed at voters immersed in a rapidly growing and changing local economy, neither party could count on a stable electoral base.

To voters outside the city of Viacha, however, politics looked very dif-ferent. Spokesmen from Villa Santiago de Chacoma, Rosapata, and Názacara reported that no local people had been put forward as candidates in the previous elections. All were "foreigners" to them, city folk they suspected. With no knowledge of how candidate lists were set, all three communities viewed political parties as "vehicles of business and rich people's interests."[104] And the elections they competed in were a dirty affair. Representatives of Chama, District Five, and District Six complained that fraud, though less common than before, continued to mar elections. The ultimate result of such behavior was both widespread throughout the municipality and unsurprising. "People are voting less and losing interest in elections," said Santa Ana de Machaqa, "as they lose faith in politicians."[105]

Community and Grassroots Organizations

With a huge area that extended from the urban factories of Viacha–El Alto to the cold, empty highlands adjoining Peru, Viacha in 1997 had an economically and socially diverse population that embraced a wide variety of cultural and organizational patterns. It is possible to array Viacha's communities along a scale of increasing urbanness where rural communities that retain their traditional *ayllu* and *mallku* authorities define the rural extreme, and Viachans who live in the city but work in La Paz occupy the urban extreme. On this scale, rural communities that organize themselves as peasant unions, and rural-dwelling day migrants who find work in the informal economy of the city, would lie somewhere in between.

This schematization along a continuum should not obscure the fact that the major divides in Viachan society were first between city and countryside, and second, within rural Viacha, between the Machaqas region and the remainder. These differences are a product of communities' economic activity, environment, history, and to a lesser extent language and culture. They resulted in the adoption of organizational forms for neighborhood and community self-governance that differed widely by area. Not surprisingly, the demand for public services also varied significantly over such a diverse region, as did political views and affiliations.

The superiority that Viacha's city folk felt toward their rural neighbors, with whom they had never felt any affinity and who had only very recently been made part of their district, is documented above. The insulting views that many in the city had of their mayor and councilmen are only the most blatant examples of the low regard in which *viacheños* held villagers and rural migrants generally. The resulting tensions in social relations, and unwillingness or inability of urban whites to cooperate with peri-urban migrants and rural villagers, were evident in everyday city life and became a barrier to the smooth operation of the institutions of government. When OC2 denounced corruption on the part of the mayor, for example, they were widely and automatically dismissed as the rantings of racially prejudiced city folk; not even the documentation they produced to substantiate their claims was enough to convince many. The contempt with which insular urbanites viewed the villages and their problems was tempered only by their determination to ignore them altogether.

Rural Viacha contained its own fault lines as well. As a number of community spokesmen pointed out to me, all of Viacha is Aymara, but the rural area was divided into two sectors, the Machaqas and the rest. The Machaqas, a large area in the western part of the district around Jesús de Machaqa and San Andrés de Machaqa, is a distinct region with a strong identity and long history of rural uprisings against both the Spanish colonialists and the *criollo* republic that followed. The *machaqueños* supported numerous uprisings against successive regimes throughout the eighteenth, nineteenth, and twentieth centuries, culminating in the fatal rebellion of 1921 in which a new Republican government—which had acceded to power pledging to defend indigenous communities—instead turned on them and slaughtered them in the massacre of Jesús de Machaqa.[106] Whereas in the rest of rural Viacha communities are organized around the general secretariats of the peasants' union movement, modernizing and "rational" forms of social organization that spread throughout Bolivia after the revolution of 1952–53 and were meant to break the social relations of the past, in the Machaqas the traditional *ayllus* and *mallkus* predominate. The former think of themselves as one of the progressive forces that ended the oppression of the indigenous majority by a small, white elite 60 years ago; the latter base their legitimacy in ethnic pride and traditions that predate the arrival of the Spanish in South America. Aymara is by far the prevalent language in the Machaqas, whereas elsewhere a mixture of Spanish and Aymara is spoken. And the ferocity remains. "The Machaqas are rebellious and conflict-prone," one observer told me. "They still have 'whipping-justice' there."[107]

Community life in the city was organized around neighborhood councils. These organizations were riven by the conflicts that divided and paralyzed the oversight committees, as described above. Hence Viacha had two rival sets of neighborhood councils, and rival representatives to the federation of neighborhood councils at the departmental level.[108] While these conflicts were partly due to hostilities particular to Viacha's urban population, they were also due in part to the ethnic cleavages that divided the city. As a result, when the mayor appointed a migrant from Potosí to head his own OC, the peri-urban population of Viacha did not voice disapproval. And the "authentic" *viacheños* determined to oust both mayor and OC1 visibly failed to carry this large and growing population. Despite their relative wealth, high living standards, and the amenities of living in a city, the residents of Viacha were unable to form community organizations that adequately represented their interests before local government.

The reality in rural areas, by contrast, was very different. The leaders of the communities of Chama, District Five, and District Six reported successful participative planning exercises, where the community met to discuss and prioritize their requests for public investments. The three representatives appeared to take their jobs very seriously and were familiar with the financial and technical details of projects being carried out in their communities. They had convened popular assemblies to approve project designs, and had participated in the various legal steps involved in launching the projects.[109] Santa Ana de Machaqa, among many other communities, boasted a democratically elected work committee to manage projects and mobilize community contributions. In this village projects were chosen via communal assembly, which prioritized them democratically and informed city hall.[110] And the practice of community contributions to projects worked well throughout rural Viacha. "There's a big difference between how projects are implemented in the city and how it's done in the countryside," said Titik'ana Takaka. "In the city people don't lift a finger for their projects, whereas in the country we build everything ourselves" with materials purchased by the municipality.[111] The leaders of Názacara were also concerned with the needs of their people, and in particular with those who migrated to Viacha and El Alto in search of work. "In the city people suffer," they told me. "What people want is a job *here*. . . . This region has great potential."[112] They proposed that the university establish an institute locally to bring them new crops and improved agricultural techniques. And rural communities were able to cooperate among themselves to at least some extent, something impossible in the city. Titik'ana Takaka explained that Jesús de Machaqa owned a truck that communities within the jurisdiction shared to transport materials and people. It was not clear whether cooperation extended to non-*machaqueños*, however. Despite poor language skills in some areas, and low levels of human capital in others, rural communities in Viacha shared a social legitimacy and capacity to mobilize that were utterly lacking in the city.

But strong village structures were insufficient to make government work effectively where government had little interest in villages. Even where communities were well organized and levels of participation and cooperation were high, the requests that communities made to local government were ignored, and local needs were not taken into account in municipal policy decisions. Hence in Villa Santiago de Chacoma, where leaders gathered the entire community to discuss its needs in a meeting open to all, and decisions were taken by acclamation, requests for local investment were rejected by the municipality without explanation.[113] Santa Ana de Machaqa's petition for a schoolhouse was rejected in favor of public urinals made of surplus materials from an urban construction site.[114] And in Titik'ana Takaka, the municipality decided to build schoolhouses with a large community contribution without consulting the community, despite the fact that three good schoolhouses were already in operation there.[115] Even when government did fund projects that satisfied locals, villagers had to negotiate a labyrinth of corruption involving extraofficial payments to municipal engineers, architects, workmen, and drivers in order to persuade them to take measurements, provide technical drawings, and deliver materials.[116] Not surprisingly, public opinion was unenthusiastic about decentralization throughout the Viachan countryside. District Five, District Six, and Chama said the LPP had improved things "to a tiny degree" only, and complained that too many popular participation resources remained in Viacha.[117] Titik'ana Takaka broadly agreed. In the view of Názacara, "Popular Participation has mainly benefited the wealthy—doctors, lawyers, not people like us,"[118] while Santa Ana accused municipal employees of being the principal beneficiaries of the LPP.[119]

The many failings of Viachan local government also had two unintended and interesting social consequences. The first was a vocal demand among the communities of Jesús de Machaqa for training their grassroots leaders in the processes and norms of modern government: budgeting, the legal and regulatory framework, and so forth. They also requested that local government post municipal officials in their jurisdiction, "in order to be closer to the people."[120] Far from disillusioned with decentralization, the residents of Jesús de Machaqa reacted to its shortcomings by demanding that it be deepened. This culminated in a movement within the jurisdiction to secede from Viacha and become the fifth municipality of Ingavi Province. Given the history and strong local identity of Jesús de Machaqa, this was in retrospect a natural response to the indifference of government in Viacha.

The second consequence of decentralization was much less predictable, and involved the autonomous reorganization of society at the village level. Titik'ana Takaka was a case in point. The community had been part of an *ayllu* that was divided into three affiliates of the peasants' union by the syndicalist movement of the 1950s. But these *sub-centrales* began regrouping with decentralization, and by 1997 they were returning to their traditional forms of authority and representation. The residents of Titik'ana Takaka hoped to increase their political weight by banding together with nearby communities, and so improve their ability to capture resources and tend to local needs.[121] In doing so they rejected the social forms of the twentieth century in favor of those of five centuries earlier.

Another, deeper motive was that decentralization changed the logic of social organization in Bolivia. A lasting legacy of the revolution was that between 1952 and 1994 the means for sharing out public resources were national negotiations, strikes, and lobbying conducted in La Paz between representatives of government, business, and labor, each organized in its own "peak association."[122] Economic identity was thus much more important to rural dwellers than where they lived. After 1994, by contrast, bargaining over resources was largely conducted at the municipal level among community representatives. Whether citizens fished, farmed, or drove a truck no longer mattered. Where they lived, and how well the leaders they elected negotiated the division of resources across municipal space, became paramount. The effects of this change reached deep down into village life and made the way in which communities were organized much more important.

Other Actors—The Military and the Church

In the past the armed forces and Catholic Church had loomed large in Viachan life, but their shared history of association with an oppressive white minority under both colony and republic conspired to make them insignificant forces in the local democratic context of 1997. Of the two, the military's role in oppression was by far the more direct. For centuries the army was the state's instrument of domination for the benefit of a landowning and mining *criollo* elite. The government in the capital legislated, regulated, and taxed the countryside so as to push Aymara communities off their traditional territories, allowing latifundistas to purchase the land at convenient prices. It also enforced the *mit'a*, a distortion of the ancient practice of communal labor by which young men were extracted from peasant communities throughout the altiplano and forced to work in the silver and tin mines of Potosí.[123] When the peasants revolted, the army was sent to put them down, which they did with a ferocity made easy by superior armor. These events were seared into the memory of the *campesinos* and became important touchstones in their ethnic history and identity. Even today the residents of Jesús de Machaqa take pride in their rebellious past and continue to celebrate their doomed uprising that led to the 1921 massacre.

By 1997 the military found itself in quite a different position in Viacha. The revolution of 1952–53 had largely ended the systematic military repression of the peasantry, and the restoration of an open, democratic regime in the 1980s had returned them to their garrisons. Years of curtailed military spending had reduced the army unit based in Viacha to a distressed state, with outdated equipment and insufficient resources for training. Its commander was Lt. Col. Adolfo Dávila, a native of Viacha, who led the 2,000 soldiers of the army's 1st Division GADA 231 unit, based only a few blocks from the city's central square. A confident, well-spoken man, he was a keen observer of local affairs and well-versed in the workings of local government. Unusually for Bolivia, he and the mayor had found no way in which to cooperate, and if his relations with local government were cordial they were also largely empty. The commander complained about the government's inefficiency and described the schemes by which senior officials misappropriated public funds, but in the end his power to affect local events was very small.[124]

The Viachan Catholic Church stands silently at one corner of the central plaza, itself the very symbol of a "civilized" urban society that defined itself in opposition to the indigenous countryside.[125] On both sides of the ethnic divide the church was traditionally and strongly associated with the dominant white and mestizo classes. Throughout the colony and the republic local authorities allied themselves repeatedly with the church and used this alliance to amass rural landholdings for the church and themselves.[126] The church was regarded by *campesinos* as a foreign institution, and in the uprising of Tupaq Katari in 1781 rebels killed the local priest. Despite this, the evangelical efforts of the church over 500 years were not in vain, and the church was also an integral part of daily rural life, with "the sacred role to bless, celebrate baptisms, festivals, and many other rites that, from as early as the 18th century, were already part of Aymara daily life."[127] Aymara and Quechua speakers throughout the altiplano internalized many of the doctrines and symbols of Catholicism in a sui generis religious form that intertwined them with elements from traditional indigenous spiritual beliefs.[128] Thus, for example, the Virgin Mary was viewed by many as a manifestation of the Pachamama,[129] and the lightning that made stones sacred and revealed the identity of yatiris[130] was thought to come from the apostle Santiago.[131]

Beginning in the late 1960s, the Aymara Church movement sought a more explicit reconciliation with its indigenous flock, introducing the Aymara language and music into liturgical celebrations. The parish priest of Jesús de Machaqa was one of the founders and principal exponents of this movement. This represented a significant change from the historical pattern of relations between the church and the rural masses, and an important attempt at outreach. Unlike comparable developments elsewhere in Bolivia, it was more a religious than a social or political movement. It was, indeed, a product of the withdrawal of the church from political life to concentrate on the spiritual and evangelical. Fr. Justino Limachi, the Viachan parish priest, confirmed that the church had little interaction with Viacha's government. "We don't work with the municipality. There was talk of church involvement early on, but people go into local government to steal, so the church didn't participate."[132] In his view municipal events were driven by politics, and this was an area that the church no longer engaged.

Summary: How Government Worked in Viacha in 1997

The evidence strongly indicates that local government in Viacha was of very poor quality. The institutions of government varied between merely ineffective and fully corrupt, and the interplay among them produced service and policy outputs that were insensitive to local needs and unsatisfying to local voters. There is substantial evidence that Mayor Callisaya was inadequate as a manager: he expanded his payroll by over 100 percent without significantly increasing the administrative ability or technical skills of the local executive branch, and he squandered huge sums of money on pet urban development projects, like a municipal coliseum, the toboggan, and municipal sewerage, that suffered significant cost overruns and were badly conceived and badly executed. These white elephants stood unfinished or broken, in ugly testimony to his administration's penchant for gesture over judgment. Unfortunately, the charges against Callisaya did not end there. Numerous sources, including public officials, municipal councilmen, and even the mayor's political boss at the CBN, testified to Callisaya's corruption, and a national audit of municipal accounts charged him with malfeasance. And the example the mayor set spread throughout his administration, until it formed a chain of corruption in which everyone from municipal truck drivers to experienced technicians demanded paybacks before they would unload supplies, draw up technical studies, and otherwise provide the services funded by city hall.

Across the hall from the mayor's office, the municipal council was a good-natured and ineffective bunch. The councilmen themselves readily admitted that they had little knowledge of the workings of their municipality, and displayed no interest in informing themselves. Regardless of party, councilmen were oblivious to the powers and privileges inherent in their post as municipal legislators and were content to react to the requests they received from time to time from the mayor's office, or occasionally from a community organization. Authoritative observers in Viacha called the municipal council "ignorant and imperceptive," unsophisticated and easily manipulable. One could only expect uninformed councilmen who showed so little initiative to be uncritical agents of the parties that got them elected. Respondents from both the city and countryside testified that the council was indeed insensitive to local needs, unresponsive to community requests, and beholden to their parties. And increasingly their loyalties belonged to just one party. When opposition representatives began to question municipal policy, the CBN/UCS hired them and members of their family, and the councilmen were thereafter quiet. The Viachan municipal council was thus the residual in the local political equation, unable to act as an independent deliberative and policy-setting body. It offered no institutional or political counterweight to the power of the mayor, and it effectively short-circuited the first layer of checks and balances designed to protect local government against executive abuses of power.

The next layer of checks and balances was based on the oversight committee and its interactions with the mayor and municipal council. But in Viacha this tier was broken, and Viacha suffered from two OCs. OC1, the "official" OC recognized by both city hall and national government, was completely uninformed and operationally inert. Its president was unaware of the financial details of the projects initiated during his tenure, and professed no knowledge of such basic information as how many people the municipality employed, what their salary levels were, and whether or not any information or accounting systems had been implemented recently. An ex-miner recently arrived in Viacha, he did not even know the results of the previous elections. Rural community leaders testified that OC1 was ignorant of their needs and ignored their requests, and prominent urban observers were unaware of its existence. Uninterested in municipal affairs and insensitive to public opinion, he not only failed to counterbalance the mayor's power but actively endorsed his demagogic manipulations, including notably the beer-soaked planning exercise that led to theft and death. In this way he earned the illegal salary that the mayor paid him. The opposition OC, by contrast, was considerably more active, intent on providing local oversight. And despite the mayor's attempts to sideline them, they were surprisingly well-informed, brandishing the municipal budget and readily quoting project details. Unrecognized by the national and local state, however, and thus excluded from the processes of local government, OC2 was ultimately powerless to intervene in the formulation of municipal policy.

The institutional mechanism for the production of local government in Viacha was thus doubly short-circuited. Having freed himself from political oversight, the mayor was able to block social oversight of his activities by dividing civil society against itself, neutralizing its mechanism for accountability, and hiring his own. The stress placed on Callisaya's role is intentional. These events were neither coincidental nor casual but rather engineered deliberately by a canny political strategist in order to free his hand. The corruption of the entire municipal apparatus subsequently, and naturally, ensued. And the policies and investments that local government carried out in Viacha were grossly inefficient, largely ineffective, and, more important, bore little relation to public need.

This story begs the deeper question of how such a situation came about. What incentives were there for such behavior? What social and economic factors sustained a municipal government that should have collapsed under the weight of its own ineptitude and corruption? The dominant actors in Viachan society were potent industrial-political groups that had stormed into the vacuum left by the withdrawal of the church and military from public life. The most powerful of these were the CBN-UCS and SOBOCE-MIR complexes. In order to understand their role it is important to consider first how Viacha fit into the larger context of Bolivian national politics. Viacha's proximity and ease of travel to La Paz, and the increasing migration of the owners of its factories and businesses to that city, made its politics the by-product of the political strategies and dynamics of the capital. Viachan local parties were mere franchises of their national organizations. They were not mechanisms for aggregating individual preferences and transmitting them to the institutions of local government, nor did they champion local causes. They were, rather, the tools by which the consequences of national struggles for power and influence were played out locally. Local party leaderships were made and unmade on the whim of national and departmental leaders based on loyalty, electoral success, and subservience. The MIR, for example, was not permitted to hold a meeting without explicit approval from La Paz. The only exception was the UCS, which was run out of the CBN bottling plant.

National party bosses expected their local operatives to conduct electoral campaigns while doing nothing to constrain the party's strategies in La Paz. They were uninterested in the problems of government in Viacha and provided local leaders with minimal resources with which to do their jobs. Of the two imperatives, the latter was by far the more important—silent electoral ineptitude was preferable to winning elections and causing a stir. The leaders of the MIR, for example, essentially closed down the local party after losing a heated political battle against a UCS mayor, among others, over the cement factory's pollution. The battle had been politically costly for a leftist party with environmentalist pretensions, and the owner of SOBOCE wanted no surprises to upset his vice presidential ambitions.[133] The retirement from politics of the only force capable of acting as a counterweight to the CBN-UCS freed it to pursue its interests without external constraint. In Viacha the party's interests were identical to those of Juan Carlos Blanco, its paramount leader. His goal was to improve his standing within the party by delivering large majorities in Viacha,[134] and he exploited the considerable resources of the bottling plant, as well as the municipality, to win over voters. And in the CBN Blanco had a business, with its large labor force, its wide distribution network, and the enticement of beer, that was particularly suited to proselytism. With such a narrow objective and a time horizon never more than an election away, the UCS proved as uninterested in Viacha's collective welfare as it was in its long-range development needs. That local government proved a disaster is thus not surprising.

The Dénouement

By 1997 Viachan civil society seemed absent from the government process, cowed by the tight grip of party, government, and brewery on local affairs. Callisaya had skillfully manipulated the hostilities between city and countryside and set them fighting against each other, and there was, it seemed, no remedy to UCS misrule. Then, to the surprise of many, the grass roots flexed their muscle and proved that they were not powerless after all. Rural communities might be too distant and poor to confront their government, but urban society was not. Following a series of town meetings that aired their grievances, on 22 March the people of Viacha rose up against their mayor and marched on city hall demanding his resignation.[135] A crowd of several hundred people[136] paraded through town and then massed in the central square opposite Callisaya's office loudly and angrily demanding his departure. A few days later he resigned. In the June general election Viacha recorded a huge swing from the UCS to Condepa. It added insult to injury and, coming after an expensive and frenetic electoral season, was a slap in the face to a party that had, literally, given so much away. The experience suggested that in the new context of local government in Bolivia no local government, no matter how rich or powerful the interests that supported it, could govern against its people for long. The UCS had taken voters for fools, and the voters had had their revenge.

CHAPTER 3

Local Government at the Extremes: Charagua

Introduction: 1997

The road to Charagua is an orange ribbon of earth that carries travelers away from the exuberance of Santa Cruz's tropical flowers and swaying palms, deep into the Chaco. The bouncing and banging of your jeep along the dusty road is interrupted occasionally by silence as you slip into pools of mud. Gradually the sun's relentless glare melts the lush green surrounding the city into the scrubgrass and low twisted bushes of the arid plain. The journey takes five hours in the dry season and becomes impossible during the rains.

Located in the southeastern corner of the country, Charagua is the second municipal district of the Cordillera province and shares a long border with Paraguay. It was overrun by the Paraguayan army during the Chaco War of 1932–35, and the memory of violence lives on in the stories of village elders and the statues of the central square. It boasts the biggest municipal area in Bolivia—its 74,424 square kilometers make it larger than Holland, Costa Rica, or Denmark, and twice the size of Belgium. Only 13 percent of its 18,769 inhabitants live in the town of Charagua, with the rest scattered across 88 indigenous and rural communities, a handful of newer Mennonite "colonies," and the smaller town of Charagua Station. The economy is rural, with agriculture, cattle ranching, education in the form of a teacher-training college, and commerce the main sources of income. Of these only cattle ranching achieves a respectable scale, with a few families raising thousands of heads of cattle on tens of thousands of hectares. By contrast Charagua's agricultural sector is planted firmly in antiquity, with Guaraní peasants farming communal lands without the benefit of the plow, let alone tractors or irrigation, relying on their traditional stick method to break the earth.

The population of Charagua is overwhelmingly Guaraní, with Ava-Guaraníes in the northern foothills and Tupi-Guaraníes in the south, especially the Isoso region. Although official business is conducted mostly in Spanish, the principal language of the region is Guaraní. Quechua, a distant third, is heard primarily in the urban market, where recent migrants from the altiplano ply their trades, and in the few rural communities where they have settled. The town of Charagua lacks industry and has little commercial activity. Its importance comes rather from the fact that it is the seat of power of the landowning cattle families who traditionally dominated the region and its inhabitants. Charaguan townspeople think of themselves as either white or mestizo, in strict opposition to the Guaraní hinterlands, a division that is clear in the minds of townspeople and Guaraníes alike.

Despite the huge landholdings of some Charaguans, the town itself retains a curiously classless, colorless air, its low one- and two-story buildings fronted by shaded porches often in need of a coat of paint. There are no conspicuous displays of wealth or poverty. This is probably due to the fact that its richest inhabitants maintain only secondary homes in town and give most of their time and attention to their farms, where their *estancias* are. But it is also indicative of the crisis affecting the rural economy, with low commodity and land prices and an exodus of the ranchers' most talented children to the city. This crisis had been going on for over a decade, and looked likely to deepen; we return to it below. Despite its unprepossessing appearance, the town benefits from a significantly higher level of public service provision than the surrounding communities. Charagua town's index of Unsatisfied Basic Needs is 0.453, tenth best for Bolivia as a whole and very similar to the scores of Bolivia's three main cities. By contrast, the value for rural areas is 0.926, which would rank 100th among Bolivia's 311 municipalities.

A principal problem of landowning wealth is illiquidity, and this is to a great extent Charagua's problem too. With few businesses in the entire district, the opportunities for charging license fees are very limited. And the small quantities of land that change hands in any given year make assessing property taxes difficult. Until 1997 this was compounded by cattle ranchers' practice of paying property taxes via their association headquarters in Santa Cruz. Hence tax revenues accrued to the departmental government, with little returning to Charagua. Charagua's own resources amounted to only Bs. 49,000 in 1996 out of a budget of Bs. 2,328,060, or a tiny 2 percent of the total. And given the subsistence economy of Guaraní agriculture, essentially all of these revenues came from the town. "The Guaraníes don't pay taxes," the mayor declared with a twinkle in his eye, "they just procreate."[1]

Despite this lack of resources, by the middle of 1997 Charagua had acquired a reputation within the department of Santa Cruz, and increasingly nationally, of being well run by a competent and enthusiastic mayor. The mayor came out on top in a ranking of all mayors in the department. "He is a very good administrator," said the departmental head of the Social Investment Fund, "and a very active person. . . . He has a very good image—even people from rival parties recognize this."[2] Decentralization had increased municipal resources by some 6,500 percent year over year, and yet the funds appeared to be well spent. Local government had resisted the temptation to inflate and had managed to keep operating costs to just 4 percent of total budget. A series of municipal audits carried out by the national government on medium-sized municipalities supported this view, finding no deficiencies in Charagua's operational programming, administrative organization, budgeting, personnel administration, administration of goods and services, treasury management, accounting, and internal auditing and control.[3]

The foundation of good local government in Charagua was a strong social consensus that upheld a political coalition between the center-left Movimiento Bolivia Libre (MBL) party and the center-right Acción Democrática Nacionalista (ADN) party. This consensus consisted of two closely related components: (1) a political covenant between the MBL and the Guaraní People's Association (APG), whereby the former allowed the latter to choose candidates for its local electoral list in exchange for Guaraní votes in municipal elections; and (2) the animosity felt by rural inhabitants of Charagua toward the MNR party and its previous mayor, who was widely accused by Guaraníes of racism and brutality toward rural villagers.[4] To this second point was added a more general, if less acute, rejection of the local MNR by townspeople who associated it with an increasingly unpopular national government. The nature of this social and political consensus is central to understanding the success of local government in Charagua, and we examine its components in detail below. Its immediate results were to allow the MBL, which had never done well in Charagua, to win almost as many votes as the first-place MNR, and then to propel the ADN and MBL into coalition government behind an MBL mayor, thus excluding the MNR from power. In a municipality where Guaraníes did not vote and the MNR traditionally beat the ADN into second place in town, this was a shocking turn of events for many.

The ADN-MBL coalition proved surprisingly robust in practice and provided the mayor with a strong political base for his administration. By his own account this was fortuitous. "Never before have so many distant communities received so much" in public services and investment, he said, explaining a planning and budgeting system built around the principle that each community in the district must receive an equitable share[5] of the municipal budget over a multiyear cycle.[6] But the effort needed to run a planning system in which communities discussed their needs and prioritized their own projects in a municipality as big as Charagua was immense. "It took two months just to meet all the indigenous communities and agree on their needs," he explained. "The workload is very heavy for many municipalities that weren't used to so much responsibility. . . . Every year we have to re-structure ourselves better." It is doubtful that the municipality would have achieved the results it did without the unwavering support that the municipal council provided the mayor.

The deeper background to Charagua's municipal dynamics is a Guaraní cultural renaissance that began in the early 1980s and gathered pace in the 1990s. The Guaraníes, who as a people had managed to survive Spanish colonialism for over three centuries, succumbed throughout the nineteenth century to the *criollo* republic's potent mix of Christian conversion, government territorial annexations, and cattle ranchers' land purchases and confiscations, all backed by repression of the Bolivian army.[7] With their spears and arrows the Guaraníes were no match for the firearms of the state, and at Kurujuky in 1892 an indigenous uprising led to a massacre that almost destroyed the Guaraní culture.[8] Coming as it did after a long string of setbacks, the massacre of Kurujuky cast the Guaraníes onto the margins of society, where they survived as the perpetually indebted slaves of large landowners or as subsistence farmers in isolated rural communities. The Guaraníes spent the better part of a hundred years in material and spiritual deprivation, a proud and bellicose people beaten into docility, lost in a sort of collective amnesia triggered by defeat.[9]

After the chaos of successive coups d'état and hyperinflation, the 1980s witnessed a rebirth of Guaraní consciousness and Guaraní pride, discussed in detail below. The Asamblea del Pueblo Guaraní (APG) was formed in 1986–87 to coordinate Guaraní affairs, foment cooperation among communities, and articulate Guaraní interests.[10] The moment was ripe for such an organization, and the APG flourished and quickly established a central role throughout the Guaraní world, from the most mundane community tasks to the international arena via its representation of Guaraníes across Bolivia and Paraguay. Thus when the MBL sought to mount an electoral coup in Charagua by capturing the hitherto ignored Guaraní vote, it found in the APG an interlocutor that not only spoke with authority but possessed the legitimacy and organization to mobilize a highly dispersed population. When Guaraníes voted for the MBL, they also voted for the Guaraní candidates that the APG had chosen. The party's vote increased by over 360 percent in the 1995 local election.[11] Rural voters and community leaders that I spoke to reported satisfaction with their electoral success and the subsequent government's performance. With the presence of Guaraníes on the municipal council for the first time, they felt not only that their voices were heard but that they had assumed control of the municipality. "Councilmen are sent to represent *us*. They pay attention to us and not to the parties— they do what *we* want."[12] Quietly, tenuously, but with evident pride, the Guaraníes were emerging from obscurity to take their rightful place at the center of Charagua's political life.

As with Viacha, the rest of this chapter considers the quality of local government in Charagua through the prism of its main governing institutions: the mayor, municipal council, oversight committee, and departmental and national governments. We then examine deeper determinants of local governance: the private sector, political parties and elections, and community and grassroots organizations.

Box 1: The Slavery of Captive Communities

Councilman Solano explained that some of the migrants to Charagua were from Ivo, Boyuibe, and Huacareta. "They come without land or money, and the locals here tend to the needs of brother Guaraníes." The source of these desperate arrivals are the "captive communities" deep in the Chaco, where modern slavery flourishes. The CIPCA's Núñez explained how it works. There are towns

where the rich families run everything and occupy all the important posts. . . . They have between 10 and 30 Guaraní families living on large properties where they are kept as slaves on the land and aren't paid for their work. . . . The *patrón* keeps them in debt. They can't leave before paying or they're put in jail.

The debt is passed down from father to son, and Guaraní families are allowed neither education nor contact with the outside world. "These [rich] families have radio communications among themselves," Núñez continued. "They set up roadblocks and radio warnings to each other when an outsider appears. Then they send the Guaraníes up into the hills with the cattle, and the outsiders are told no one lives there." The *patrones* even had the gall to register themselves as a rural community so they would not have to pay taxes. "Now these rich families have formed a GRO and are able to demand public money for wells, roads, etc. on their private property. And they put Guaraní families on their lists of GRO members." CIPCA has purchased the freedom of some captive Guaraníes at a price of around Bs. 1,000 each. The APG has proposed the wholesale liberation of these slaves, but successive governments have been afraid to tackle the issue.

Local Government Institutions

The Mayor and the Local Executive Branch

Prof. Luis Saucedo Tapia is a retired schoolteacher originally from Villamontes, on the southeastern edge of the Chaco in Tarija. He has lived in Charagua since 1967, working for most of that time in the town's large educational establishment. A sympathizer of the center-left MBL party and its brand of politics emphasizing human rights, rural development, and periodic anticorruption drives, he became mayor when the APG nominated him to the top position of the MBL's electoral list. "The Guaraníes borrowed a *karai*[13] as candidate for mayor" in order not to scare Charaguan townspeople, explained the president of the oversight committee. All of the other names on the list were Guaraní, and the APG made an implicit bargain with the town to control Charagua through one of them in exchange for the support, or at least restrained hostility, of the white elite.[14] Saucedo agreed with this, explaining that "the town demanded that the ADN give me their vote in the municipal council. Now they've turned against me because they say I give all the money to indigenous people."[15] But the countryside continued to support him, he added.

Saucedo was relaxed and patient during various lengthy interviews that spanned several months. With a thorough grasp of the administration over which he presided, he easily rattled off population and investment figures, project names and budgets, and much other municipal information in detail without reference to notes. "Our plan is to attend to the basic needs of all of the communities first," he explained, "and *then* to invest in productive projects that raise future income."[16] To this effect the municipality's 1997 budget prioritized the following areas, in order of importance: (1) Education—14 schools throughout the district; (2) Health—the Mother and Child Health Insurance scheme and an anti-Chagas program; (3) Water and Sanitation—a number of new wells in rural areas; and (4) several tourism projects and heavy road maintenance. Saucedo noted that Charagua was investing half its municipal budget in human development, compared to the 30 percent that central government guidelines recommend. He reported municipal investments in all eight of the sectors about which he was questioned, and judged the results obtained so far as good in six of these and bad in two.

Saucedo was most emphatic about the distribution of resources in his municipality. "This has undeniably improved since the Popular Participation Law—there's no comparison." He described a planning system that breaks the municipality into four zones and allocates resources to each strictly by population. Thus Charagua Norte received Bs. 500,000, Charagua Sur Bs. 350,000, the Isoso Bs. 650,000, and the town and surrounding Guaraní and Mennonite communities Bs. 900,000. He then recited the population of each region to prove his point. Within these limits, specific projects and policy interventions are decided by local meetings in each community. These agree on local priorities and send a list of each community's preferences to the oversight committee and the mayor. The mayor and OC preselect which of these projects they will undertake. The municipality then hosts general meetings in each of the four zones to discuss projects requested, make the final selection, and establish an investment plan for each. From these meetings the municipal Annual Operating Plan emerges. This AOP cannot be modified by the municipal council or mayor alone—it requires a written resolution from community leaders or the OC before changes can be considered.[17]

Other local authorities confirmed Saucedo's outline of the planning system, and all stressed the high degree of grassroots participation that made it successful. "Each zone demands a share of the budget proportional to its population," the mayor explained. But it did not end there. "Even after the AOP is finished, some groups want to benefit always. They send written requests for more projects and stage demonstrations" to voice their demands.

These are analyzed by the mayor, municipal council, and OC; they may lead to reformulations of the entire AOP. Grassroots leaders are also instrumental in setting the level and type of community contribution that financing agencies like the FIS, the World Bank, and others demand, according to the president of the OC. And once the project is going, "they press for the FIS, the municipality, and the contractor to deliver on their obligations as well."[18]

MNR councilman Julián Segundo Chipipi described an atmosphere of cooperation and accommodation in zonal meetings. "The money of communities that have already satisfied their needs goes to other communities. They understand this and are in agreement."[19] "Peasants today aren't like they used to be," added the (ADN) president of the municipal council. "Now they're learned, able, awake, and agile," and can easily handle complex negotiations among distant communities.[20] Despite the mayor's protests that this planning system was still new, its results—the municipality's AOP—satisfied all of the rural communities that I interviewed in Charagua. Only civic leaders from the town itself complained that the 1997 AOP represented the municipality's wishes and not communities' greatest needs.[21] But this was probably due to resentment of the shift in resources and priorities away from the town that Popular Participation had brought about. "It's the Guaraníes who are most successful in extracting resources from the municipality," admitted Saucedo.

The mayor was obviously pleased with his success in Charagua, declaring merrily, "This system of programming funds is good! It's right to do things this way."[22] But he also worried that managing the process was stretching his municipal government to the breaking point. Even though it had increased in size from four to nine employees, the administration was still too understaffed to provide effective local government to an area twice the size of Belgium. The mayor had three executive, four operational, and two support staff working for him, plus a few occasional employees hired for specific projects. The highest qualification required—for the executives—was a high school diploma, and salary levels were too low to attract technically trained staff from the city. And to make matters worse, they were building institutional capacity on a nonexistent base. "Before Popular Participation," said Saucedo, "there were no educational requirements for hiring people. Any cripple who limped past was given a job." The mayor then earned a derisory Bs. 250/month, and the others less. With no salary, no staff, and no budget to work with, those who had served in Charagua's government were motivated by a sense of civic duty, not by hopes of what they might achieve.

After decentralization, various central agencies attempted to strengthen the municipality by installing the SICOPRE and SICOM information systems and training staff in their use. But the mayor did not hold out much hope for these. "In the end no one understood SICOPRE," he admitted. "And they're implementing SICOM now," he added, shrugging. Instead Saucedo opted to hire CIPCA (the same NGO encountered in Viacha) for institutional development and technical advice. CIPCA is a left-of-center group that established itself in Charagua some years earlier under the leadership of a group of politically active university graduates, who then took over the ailing branch of the MBL.[23] CIPCA signed a covenant with the mayor to provide technical support for the formulation of the AOP, advise on relations with rural communities, and help with administrative development. In practice CIPCA quickly became involved in most aspects of daily business, helping the government to design and find financing for projects, formulate its five-year Municipal Development Plan, and assist in relations with the various national development funds (e.g., FIS). Some local observers, such as the parish priest Fr. Luis Roma, lauded CIPCA's role, saying "The good shape the municipality is in is due to CIPCA. The mayor blindly does what CIPCA tells him to do." But others, especially in town, complained that CIPCA's influence was too strong, and that it had become a parallel government. The president of the OC, the man perhaps in the best position to know, countered this, explaining that CIPCA supported the local planning procedure only and was not involved in the decision-making stage.[24]

But not even Charagua's careful planning system or the widespread goodwill that it engendered among civic and political leaders could guarantee success. In order to multiply his investment budget, the mayor had obtained cofinancing for school construction projects from the FIS. But a number of these suffered delays in late 1996, and by mid-1997 construction had stopped at 10 of them as the FIS sued the contractor for damages. The mayor, municipal councilmen, and many of the community leaders interviewed attributed these suspensions to the particularly heavy rains that had affected the region that year, washing out roads and paralyzing even the trains. The mayor also cited the contractor's weak cash flow, which made it unable to operate 10 construction sites simultaneously and led it to demand larger community contributions than had been initially agreed upon. In both cases the mayor lay blame squarely at the FIS's door. He argued that the FIS worked backward—using the dry season to complete project paperwork and initiating construction at the onset of the rains; and he complained that the FIS should never have awarded 10 projects to a single firm in the first place, especially one only recently formed and with little experience building schools to the FIS's comparatively high specifications.[25]

Saucedo was quick to point out that the rest of his investment program had gone well and was largely completed. But these schools represented one-half of Charagua's yearly investments, and their interruption froze Saucedo's budget and crippled his government. Large swaths of rural Charagua had agreed to expect nothing more from local government than a school. The projects' suspension broke local government's credibility in the areas affected, and undermined its claim to be focusing resources on rural problems more generally. Although local authorities such as the district director of education and the president of the OC defended the municipality and accused the FIS and the contractor of poor planning,[26] their view was not shared by all of the grassroots leaders I spoke to. At the community level people seemed disillusioned by the turn of events and unsure whom to blame. As time passed and no solution was found the public began to lose patience with the mayor and his municipal council, and in some quarters opinion turned hostile.

That the Charaguan government retained significant credibility among voters despite these setbacks, and that many civic leaders seemed prepared to suspend judgment for a time, is probably due to the stark contrast between the MBL administration and the MNR regime that preceded it. According to Mr. Núñez of CIPCA, "The previous government was absolutely urban—rural communities weren't represented. . . . Its AOPs were drawn up for it by the Office of Municipal Strengthening in the Santa Cruz Prefecture. The communities complained that their needs weren't in it."[27] Saucedo paints a much more dire picture of the state of affairs.

> The previous government was taking Charagua to the brink of disaster. The FIS could find nothing in Charagua to finance in 1994 and 1995. Finally the municipality began sending money directly to the communities because projects would not materialize. Some spent well, others badly. . . . This distorted the local idea of what revenue-sharing means.[28]

But more important perhaps were the purely political elements of government. "Rolando Gutiérrez [the previous MNR mayor] had serious problems with the Guaraníes. He had been a policeman here. He was one of those who went to Guaraní villages to demand labor, and if they didn't comply he beat them and put them in jail."[29] It is not surprising that Guaraníes voted overwhelmingly against the MNR and were happy to see the party defeated. I attempted to interview Mr. Gutiérrez about these allegations but he would not speak.

In the rural communities where most Charaguans live people displayed a lively pragmatism, judging the mayor and his administration on their performance and little else. When asked about the legal provision that allowed the municipal council to overturn the mayor after his first year in office, the common view was that this was positive and should be freely used if the mayor did not satisfy expectations. According to the leadership of La Brecha, "This measure is necessary. Municipal projects must benefit everyone. The municipality either works or it doesn't work."[30] Respondents in the community of Yapiroa made the point, "We know how much we're due from the Law of Popular Participation—it's according to our population. If this isn't disbursed, then we must get rid of the mayor."[31] Civic leaders in Kapiwasuti, Taputamí, and Akae echoed these sentiments, stressing that the decisive criteria for such decisions must be municipal performance at the community level and official responsiveness to community needs.

The general view from the communities was that municipal performance had been at least satisfactory, and for the most part good. Representatives from Kapiwasuti reported projects in four of the eight sectors queried, and judged all of them good. "Popular Participation has increased the distribution of money in this municipality. . . . And the municipality is investing well. They're not wasting money. These aren't bad investments."[32] Leaders from Taputamí held a similar view, reporting investments in two sectors, both good. The villages of Yapiroa, Akae, and El Espino all suffered from the school suspension debacle and did not hesitate to express their disappointment. But despite this, all reported satisfaction with a local government that listened to their needs and at least attempted to respond to them. The response of El Espino's leader was typical, reporting projects in four sectors: three good and one mediocre. But despite the travails of the school, he praised the municipality for responding to a genuine need. "We chose the school in a community meeting," he explained, "according to greatest need. Because there are many students here, and the nearest schools are far away."[33]

But perhaps the most surprising response came from the community of

La Brecha. As of mid-1997, this community, the traditional capital of the Isoso region, had received nothing from its municipal government. And yet local spokesmen lauded the law and their local government for the schools it had built and the road it had improved elsewhere in the Isoso. Referring to one school in particular, they said "all of the Isoso benefits because that school is a nucleus.[34] And the road runs the full length of the Isoso. . . . These projects are necessities that emerge from the community itself, which has prioritized their greatest needs. They're discussed and analyzed in a community meeting."[35] They went on to describe how the needs of the entire Isoso were discussed in a meeting of the region's civic leaders. Largely because of this consensual process, the projects that were approved were seen as belonging to the entire region. The local concept of "community" had expanded to include villages hours away by jeep. "Things that were never seen before have been seen now," they enthused. The strong Guaraní identity, and the social bonds that link Isoseño communities, allowed even a village that had seen no municipal investment to appreciate local government's work elsewhere.

By contrast, this attitude was missing among the Charaguan townspeople. Of the five sectors in which they had received municipal investment, they judged one good, three mediocre, and one bad. Local leaders approved grudgingly of the main public investments there, a new motor for the electricity generator and the renovation of the town square, but complained that other urban priorities were being ignored in favor of investment in rural areas. "Sewerage, domestic gas, street paving, storm drainage, waste recovery and treatment—they're all expensive projects and there's not enough money," they groused.[36] The fact that their existing public services were far superior to those of any rural community in Charagua did not prevent them from resenting the investments the latter received. And when queried about neighborhood construction officers and the arrangements they'd made for the plaza's upkeep, they admitted that there was no civic oversight of project finances, quality, and so forth, and that maintenance of the plaza would be the exclusive responsibility of the municipal government. Unlike in the rural communities, townspeople clearly felt that the municipality belonged to them, its resources theirs to exploit. They did not conceive of local government as something external with which they had to reach accommodation.

Grassroots perceptions of larger questions of the effectiveness and equity of municipal government seemed to proceed directly from communities' appraisals of its performance at home. In most communities people noted that decentralization had brought about improvements in the effectiveness of government that ranged from modest to large. Community leaders in Copere Brecha, Yapiroa, Akae, Kapiwasuti, El Espino, and La Brecha all reported that municipal government had improved significantly with the Popular Participation program. The commentary from El Espino was typical.

> Things are much better with Popular Participation, because now we know how much money arrives each year. Before they said "There are royalties" but there was no way to find out [how much] and we never received anything. Now the mayor is closer [to us].[37]

"Before the money was all for the people in the local administration itself—not even for the town," added Israel Romero Macuendí and Florencio Altamirano of Akae. "Now we have people who know the laws [and can prevent this]. The communities choose the most important projects."[38] It is interesting that the leaders of El Espino and La Brecha attributed this wholesale change to the presence of three Guaraníes on the municipal council. "They control things here. Hence things aren't done so badly."[39] Other communities attributed increased municipal effectiveness to procedural changes that improved responsiveness to local needs. "The municipal government improved a lot after Popular Participation—now the municipality comes *here* to meet with the people and budget resources with them."[40] Spokesmen for other communities agreed, citing direct contact with and listening to voters as crucial attributes of an ideal mayor.

Of the 11 communities I visited in Charagua, most were fairly or very satisfied with the quality of their local government generally. Only one—Rancho Nuevo—complained government was unsatisfactory, saying, "The municipality spends its money elsewhere—not here. What it promises remains on paper only."[41] Two communities, Charagua town and Isiporenda, reported little change in the quality of government since decentralization. Two communities, Taputamí and La Brecha, were fairly satisfied with the quality of government. And the remaining six communities were very happy with municipal government, reporting significant changes since 1994. Remarks in El Espino were typical: "There are paralyzed schools here—but this is *not* the fault of municipal government. . . . Most people are quite satisfied with the municipality because they see the works that are being carried out."[42] It is interesting to note that this summary includes the deterioration in local perceptions between the first and second halves of 1997, due mostly to the paralyzed FIS schools. Chávez and the others in La Brecha, where satisfaction had dropped from high to moderate, summed up the feelings of many when he said, "Up to a year ago things really looked good. But now we see things differently because the money never arrives. The AOP—which itself is good—isn't being executed."[43]

From the outside, the mayor and the local executive branch were regarded quite positively by prominent local observers. Civic and private sector leaders alike praised the mayor for his honesty and his hardworking and transparent administration. Juan Carlos Gutiérrez, president of the local branch of the Cattle Ranchers Association of the Cordillera province, professed satisfaction with the municipality. "Local government works well as far as we're concerned. We call the municipality and they respond. The municipal council and the mayor work well together."[44] Given the very large share of the local wealth that cattlemen represented, this was an important vote of confidence. The district director of education was even more enthusiastic.

> We receive everything that local government can give us. . . . In 1995 we got almost nothing from them. In 1996 we got Bs. 4 million and this year Bs. 3 million more. . . . This mayor is good because he invests in human capital, including teacher training. He has a great will to do good.[45]

Fr. Gabriel Siquier, who worked for decades with poor Guaraní communities in the region, put it more bluntly still. "The municipality is working here like never before. It deserves our applause. . . . The Law of Popular Participation is a blessing from God."[46]

The other institutions of local government concurred. Florencio Antuni, the president of the oversight committee, was enthusiastic about the quality of the local executive. "Almost everything is being done now. Before 1994 nothing was being done—the municipality had no money. Now, with a little money from the LPP law, they can go in search of cofinancing from external sources. They can consult communities and do what the local people want."[47] In a relatively short period the mayor and his staff had proceeded from the initial resource shock to a strategic ability to leverage resources in order to obtain central government and external financing that multiplied the local budget. But Antuni's praise did not end there. "The opinions and necessities of the grass roots are being taken into account here. And for the Guaraní people this is very important," a point with which the Isoseño councilman Julián Segundo Chipipi agreed.[48] Both men joined municipal council president Vargas in declaring that the distribution of resources had improved remarkably under the present government, using words that echoed the most enthusiastic community leaders cited above. Regarding specific investment projects, Segundo judged them good in three sectors and mediocre in two, Antuni good in five sectors, and Vargas very good in five sectors. But Vargas pointed out that institutional weakness was still a significant problem. "A team of advisers financed externally should come for at least a year and provide technical and legal advice. . . . And the municipality needs to pay better salaries to attract better people—especially technicians and functionaries. They need money . . . to hire financial and administrative officers to run the local administration."[49] He recommended a sort of apolitical municipal civil service that would maintain local service standards through local and national changes of government.

The mayor himself was sanguine, and even modest, about his role in the transformation that his municipality had undergone over the previous three years. "In the beginning *no one* understood what Popular Participation was—including the municipality. Now we're beginning to reap the fruits of the LPP."[50] But he did not underestimate its importance. He thought decentralization had visibly and "undeniably" improved municipal government in Charagua. "We see better civil works; the necessities of the people are being attended to." Of the 88 communities in the district, over 50 had received new investment since 1994, and the rest had benefited in other ways, via building repairs, road improvements, and the cleaning of public areas. But more important than the projects were the changes to the process of governance itself.

> Now the people that run the show are the common, rural people. Classist principles are being abolished here. Marginalized people are entering the political realm. Before the cattlemen ruled here. Now it's the indigenous villages and marginalized people who reap most of the benefits of Popular Participation.[51]

This shift in power relations had permitted a change in the relationship between government and its citizen-beneficiaries. No longer were rural communities cast in the role of supplicants, making formal requests to local representatives of a state that might never deign to answer, for public services that in the best circumstances would be bestowed from on high upon a grateful populace. Responsive local government responded to the people by working with them. "The municipality has to help people with the greatest needs. But we must not be paternalistic. We give but we make demands as well—that those who benefit work, produce, etc. There must be counterparts. Nothing should be given freely."[52] And the concept of counterparts was much broader than community contributions in building materials and project costs. "If we build them a school then they must educate themselves."[53] But the mayor kept the process in perspective, his gaze clearly fixed on his ultimate goal. Charagua had for decades suffered high levels of poverty and deprivation, with a highly dispersed rural population mired in a trap of ignorance, endemic diseases such as Chagas and tuberculosis, and the low productivity of a subsistence economy. His goal was to increase the human capital of his poorest voters and then invest in public infrastructure to increase their incomes. "All of these productive projects serve to keep the Guaraníes from having to beg," he explained. After much municipal investment, for example, "Charagua Norte is now producing large quantities of corn." Change was possible, he believed. "It all depends on how you invest the money."

Municipal Council

Voting patterns in the town of Charagua remained largely stable in the 1995 municipal elections, with the MNR and the ADN vying for first place among urban preferences. But the inclusion of a large rural area in the Charaguan district space changed municipal voting patterns significantly, increasing the total vote by 140 percent. The MBL captured more than half of these new voters, with an especially dramatic surge in the Guaraní communities of Charagua Norte and Charagua Sur. This was the motor that propelled the party from under 10 percent to over a third of the vote districtwide and a close second place behind the MNR, increasing its representation on the municipal council from none to two. Also notable was the MNR's success in capturing votes in the Alto and Bajo Isoso regions, which partly compensated for its slump in town on the heels of a highly unpopular outgoing mayor and a somewhat less unpopular national government. Concerned that the MBL-APG electoral pact would cost it votes in rural Charagua, the MNR had reached a similar agreement with the Capitanía del Alto y Bajo Isoso (Cabi), the traditional Guaraní authority for the Isoso region,[54] which allowed Cabi to name the second candidate on the MNR's electoral list in exchange for official Cabi support. All of this left the local legislature with two MNR councilmen, two from the MBL, and one from the ADN. The latter three easily reached agreement whereby the ADN councilman supported the MBL candidate for mayor in exchange for the presidency of the municipal council and the job of chief municipal officer for his son. According to one local observer, "Vargas behaved well—he was offered money, a farm, and more if he gave his vote to the MNR for mayor. But he said 'If I vote for the MNR the town will kill me.'"[55]

Abelardo Vargas Portales, the president of the municipal council, was born and raised in Charagua town. Ex-principal of the rural teacher-training school, he has the gray hair and serious air of a man who thinks before speaking. Vargas praised the civic attitude and will to work of his fellow councilmen. "Councilmen don't wear their party's colors," he said. "They don't speak of politics. They all want the development of the community."[56] Councilman Abilio Vaca agreed and developed the point further.

> We don't have sectarian politics here. We work together for the municipality. We take advantage of the parties to move the wheels of government in Santa Cruz if things get stuck there. But there's no party politics here. It's all work, progress, and solutions to problems. . . . Parties don't get involved in local affairs. I'm here for the APG, not the MBL.

Vargas extended his praise to the opposition MNR councilmen as well. "There's no real opposition on the council—the MNR doesn't actively oppose us. Outside they do campaign against other parties, but in the council they work [with us]." This last point was quite easy to corroborate. Councilman Julián Segundo Chipipi freely admitted, "I was named to this post by the Cabi. I'm not here representing any party."[57] And Rolando Gutiérrez, the ex-mayor much hated in his own town, had virtually disappeared from sight and ceased to play an active role in local politics.

Segundo, a Guaraní farmer and civil registrar from the town of Yapiroa, had never been active in politics until the 1995 election. He explained the dynamic within the municipal council. "The three Guaraní councilors respond more to their grass roots [than their respective parties]. They are the ones who demand that the municipality perform."[58] Behind the closed doors of the council these three cooperated, oblivious to their party and government-opposition divides, to promote service provision and investment in Guaraní villages. Councilman Crispín Solano, from the Guaraní village of Masaki, concurred, citing his own political freedom from the MBL and the absence of national party politics in Charagua. "The municipality seeks instead to work with the APG," eschewing political intrigue in favor of community development.[59]

The oft-heard phrase "responding to the grass roots" appeared to be more than a slogan in Charagua. Segundo and Vargas set out what this signified. "The peasants are very direct. If they send me a note [containing their demands] and I don't comply they'll kick me out of my job," said the former.[60] But most grassroots demands were channeled through the Cabi/APG, which played an important role coordinating requests and following them up.

> There is a good understanding on the part of the *Capitanía*. They come to see how the projects are going. They send requests [for modifications or new projects] to the municipal council. The council investigates the possibility of approving. [And at the end,] I write a letter of information directly to the *capitán*.[61]

Segundo testified that the council listened to such requests carefully and took them seriously. Vargas agreed, noting that whether civic pressures took the form of official letters or demonstrations, the council always viewed them as legitimate expressions of the popular will. The APG (including the Cabi) also coordinated community requests and lobbying of national institutions, including the FIS.

The councilmen's accounts of their own work were corroborated by community leaders throughout Charagua. Of the eleven communities questioned, only three reported that the council did not respond to their needs. The other eight expressed satisfaction with a local legislature that, in their opinion, listened to and worked for them. Spokesmen for Kapiwasuti said simply, "Councilors respond to the people who voted for them,"[62] and those from Yapiroa, "Councilmen are sent to represent *us*. They pay attention to us and not to the parties. They do what *we* want."[63] El Espino attributed this to the way in which candidates for the council were selected, indicating that information on the electoral deals that had been struck—and the resulting political dynamic—had penetrated to the village level in Charagua. Community leaders were well aware of where they stood vis-à-vis local government, and were eager to exploit their advantage. "Politicians have opened their eyes and seen that they have to work," noted La Brecha. "Their behavior has improved."[64] And in Isiporenda, "The municipal council's job is to approve everything that is formally requested by the communities. The *capitanes* direct only just requests to the council."[65]

Only Isiporenda, Rancho Nuevo, and Charagua town expressed dissatisfaction with the council. "Currently councilmen obey the commands of an NGO and not their parties nor the people," García and Cortez from Charagua explained, referring to CIPCA. They qualified the work of the municipal council as no better than mediocre "on account of the inexperience of the three Guaraní representatives, not because of bad will or negligence."[66] Even enthusiastic communities admitted that the councilmen required assistance. "The council needs to be well advised because the Guaraníes aren't well educated and need advice in order not to regress,"[67] said El Espino. Charagua town recommended training in planning, legal matters, and parliamentary procedure in order to foster a nonpolitical atmosphere in the council. Other communities agreed.

Outside government, local authorities also rated the municipal council highly. One of the cattle ranchers, Gutiérrez, declared that the council worked well and that he was pleased with it. "One of the councilors is an ex-leader of the cattle ranchers. He clarifies things for us when necessary," thus facilitating trust and a smooth flow of information.[68] Some esteemed the municipal council more highly than the mayor. "The council is better than the mayor—it is more equitable because of the Guaraníes and the presence of Vargas, who is an honest and dependable man," said the parish priest of Charagua.[69] The mayor and the president of the oversight committee agreed that the presence of the Guaraní councilors was the key to the council's effectiveness. Saucedo echoed the councilors' thoughts about the absence of party politics in the council, explaining that the councilmen had made a joint commitment to resign if they campaigned actively in national elections. "Councilmen respond to the interests of the region. It's the ethnic factors that unite them in this way. There are no political fanaticisms, no frontal fights. This is a stable municipality despite the diversity of its composition."[70]

The dynamic described by prominent local observers, community leaders, and councilmen alike was of a well-organized civil society expressed through representative and legitimate institutions working closely with the municipal council to detect and prioritize local needs throughout a large municipal area. This close cooperation, once established, allowed a process of feedback to develop in which municipal plans could be constantly reviewed and altered to respond better to changing community conditions. The policy outputs of this system, in the form of municipal investments, commanded the respect and enthusiasm of voters even in far-flung communities as citizens felt that their concerns were being addressed. And where projects were delayed or suspended, grassroots pressure on the municipal council was intense. For such favorable dynamics to emerge, was it necessary for an APG-like institution to virtually take over local government? We return to this issue below.

Oversight Committee

Charagua's oversight committee was the preserve of the Guaraníes, with seven of its eight members from rural villages and only one *karai*, the secretary—an orthodontist from the town. The president of the OC was Florencio Antuni Sánchez, a peasant farmer from Akae and member of the MBL. Although he has only a fourth-grade education, Antuni is an impressive man—rapid, with intelligent eyes and a speaking style that is direct and succinct. I met him the day after he stepped down as president of the APG. He sat sideways in his chair, tilting against the wall and swinging his legs, cheerful and relaxed with a confidence born of experience. Unlike other municipalities in Bolivia where OC presidents often had little relevant experience, Antuni entered the job with an extensive preparation in leadership, administration, and politics.

Is the oversight committee active here? "Oh yes—I'm very good," Antuni said smiling, and then more seriously, "Up to now there hasn't been even one letter of complaint against me. Never—because we work well there aren't any conflicts."[71] He went on to describe how the OC met regularly with the full municipal council to discuss and solve problems that cropped up throughout the municipality. But he also stressed that there was much room for improvement.

> The oversight committee has no money, no means for moving about the municipality, etc. Oversight committees should be supported. Most members are peasants who are forced to return to their homes because there's no money for the OC to carry out its activities.

He explained that the work of the OC requires it to travel throughout the municipality in order to plan investments, review ongoing projects, and respond to local concerns. In a municipality the size of Charagua, this implies significant expense just to reach far-flung communities. But the OC had no budget, its representatives received no salaries, and there was no vehicle at its disposal. The mayor lent the OC his official car on occasion, but it was old and unreliable, constantly in use, and lacked the four-wheel drive necessary to travel around the district during the rainy season. Antuni stressed that the provision of operating funds for the OC was a key way in which to improve the quality of local government in Bolivia. His plea found an echo at the grassroots level. "The president of the OC is a hidden mayor. He's given a bigger responsibility than that of the mayor, but he doesn't have Bs. 1 to do it with," said Charagua town. "What is he supposed to eat? He has to leave his work in order to do that job."[72] Interestingly the central government also agreed, and in mid-1997 decreed that 1 percent of all devolved funds should be earmarked for the operating costs of oversight committees.

The division of the responsibilities of local governance between mayor, municipal council, and oversight committee seemed very clear to Antuni, as was the power that lay in his hands. "If there's corruption . . . then we must get rid of the mayor. . . . In the house of the people you cannot take possession of what isn't yours."[73] He was not shy about the possibility of confronting the mayor in a direct battle for local power, if necessary, and confident that he would prevail. This was based on the strength of his mandate, which in turn depended upon the high degree of legitimacy and representation of the APG system that selected him. In any local fight for resources or power Antuni could rely on an organization that reached down into the smallest community, for support that in principle was comprehensive, unambiguous, and untainted by the horse-trading and compromises of party politics (see below). Antuni stressed this last point. "Politics screws everything up. The MNR pushed and pressed town hall about the [restoration of the] plaza. They held loud street demonstrations about it demanding action." But nothing came of it. Local people showed little interest, spurning public meetings called by the party, and the MNR's claims to voice local anger were shown to be nothing more than *politiquería*.[74] In Antuni's opinion, the apolitical nature of the OC system of representation was one of the keys to its success, at least in Charagua.

At the grassroots level Charaguans testified to the importance of the work of the oversight committee for effective local government, and vouched for the quality of the previous OC leadership, but were divided in their judgment of the current OC. Taputamí and Isiporenda were most positive. "The OC *does* work here—it *does* oversee municipal funds. Requests from the community to change projects are taken up by the OC and reviewed with the mayor. Then they meet with the municipal council to make a decision."[75] Other communities, while lauding the work of the previous OC, noted that the current leadership had not yet made its weight felt. "The OC has stumbled this year—it doesn't report on municipal expenditures like an OC should," complained the leaders of Antuni's village of Akae.[76] El Espino concurred but refused to condemn the OC, noting that "the current OC is still new—only two months old," and it was still too early to judge.[77] Kapiwasuti, Yapiroa, and Charagua Station agreed that the current OC had not yet reached the standard set by the previous one. But the leaders of El Espino put this issue in perspective. "Before 1995 there was no OC—and the municipality paid no attention to us then." Even if the current OC was not yet fully satisfactory, its very existence gave rural communities additional weight in the competition for public resources.

At the other end of the spectrum, Charagua town and La Brecha agreed that the previous OC had been effective, but condemned the inaction of the current one. "It *does not work*," said Charagua.[78] La Brecha saw evidence of a sinister dynamic behind the OC's declining effectiveness. Alleging that the OC president was a member of the ADN, and its vice president a member of the MBL, they accused the OC of conspiring with the mayor and municipal council to ignore community requests and cover up local complaints. Instead of representing rural communities during the last round of participative planning to draw up the AOP, "the OC became a supporting agency for the mayor's office. . . . The parties have become so powerful that they have been able to co-opt civil society," they explained. "The APG is being undermined here by politicization."[79] Such a development would be serious, with the potential to undermine accountability in local government. But this accusation was not voiced by any other respondents that I interviewed in Charagua. And indeed, with Guaraníes appointed by the APG and Cabi making up a majority on the municipal council,[80] it is difficult to conceive of political parties conspiring to co-opt the OC in order to have it collaborate with municipal government against the interests of Guaraní villages. In Charagua the co-opting would seem to have worked in the opposite direction.

Other local authorities had a favorable opinion of Antuni and the work of his OC. Mayor Saucedo weighed in without reservation.

> The OC is working well, without problems. It's structuring itself better in order to meet more often. And its members are receiving training. . . . They have many criticisms [of investment projects] and demand modifications. But they don't have the money to comply with their obligations—especially to mobilize themselves. . . . The bureaucracy thinks they're peons whose time is free.[81]

Gutiérrez affirmed that the cattle ranchers worked well with the OC, a sentiment that Antuni reciprocated. Councilman Vargas described the OC as an effective body. "They're Guaraní—" he explained meaningfully, "they're vigilant and they watch over things."[82] He noted that the OC had not fought with the municipal council yet and ascribed this to the presence on the council of three Guaraníes, whose strong cultural tendency was to reach consensus at any cost in order to avoid open conflict (see below). Saucedo was eager to promote the institutions he judged necessary for good government, but unsure how to approach the problem of the OC. "If you don't give them money they're against you," he pointed out, "but if you do they're beholden to you."[83]

Other observers mentioned the deterioration in OC performance noted above. "The OC is not so active lately," said councilman Segundo. "Their presence hasn't been in evidence."[84] Chief municipal officer Vargas agreed with this assessment and noted a quiet shift in the institutional dynamic of the town. "The Guaraníes are in the majority here, and named a Guaraní directorate of the OC. But they're uneducated peasants and hence timid and unchallenging before the municipal government."[85] Concerned that their interests were being ignored by the OC, and seeking a voice of their own with which to address the municipality, the nine neighborhood councils of Charagua and Charagua Station joined to form the Community Association. This was a new institutional interlocutor with no standing in law, but one that nonetheless proved adept at representing urban Charagua's concerns. "The Community Association is more active in meeting with the mayor and asking what's going on," said the chief officer. "The OC has allowed its functions to be usurped by the Community Association. . . . The town is dominating the participatory element of the Law of Popular Participation." This association thus afforded Charaguans a tool with which to redress the rural bias that they felt themselves subjected to. It is interesting to note that the system of local government established by Bolivian decentralization was sufficiently flexible to allow for the emergence of new institutional forms to fill the vacuums of representation and voice that might occur from time to time.

Interestingly, the role of the oversight committee in the institutional dynamic of Charagua's local government can be summarized by two semi-contradictory facts. The first is that in the OC, as opposed to the municipal council, Guaraní leaders did not feel the need to disguise their preponderance behind a white figurehead in order to comfort the urban elite. They regarded the OC, built on a foundation of grassroots organizations, as their natural habitat and simply took it over. They felt no need to compromise on its administration or the form that social representation took. This was not true of the mayoralty or the municipal council, with their urban seats, political parties, and electoral campaigns, which were claimed by the town and seemed alien to many Guaraníes. This view was repeatedly confirmed to me by rural leaders, independent urban observers, and other local authorities, who acknowledged the OC as "theirs" and saw the three indigenous councilors as a natural bridge between "them" and the council. It was also confirmed by the complete absence of Mennonite participation in OC activities, elections, and so on, and by the urban neighborhoods' decision to break away from the OC and form a separate body. Indeed, the identification of the OC with Guaraní interests explains why non-Guaraní spokesmen in Charagua had so little to say about it and sought separate, parallel channels of influence over local policy-making.

The second, more striking fact is that the need for an OC dominated by rural Guaraní-dwellers was low in a municipality like Charagua. The presence of three Guaraníes among the five councilmen, and a mayor selected by the Guaraní People's Association, ensured that the interests of the indigenous rural majority would be well represented in local government even without the participation of the OC. In an institutional framework built around checks and balances,[86] the role of the OC was essentially oppositional, based on the power to hobble municipal finances if the OC disagreed with local government decisions. As a representational vehicle it was structurally different from the mayor and municipal council, and intended to give voice to groups underrepresented therein. But there was little scope for such opposition in a municipality in which the OC and municipal council were both rooted in the social network of the APG. This eliminated many of the key functions of the OC, rendering it in these respects redundant. The conspiracy theory voiced above by residents of La Brecha is probably due to this phenomenon, and not to any political party's success in manipulating the organs of local government. In this respect the efficacy of the OC in Charagua, while interesting in the abstract, was a second-order concern.

National and Departmental Government

Unlike Viacha, Charagua's status as the second municipality in the Cordillera province did not merit a subprefect or other direct representative of the departmental government.[87] The highest central government representatives resident in town were the district directors of education and health. Satisfied with local government's focus on investment in primary health and education, both authorities professed good relations with the municipality individually and throughout their respective sectors. "The municipality . . . supports us paying salaries, supplying personnel, and helping with the costs of the hospital," said Dr. Wilfredo Anzoátegui Vaca.[88] No conflicts between local and departmental or national government were evident in either sector. Local community leaders supported this view and went further. When questioned about the change in national (and departmental) governments after the 1997 election, spokesmen from throughout the district replied that there had been no effect on the day-to-day operations of local government. "We have seen no difference since the change of government," affirmed La Brecha, reflecting the near-universal view that national politics simply did not matter for local affairs. Of the 11 communities visited, only Rancho Nuevo dissented, saying, "It's politics as usual— we'd like to change to an ADN mayor so things work better than with the MBL one we have now."[89] But his omission of any specific failures of coordination implied that this was a general impression based on expectations or even political bias, and not a complaint founded in experience.[90]

Among local government authorities—those in the best position to know—the view that little had changed prevailed. Councilmen Vaca, Vargas, and Solano all asserted that "things are the same after the change of government. Popular Participation is working the same."[91] It is telling that these three represented both the incoming (nationally) ADN and outgoing MBL parties. Vaca and Vargas went further, accusing the prefecture of ignoring Charagua, a charge echoed by Edgar Gutiérrez, leader of the local ADN, who testified that his local work was quite unsupported by the ADN prefect in Santa Cruz.[92] The mayor provided a more nuanced view of the state of affairs.

> There have been few concrete changes, but relations with the prefecture have improved [since the change of government]. Before the MNR waged war on us because of our alliance with the ADN.[93] But the new ADN prefect has pledged not to treat us as opposition despite being MBL.[94]

"The *ADNistas* made a lot of noise after the national election and turned up wanting to govern," added Antuni. "But they were told that for that they have to win *local* elections, and from then on they were quiet."[95]

These political (non-)dynamics took place in a deeper context of the relative power and legitimacy of local and regional governments respectively. And on this point Charaguan opinion was unanimous. "Municipal government is autonomous and free of the prefecture," explained Solano. "The prefecture is not a departmental government because it's not elected, unlike local government."[96] Vaca and Vargas agreed. "The municipality is autonomous—no outside authority can impose itself on it. It's never happened."[97] Opinion in the villages was both informed and in agreement. "The municipality is stronger," was the response of Isiporenda, typical of the 11 communities. "It's based on elections."[98]

Deeper Determinants of Local Governance

Private Sector

With nothing else to sustain the local economy but teacher-training schools and small-scale commerce, cattle ranching and the private sector were synonymous in Charagua. The Cattle Ranchers Association of the Cordillera province (AGACOR) represents the ranchers of Charagua and neighboring districts. AGACOR had 200 to 250 members, each with an average of 2,500 hectares; collectively AGACOR claimed some 50,000 head of cattle and controlled over a half-million hectares of land. In addition to being a voice for ranchers' interests locally and regionally, AGACOR is a self-help group dedicated to providing *ganaderos* with technical assistance and disseminating best practice among them. One of its most important programs in 1997 was a campaign to eradicate hoof-and-mouth disease. Juan Carlos Gutiérrez, president of the local branch, assured me that the Cordillera would be the first region in Bolivia to accomplish this, and to this end AGACOR was working with local ranchers whether they were members of the organization or not. He went on to explain that the region's cattle were grass-fed and hormone-free. "Our meat is ecological," he said, with evident pride.[99] But there were also dark clouds on the ranchers' horizon, as Pedro Ribera of AGACOR's directorate explained. "With MERCOSUR the meat market will open up, and we will face competition from better quality and cheaper meat. And we face high interest rates and a high cost of transport here."[100] Business was set to become considerably more difficult for the cattlemen.

Although it was generally agreed that the cattle ranchers were predominantly *ADNistas*, they were known for supporting all of the main political parties, donating cows during electoral campaigns for candidates to serve up at political barbecue rallies. "Even the MBL gets cattlemen's support for their *churrascos*," said Antuni.[101] In the same catholic spirit, Gutiérrez declared his support for distributing municipal resources evenly throughout the district. "All of Charagua benefits from rural schools and roads—the town should not get everything." But he hinted that the authorities were not taking advantage of their resources as they could. "They need to learn how to leverage their funds, to turn 20 into 100. We need strategic associates for community development."[102]

Under Gutiérrez's leadership, AGACOR sought to be one such partner, contracting to drill wells in rural areas for the municipality for significantly less than commercial drillers charged. "In 1996 we hired a private company to drill and lay pipes for us," the mayor reported, "for about Bs. 100,000 [per well]. This year the cattle ranchers are doing the same for Bs. 35,000 each."[103] "We've had success recently drilling wells at 60–120 meters in a region where the experts said there was no water above 300 meters," Gutiérrez said, smiling, and explained that they developed this expertise providing technical aid for AGACOR members. "This 'Dry Chaco' is a myth." But Gutiérrez's vocation stretched beyond the mayor's finances. "One way we help indigenous people is by drilling wells for them. I told the mayor to ask for anything and we'll give it to them."[104] Gutiérrez's offer was certainly generous. But it also denoted the "gift" logic of public action that the *ganaderos* espoused, which was born in and reinforced the traditional relationship of dependency between ranchers and Guaraníes. Commenting on their continuing political power, Ribera hinted that this relationship was not yet dead. "We have ways of making ourselves felt," he assured me.[105]

One of the instruments of AGACOR's local power was its control of the flow of tax revenues. Ranchers traditionally paid their taxes to AGACOR, which in turn transferred them to the Eastern Agricultural Congress (CAO), the peak association for Santa Cruz's farmers and ranchers. The CAO was headquartered in the city of Santa Cruz, and all revenues it collected were paid to the departmental government there. But the agricultural reform law that followed Popular Participation obliged ranchers to pay tax locally instead. Though still unimplemented in mid-1997, the effect of this measure would be to increase local tax revenues significantly at the expense of the prefecture. Gutiérrez made the case that AGACOR should be named payments agency, collecting taxes on behalf of the municipality. In addition to showing his willingness to work with the municipality, his offer reflected ranchers' desire to remain in control of their affairs in a changing institutional and legal environment. This was especially true on an issue widely viewed as the thin edge of a wedge that might ultimately deprive them of their landholdings and hence their base of power.

If the *ganaderos'* future allowed for some uncertainty, their past was unambiguous. Community leaders, municipal authorities, and local observers voiced a consensus notable for its unanimity on the dominance of the ranchers in the past. "Landowners used to run the show. They imposed their will. One of them arrived with two revolvers and he was the boss," explained La Brecha.[106] Councilman Segundo described a power that was both economic and political.

> Before the cattlemen and whites ran the show. They had the right to make Guaraní men and women work without pay, and they didn't allow them to go to school to get educated. . . . Before the *karai* beat peasants [who voted the wrong way]. Even today old people refuse to vote because they think this will happen again.[107]

The white elite in town used legal requirements on voter registration and identity papers to their advantage, keeping Guaraníes away from the ballot box and out of public office. But they were not alone in this project. "Ranchers ran to the army to fix their problems with their employees and servants," said Núñez.[108] The district director of education agreed, arguing that under the Banzer dictatorship, "ranchers and the army divided up [public] lands between them according to their taste and pleasure."[109] And they availed themselves of the local institutions as well. "Local power was in the hands of three or four families that occupied all of the 'spaces of power' locally—the electricity and water cooperatives, the television station, and AGACOR."[110] Through their control of resources, political power, and local institutions, the landowning elite acquired a stature that tended to legitimate and perpetuate their position.[111] "The people saw them as [natural] leaders too."[112]

But the twin forces of economics and the sociopolitical emergence of the Guaraníes from what Albó describes as a sort of spiritual exile[113] conspired to change the Charaguan panorama. Roma explained that the ranchers continued to exercise power,

> but much less aggressively than before. It's less visible here than in the Beni, for example. This is because the profitability of their farms is much lower. Farming is only feasible on a large scale now. So the sons of the *ganaderos* go to the city [instead of staying on the farm]. . . . The triangle of power—jobs, power, money—has been broken.[114]

The ranchers' decline is mirrored in that of their traditional political vehicle as well. "The MNR used to dominate also, but as it has lost power so has that old class."[115] Though Roma argues that these changes began well before the LPP, the law contributed to them and earned the landowners' enmity. Respondents from the villages agreed that the ranchers' dominance was over. "Here anyone who wants to order others around is chased out," announced La Brecha triumphantly. "Huasca!"[116] But respondents differed on the origins of their decline. Many, such as Kapiwasuti and La Brecha, dated it to the Chaco war, which opened the doors of a closed society and its ways to a huge influx of people from distant parts of Bolivia. Others, such as El Espino, thought the change happened later. "Very recently this has finished—because of people in the communities organizing themselves. Now the people don't go out to the ranches to work anymore."[117] But there was widespread agreement that both the landowning elite no longer held the town in its grip, and the interests of the Guaraníes were now effectively safeguarded by the APG and its representatives in local government. The Law of Popular Participation had contributed to and accelerated this dynamic, but the fundamental change in the power structure was under way from well before 1994. Antuni summed things up with three illustrative facts.

(i) It would be difficult for someone to force you to chop wood for him these days. Before you had to chop five meters of wood in exchange for a piece of bread and an ounce of coca leaf. . . . (ii) People no-one thought would *ever* enter town hall now sit on the municipal council. . . . (iii) Cuéllar, Gutiérrez, Pantoja, and García [the most prominent cattlemen] no longer rule the roost. Now they're my friends—or at least I don't have problems with them.[118]

The new Charagua incorporated all of its inhabitants, rich and poor, into its political life, and the various actors treated each other with civility and even respect. The private sector appeared eager to work with local government on projects for the common good, and publicly elected and accountable officials, not ranchers, were the final arbiters of local policy and the use of resources. The list of practices and abuses that were commonly accepted before and had now disappeared was a long one, but perhaps the most telling change in Charagua was in the general climate of relations between townspeople and villagers. This change was both difficult to characterize and obvious and pervasive even to the unaccustomed eye. "The *ganaderos* lead on initiatives because they have money—for any initiative the town knocks on their door. But they don't impose themselves on Charagua," assured Lt. Col. Villaroel, commander of the local garrison. "Town hall runs things now."[119] Gutiérrez described the accommodation.

We've had a few problems with the APG over land rights. When the land reform law came into force there was confusion on both sides. But problems were resolved through talk, through negotiation. . . . Keeping the peace here is priceless.[120]

"Here there are many *ganaderos* who are Guaraníes or mixed," he continued, explaining that AGACOR and the APG had good reason to get along well. And for good measure, "It's as if everyone was a millionaire here—you can drink a beer and a humble person sits down next to you and speaks to you, just like that."

Political Parties and Elections

The political topography of Charagua before decentralization was relatively well-defined, according to local political leaders. The MNR was "the party of the old guard—old professors, old cattlemen. Some Guaraníes are grateful for 1952[121] and still vote MNR in the communities."[122] The party was highly centralized, with local candidates named directly by departmental leaders in Santa Cruz. Cattle ranchers dominated the ADN, electing local leaders from among their senior figures. Some rural communities were allowed to name candidates directly (*a dedo*) onto the lower parts of the list.[123] The MBL, the insurgent that upset the ruling duopoly, was a traditional also-ran in Charagua, depending for its support on the goodwill generated by rural NGOs associated with it. It was able to advance beyond the third rank of local politics when a new generation of activists arrived from Santa Cruz to displace an entrenched and ineffective leadership.[124] They revitalized the party by holding meetings with representatives of Guaraní areas and inviting them to name from among themselves the top candidates to the MBL electoral list (see above).[125] Thus a movement that began in dialogue ended taking over local government. The other national and regional parties, including Condepa, MIR, and the UCS, commanded little support locally and were not serious contenders for power.

Although the MNR consistently won three of five seats on the local council, it traditionally eschewed internal elections, leaving little room for local activists or the development of local leadership. The head of the local branch of the MNR in mid-1997 was a native of the town, Nelson Eguez Gutiérrez, who was unemployed at the time.

> Santa Cruz always wants to order us around. I proposed that the local *commando* designate candidates directly, but Santa Cruz named the ex-mayor [Rolando Gutiérrez] instead. I tried to get rid of him but couldn't—that's why we lost so many votes. . . . People don't like the MNR candidate.[126]

Cattle ranchers and businessmen were also kept at arm's length. Some donated money or lent vehicles for campaigns, but there was no consultation with private interests for the selection of MNR candidates. Eguez blamed this political arrogance for the party's disastrous performance throughout the province in the last elections. What the party lost in this way it then tried to recoup through bribery, allegedly offering the ADN $30,000 for supporting the MNR candidate in the municipal council. But the local ADN leader had received an order to support any party other than the MNR, and the ADN's vote went to Saucedo.[127]

Unlike MNR *comandos* in the altiplano and valleys, where the powerful legacy of the agrarian reform filled party rosters with indigenous and mestizo names, Guaraní communities played almost no part in party affairs before 1995. In that year's local campaign, the MNR realized that the MBL was on the verge of capturing a large share of the Guaraní vote and negotiated a defensive agreement with the Cabi, which resulted in the election of Julián Segundo to the municipal council (see above). The residents of La Brecha and Isiporenda confirmed that this strategy was at least partly successful. "There was a general assembly to select candidates for the MNR and MBL, to see who best represents the peasants. . . . The MNR and MBL had peasant candidates—not the others. . . . Peasants voted for them to vote for their own people."[128] The MNR's lack of a strong rural base can be explained by the failure of land reform to make significant inroads in the Cordillera province (see box 1). "Agrarian reform changed things very much in the altiplano and Cochabamba. But here the big landowners appropriated the revolution of 1952 by becoming *MNRistas*. And in that way they were able to protect themselves" and their *estancias* from the state confiscations promulgated throughout most of the rest of the country.[129] Thus, while the party's political history bequeathed it a large peasant following in the rest of the country, the elite's appropriation of the revolution in the Chaco made the MNR into a different sort of vehicle there.

Edgar Gutiérrez, the local ADN chief in mid-1997, is a jovial man with a large walrus moustache. Known as "Chipi," he is a native *charagueño* and restaurant-hotel owner who worked in the regional development corporation in Santa Cruz for fourteen years until the MNR returned to power in 1993 and threw him out. "The ADN is organized in all 67 communities in Charagua. We have a political committee in each ranch,"[130] he explained, revealing his party's lack of organization in Guaraní communities and its status as the preserve of the landowning elite. As elections draw near, "the departmental order comes to draw up electoral lists. Two or three candidates present themselves and party members vote. . . . About twenty people go to meetings to elect candidates," he explained, describing the cozy atmosphere in the local party. "There's not much rivalry within the ADN—not much competition."

But Gutiérrez also complained of a complete lack of support at the departmental level. "Santa Cruz sent no money [for internal elections]. I had to finance it all myself." And as if to rub in his lack of resources, "then our second candidate switched to the MNR for $300 plus a job at ENFE [the national railroad corporation]." The regional party's neglect of its Charaguan branch stretched well beyond the setting of electoral lists. "There's little contact between them and us. We have to go to Santa Cruz to inform ourselves of what's going on." The problem continued even into elections. "They sent us $600 for national elections. But you need at least $3,000 for good results." Other parties sent considerably more. Gutiérrez was very disappointed that the Santa Cruz leadership did not get involved with the local party or the municipality, and did not manage to pay him a "decent" salary for his efforts. "Now I'll be *corregidor*[131] and will earn Bs. 1,300/ month. I have a daughter studying in Santa Cruz and another who leaves next year," he said plaintively, explaining why he could not afford to retain his political independence.

It was perhaps Gutiérrez's disappointment that led him to a surprising conclusion. "The MNR knows how to govern. We do not. Look now! Nothing's happening," he said, referring to the newly elected ADN president. "The government hasn't changed anyone yet in the local institutions. I've traveled to Santa Cruz to speak to the prefect and leave lists [of names] with him, but all the same people are still working in health, education, etc." So the smiling "Chipi" revealed his conception of politics as a naked game of power and patronage, where political tribes compete to gain control of government in order to share out its resources among themselves. And his tribe was a white tribe, and the game was tinged with racism. He freely referred to his party's electorate as "we the white people."[132]

> CIPCA teaches the peasants not to deal with whites—to fight the whites. There's going to be a conflict here. Money comes to the MBL from outside. No one controls this. The priests are also MBL to the death. The professors are almost all MBL. That's why we *must* change the people in local institutions!

In this sense Councilman Vargas, perhaps because he is a former professor, represented a different wing of the local party—one that conceived of the municipal interest more broadly and was willing to work alongside Guaraní leaders. But the danger remained that the party's core constituency would eventually depart from his path.

The leader of the Charaguan MBL, and the man who oversaw the opening of its electoral lists to the APG, was Eulogio Núñez of CIPCA, a young man who dressed casually and carried the air of an intellectual in the wilderness. He described the ease with which he was able to negotiate the

MBL's accord with the APG, and how it caused a chain reaction in the local political establishment. "The MBL opened its list completely to the Guaraníes, and other parties that had closed their lists grew afraid and included Guaraníes in theirs—the MNR in the second slot and the ADN at number five."[133] The entry of Guaraníes into the municipal council provoked another negotiation, however, this time with the elite in town. "Crispín Solano was the first president of the municipal council. But the cattle ranchers couldn't accept that a former servant of theirs now led the meetings." So Vargas took over the presidency and Solano became vice president of the council. The cattlemen's distrust was in part prompted by the Guaraní representatives themselves, who behaved in council as an ethnic group and not as members of political parties. "They don't pay the 10% to their parties," explained Núñez. "And they speak in Guaraní so the others [on the council] can't understand." As cattle ranchers had always molded local policy to their liking, and continued to lead the two principal parties in town, this flouting of political convention by Guaraní councilmen threatened the parties with a loss of control over local affairs. Crispín Solano cheerily confirmed their fears. "I came in via an electoral accord with the APG. I report to the APG," he declared, and not to any party.[134]

Despite not being Guaraní himself, Saucedo echoed these sentiments at the mayoral level. "We don't pay any attention to the parties," he said. "I support the MBL through my way of being mayor."[135] But unlike how other parties might have reacted, the MBL gave Charagua its full support, providing volunteers to convoke meetings and mobilize people for planning exercises. Otherwise, "I have my hands free to run the municipality as I want. It's always the people first—the party doesn't interfere." The explanation for this attitude lay largely in the MBL's symbiotic relationship with rural NGOs, many of which were active in the region. The party had split away from the larger Movement of the Revolutionary Left during the 1980s and had taken with it its left-leaning anthropologists, agronomists, and rural development practitioners. After years of working with MBL-affiliated NGOs, communities throughout Bolivia's foothills and eastern regions had come to trust the party and identify with its values, and provided it with a natural constituency. For its part, taking over local government was for the MBL a natural scaling-up of the rural development activities carried out by its affiliated NGOs. As the NGOs were an important component not only of the party's ideology but also of its electoral success, it was happy to give its elected officials a relatively free rein to invest municipal resources in community development. The experience of CIPCA, whose officers also led the local MBL, provides a good illustration of this dynamic. Having negotiated with communities that knew them well to elect their candidate mayor, CIPCA then provided technical assistance to the mayor's office, focusing on a planning and investment strategy that was firmly focused on rural areas.

Charaguans were also happy with the more general changes that had occurred recently in their local political system. Respondents from Taputamí, Yapiroa, El Espino, Akae, La Brecha, and Charagua town agreed that the most recent elections had been clean—a welcome change from how things used to be. "Before they hit the peasants and obliged them to vote for the party of the rich man by removing all of the ballots naming the parties favored by the poor. Then they showed the *campesinos* the door. That no longer happens."[136] And where the voting was fair, "results from here never made it to the capital. Ballots were thrown away and replaced with others."[137] "But now they can't do that," explained El Espino. "The votes are counted here and radio and press reporters are present, observing."[138] Recent electoral reforms allowing more voting stations to be located in rural areas also pleased Charaguans and increased turnout. "Now we vote here," said Akae with satisfaction. "Before we had to go to Charagua 8 kilometers away."[139] Related reforms aimed at providing rural citizens with identity papers had also helped. Since women formed the majority of undocumented Bolivians, this had had a disproportionate effect on women's voting, as had rural literacy campaigns, where much the same was true. The aggregate effect on voter turnout was dramatic in some areas, increasing from one-quarter of eligible voters in La Brecha to about three-quarters in the previous election.[140] Overall these changes generated a virtuous circle in which voting became feasible or significantly easier for rural Charaguans, who then took an increased interest in local politics. Local politicians accordingly took an increased interest in them, and for the first time municipal policy and life in the villages began to interact.

But the deep-seated suspicion harbored by rural dwellers for things political did not disappear. "Here in the community there are no politicians," said El Espino, and the sentiment was echoed in La Brecha. "Where there are politicians people fight a lot."[141] Mennonite colonies continued to shun politics in all its forms. Even the residents of Charagua Station argued for "a pure representation of the people. Parties get in the way. We should get rid of the parties and allow communities to nominate councilmen directly. This would better represent the interests of the people."[142] Such an attitude was surprising in a community that regarded itself as an urban satellite of Charagua town, where the parties were embraced as their own.

Community and Grassroots Organizations

The maximum expression of Guaraní social organization in Charagua, and indeed throughout the Chaco, is the APG, which acts as the voice of Guaraní interests. But to understand how it works and the legitimacy it has locally, it is important to consider its roots in the organization of rural communities. Guaraní communities benefit from a traditional system of self-government. Leadership is rotational, and indigenous communities change their leaders every year. Communities nominate individuals, according to ability and interest, as community officers responsible for priority tasks.[143] "Of 100 [villagers], there's always one who loves a particular type of work," explained Antuni. "So the community names an education officer, for example. He has the keys to the schoolhouse and decides how it's to be used and keeps it in good repair. He lends it out for meetings."[144] And so too for health, irrigation, and so on. Each community has its own statutes setting out the responsibilities of community officials, how they are selected, and how it is governed. "They operate via assemblies," explained Muñoz of the FIS. "Everything is consensual. There's no majority voting, nothing like that. They spend days and days talking in order to reach a decision. But once they do agree, that decision is very strong—no one can later say 'I did not want it so.'"[145]

Until the 1980s, Guaraní communities labored in isolation and with an acute lack of resources. But beginning in 1983, a diagnosis of Guaraní poverty and exclusion carried out by the Santa Cruz Regional Development Corporation, CIPCA, and others resulted in the adoption by Guaraní leaders of PISET as the guiding principle for their local development efforts.[146] The concept of PISET, the Spanish acronym for production, infrastructure, health, education, and land/territory, makes up a system of work that defines how the community should progress. "They have a directorate at the regional level that directs PISET efforts. They work PISET at each level from the community up to the department and beyond."[147] Siquier placed great emphasis on the emergence of this consensus. "PISET marks the opening of a new historical process here . . . a re-birth of Guaraní culture" after the Battle of Kurujuky.[148]

Box 2: Building Consensus in Guaraní

I arrive on a golden late afternoon to speak to the leaders of Taputamí. We shake hands and retire to a badly kept classroom to conduct the interview. Numerous onlookers and passers-by squeeze into the little room with us, sitting in desks meant for eight-year-olds and crouching on the floor. I count 13 inside, and perhaps 10 more peering in at both windows and the door. They are badly dressed and look poor. Their curiosity blocks the light and I find it difficult to see what I am writing. Later night falls, someone brings a flashlight, and the interview continues. I scribble in its pallid beam and they sit still in the darkness. Many of my questions trigger long discussions in Guaraní. The strange, lyrical tones linger in the night air, and when they have finally reached agreement one or two explain the answer to me in Spanish, which they all seem to speak.

The scene is similar in La Brecha. Deliberations are invariably followed by a broad smile as the one sitting nearest turns to me and begins, "Well, I think . . ." The rest listen to the collective verdict with approving nods—the Guaraní system of consensus.

The Guaraníes' success in integrating local PISET efforts into a regional development strategy inspired the creation of the national APG in 1986–87. From its very inception, the APG built its organization on the preexisting social structure of Guaraní communities; it benefited from the deeply ingrained legitimacy of autochthonous village institutions founded in consensual decision making. According to both Muñoz and Antuni, the APG was energetic and achieved a great deal in its first years of existence. "In less than two years the Guaraníes produced 500 high school graduates," Antuni cites as an example. "We'd thought that would take us until the year 2000."[149] And by serving as a credible voice for Guaraní interests, it was for the first time able to mobilize external resources, including notably those of the FIS, in favor of Guaraní needs. New schools and health posts appeared in the Charaguan countryside alongside irrigation and other productive projects. The APG's initial attainments combined with the weakening of landowners and modest economic growth during this period to produce gradual but steady improvements in the lives of Guaraní peasants. Whereas before most Guaraní men had been forced to leave their homes for the sugarcane harvest, for example, now few did. "Before Guaraníes were employed as servants. Now there are very few Guaraní domestic employees. The rich bring them from elsewhere."[150] The APG's structure, which reached deep down into the smallest Guaraní communities and was based upon sponta-neous forms of self-government, was largely responsible for what it achieved. "The Guaraníes' incredible unity is the source of their success," the FIS's Muñoz declared.[151]

Both the degree of social organization and its effects were on display in villages throughout Charagua. Unlike Viacha in 1997, communities here were well informed about the costs, schedules, and counterpart contribu-tions of projects being implemented locally. In Kapiwasuti, for example, the entire community discussed and agreed on plans for an irrigation project for local farmers, and then approved the design that CIPCA had drawn up.[152] And villagers were able to overcome the free-rider problem by mobilizing themselves to provide services for the common good. Thus Akae boasted three production teams called "work communities"[153] that planned, orga-nized, and worked communal lands for the benefit of all.[154] And this was not limited to more prosperous areas. Even the poorest communities such as El Espino and Taputamí, where respondents wore no shirts and scarcity was evident, had village presidents, work communities, and PISET officers. These institutions permitted villages to coordinate relatively large and com-plex projects, and so attain a considerable degree of self-reliance. Thus Taputamí was able to design and build a 100-meter bridge over a local stream entirely on its own. The strength of indigenous institutions was demonstrated in Kapiwasuti shortly after decentralization, when villagers set about organizing a "grassroots organization" (GRO) as the law stipulated. But Kapiwasuti already had a community president, and he retained the people's support. "The GRO shriveled and the community president took over as de facto GRO," the villagers said, explaining how they preferred their own institutional forms to the foreign ones of the Bolivian state.[155]

The organizational capacity of Guaraní communities was largely based on feelings of solidarity among villagers. And these feelings extended far and wide through the ethnically homogeneous Guaraní countryside. Thus many villages reported working with neighboring villages on joint projects. "The people from neighboring communities are the same as us—they have the same customs," reported Isiporenda.[156] Copere Brecha agreed, adding that they participated in meetings of the huge upper and lower Isoso to co-ordinate activities and plan joint projects.[157] Yapiroa went further, affirming its willingness to forgo further municipal investments for the benefit of other communities. "There's a lack of money in the municipality, and other communities have needs too."[158] This solidarity persisted despite the historical and cultural differences between the Ava-Guaraníes of the northern Charaguan Serranía Aguarague and the Tupi-Guaraníes of the Isoso farther south.

To the outsider these differences are difficult to perceive. The Guaraníes themselves refer to each other as cousins very similar in appearance, discernible only by the "echo" in their speech.[159] A more telling distinction lies in the organization of their communities. Tupi-Guaraníes retain the traditional *capitanías* of their forebears, while Ava-Guaraníes' local authorities are called local mayors, *corregidores,* and so on. Village *capitanías* are subordinate to the authority of the Capitanía del Alto y Bajo Isoso (Cabi)—headed by the *Capitán Grande*—while local Ava-Guaraní authorities are integrated directly into the APG. The Cabi is also formally part of the APG but maintains its distance and prefers to think of itself as a separate entity. The differences between the two surpass the semantic and the symbolic. "The Cabi has an autocratic structure, while the APG is more democratic," the mayor explained to me. "With the *capitanes,* all that they get[160] is for themselves and the people go hungry."[161] Antuni was more explicit.

> Boni [the *Capitán Grande*] takes the men out to work in the sugar harvest in Santa Cruz. He charges Bs. 10/head, supposedly for the benefit of the *capitanía.* But it's all for him. You'd think they'd have at least one building after thirty years of this. . . . And the *Capitán Grande* has a woman in each community.[162]

Avas saw themselves as more modern, while Tupis thought themselves more authentically Guaraní. But the solidarity among them overcame this divide. Village spokesmen throughout the countryside reported good relations and numerous joint projects with nearby rural communities. Tupi and Ava families alike identified with the larger Guaraní cause.[163] There was neither visible resentment nor a struggle for resources between the two groups. But even among rural peoples, solidarity ended at the racial barrier. "We have good relations with other communities," said La Brecha, "but few relations with the Mennonites."[164] All of the villages I spoke to with Mennonite neighbors agreed. Some complained about the Mennonites' farming methods, and others seemed worried that they were buying up land. But none reported more than minimal, strictly commercial relations with them.

Civic activity in town, on the other hand, took on a very different character. Communities were organized into neighborhood councils and focused their attention on infrastructure and urban development—much narrower concerns than in rural communities, where authorities' concerns extended to residents' livelihoods and cultural identity. They operated not as community governments but as interest-group lobbies competing for municipal funds. Indeed, according to the MNR's Eguez, neighborhood councils did not exist before 1994. "All of them were formed specially for the LPP."[165] The councils' formation of the Community Association (described above) as a means of increasing their political weight and wresting the initiative from the Guaraní-dominated OC is a telling sign of their underlying concerns. They were not motivated by social solidarity but rather by the refinement of political antagonism as a tool for controlling the public purse. It is ironic that the town, in creating new representative institutions, was following the example of the Guaraníes in form even as it betrayed it in substance. The responses of both neighborhood councils and rural communities to general questions of governance support this view. To the question of how to improve local government, townspeople proposed granting official functions to the civic committee—a sort of local chamber of commerce—as well as urban social and educational organizations. "The OC is being politicized . . . , and we must involve other organizations in local administration. . . . White people are better at leading . . . because we can't be influenced as readily," they affirmed.[166] Their intent was essentially to exclude the OC, and hence the peasant majority, from government.

In answer to the same question, by contrast, spokesmen for El Espino innocently proposed organizing the APG in the town itself. "It still doesn't work there—they need officers in charge of education, infrastructure, etc."[167] Though naive, this idea was based on a concept of community organization that springs from the grass roots upward, and that is deeply rooted in the Guaraní mentality.[168] Respondents throughout the Charaguan countryside invoked it responding to a variety of questions about governance and identity. When asked what caused a community organization to be bad, for example, Copere Brecha replied, "A grassroots organization is *always* good. It is able to work for the community."[169] They did not admit the possibility of a bad GRO. For them a GRO is the institutional expression of the community and all of its inhabitants. A GRO could not be bad any more than a community could be bad, though it might prove more or less effective over time. This essentialist view of community organization as an expression of the collective will contrasted sharply with the townspeople's view of GROs as interest group lobbies immersed in pork-barrel politics. It was founded in a deeper, Hegelian notion of historical progression.[170] "We always wanted education," pleaded Yapiroa. "We want to advance as a people. The older generations eliminated slavery. Now we want to continue to move forward."[171]

Other Actors—The Military and the Church

The last two actors of any significance on the Charaguan political scene are the military and the church. The local army garrison traces its history to the soldiers who bravely fought back the invading forces during the Chaco War and retook Charagua from the Paraguayans. But years of small military budgets left their installations in poor condition, with no funds for equipment and inadequate resources for training. The garrison commander, Lt. Col. Fair Villaroel, boasted of good relations with the municipal government, with numerous projects on which the two had cooperated. For example, the garrison provided a large part of the labor for the plaza renovation and park projects. "They provide the cement and we provide the rest," Villaroel said.[172] The army had also helped to clean the cemetery and the streets of the town, and had provided manpower for several health campaigns.

Villaroel had in effect taken advantage of an ambitious municipal government to substitute the combat training he could not afford with civic exercises, the running costs of which the municipality paid. This work broke the tedium of barracks life and afforded his officers the chance to develop their organizational skills and instill discipline in the rank and file. The commander's only complaint was of too few such opportunities. "We'd like to do more," he declared, "but the mayor is a little disorganized." The garrison's civic spirit also extended into the Guaraní hinterland. "We have very good relations with the Guaraníes and the APG," said Villaroel, explaining that he sent a doctor and dentist to the Guaraníes' medical center regularly, and that "any community that requests help gets it." Mindful of the army's historical role in the repression of the Guaraní people, Villaroel sent officers to village festivals and ceremonies, and tried to ensure that his soldiers did not disrupt Guaraní life. Local observers were not in disagreement with the picture Villaroel presented, observing that after many years the army had returned to the barracks and now played a benign role in the affairs of the municipality.[173]

The leader of the Catholic Church in Charagua in mid-1997 was Fr. Luis Roma, a Spanish priest who had worked for 40 years in Bolivia, 3 of them in Charagua. In addition to overseeing the parish, Roma was responsible for the school run by Fe y Alegría, a Catholic NGO dedicated to education. Roma professed good relations with the municipal government, the army, rural villages, and the townspeople, an impression that was shared by each of these in turn. But the Church's role had not always been impartial or benign. "Before 1955 local power was held by the landowners and the Church, plus the politicians in power at the time," explained AGACOR's Ribera, himself a landowner. "But after the revolution the Church changed and took up popular causes and began working with marginal populations."[174]

The Church had previously formed part of the *criollo* establishment, sanctioning the violence of the state against the non-Christian Guaraní people. But then it changed, and its new attitude was exemplified by such men as Albó, Siquier, and Roma—foreign-born activist priests who had crossed the globe to work with the rural poor and dispossessed. They employed a new, highly involved form of outreach that addressed not just the spiritual needs of Guaraníes but their physical and cultural concerns as well. Their instruments were traditional church-centered community activities, parish programs in the villages, and a range of church-supported NGOs dedicated to education, health, and rural development. Fe y Alegría and CIPCA were two prominent examples; a third was Teko-Guaraní, led by Jesuits and dedicated to bilingual education for Guaraníes as a form of cultural assertion. No longer seated at the right hand of temporal authorities in town, the Church's profile was much reduced, its power greatly diffused compared to a half-century earlier. But it remained an important and influential actor in Charaguan daily life.

Summary: How Government Works in Charagua

The evidence points overwhelmingly to the conclusion that local government in Charagua was of high quality. Through dozens of hours of interviews with authorities and citizens from all walks of Charaguan life not a single accusation of official corruption surfaced. This is surprising given the state of public disaffection with elected authorities in Bolivia, as well as Charagua's inexperience managing large financial flows. Respondents from communities scattered throughout the municipal area reported satisfaction with their local government, and felt that their concerns were being addressed by municipal policy. The mayor, working in concert with the oversight committee, had implemented an investment planning system that the authorities and grass roots alike agreed was transparent, equitable, and highly participative. The projects that resulted from this process pleased citizens both because they responded to real needs and because of the importance given to local opinions in their conception and design. Informed observers with a variety of political and organizational affiliations agreed that municipal authorities were well-meaning and effective, and that the quality of the investments and services they provided were correspondingly high.

Good government resulted from the interplay of the institutions of local government—the mayor, municipal council, and oversight committee—operating in a political context dominated by the principal actors in Charaguan society—cattle ranchers and the APG. The mayor's office, the executive branch of local government, was institutionally weak in Charagua, suffering, as Saucedo admitted, from poor human resources and relatively low administrative capacity. This was largely compensated by the virtues of the mayor himself, who was widely admired as energetic, honest, and ambitious for his municipality. The strength of his electoral mandate was an additional advantage. Handpicked by the APG leadership, Saucedo was the white face of Guaraní political power in Charagua. His nomination by an organization that embraced the majority of the population and reached deep down into its community structure conferred upon his office immense legitimacy. At the lowest, grassroots level, the people trusted their mayor. This proved instrumental in eliciting the ideas and preferences for municipal investment of communities more used to the violence of the state; their subsequent cooperation during project implementation was similarly forthcoming. And so the mayor was able to integrate the demand from dozens of rural communities into an investment strategy that reflected their needs: human development, productive projects, and road maintenance. And he was also able to make demands of them—to donate labor and materials, but more importantly to exploit public investment to their benefit. If a school would be built, they had to get educated. The fact that the municipality now spoke with the voice of the poor illustrates the degree to which power had shifted in Charagua. Town hall was no longer the domain of the *ganaderos*.

Like the mayor, the council worked closely with community leaders and listened carefully to grassroots demand. Like the mayor, councilmen were held in high esteem in their constituencies as hardworking, honest, and able. Villagers judged them effective and were pleased with the outcome of their work. But in institutional terms the municipal council was perhaps more remarkable than the mayor, as the APG's influence crossed party boundaries and overcame well-established political and ideological rivalries. The two MBL and one MNR Guaraní councilmen essentially ignored their parties once elected, admitting enthusiastically that they reported to their superiors in the APG and no one else. They formed a majority on the council of five and worked, along with the ADN representative, to advance the interests of rural communities. The presence of the Guaraníes and the way in which they operated were clearly key to the council's effectiveness. Once again, the foundation of its electoral mandate in the APG, and the legitimacy this bestowed on its efforts, allowed it to work closely with village authorities to detect and prioritize needs throughout a large municipal area. This led to a process of feedback in which municipal plans were constantly reviewed and revised to better respond to changing community conditions.

If the Guaraníes controlled the municipal council, they completely dominated the oversight committee. With seven Guaraníes out of eight members, the OC was essentially an arm of the APG cast in the guise of a municipal institution. Its authorities were APG authorities, and its president, Florencio Antuni, spent the first part of his term as president of the APG as well. Whereas the mayor and municipal council represented the APG's positions in local government, the oversight committee essentially was the APG. Whereas Guaraní interests were able to transcend party politics in the municipal council, the OC was overtly apolitical. The grass roots perceived the OC as they did the APG—representative, honest, and practically an extension of their will. Antuni could exploit the APG's organization directly to ascertain village opinion and to mobilize Guaraníes from the grass roots upward. This placed him in a strong position with respect to the mayor and municipal council, and he knew it.

But ironically, the electoral underpinnings of power in Charagua were such that the OC did not find it necessary to assert itself. Bolivian local government is designed around checks and balances, where the different institutions of government represent competing interests. The role of the OC is as a veto-wielding upper house of parliament where rural populations are overrepresented; it is able to paralyze municipal business if government proves corrupt or insensitive to its constituents' needs. But in a municipality where both municipal council and mayor sprang out of the APG, the interests of the rural majority were already well represented. There was little role left for an OC that also spoke for the countryside. Its mere existence probably gave rural communities greater weight in the competition for public resources. But its efficacy was ultimately of second-order importance to the question of government effectiveness. With their complementary roles in policy planning and execution, it was the mayor and municipal council that jointly determined local government's success in Charagua. Of these the mayor, the protagonist who helped to plan investment and then carried it out, was probably more important. To the extent that the council provided oversight for a mayor already watched over by the APG, it was somewhat redundant. But the common political roots of the two institutions render such distinctions both difficult and ultimately futile. The strength of the mayor was based on the social consensus represented by the governing majority in the municipal council. Both institutions were ultimately founded in the social network of the APG.

Organization or Ethnicity?

The Guaraní assault on local politics began only in 1995. Their history over the previous hundred years was a long, sad tale of official oppression and abandonment. What changed? What underlying economic and social conditions allowed the Guaraní people to successfully occupy the central spaces of local power? This is fundamentally a story of organization building, not ethnicity. After all, Guaraníes had resided in Charagua for generations with no political projection whatsoever. During that century they were not somehow "less Guaraní." Decentralization was an institutional shock that opened a space requiring organization to fill. It was their luck that Guaraníes had—quite independently—begun organizing a few years before. The form that organization took was largely colored by the preexisting social structure of Guaraní communities, which in turn contributed to the speed with which the APG gained legitimacy and organizational strength. But without the organization their consensual decision making and natural solidarity would have remained bottled up in their rural communities, unlinked to policy and power.

For the APG to have such a large impact on local affairs, one additional factor is required. The urban elite in Charagua town had dominated local life for decades, through wars and revolution, and the rise of a network of rural communities did not represent a serious challenge to their supremacy. In previous times AGACOR might have squashed the APG or easily excluded it from power. That it made no such attempts in 1995 is indicative of the depths that the cattle economy, and cattlemen's morale, had plumbed. Once the rulers of the southern plains, with vast landholdings and herds that numbered in the tens of thousands, Charagua's *ganaderos* were by 1995 the dispirited victims of years of agricultural crisis that had slashed food prices, incomes, property prices, and borrowing ability. As economic power passed from the countryside to the cities, the children of the ranchers left the farm in search of education and careers in the city. The ancient certainty of rich farms and perpetual prosperity passed from father to son was broken; no longer would land be the sustenance of generations of rancher families stretching into the indefinite future. For many, farming would become a hobby. As the value drained from the land, the *ganaderos* found they had much less invested in their farms, and thus much less interest in controlling local politics. And thus when a conciliatory APG emerged to claim the municipality for itself, they found that they had no strong reason to oppose it.

AGACOR retained its importance as an institution, with control over a large budget and good technical and human resources. But as a political protagonist and defender of interests it was lost in the new Bolivia. One sensed that even the ranchers regarded themselves as a dying breed. Whereas AGACOR's will once echoed in the town hall, it now found little place for itself in the new institutional context. One interpretation of the townspeople's formation of the Community Association is as an attempt to find an organizational form that might fit into the new scheme. But even this was not so much a strategy as a response to the APG's success, a sign of their ambivalence, and a groping attempt to regroup. In an era when history and ideology had stripped the ranchers of their traditional allies, the armed forces and the Church, and they found themselves lost in a sea of change, the APG was able to stroll into town and simply take over.

CHAPTER 4

Decentralization and Responsiveness across Bolivia: A 21-Year View

Chapter 1 presented simple but powerful descriptive statistics implying that decentralization changed sectoral and spatial patterns of public investment. Decentralized governments invested in different places and different sectors than centralized government had before, shaping national investment patterns that became more responsive to real local needs. But such descriptive statistics, though often compelling, are analytically rudimentary. Deep qualitative evidence in chapters 2 and 3 showed that decentralized governments were as capable of corruption and ineptitude as of efficiency and responsiveness. What is the balance of decentralization's effects on the nation as a whole? Can more rigorous evidence tell us whether decentralization made government systematically more responsive to local needs, less responsive, or enough of both that there are no systematic effects?

This chapter takes up the challenge with econometric tools and an original municipal-level database that contains yearly information on local investments for all Bolivian municipalities for the period 1987–2007. This doubles the size of the sample on which my previous work on Bolivia[1] was based (1987–96). Hence the estimations provided below incorporate far more information than any of my previous work on Bolivian reform. More interesting, the longer time span examined here allows us to explore how decentralization's impacts changed over time.

In addition to financial data, the database includes demographic, social, economic, and geographic data, local electoral results, and institutional and procedural data from the innovative Censo Municipal. Unfortunately, changes in the wording of many census questions between 1992 and 2001 make it impossible to compare a number of specific answers across time, leaving us with only one observation for a number of key sectoral variables during the 20-year period. How then can we investigate decentralization's effects given good time-series data on national and local investment flows, but cross-sectional-only data for some key variables? This chapter provides an econometric methodology for doing so.

It also develops a theoretical model in which public goods are jointly provided by central and local governments. This serves as an aid for interpreting the econometric results, and as a consistency framework for thinking about some of the key trade-offs between local versus central provision of public goods more generally.

The question of decentralization and responsiveness to need brings us back to the curious discrepancy discussed in the introduction between enthusiasm for decentralization among governments and policy analysts across the world, and the weak and contradictory evidence on its effects. In particular, the literature records little econometric analysis of the effects of decentralization on government responsiveness to local needs, and relevant anecdotal evidence is ambiguous. This is especially surprising given that increased responsiveness constitutes one of the central claims in favor of reform. Furthermore, I have not found any studies in the literature that follow the process of decentralization with rigorous evidence over any significant span of time.

This chapter seeks to fill these gaps by examining decentralization's effects on government responsiveness to local need over 21 years in a careful, methodical way using abundant data from Bolivia. Focusing on one country allows me to control for political regime, external shocks, and other exogenous factors more systematically than a cross-country approach can. And Bolivia is particularly appropriate since reform was comprehensive and sustained, and so constitutes a social experiment. The remainder of the chapter is organized as follows. The second section models the joint provision of local public goods as a Stackelberg follower game in which political competition provides local governments with better information on heterogeneous local preferences, but central government is more productive. The third section presents the data and develops a methodology for estimating the effects of decentralization on government responsiveness to need when financial data is extensive, but social, demographic, institutional, and other data are not. The fourth section tests whether decentralization changed public investment patterns across Bolivia's 311 municipalities and then examines the determinants of these changes focusing on variables of need. The final section concludes.

The Model

As in many countries, Bolivia's local services are jointly provided by central and local governments. The evidence in the fourth section below thus focuses on the effect that local institutions and control of local budgets have on the responsiveness of municipal investments to real local need. But before delving into the empirics of the question, it is useful for the sake of conceptual clarity to formalize the interplay between center and periphery. To better understand how interactions between them affect provision of a common local public good, this section develops a simple model of joint provision, following Varian (1994) and Batina and Ihori (2005), in which central government moves first, and local government is a Stackelberg follower. Rather than compare two theoretical extremes in which public services are provided *either* by central or local governments, as I did in my 2004 article, I model provision more realistically as the joint product of central and local investment decisions.

The key trade-off is that local governments have better information, but central government is more efficient in the production of public goods. The former is due to local political competition, which we can think of as election cycles and the lobbying, campaigning, and related dynamics these entail, that provide local governments with information about local preferences. Political competition does not, by contrast, provide central government with useful information about local preferences. This is because national elections do not focus on local issues and specific local policy options in the way that local elections do. The latter half of the trade-off may be thought of as traditional economies of scale, or as technological or organizational advantages over local governments in the production of public goods. In many countries, for example, the most capable public sector professionals work for central, not local, government. This allows central agencies to design, plan, and implement interventions that are higher quality, more cost effective, or both.

Assume a country made up of T districts, each with population n_j where j denotes district. Individuals have linear utility $U_i = \ln(x_i) + \theta_i \ln(g_j)$ where x_i is the amount of private good consumed by individual i, g_j is the amount of public good available in district j, and θ_i is individual i's preference for public good g_j. Central and local governments' contributions to the common public good are denoted g_j^c and g_j^l, hence $g_j = g_j^c + g_j^l$. We denote the local median preference for the public good in district j as θ_{mj}. Local welfare is defined as median utility, $U_{mj} = \ln(x_{mj}) + \theta_{mj}\ln(g_j)$.

The function of government is to provide public goods, which it finances with a local head tax. Local government ascertains θ_{mj} with probability p_l and θ_{-mj} with probability $(1 - p_l)$, and central government ascertains θ_{mj} with probability p_c and θ_{-mj} with probability $(1 - p_c)$. Probability varies as $p_{l,c} \in [0,1]$, and θ_{-mj} is defined as an unrestricted value of θ other than θ_{mj}. By assumption (see above), p_l increases with the amount and duration of political competition in a municipality, whereas p_c does not. For notational simplicity political competition is proxied by e, the number of elections since the inception of local government in a municipality. Hence

$$p_l = f(e), \quad \frac{dp_l}{de} > 0, \text{ and } \quad \frac{dp_c}{de} = 0.$$

Central government's superior efficiency is modeled as a cost advantage in the provision of a given public good. The head tax needed to finance a given level of provision under central government is thus $\alpha g_j/n_j$ with $0 < \alpha \leq 1$, lower than local government's tax g_j/n_j.

In this variant of the Stackelberg game, central government is the leader and announces its level of provision first. Local government observes this and calculates its optimal reaction, which it then provides. The solution is via backward induction, and so we begin with local government's reaction. For any g_c that central government chooses, local government's problem in district j is

$$\max_{g^l} \left[(p_l\theta_m + (1 - p_l)\theta_{-m})\ln(g^l + g^c) - \frac{g^l}{n} \right] \quad (1)$$

where for convenience we drop subscripts j. We take first-order conditions and simplify the expression without loss of generality by letting $\theta_{-m} = 0$. Rearranging provides local government's optimal response

$$g^{l*} = n\theta_m p_l - g^c \quad (2)$$

Central government sets its level of provision independently. This reflects common practice and may be thought of as bureaucratic convenience of the center. In the real world it may be motivated by the relative variabilities of central versus local allocations over time, their relative size, the different allocation criteria used at the central versus local levels, or the simple fact that the center moves first and local politics can be unpredictable. Central government's problem over T districts is

$$\max_{g_1, \cdots, g_T} \left[\sum_j (p_c \theta_{mj} + (1 - p_c) \theta_{-mj}) \ln(g_j^c) - \sum_j \alpha \frac{g_j^c}{n_j} \right] \quad (3)$$

Solving for district j, we take first-order conditions and once more simplify by letting $\theta_{-m} = 0$. Rearranging, we get central government's optimal level of public good provision

$$g^{c*} = \frac{n\theta_m p_c}{\alpha} \quad (4)$$

which reflects central government's superior efficiency.

Substituting (4) into (2) and letting $\tau = p_c/p_l$ we get

$$g^{l*} = n\theta_m p_l (1 - \frac{\tau}{\alpha}). \quad (5)$$

We can think of τ as the center's sensitivity to local preferences expressed in terms of local government's sensitivity. Local government will only provide a positive quantity of public good g^{l*} when $\tau < \alpha$, that is to say when local government's relative accuracy in sensing local preferences more than offsets the center's superior efficiency. In this case it is efficient for local government to provide some share of the public good, a share that rises as the value of τ/α falls. If $\tau \geq \alpha$, by contrast, then g^{l*} will be zero, and all public goods will be provided by the center.[2] These results provide a simple guide to what sorts of public goods and services should be decentralized and which ones provided by the center, if the central trade-off of our model is correct.

TABLE 2.

Condition	Result	Implication
$\tau = p_c/p_1 < \alpha$	$g^{l\ast} > 0$	Joint central-local provision is efficient
$\tau = p_c/p_1 \geq \alpha$	$g^{l\ast} = 0$	Centralized provision is efficient

For further implications, consider that parameters τ and α are characteristics of the specific good or service in question (e.g., primary education, local roads, sanitation), not of the locality. For services where production is small-scale and dispersed, such as primary education and primary health care, we can reasonably expect the center's efficiency advantage over local provision to be relatively low (i.e., compared to tertiary education, trunk roads, or environmental protection) and dominated by local government's ability to better sense local preferences; hence $\tau < \alpha$. Such services make up a category in which individuals are well placed to assess their own needs (contrast primary education with, for example, environmental protection), and local governments are closer to individuals than central government. Hence we expect $g^{l\ast}$ to have a positive value for primary education and health, and indeed to increase over time as successive elections drive p_l closer to 1. Other services, such as tertiary education, environmental protection, or indeed national defense, rely on more specialized knowledge and/or display greater economies of scale. Central government will have a larger advantage in the production of such services, and local governments less of an advantage in sensing locals' needs.

These results imply that, for goods where $\tau < \alpha$, decentralized provision will be more responsive to local needs than centralized provision. We test this prediction empirically by comparing both central government investment patterns before 1994 and local government investment patterns since 1994 to objective indicators of local need.

Data and Methodology

Data

My database is compiled from official government sources and is as far as I know the only such database in existence. Data come from the Controller General's Office, General Accounting Office, Ministry of Finance, National

Electoral Court, National Institute of Statistics, National Secretariat of Rural Development,[3] Political Economy Analysis Unit, Social Investment Fund, Social Policy Analysis Unit, Vice Ministry of Popular Participation, and the Vice Ministry for Public Investment and External Finance. The database covers the universe of Bolivian municipalities, territory, and people.[4]

Compiling the database was not straightforward. Before 1994, the vast majority of public investment in Bolivian villages and towns was undertaken by central government. But financial records of these projects—voluminous and very detailed—do not include information on which municipality they (would eventually) belong to. This is not surprising, as most municipalities did not exist even in statute, let alone in any real administrative or budgetary sense. Hence local experts in geographic information systems were engaged to allocate the thousands of public investment projects in the 1987–93 Public Sector Investment Budget to Bolivia's municipalities, as created or expanded by the 1994 reform. This data was combined with postreform data reported by municipal governments to create the 1987–2007 Bolivia Municipal Investment Dataset. This data set is available on my personal webpage[5] and is one of the primary contributions of this research.

Budgetary and investment data are panel data. Electoral data from the 1993, 1995, 1999, and 2005 elections are periodic and cross-sectional. Social, demographic, economic, and geographic data are cross-sectional from the 1992 and 2001 national censuses. Institutional, infrastructural, and procedural data from the innovative 1997 Censo Municipal—a special exercise that inventoried municipalities' physical and institutional infrastructures as well as their decision-making procedures—are cross-sectional. Their use constitutes one of the innovations of this study. The database retains data integrity by source.[6] Econometric estimations in this chapter use similar variables from different sources in alternative specifications as robustness checks. The models prove robust.

Methodology

My objective is to test whether decentralization made public investment more responsive to local needs in Bolivia. This can usefully be decomposed into two questions: (1) did the patterns of public sector investment change with decentralization? and if so, (2) do indicators of need determine those changes? It is possible that public investment did not change with decentralization—that the structure of Bolivia's public administration was significantly reformed, but local investment patterns and policy decisions continued much as before. If so, decentralization and centralization would be largely equivalent from an economic perspective, though one might be preferable to the other on political or other grounds. If decentralization did change investment patterns it becomes important to try to characterize these changes in terms of welfare and distribution and to identify which social and institutional factors are most associated with these changes.

Ideally public goods would be measured in quality-adjusted units of output, separated by type. But such information is (unsurprisingly) unavailable for Bolivia, and instead I measure investment inputs in the form of resources expended on public investment projects. This approach has the advantage of using natural, noncontroversial units, and of facilitating comparisons across different sectors. I separate these flows into 13 distinct sectors, of which I analyze 10 (see table 2).[7]

Using the panel data described above, I estimate the model

$$G_{mt} = \beta_1 \alpha_m + \beta_2 \alpha^*_m + \beta_3 \delta_t + \varepsilon_{mt} \tag{6}$$

where G_{mt} denotes public investment by sector (education, health, etc.) measured in thousands of constant 2000 bolivianos,[8] α_m and δ_t are vectors of state and year dummy variables, and $\alpha^*_m = \alpha_m D_t$, where D_t is a decentralization dummy variable that takes the values 0 before 1994 and 1 after, all subscripted by municipality m and year t.[9] Investment patterns are thus decomposed into three terms: a year effect, δ_t, which captures year shocks and time-specific characteristics; a state effect, α_m, which captures all of the characteristics of a state fixed in time; and a decentralization-interacted state effect, α^*_m, which captures state-specific characteristics that begin in 1994.

Any systemic changes in Bolivia's politics or economy that affect all municipalities similarly, such as a national policy initiative or an external shock, will be captured by the year term, δ_t. Effects related to municipalities' fixed characteristics, such as their size, location, or environment, will be captured by the state term, α_m. And any locally specific effects that kicked in only after decentralization are captured by the α^* term. Knowing what we do about Bolivia as described in chapter 1, the most reasonable interpretation of this last term is that it captures two kinds of effects: (1) local governments, local civic associations, and other local institutions created by the reform, and (2) preexisting local actors and forces made relevant by decentralization—that is to say, those able to affect policy-making at the local, but not central, level. Note that this is so by construction, and not by assumption. I use Tobit estimations for equation (6).

Because α_m and α^*_m are dummy variables, one for each of Bolivia's 310 municipalities, equation (6) will produce 310 separate β_1's and 310 β_2's. I then perform three tests.

1. $\beta_2 = 0$ A t-test of whether the mean of the coefficients of α^*_m are significantly different from 0, for each sector. An insignificance result, that is, $\beta_2 = 0$, is evidence that decentralization did not change investment patterns in a given sector. Statistical significance, that is, $\beta_2 \neq 0$, provides evidence that decentralization did change national investment patterns through the actions of local governments and newly empowered local actors.

2. $\beta_{2m} = 0$ An F-test of whether the coefficients of α^*_m are statistically different from 0 municipality by municipality, for each sector. Significance implies that decentralization changed local investment patterns in a particular municipality. Significance in many municipalities constitutes stronger evidence that decentralization changed national investment patterns in a given sector.

3. Last, I use the values of β_{1m} and β_{2m} to estimate the model

$$\beta_{2m} - \beta_{1m} = \zeta S_m + \eta Z_m + \varepsilon_m \qquad (7)$$

for each of ten sectors, where the LHS is the *differences* in state dummy coefficients from equation (6), **S** is a scalar or vector of the existing stock of public services (variously defined, as we will see below) when decentralization began, and **Z** is a vector of institutional and civic variables, both indexed by municipality m.

This approach isolates the changes in investment patterns resulting from the move to a decentralized regime and then examines their determinants. Its principal advantage is that it provides a natural way to estimate the determinants of decentralized policy-making when budgetary data are time series, but institutional, civic, and need-type variables are cross-sectional. Notice that equation (7) is a general-form and not structural model, and hence the results will not be sensitive to specific theoretical assumptions. The LHS variable should by construction be unrelated to all factors that remain constant between the two periods, and I thus omit socioeconomic, regional, and other variables that do not vary between the centralized and decentralized regimes.

Literally hundreds of variables that might be included in the Z vector are available for Bolivia. To facilitate analysis, and in order to combine very specific Z-type variables into more meaningful and conceptually defensible indicators, I characterize them by type into the groups in table 3 and construct principal component variables (PCVs) for each.

This is a data reduction process that allows me to distill a small number of summary variables from a large number of highly specific indicators with minimal loss of information. The process is explained in detail in appendix 1, where PCVs and their constituent variables, as well as variables of need, are also summarized. Equation (7) can thus be written

TABLE 3. Principal-Component Variables and Their Interpretations

PCV Group	PCV No.	Interpretation—Variable Increases in . . . Listed in Order of Importance, where Applicable (see the appendix for details)
Civic Organizations	1	Number of local civic grassroots organizations (GROs)
	2	Number of indigenous groups (as distinct from urban GROs)
	3	Number of urban neighborhood committees
Private Sector Organizations	1	Number of firms in the restaurant and hotel, commercial transport, electricity, and finance sectors
Project Planning	1	Project planning procedures based on detailed sectoral information that follow consensual and open procedures
Training & Capacity-Building	1	Number of training and capacity-building efforts undertaken (as opposed to requested) by/for local government in specific areas of planning, budgeting, and adminstration
	2	Number of such efforts requested (as opposed to undertaken)
Information Technology	1 and 2	IT systems—hardware and software—in use by municipalities and how municipalities access them
Engagement with Central Government	1 and 2	Central government investment dummy; central reports and audits on local government activities

$$\beta_{2m} - \beta_{1m} = \zeta S_m + \eta_1 Z_{1m} + \cdots + \eta_6 Z_{6m} + \varepsilon_m, \tag{8}$$

where subscripts 1 to 6 denote the groups above.

The main coefficient of interest is ζ, which I interpret as a district's need for additional public investment at the outset of decentralization. This is rooted in the assumption of decreasing marginal utility of a public service as the level of provision of that service rises. In the language of the model, let $\theta_m = U'(g) < 1$. I use two types of information as indicators of the stock of public services: (1) the penetration rates[10] of public services or benefits in the local population, r, or the population without access to the same, $1 - r$,[11] and (2) the initial per capita stock of infrastructure (at the outset of decentralization). Examples of these are (1) the literacy and illiteracy rates, the share of population without water or sewerage; and (2) the number of sports facilities and markets per capita in 1994. Of these, type 1 variables can be considered truer indicators of need, as they better capture the criterion of public service use by the population and are likely to be better measures of the flow of benefits produced by public investments. Type 2 variables indicate existence more than exploitation by the local population and hence should be less accurate indicators of need. I use type 2 variables when type 1 variables are unavailable. It is also important to note that need here is a relative concept, rising and falling with $U'(g)$. This is an important distinction, as the semantics of its common usage imply that need is an absolute, and even discrete, concept, existing in some places (at some times) but not in others.

Following the argument in the second section, I expect ζ to be negative and significant when S_m is measured by the penetration rate r, and positive and significant when S_m is measured by $(1 - r)$. If S_m is measured by r, a negative coefficient suggests that decentralized government invests more heavily in a type of public good where it is scarce, and hence presumably where it is more strongly preferred. Decentralization would thus lead to a more progressive investment pattern in terms of objective need than obtained under centralized government. A positive coefficient would imply that decentralized government behaves regressively, accentuating preexisting differences in public goods endowments. I interpret such a result as evidence that the relationship posited in the second section is backward, and central government allocates public investment with more sensitivity to need than local government. A coefficient equal to zero would suggest that local government does not take the existing stock of public goods into account at all in making its investment decisions, implying that local preferences should not appear in the expression.

The variables in Z are not included as mere controls, however. Their coefficients, η, are of interest insofar as they help unlock the black box of local investment decision making. Which factors were important in determining the investment patterns described in tests 1, 2, and 3? The case put forward by political scientists for decentralized government's superior assessment of local needs includes a greater sensitivity to grassroots demand and greater access by local lobby groups to the decision-making process. These factors combine to produce greater political accountability of local officials to the local population.[12] Accordingly, I include indicators of local civic and private sector organizations in all of the sectors examined below (test 3). I return to this theme in much greater detail in the chapters that follow.

Other factors that may affect municipal investment outcomes where they are available include the use of project-planning techniques, training, and capacity-building measures, and access to information technology. Last, local investments may be affected by municipalities' engagement with central government, such as central cofinancing schemes, or audits, reporting, and other centralized oversight of local activities. I thus include such variables in selected models in all of the sectors I analyze below. These terms may be placed on the RHS of equation (7) because they represent either programs that did not exist before 1994 or factors that were not relevant to investment decisions made at the center. Positive coefficients on these PCVs provide weak evidence that local government assesses preferences more accurately than central government ($p_l > p_c$).

Empirical Results: Decentralization and Investment

Tests 1 and 2: Did Decentralization Change Public Investment Patterns?

Table 4 shows the results of test 1, $\beta_2 = 0$. Test statistics for $\beta_1 = 0$ are also included for purposes of comparison. Mean values are significantly different at the 0.1 percent level for eight of the ten sectors: education, transport, agriculture, energy, communication, urban development, water & sanitation, and health, and at the 10 percent level for water management. Only

TABLE 4. Did Decentralization Change Local Investment Patterns?
(Test 1: $\beta_2 = 0$? $\beta_1 = 0$?)

Sector	Variable	Mean	Std. Error	Test t-Statistic	Test P Value
Education	D-state dummy β_2	0.02253	0.00183	12.34170	0.00000
	State dummy β_1	0.00805	0.00142	5.66610	0.00000
Transport	D-state dummy β_2	−0.16890	0.01475	−11.45060	0.00000
	State dummy β_1	0.18026	0.01204	14.97770	0.00000
Agriculture	D-state dummy β_2	−0.02835	0.00304	−9.33570	0.00000
	State dummy β_1	0.03594	0.00245	14.64660	0.00000
Energy	D-state dummy β_2	−0.03369	0.00370	−9.10040	0.00000
	State dummy β_1	0.03691	0.00302	12.23910	0.00000
Communication	D-state dummy β_2	−0.00602	0.00069	−8.71880	0.00000
	State dummy β_1	0.00524	0.00057	9.15270	0.00000
Urban Development	D-state dummy β_2	−0.01618	0.00201	−8.05070	0.00000
	State dummy β_1	0.01206	0.00165	7.30610	0.00000
Water and Sanitation	D-state dummy β_2	−0.00643	0.00152	−4.22130	0.00000
	State dummy β_1	0.01484	0.00122	12.17050	0.00000
Health	D-state dummy β_2	0.00256	0.00075	3.42380	0.00060
	State dummy β_1	0.00742	0.00058	12.73260	0.00000
Water Management	D-state dummy β_2	0.00076	0.00043	1.79000	0.07350
	State dummy β_1	0.00233	0.00034	6.83000	0.00000
Industry and Tourism	D-state dummy β_2	0.00146	0.00127	1.14890	0.25070
	State dummy β_1	0.00687	0.00103	6.67470	0.00000

Note: N = 4,340.

one sector, industry & tourism, clearly fails the test. This implies that decentralization changed national investment patterns in the first eight sectors, and perhaps in water management as well. These results are very similar to those of my 2004 paper, only somewhat stronger.

Examination of the β_2 values indicates that decentralization increased investment in education, health, and water management, and decreased investment (by value) in transport, agriculture, energy, communication, urban development (which is puzzling given the descriptive statistics of chapter 1), and water & sanitation. To understand these results consider also table 5, which shows that the number of municipalities investing in these sectors increased massively across the board. This implies that the concentration of investment fell after decentralization, as more municipalities invested in many more, smaller projects than central government had before.

Table 6 shows results for a more demanding test: the number of individual municipalities where we can reject the hypothesis $\beta_{2m} = 0$, that is, the number of municipalities where decentralization changed investment pat-

TABLE 5. Number of Municipalities Receiving Investment, by Sector (in municipality-years)

Sector	1987–93	1995–2001	% Change
Urban Development	66	1,646	2,394%
Education	75	1,576	2,001%
Health	96	1,269	1,222%
Industry and Tourism	44	564	1,182%
Water and Sanitation	202	1,390	588%
Energy	180	815	353%
Transport	371	1,376	271%
Water Management	46	146	217%
Agriculture	343	1,037	202%
Communications	38	83	118%

Note: The postdecentralization period is truncated in 2001 in order to compare similar time spans.

TABLE 6. Test 2: Number of Municipalities where F-Test Rejects $\beta_{2m} = 0$ and $\beta_{1m} = 0$ Hypotheses

Sector	$\beta_{2m} \neq 0$	% of Total	$\beta_{1m} \neq 0$
Education	117	38%	1
Water Management	108	35%	4
Industry and Tourism	89	29%	4
Health	69	22%	9
Agriculture	55	18%	37
Transport	34	11%	36
Water and Sanitation	27	9%	21
Energy	10	3%	8
Communication	6	2%	4
Urban Development	2	1%	6

terns significantly after 1994. Test statistics for $\beta_{1m} = 0$ are again included for purposes of comparison. Thirty-eight percent of municipalities pass this test for education, one-third of municipalities for water management and industry & tourism, one-fifth of municipalities for health and agriculture, and one-tenth of municipalities for transport and water & sanitation. Three percent of municipalities or fewer show significant results for energy, communication, and urban development. This test leaves us in little doubt that investment patterns did change significantly in the first five sectors and did not change significantly in the lower three (shaded), with transport and water & sanitation straddling the border between stasis and change. Taking the results from test 1 into account allows us to resolve the straddlers—local investment in transport and water & sanitation did change with decentralization, although less dramatically than the other sectors.

Why did industry & tourism fail test 1 but pass test 2? This is due to the averaging effect of test 1: investment rises in 300 municipalities are largely canceled out by investment falls in 9 that are between 10 and 1,000 times larger in size, leaving the average effect insignificant. The latter are the favored few places where central government invested huge sums prior to reform. The closer, one-by-one look of test 2 captures what the broader-brush approach of test 1 misses.

Some readers may notice that the number of municipalities passing test 2 is generally lower than reported in my 2004 article. There are two reasons for this: whereas the earlier study used current bolivianos over a much shorter period of time, the longer time span here obliges me to measure investment in constant 2000 bolivianos. Second, as noted in chapter 1, the period immediately following decentralization (1994–96) shows the largest differences in investment patterns compared to central government's priorities, as investment becomes hugely concentrated in just two sectors that the center had largely ignored: education and urban development. This is precisely the period that my earlier study focused on. After 1997 municipal investment encompasses a broader array of sectors,[13] and so test results are bound to be less dramatic.

Last, and in terms of the broader context in which local governments operated, it is interesting to ask how central government policy priorities changed during this period. My methodology associates such changes to the year dummy variables and quantifies each yearly effect. Note that these are nationwide changes that by definition would have affected all municipalities (due, e.g., to changing national policies or external shocks) and thus are not attributable to local government decisions. Table 7 presents the results.

The only sector showing important changes is industry & tourism, where three-quarters of year dummies are statistically significant. All of these are negative in sign, implying that the center deprioritized this sector consistently between 1991 and 2005. Significant nationwide changes in investment occurred during only three years for both energy and health, first in 1992 (before decentralization), and then in 2006–7, when Bolivia was enjoying a natural resource boom. All of these changes were positive, implying investment increases, which was likewise true for communication in 1995 and 2007.

TABLE 7. Year Dummy = 0? Number of Municipalities where *F*-Test Rejects Hypothesis (omitted/comparator year: 1987)

Sector	β_{3m} No. Significant	% Significant	Years
Industry and Tourism	15	75%	1991–2005
Energy	3	15%	1992, 2006–7
Health	3	15%	1992, 2006–7
Communication	2	10%	1995, 2007
Education	2	10%	1994, 2007
Water Management	1	5%	1994
Agriculture	0	0%	
Transport	0	0%	
Urban Development	0	0%	
Water and Sanitation	0	0%	

It is notable that for education the 1994 year dummy is significant and *negative,* implying a central decrease in investment, followed by an increase in 2007. The former is also true of water management. This is less surprising when we consider that Bolivia's decentralization gave primary responsibility over these two sectors to municipalities, and thus a certain degree of central withdrawal is natural. These results directly contradict those who claim that the large changes in investment priorities chronicled above and in chapter 1 are somehow due to changing policies at the center, and not to the decisions of local governments. In the case of industry & tourism, where systemic effects are greatest, the largest year effect is smaller than the state-specific effects of fully 302 municipalities. In even this sector, the actions of local governments collectively swamp those of central government. Investments in sectors such as education and health did not rise dramatically across Bolivia because the center willed it. They rose dramatically in spite of central inaction or even—in the case of education—in spite of central retreat.

Test 3: Responsiveness to Need

Test 3 investigates the determinants of the difference in state dummy variables, $\beta_{2m} - \beta_{1m}$, equivalent to the changes decentralization caused in local investment. I focus henceforth on those sectors that satisfy two criteria: (1) investment patterns changed significantly after decentralization, and (2) good sectoral indicators of local need are available. This leaves us with six sectors to examine: education, water & sanitation, health, agriculture, water management, and urban development. Results are examined by sector, beginning with education. The full justifications for the need variables used below are the same as those provided in chapter 1. In the interest of avoiding repetition I only summarize them here.

Education

Decentralization increases investment where illiteracy is higher and where school attendance is lower. As we saw in chapter 1, education investment increased strongly across Bolivia with decentralization. But in those municipalities where illiteracy was particularly high, or school attendance particularly low, investment rose even more. I interpret these results as evidence that decentralized investment was progressive in terms of need, and thus

TABLE 8. Is Decentralized Education Investment Responsive to Need?
(Test 3: $\beta_2 - \beta_1 = \zeta S_m + \eta_1 Z_{1m} + \cdots + \eta_5 Z_{5m} + \varepsilon_m$)

	Model					
	1	2	3	4	5	6
Need Variables						
Illiteracy rate (over-6's)	0.0006758***		0.0007912**		0.0007847**	
	(2.680)		(2.300)		(2.470)	
Illiteracy rate (over-15's)		0.0003463*				
		(1.810)				
Illiteracy rate (adult)				0.000301*		
				(1.900)		
School attendance rate						−0.0012798**
						(−1.970)
Civic, Private Sector, and Institutional Variables						
Private sector PCV1	0.0027345**	0.0021328**	0.0012544	0.0006825	0.0017898*	0.0028344*
	(1.980)	(2.000)	(1.050)	(0.510)	(1.870)	(1.660)
Civic organizations PCV1	−0.0010635	−0.0009121	−0.0026732**	−0.0024499**	−0.0025439**	−0.0009748
	(−0.600)	(−0.490)	(−2.260)	(−2.260)	(−2.300)	(−0.570)
Information technology PCV1			0.0095486	0.009281		
			(0.930)	(0.920)		
Engagement with central government PCV1					0.0062212	
					(1.110)	
Constant	−0.0019903	0.0056504	−0.0041216	0.0038268	−0.0040883	0.1043142***
	(−0.110)	(0.420)	(−0.210)	(0.240)	(−0.210)	(2.980)
R^2	0.001	0.0003	0.004	0.0031	0.0021	0.0042
Prob > F	0.0297	0.1176	0.0655	0.1131	0.036	0.0162
N	295	295	295	295	295	294

Note: *, **, *** = coefficients significant at the 10%, 5%, and 1% levels.

that local governments proved more sensitive to local need than central government was before. The finding is not sensitive to specification or to the measure of need used (school attendance is significant and negative). In terms of the model of the second section, the results imply that $p_l > p_c$, and hence that local government assesses local preferences more accurately than the center does.

Educational investment increases where there are more private sector firms, but—curiously—decreases where there are more civic organizations. The latter is most likely an artifact of the phasing issue discussed above and in chapter 1. After a few initial years of booming education investment, civic organizations began pressing municipalities to invest in other sectors. The presence of a budget constraint means that this necessarily came at the expense of the largest two sectors during the first phase of reform: education and urban development. The evidence below supports this interpretation, with positive coefficients for civic organizations in health and water management, and negative coefficients (but significant only at the 15 percent level) in urban development. Evidence from my 2004 study is also in agreement: there civic organizations had a consistently positive effect on education investment. This supports the idea that education was initially one of Bolivians' highest priorities. Once satisfied, civic groups pushed municipalities to attend to other needs.

Neither information technology nor the level of engagement with central government seems to have any effect on investment. The same is true of project-planning methodologies and training and capacity-building activities (results omitted to conserve space).

Water & Sanitation
Investment is higher under decentralization where fewer people have access to sewerage. I interpret this as evidence that local governments invest more where need is greatest, and thus investment is progressive in terms of need. This implies that $p_l > p_c$ in the model above. The far smaller number of potential need indicators available for this sector means that, unlike education, I cannot confirm this result with a number of similar variables. Open and informed project-planning methodologies are associated with decreasing investment, as are training and capacity-building activities. Indicators of private sector and civic organizations are both insignificant.

TABLE 9. Is Decentralized Water and Sanitation Investment Responsive to Need?
(Test 3: $\beta_2 - \beta_1 = \zeta S_m + \eta_1 Z_{1m} + \cdots + \eta_5 Z_{5m} + \varepsilon_m$)

	Model			
	1	2	3	4
Need Variable				
% population lacking	0.0010887*	0.001045*	0.0008989*	0.0006972*
sewerage	(1.750)	(1.750)	(1.690)	(1.670)
Civic, Private Sector, and Institutional Variables				
Private sector PCV1	−0.0111272	−0.0091076	−0.0110392	
	(−1.480)	(−1.250)	(−1.490)	
Civic organizations PCV3	0.0228963	0.020011	0.0225832	
	(1.190)	(1.080)	(1.190)	
Project planning PCV1		−0.0142177*	−0.0118762*	−0.0136691**
		(−1.800)	(−1.790)	(−2.040)
Training and capacity			−0.0088149*	−0.0077744
building PCV1			(−1.680)	(−1.540)
Constant	−0.1058673*	−0.1019036*	−0.0901295*	−0.0744243*
	(−1.820)	(−1.830)	(−1.800)	(−1.910)
R^2	0.0167	0.0287	0.0369	0.0305
Prob > F	0.0257	0.0229	0.0797	0.1766
N	294	294	294	309

Note: *, **, *** = significant at the 10%, 5%, and 1% levels.

Health

Decentralized health investment rises with the number of households that use private and "other" providers as their primary sources of health care. "Other" is defined in the Bolivian census as health-care providers other than the state, private clinics and insurers, NGOs, churches, or pharmacies. Investment is also higher in localities that have health posts, the lowest level of public health provision (usually staffed by a nurse or health worker); above this level the coefficients go to zero. This provides evidence that decentralized investment was more responsive to local need, rising disproportionately in places where only the most basic state facilities exist and where few households have access to public health services and must rely instead on private or "other" providers.

Investment is higher in districts where civic organizations are more plentiful, but—curiously—lower where a local health authority is present. Private sector firms do not appear to have an effect, nor do project planning or training and capacity-building activities.

TABLE 10. Is Decentralized Health Investment Responsive to Need?
(Test 3: $\beta_2 - \beta_1 = \zeta S_m + \eta_1 Z_{1m} + \cdots + \eta_5 Z_{5m} + \varepsilon_m$)

	Model		
	1	2	3
Need Variables			
Private health care,	0.0005828**		0.0005844**
% households using mainly	(2.230)		(2.120)
Other[a] health care,	0.0006946**		0.0006181**
% households using mainly	(2.270)		(2.140)
Number of health posts (lowest		8.459288***	
tier) per capita		(3.530)	
Number of doctor's offices (2nd		−33.85788	
tier) per capita		(−0.560)	
Number of health centers (3rd		−6.560385	
tier) per capita		(−0.750)	
Civic, Private Sector, and Institutional Variables			
Private sector PCV1	−0.0004089	0.0011388	
	(−0.910)	(1.010)	
Civic organizations PCV2	0.0019996***	0.0018358**	0.0022228***
	(2.690)	(2.460)	(2.620)
Project planning PCV1			−0.0029072
			(−1.640)
Training and capacity building PCV2			0.0001196
			(0.030)
Local health authority dummy	−0.0142263**	−0.0128173**	−0.0118982**
	(−2.320)	(−2.060)	(−2.150)
Constant	0.0008407	0.006274*	−0.0005941
	(0.150)	(1.790)	(−0.070)
R^2	0.0119	0.0111	0.0157
Prob > F	0.0011	0.0035	0.1406
N	295	294	303

Note: *, **, *** = coefficients significant at the 10%, 5%, and 1% levels.
[a]Nonstate, nonprivate, non-NGO provided health care.

Agriculture

Investment increases with the rate of malnutrition, a finding that survives alternative specifications. This implies that decentralized municipalities invested disproportionately where the need to increase food productivity was greatest. Open, informed project-planning techniques once again decrease agricultural investment, while private sector and civic organizations appear to have no effect. Decentralized investment is similarly unaffected by training and capacity-building programs and engagement with the central government.

TABLE 11. Is Decentralized Agriculture Investment Responsive to Need?
(Test 3: $\beta_2 - \beta_1 = \zeta S_m + \eta_1 Z_{1m} + \cdots + \eta_5 Z_{5m} + \varepsilon_m$)

	Model			
	1	2	3	4
Need Variable				
Malnutrition rate (mild)	0.0022277	0.0024655*	0.0028989*	0.0024397*
among boys	(1.630)	(1.690)	(1.770)	(1.780)
Civic, Private Sector, and Institutional Variables				
Private sector PCV1	−0.0013536	0.0011323	0.0024298	
	(−0.480)	(0.260)	(0.470)	
Civic organizations PCV2	0.0052246	0.0070434	0.0083226	
	(1.320)	(1.460)	(1.460)	
Project planning PCV1		−0.030547*	−0.0327134*	−0.0290876*
		(−1.710)	(−1.720)	(−1.690)
Training & capacity		−0.004469	−0.0040023	
building PCV2		(−0.330)	(−0.300)	
Engagement with central			0.0326923	
government PCV2			(1.270)	
Constant	−0.1218982***	−0.1248753**	−0.1356345**	−0.1240206***
	(−2.600)	(−2.530)	(−2.450)	(−2.770)
R^2	0.002	0.016	0.025	0.0143
Prob > F	0.1336	0.045	0.1237	0.0876
N	280	280	280	294

Note: *, **, *** = coefficients significant at the 10%, 5%, and 1% levels.

Water Management

Water management concerns the management of river, lake, and underground water resources, and includes, for example, reservoirs and wastewater treatment lagoons, levees, and storm drainage works. Only three indicators of need are available for this sector, and none is significant. One of these is storm drainage per capita, which estimates I provide below. Decentralized investment in water management thus appears to be unrelated to need. In the language of the model, we cannot say whether $p_l > p_c$ or $p_l < p_c$. Of the other variables in the models, only civic organizations are significant—at the 1 percent level, and positive. Civic groups thus appear to promote investment in this sector, perhaps as a follow-on once educational and urban priorities have been attended to, as discussed above. No other variable was significant for this sector.

Urban Development

As in chapter 1, I use the initial (pre-decentralization) stock of relevant infrastructure as my indicator of need in this sector. Investment under decen-

TABLE 12. Is Decentralized Water Management Investment Responsive to Need?
(Test 3: $\beta_2 - \beta_1 = \zeta S_m + \eta_1 Z_{1m} + \cdots + \eta_5 Z_{5m} + \varepsilon_m$)

	Model			
	1	2	3	4
Need Variable				
Storm drainage per capita	1.120977	0.1766506	−0.8378111	−1.656368
	(1.250)	(0.340)	(−0.640)	(−0.950)
Civic, Private Sector, and Institutional Variables				
Private sector PCV1	0.0010271	0.0017974	0.0014235	0.00236
	(0.350)	(0.510)	(0.440)	(0.640)
Civic organizations PCV2	0.0016861***	0.0018099***	0.0019376***	0.0020494***
	(3.680)	(3.340)	(3.160)	(3.150)
Project planning PCV1		−0.0021492	−0.0021763	−0.0024551
		(−1.040)	(−1.040)	(−1.080)
Information technology PCV2			−0.0027533	−0.0022695
			(−0.970)	(−0.900)
Engagement with central government PCV2				0.0042239
				(1.440)
Constant	−0.0016212	−0.001416	−0.0012638	−0.0012477
	(−0.500)	(−0.470)	(−0.430)	(−0.430)
R^2	0.002	0.0054	0.0088	0.0167
Prob > F	0.0021	0.01	0.0077	0.0014
N	288	288	288	288

Note: *, **, *** = coefficients significant at the 10%, 5%, and 1% levels.

tralization increases as the number of markets per capita increases, a finding that is repeated for museums, greenhouses, and theaters. These results
imply that investment is regressive in terms of need, increasing in municipalities that are already better provided. This finding survives a number of
different specifications, some of which are provided here. But when I use
storm drainage (which projects can be classified as either water management or urban development) as my variable of need the results invert, becoming much more significant and much larger in magnitude. Bolivian
municipalities invested more in storm drainage where existing provision
was lower, implying that investment responded positively to need.

How can one explain this contradiction? Urban development is a loose
grouping, encompassing a far broader array of activities than education,
water & sanitation, health, or agriculture; in this regard only water management comes close. Markets, theaters, and storm drainage are fundamentally
different kinds of investment activities, and may very well be approached by

TABLE 13. Is Decentralized Urban Development Investment Responsive to Need?
(Test 3: $\beta_2 - \beta_1 = \zeta S_m + \eta_1 Z_{1m} + \cdots + \eta_5 Z_{5m} + \varepsilon_m$)

	Model					
	1	2	3	4	5	6
Need Variables						
Number of markets per capita	0.1168764**	0.1557067**	0.1616904**			
	(2.060)	(2.260)	(2.180)			
Number of museums per capita		19.89929*				
		(1.750)				
Number of municipal greenhouses per capita			6.04144*			
			(1.780)			
Number of theaters per capita			23.61572*			
			(1.700)			
Storm drainage per capita				−42.73767***	−41.58996***	−41.40935***
				(−7.150)	(−5.980)	(−5.960)
Civic, Private Sector, and Institutional Variables						
Private sector PCV1	0.0037143	0.0035695	0.0036899	0.0115908		
	(1.470)	(1.430)	(1.640)	(0.840)		
Civic organizations PCV3	−0.006705	−0.006515	−0.007			
	(−1.450)	(−1.430)	(−1.250)			
Training and capacity building PCV1		−0.001638*	−0.001743*	−0.010214		
		(−1.650)	(−1.800)	(−1.280)		
Project planning PCV1				−0.004908		
				(−1.180)		
Information technology PCV2					−0.000284	
					(−0.090)	
Engagement with central government PCV1					0.0018454	
					(0.280)	
Constant	−0.010859***	−0.011282***	−0.011479***	−0.02327*	−0.024757	−0.024833
	(−4.330)	(−4.210)	(−3.790)	(−1.650)	(−1.610)	(−1.610)
R^2	0.0192	0.0253	0.0279	0.0336	0.0276	0.0275
Prob > F	0.2249	0.285	0.1984	0	0	0
N	291	290	286	293	301	301

Note: *, **, *** = significant at the 10%, 5%, and 1% levels.

the same local governments in very different ways. In addition, it is likely that central and local governments have different advantages in assessing the need for, designing, and executing these different types of projects, as argued in the theoretical section above.

The evidence supports this argument. Local governments invested more in markets, museums, greenhouses, and theaters where the need for each was lower, but in storm drainage where need was higher. Thus it would seem to be central government that more accurately assessed local need for markets, and so on, while local government better assessed the need for storm drainage.

Of the other variables included in the six models, only training and capacity building was significant, and then only twice and at the 10 percent level. This result is too weak to allow for much interpretation. Investment appears to be unaffected by private and civic organizations, project-planning techniques, available information technology, and engagement with the central government.

Conclusions

Decentralization caused large changes in national public investment patterns in Bolivia. Investment changed significantly in education, water management, industry & tourism, health, and agriculture after the 1994 reform, and to a lesser degree in transport and water & sanitation as well. These shifts are strongly and positively related to real local needs. In education, water & sanitation, health, agriculture, and at least one kind of urban development, post-decentralization investments are higher where illiteracy rates are higher, sewerage connection rates lower, malnutrition a greater risk, and so on respectively. These relationships are robust and insensitive to specification. Decentralization thus led to higher investment in human capital and social services as poorer, needier regions of the country chose projects according to their greatest needs.

Few terms other than need are consistently significant across the sectors analyzed. Only civic organizations have a statistically significant effect in at least three of the six sectors, working to transfer resources from education to health and water management. This is particularly interesting as it contradicts my earlier findings from the first years of decentralization (Faguet 2004), where the only statistically significant effect of civic organizations was to *increase* education investment. The best explanation for this apparent contradiction is that both results are true. Education investment initially surged after decentralization out of all proportion to what central government had invested previously. Close examination of those first three years shows that civic groups strongly supported this rise. But in the years that followed, faced with tight budget constraints and extensive needs, civic groups in poor communities pressed local governments to transfer resources from education to other sectors where local needs were similarly large, which centralized government had also ignored.

By contrast other institutional and procedural variables are infrequently significant across sectors and seem to account for little total variation. Indicators of both the number of private sector firms and training and capacity-building activities are significant in only one sector each, while access to information technology and central government engagement are insignificant in all sectors. This implies that the broad changes in investment patterns chronicled above are fundamentally driven by local needs, and these needs are at least partly mediated by the actions of civic organizations. Investment patterns are not fundamentally driven by training programs, information technology, or any of the other institutional characteristics for which I have information.

These results can be combined with the findings of chapter 1 to distinguish between the cost advantage versus needs assessment trade-off at the heart of the theoretical model. Remember that the number of municipalities investing increased after 1994 in every sector, and the effect of local government on average investment was positive for primary social services and negative for economic infrastructure and agriculture. The average rise in investment (i.e., across all municipalities) in education, health, and water management after decentralization can be interpreted as evidence of local government's superior responsiveness to local needs, an effect that is greater in magnitude than any productive advantage the center may enjoy in these sectors. The fall in average investment by value in water & sanitation, agriculture, and urban development, combined with an increase in the number of districts investing and the significance of need, implies that the central government concentrated investment in too few projects and districts (and perhaps the wrong projects); local government thus reallocates resources in a larger number of smaller projects where need is greater. And last, the systematic fall in investment by value throughout Bolivia in transport, energy, and communication, combined with the irrelevance of need,[14] implies weakly that the center may have had a cost advantage in these sectors, causing resource flows to fall after decentralization.

By demonstration, this chapter seeks to make a case for conducting empirical research on decentralization and fiscal federalism in the manner employed here. Much of the empirical work on decentralization to date focuses on the share of national expenditures conducted by different levels of government, and ignores the many insights waiting to be uncovered by moving down to the level of the local political economy and conducting a careful comparison of spending and investment patterns with economic, institutional, social, and demographic indicators. The data presented here are from one of the poorest countries in the Western hemisphere and took two years to collect, clean, and organize. But as this chapter demonstrates, its quality is sufficient to permit significant and counterintuitive results. Applying a similar methodology to more sophisticated countries in the region, not to mention Europe and North America, could prove very fruitful.

I conclude with the observation that the Bolivian experience, where decentralization led to an investment increase in municipalities with the worst demographic indicators and infrastructure endowments, is exactly the opposite of what many academics and policymakers predict, and what other researchers have found in the past. To understand how these changes came about it is important to investigate the microlevel social and institutional mechanisms by which local governments sense local demands and respond to local needs. These questions are explored in the chapters that follow.

CHAPTER 5

The State of Knowledge on Decentralization

Decentralization redirected public investment in Bolivia away from production toward human capital formation and primary social services. It distributed resources far more equally across space, and it made government strongly responsive to local needs. Strikingly, this last comparison is the difference between local governments that invest in areas where need is high versus a central government that invested without reference to need, or—worse—concentrated resources in places and sectors where need was low.

Where does Bolivia fit into the decentralization literature? Why do these results differ so strikingly from what the literature as a whole has found? Descending beneath the national frame to local-level analysis allows us to see in detail how responsiveness and accountability came about, but also how local government processes can be distorted and subverted, leading to government that is unresponsive and corrupt. How do we understand the apparent contradiction of a decentralization program that generated both Viacha and Charagua? Can the literature help us understand Bolivia's reform better? Can Bolivia help us better understand decentralization?

This chapter provides a broad review of the state of knowledge about decentralization beginning with theory and then moving on to the empirical literature. This is an enormous literature numbering hundreds of academic studies; including the policy ("gray") literature the number rises literally into the thousands. The paragraphs that follow give what I hope is a good account of the main theoretical arguments. Treatment of the much larger empirical literature is necessarily more synoptic. The overarching theme of the chapter is the central paradox of a policy phenomenon—decentralization—that has solid theoretical arguments in favor and enormous real-world enthusiasm but about which empirical results are decidedly mixed. How can evidence about a reform that should work, and that policymakers love, be so inconclusive?

An important part of the answer, I shall argue, is that much of the study of decentralization has proceeded—ironically—in a centralized, top-down fashion, treating reform as a sort of policy lever and searching for symmetric effects. Decentralization should be approached instead as a common institutional shock that generates diverse, contingent outcomes—outcomes that will differ as much as localities' economies, politics, and societies do.

Theoretical Arguments

Enthusiasm for decentralization is not unfounded. Arguments about the benefits of devolving authority to subnational units of government stretch at least as far back as *The Spirit of the Laws* (Montesquieu 1748) and *The Federalist Papers* (Madison, Hamilton, and Jay 1788). The belief that the natural or most advantageous organization of society involves multiple hierarchical tiers goes back much further. Aristotle (350s–340s BC) deconstructed the Greek city-state "into a three-tier hierarchy of households, villages, and the polis, each of which aims at a different good."[1] Building on classical reasoning, Dante (ca. 1314–20) argued, "Only in a pyramid of different-sized, nested communities could the full multiplicity of human potential be realized all at once."[2]

Modern claims about the advantages (and disadvantages) of decentralization follow this gist but are far more numerous and specific. Although they span a number of disciplines, they are mostly concentrated in the policy[3] and public economics literatures, on which this chapter therefore focuses. Because the terminology and styles of argumentation are quite different between the two literatures, it makes sense to review them separately.

The policy literature is huge, and its arguments come in many variants. The most important of these positive and negative effects of decentralization, however, can be grouped as follows.

Arguments for
i. increase citizen voice and participation
ii. improve government accountability and hence responsiveness
iii. deepen democracy
iv. strengthen individual liberties
v. improve economic performance
vi. increase policy stability

    vii. reduce bureaucracy
    viii. decrease public spending
Arguments against
    i.   decrease efficiency in public goods production
    ii. decrease the quality of policy-making
    iii. increase graft and corruption
    iv. facilitate elite capture of government
    v.   increase fiscal deficits and hence macroeconomic instability

The Policy Literature: Arguments For

i.–iii. Improve Accountability and Responsiveness

The first three are tightly intertwined and can be bundled together as "accountability and responsiveness." In my view these are the most important and powerful of all the arguments concerning decentralization, and hence what this book will concentrate on. In various forms and with different language, Mill (1993 [1895–61]), Montesquieu (1989 [1748]), Rousseau (1978 [1762]), and Tocqueville (1994 [1835–40]) all debated these points. They appear frequently in the popular and policy literatures as well, often referred to as "bringing government closer to the people." The latter is more slogan than argument, although there is an unfortunate tendency in that literature to present it as an argument. The more serious version of Wallis and Oates (1988), widely cited, holds that decentralization makes government more responsive to local needs by "tailoring levels of consumption to the preferences of smaller, more homogeneous groups" (5). While this account is descriptively correct, it is analytically insufficient. Why does homogeneity imply responsiveness? Is the fundamental problem one of scale? It is my view that the sources of responsiveness lie deeper, in the incentives that officials face in decentralized versus centralized government regimes.

The fundamental logic is as follows: By devolving power and authority from upper (usually central) to lower (regional or local) levels of government elected by their respective constituencies, decentralization fundamentally changes the incentives that local authorities face, and thus—not surprisingly—their behavior. (For ease of exposition, all subnational levels of government are henceforth referred to as "local" government.) Under centralization, those who hold authority over local matters are not elected by local citizens but rather *selected* by higher-level authorities, regardless of whether they are physically located locally or in the capital. Immediate accountability for their performance is thus upward to the central government officials who have power over their salaries, careers, and broader professional prospects (Riker 1964). Accountability does not run downward to the citizens who consume the public goods and services they are meant to produce except at one or more removes, in the sense that central government officials are ultimately beholden to national electorates. "Local" officials thus face clear, strong incentives to respond to central government priorities and concerns, and weak, muffled incentives to respond to local citizens' needs.

The most important effect of decentralization is to reorient these incentives. "Local" officials become local officials, whose tenure and career prospects are in the hands of the local citizens they serve, who elect them. The incentives that govern their performance are no longer received from on high but rather are determined by those most directly affected by what they do. And accountability to local citizens is direct, no longer running through a national administration or various layers of bureaucracy.

This supply effect in the constitution of local authority generates a complementary demand effect. Citizens see the change in local officials' performance, understand the incentive change that has occurred, and become more involved in local politics. They vote and exercise voice more because both tools are more powerful than before. Elected officials, being largely rational, respond better to citizens' demands—not just because they "should" but because it is in their interests to do so. The net effect is to shorten and tighten the loop of accountability between those who produce public goods and services and those who consume them.

One of the main points of this book is that decentralization works—if and when it works—through a fundamental effect on officials' incentives, and thence on government accountability to the governed. Surprisingly often, both enthusiasts and critics of reform omit this basic point in favor of second- and third-order arguments about whether decentralization can increase growth or reduce ethnic conflicts, a point to which I return below. Many of these things, such as inflation, the fiscal deficit, and ethnic conflicts and political stability in a nation more broadly, are important, and decentralization may indeed affect them. But it does so via incentives and accountability; there is no direct effect. In the best cases, the new equilibrium that emerges after reform features greater citizen voice and participation and greater government responsiveness. It is one in which democracy has been both deepened and strengthened.

iv. Strengthen Individual Liberties

Scholars from Tocqueville (1835–40) and Hamilton (1769–1804) to Weingast (1995) have argued that in a decentralized or federal system of government, strong, legitimate local governments can protect individual freedoms by checking central government abuses. They can use their resources to resist or counteract specific government actions (e.g., by suing central government, or implementing a countervailing tax or credit) and can threaten the center financially by witholding tax receipts, in defense of their citizens. Diaz-Cayeros (2006) relates how, in late nineteenth- and early twentieth-century Brazil, repeated attempts by the center to encroach on state power and independence were resisted using such means plus the credible threat of violence. In Brazil, state-level police forces, especially of Minas Gerais and São Paolo, "constituted true armies that could effectively challenge the federal government" (211).

v. Improve Economic Performance

By increasing local governments' share of tax revenues, decentralization gives them a larger stake in the performance of the local economy. This motivates local officials to implement policies that support businesses and promote growth for two reasons: (1) economic growth increases local tax receipts and hence officials' freedom of action, and (2) growth increases officials' popularity. The effect is to make local governments compete for mobile capital by reducing public sector waste, inefficiency, and corruption, and by providing infrastructure. When this happens nationwide, efficiency rises and the economy grows faster (Brennan and Buchanan 1980; Hayek 1948; Jin, Qian, and Weingast 2005; Roland 2000).

vi. Increase Policy Stability

Decentralization increases the number of actors in a governmental system, as alluded to in (iv), who must coordinate for maximum effectiveness, especially when attempting policy change. This increases the number of actors with veto power over policy and so tends to make change more difficult. Greater policy stability is the result (see Tsebelis 2002 and Proudhon 1979 [1863], both cited in Treisman 2007).

vii. Reduce Bureaucracy

This claim appears at first sight paradoxical, as decentralization unambiguously increases the number of instances of government, and in many if not most cases the number of government officials as well. But from the point of view of a citizen with specific needs, decentralization locates public officials with the authority and resources required to provide a public response in her vicinity, and more importantly aligns their career incentives with her needs. No longer will central bureaucrats with local authority transmit the request upward to higher-level bureaucrats, who in even medium-sized countries are likely to do the same again before a decision can be reached, resources allocated, and officials responsible for action identified. Hence the amount of "bureaucracy" that must intervene for a citizen to obtain a particular public action or service reduces considerably (see Brennan and Buchanan 1980; Oates 1972; Rondinelli, Cheema, and Nellis 1983; Tanzi 1995).

This argument can be falsified empirically if the local governments that decentralization empowers become slower and less responsive—that is, more "bureaucratic"—than centralized government was before them. Marlow (1988) finds strong evidence to the contrary for the United States. But as we shall see below, empirical studies of developing countries find substantial evidence both for and against this proposition.

viii. Decrease Public Spending

There is no reason to expect decentralization to lead to lower administrative costs for the state, as it is likely to result in a larger overall government headcount, and thus higher salary and overhead costs. But total public spending can still fall if local governments' unit costs are lower than the central government's. The logic is as follows: Two common empirical regularities are: (1) that the price level is higher in large cities than small cities, or towns or villages, and (2) that a country's capital tends to be far larger than its average city, and in many cases is the largest city. The devolution of resources and authority from the capital to smaller cities and towns tends strongly to result in firms in those cities and towns winning public contracts that they previously found difficult or expensive to obtain. Such firms tend to have lower unit costs than firms based in the capital because they operate in a lower-price environment. Hence public investments and expenditures executed by local governments tend to be cheaper than those executed by central government, and the question is whether or not this effect dominates higher administrative costs (Estache 1995; Humplick and Moini-Araghi 1996). Where the former case obtains, decentralization will reduce government spending.

Another, less benign form of expenditure reduction occurs when central government devolves responsibility for specific public services and investments to local governments, but not the resources necessary to fund them. These are known as "unfunded mandates" and are often a political strategy for dealing with central budget deficits by in effect shifting them to the periphery. In other cases, national politicians who decentralize insincerely may intentionally underfund in order to undermine local government legitimacy, and by extension decentralization itself. Examples of such behaviors are reported by Bardhan and Mookherjee (2006), Manor (1999), and Rondinelli, Cheema, and Nellis (1983).

Against these positive arguments are arrayed a smaller set of negative arguments that hold that decentralization will worsen a country's quality of governance.

The Policy Literature: Arguments Against

i. Decrease Efficiency in Public Goods Production

The most common and important argument against decentralization concerns economies of scale and other productive advantages (i.e., technical or organizational advantages vis-à-vis sophisticated services such as tertiary medical care, or environmental management) that make central government more efficient in the production of public goods than local governments. The analogy is often drawn with industrial production, in which larger firms with larger factories and more capital are able to reap economies of scale that smaller firms, even with the best intentions, cannot. Hence the devolution of responsibility to subnational governments is a misguided failure to reap important efficiencies that accrue naturally to central government (see Bardhan and Mookherjee 2006; Prud'homme 1995).

ii. Decrease the Quality of Policy-making

The second most common argument against decentralization is that the highest-quality politicians, technocrats, and administrators are at the service of central government, where salaries and the facilities are better and the challenges more interesting. The human resources at the service of local governments are simply lower quality; the same is true of their physical resources and technical expertise. Hence the policy decisions and implementations undertaken by local governments will tend to be worse than those undertaken by central government. Put crudely, central government is smarter, better equipped, and better informed, and so better able to govern well. (Manor 1999 and Tanzi 1995 characterize this argument; Prud'homme 1995 embraces it.)

iii. Increase Graft and Corruption

By distributing public resources and authority over many local governments, decentralization increases the number of actors with access to public resources and authority, and thus the probability that both will be abused for private gain instead of used for the public good. This is because as the size of individual "pots" of money decreases, the motivation of journalists, interest groups, and individuals to hold authorities to account for their use diminishes as well. If such "accountability motivation" decreases more rapidly than the quantity of resources, then decentralization will provide local officials with proportionally more money than oversight compared to national authorities, and corruption will tend to increase (see Manor 1999; Prud'homme 1995; Treisman 2007).

iv. Facilitate Elite Capture of Government

Now largely forgotten among the echoing calls for decentralization of the past 40 years is the underlying argument in favor of *centralization* during the decolonizations of the postwar period. Developing countries, it was argued, were beset by premodern social relations exacerbated by the poverty and ignorance of small-town and rural society. In such places local elites were very "large" compared to civil society, which was too weak to oppose them and even internalized elite priorities as their own. Decentralization would lead to weak local governments cowed and captured by local elites. The remedy was a centralized state that was comparatively wealthy and powerful—"large" compared to local elites—that could effect the sorts of nation building and rapid development activities that nations emerging from colonialism required.

Half a century later, it is now argued, social relations in smaller municipalities have not changed that much. Local elites that cannot challenge the central state can easily capture devolved local governments and abuse its resources and power for their own benefit. Decentralization will not lead to transparent, equitable local government because the local societies in which local governments operate are distorted by extreme inequalities of wealth and power. And thus reform will lessen the transparency, responsiveness and accountability of the state (see Bardhan and Mookherjee 1999, 2006; Blair 2000; Crook and Sverrisson 1999; Dreze and Sen 1996; Manor 1999; Prud'homme 1995).

v. Increase Fiscal Deficits and Hence Macroeconomic Instability

Decentralized countries face the intrinsic problem of soft budget constraints because local politicians have strong incentives to overspend and reap the benefits themselves, while nationalizing the cost of their behavior through central bailouts. Such behavior is underpinned by the knowledge that at least some of the blame for a local government default, with attendant reductions in public services, investment, and employment, would attach to central government politicians for two reasons: (1) many such services are jointly financed and voters may not clearly distinguish among responsible parties, and (2) the center could have averted a default by bailing out the insolvent municipality. Meanwhile, central government faces a commitment problem: any promise not to bail out in the future is not credible precisely because voters will punish it. All local governments know this, and hence all have incentives to overspend today in the hope of being bailed out (Prud'homme 1995; Rodden 2006; Rodden, Eskeland, and Litvack 2003; Tanzi 1995). In the aggregate, such behavior can lead to large (national) fiscal deficits, and hence macroeconomic instability. Many observers (e.g., Diaz-Cayeros 2006; Jones, Sanguinetti, and Tommasi 2000) have commented on the provinces' contribution to Argentina's economic collapse in 2001–2, when precisely such behavior was observed.

Deeper Theory: Information and Incentives

The most important case for decentralization is that it can increase government accountability and responsiveness to citizen needs, as argued above. Very, very few studies in this enormous literature deconstruct this argument; most who find against decentralization claim instead that this effect will be small, and will be outweighed by the negative effects of reform. One that does take this argument head-on and find it wanting is a learned book of theoretical clarity and rigor: Treisman's *The Architecture of Government: Rethinking Political Decentralization* (2007). Its treatment of information and accountability in chapters 7 and 9 is detailed and careful, and provides a useful template for us to follow.[4] As we shall see, the amount and quality of local information that feeds into policy-making is crucial.

Holding Government to Account

Arguments about decentralized government's superior accountability are in large part arguments about its superior information. Consider first information about what government is doing, which can be used to hold it to account. By virtue of proximity, according to advocates of reform, voters' everyday experience will lead them to become better informed about local government's performance than they can be about the performance of a national government. Treisman disputes this, pointing out that "in most real political units—both local and national—acquiring accurate information about government performance requires an investment in more systematic monitoring" (166). In this view, information about what government is doing is imperfect, in the sense that it is costly to discover. Monitoring is a kind of public good, which will have a strong tendency to be underprovided by the market. Hence effective monitoring will generally depend on the efforts of agents with extrinsic motivations, such as investigative reporters, lobby groups, or NGO watchdogs. And such monitoring will be more intense at the central level because the stakes are usually higher in central compared to local policy decisions; and perhaps too because audiences for the national media, and constituencies of national watchdog groups, are bigger than their local cousins'. Hence voters in national elections should be better informed about government performance than voters in local elections.

This argument in my view relies on a rhetorical sleight of hand. It is indeed true that the stakes are usually (much) higher for central policy-making than its local counterpart. But unless we are discussing decentralizing such issues as defense or monetary policy, the comparison is false. There is no reason to think that policy decisions about garbage collection, primary education, or street lighting *in a specific municipality* would receive more attention if taken centrally versus locally because, as the previous logic suggests, a national constituency is not much interested in such questions. Interest might rise significantly if such decisions affected all municipalities similarly. But that would violate another of the author's claims—that central government can easily implement different policies in different locations (59–61)—a claim that is both logical and empirically well supported.

The fact that the national media and national watchdog groups may be proximate to national government when it is making such essentially local decisions does not imply that they will lend them special attention. Indeed, the opposite is probably true—when such decisions are made at the center, the *local* media and watchdog groups most interested in the affairs of the municipality in question will be less able to obtain and disseminate accurate information due to greater distance and the cost this implies.[5]

The argument is also predicated on a simplifying mistake, although at bottom this is an empirical and not theoretical question. This is that voters do not gain much useful information about local government performance through their day-to-day experience of public services because any information so gained is likely to be unrepresentative (e.g., a voter may know how well maintained her street is, but not the average street). Hence information acquisition is costly at both local and central levels, and the costs are similar. While this objection is logically plausible in very large municipalities, it is less plausible for the medium-size cities and small towns that make up the large majority of municipalities the world over. In my own empirical research, small-town voters report that they *are* able to observe a significant sample of the streets, parks, public lighting, garbage collection, and other local services, either directly or indirectly through the reports of friends and colleagues. And their replies to detailed questionnaires, corroborated through independent observation and other data-gathering, confirm what they say (chapters 2 and 3 are based on such research).

It helps to consider how small nonmetropolises typically are. Take for example the United States, a highly urbanized country where we might expect most municipalities to be large. In fact, most American municipalities are very far from the nation-scale of cities like New York and Los Angeles. Even including such metropolises, the average local government serves around 3,400 people in the United States (U.S. Census Bureau 2002b, 2009).[6] In Bolivia, where the average municipal population is 26,691, fully 84 percent of municipalities' populations lie below the average, and just over a quarter of municipalities have 5,000 people or fewer (Instituto Nacional de Estadística 2001). Other countries' local authorities also seem to vary in average size between the thousands and few tens of thousands. In Morocco, for example, the average municipal population is 18,000; in Colombia it is 36,000; in the Philippines it is 1,700; the average Mexican *municipio* has 40,000 inhabitants; in India the average local authority, including urban and rural local bodies, municipal councils, and nagar panchayats, governs about 4,000 people (World Bank 2000b).

In populations and spaces that are small, the conduct of daily life allows citizens to directly observe a nontrivial share of the local services and goods provided by local government. Such information is supplemented by the reports and opinions of neighbors, family, and friends. This combination allows voters to form well-informed opinions about the performance of local government at much lower cost than in large cities.

Large cities, states, or countries differ not because life there is less romantic, but as a simple matter of scale. In large cities, the same individuals going through the same daily routines would encounter only a tiny proportion of the services and goods on offer. Supplementing with information from their personal networks would still fail to achieve the level of representation necessary for informed opinions about the (general) state of local affairs. The latter requires explicit investment in information, taking us back to the original argument about costly monitoring, which is correct but not general. This connection between municipal size and the cost of local knowledge acquisition is clearly born out in my nine Bolivian case studies.

Responsiveness to Local Needs and Tastes 1: Perfect Information

Next, consider the question of responsiveness. Would decentralized governments be more responsive to local voters' preferences and needs? The reasons for thinking they would be, as outlined above, are well established and based on a long tradition of theorizing about federations and the division of public authority. Treisman argues that this common intuition is wrong. He uses the following model.

Imagine a country in which multiple districts have heterogeneous preferences for public policy outputs, and voting is Downsian. Call the program of local public goods and taxes[7] most preferred by the median voter m. Under decentralization, the candidate who offers m as his platform wins. Political competition drives any other candidate to offer m too, as deviation leads to defeat. Hence regardless of which candidate is elected, local government is fully accountable. Under a centralized regime, candidates for national office offer identical "packages of balanced-budget vectors of local public goods and tax rates, one for each locality. . . . In equilibrium, each will offer the program in each locality that is preferred by its median voter, resulting in the same outcome as under decentralization" (182). Neither candidate has any incentive to deviate from this optimal package in even one locality because deviation hands victory to her rival. These policies are then implemented, and centralized government is—like decentralized government—fully accountable.

This argument rests on two key assumptions: (1) optimal policies can be identified in advance, and (2) these are equally known to all politicians/parties competing. These assumptions are, at the very least, strong. If we accept them, the result that all candidates choose the optimal policy mix becomes banal. This is true for a broader class of voting models that rely on similar mechanisms. *A given policy menu is objectively optimal and is known in advance.* Who would not choose it? In such a system, politicians effectively choose their voters. In a Downsian framework, where the median voter is decisive, all candidates unsurprisingly choose her. This style of thinking has the virtues of tractability and clarity, but also the vice that it assumes away the most interesting part of the problem.

In the real world, optimal policies are not known in advance of elections. If they were, there would be little need for elections. Society could go straight to the coin-toss that ultimately chooses which of the identical candidates and policy packages triumphs in such models. In the real world, politicians offer different policies from behind an electoral veil of ignorance. They are unsure how their proposals will fare in advance. They try not only to meet voters' preferences but to shape them. Through speeches, debates, and campaigning more generally, they have opportunities to sway public opinion and "shift the debate." Some succeed, others fail. Candidates try to convince voters, and voters try to convince candidates. Candidates' policies shift in ways large and small. Voters' preferences shift in ways small and large. Information is imperfect, and there is a great deal of uncertainty.

The information in question now is primarily voters' needs and tastes, as opposed to government performance. Assuming optimal policies are not known in advance but voters can be relied on to rationally choose which of the policies offered are best for them, the principal question is then, Which system—centralized or decentralized—gives them better options? Where information is imperfect and preference detection costly, national platforms will in equilibrium be imperfectly correlated with districts' heterogeneous preferences. In which districts will the match be closer? Central politicians will rationally focus their detection efforts on those districts that offer the largest electoral prizes. Districts with large and/or dense populations (those that are electorally important) may indeed be almost indifferent between decentralization and centralization, in the sense that central politicians might have strong incentives to invest in learning about their conditions and offering platforms well-tailored to their needs. But electorally less important districts can be ignored and national elections still won.

Under centralization, politicians can win national elections despite offering the "wrong" policies in district X, so long as their policy offerings are superior in more districts than their competitors. The equilibrium number of wrong policy offerings will depend on the cost of preference detection, and can be high. Furthermore, the problem of wrong policies will tend to worsen between elections, as conditions (and hence needs) change but preference revelation relies on potentially less representative means, such as lobbying, petitions, personal contacts, and so on. For example, in Bolivia under centralization 40 percent of all municipalities received no investment at all during the years before reform, and a further one-third received investment apparently unrelated to local needs (see chapters 1 and 4). Hence for small districts the choice is clear. Decentralization gives local politicians strong incentives to match policy offerings to what voters want, and hence to make government more responsive to voter needs.

Treisman replies that if "serendipitous learning" does occur in certain districts, "it may also occur for the locally based agent of a central decision maker. If the central government can get the incentives right for its subordinates, it need not decentralize decision-making authority in order to exploit such accidental knowledge" (212). But this *if* is exactly the point. Decentralization gets these incentives right by putting power in the hands of the people who benefit from serendipitous learning. Centralization does not, and so must come up with alternative means. What these means are, and how they might work, is left unclear.

Responsiveness to Local Needs and Tastes 2: Imperfect Information

Treisman then returns to the problem of imperfect information and costly information gathering, but with an assumption that both local and central governments will incur similar costs in the detection of preferences in any given locality. This is justified with the argument that both local and central governments can contract with (the same) private survey firms to discover local tastes. If such firms are unavailable and government must discover local tastes itself, then central government may even have an advantage from economies of scale in designing, running, and analyzing surveys. He presents a formal Downsian-type model adapted from Laffont and Zantman

(2002) featuring a country with two districts, and elections in which two candidates compete with credible promises to implement specific policies.

Under decentralization, "policies" consist of a level of local public good provision fully financed by a local tax rate. Under centralization, policies consist of public good levels for all municipalities, and local tax rates that fully finance each good. Candidates' payoffs for winning elections are R under decentralization and $2R$ under centralization (one for each district). Citizens' tastes for public goods are unknown, and so candidates must invest in information acquisition. This is modeled as follows. Each candidate can choose to send an agent to try to determine citizens' preferences for public goods, which are unknown and vary between those who prefer low levels of provision and those who prefer high levels of provision. Investigation costs are K in one locality and $2K$ in both localities. A given search in a locality will reveal local tastes successfully with probability ξ, and will reveal no information with probability $1 - \xi$. Candidates' investments in information are common knowledge, but the results of each search are known only to the candidate who paid for it. A candidate with no information acts on the prior that the median voter is more likely to have preferences for a high level of public good provision (see Treisman 2007, 218–21, for the full exposition).

The model is solved to show that politicians will have identical incentives to search for information about voters' tastes under decentralization and centralization. The "extent of information search at both local and central levels will depend on the value of holding office, the effectiveness of search methods, the prior probability of making a mistake, and the intensity of electoral competition" (222). As these parameters are assumed to be either constant (search effectiveness, the mistake rate) or vary symmetrically (value of holding office, electoral intensity) across local and central governments, neither architecture of government motivates politicians more than the other to seek out what local voters want from their public servants.

Although the full model is more complex than I have presented here, it remains an oversimplification of the characteristics—and especially the main differences—between central and local government. Any model is, of course, a simplification—and should be, as should theory more generally. Simplification of complex reality to the key factors and relationships in any system, physical or social, is why theory exists. But the simplification goes too far when the key relationships are misconstrued so as to give results that do not accord with observed behavior. This is the problem with this model.

The general problem is a model structure that assumes that all the key parameters either are constant across regimes or vary as a simple linear function (in this case a ratio of 1:2). If search capabilities are identical, and the costs and benefits of attaining office strictly proportional, then it is hardly surprising to find that central and local politicians behave in similar ways. While we could quibble with all of these assumptions and contest several, the most important concerns—again—information, so let us focus on that. The main tool of information discovery that real candidates employ is not contracted surveys but rather the multitude of campaigning activities (speeches, meetings, canvassing, debating, lobbying, etc.) required to obtain office, which brings candidates and voters together and provides the latter set-piece opportunities to make policy demands.

Surveys and focus groups conducted by private firms are part of the toolbox but in most countries—especially developing countries—are far less important sources of policy information than what candidates see and hear on the campaign trail. And this does not end with the election. The process of democratic governance has structural features that also serve to inform policymakers about voters' needs and wants. Politicians who wish to be reelected make efforts to meet regularly with constituents, respond to individual appeals, and listen to civic organizations and interest groups that aggregate and (perhaps) amplify the demands of important groups of voters. Elected officials do not mostly rely on private firms to tell them what voters want because voters are willing to tell them themselves. For their part, officials must have listened in order to get elected to office, and they have strong incentives to keep listening if they want to remain there.

Hence the costs of obtaining information on local preferences (of a given quality) are not constant across districts and hierarchical levels of government because they are not divorced from the costs of obtaining and holding office. For local government officials, the latter largely subsidizes the former. But the same is not true for central government officials, who do not win national elections based on the level of garbage collection or public lighting in municipality X. National campaigns provide information about the national issues that dominate them; in all but the very largest cities local concerns are swept aside. Once we accept that the costs of information acquisition do not scale up symmetrically from local to central government, Treisman's result breaks down. This key asymmetry implies that decentralization *will* lead to better-informed governments and provide incentives for policy-making better tailored to local needs and tastes.[8]

To summarize, the argument in favor of decentralization rests on information and incentives. Voters' information about government performance is superior for local government because the conduct of daily life, including exchanging information and opinions with others, provides detailed information about a broad range of public affairs in most municipalities in a way that it simply does not about national affairs. Hence voters will more easily be able to hold local than national government to account. By placing power over their electoral fate in the hands of voters, decentralization provides local politicians with strong incentives to inform themselves about what voters want and need, and to act on this information once elected. And the process of obtaining and holding local office subsidizes learning about *local* conditions in a way that central elections do not. Posting central agents to localities does not level the playing field for centralization. Their intrinsic incentives are not downward to voters but upward to the center, in the service of its priorities and needs. It might be possible to design some extrinsic institutional mechanism that realigns agents' incentives with those of local citizens. If so, how such a mechanism works should be explained— simply asserting it is not enough. With better information about government performance in the hands of voters, better information about voter preferences in the hands of government, and strong incentives for the latter to do what the former want, decentralized government has strong tendencies to be more responsive and accountable to the governed.

Last, there is a third type of information thus far ignored that is important for the provision of all public goods, and particularly important in the context of a federal system. This is specialist technical or scientific expertise—as distinct from information on local preferences and conditions—of the kind required to design and properly equip, for example, health clinics, sanitation systems, or agricultural extension schemes. Although not absent from the literature, this distinction has probably not received the attention it deserves. Some authors, myself included (Faguet 2004), have at times treated this question as "either-or," classifying public services as naturally central or local according to which type of information is most important for their provision.

I now regard this as a false dichotomy. A more mature approach admits that most if not all public services require at least some technical expertise and some locally specific information, and hence the main question should be how to combine both types of knowledge in the production of services nationwide. Ostrom, Schroeder, and Wynne (1993) provide probably the best treatment of this issue, analyzing the institutional arrangements that can bring together the inputs and efforts of local and central government for the planning and execution of public projects. I addressed this question in chapter 4 with a formal model in which central and local governments have precisely these advantages and cooperate to provide public goods jointly in different districts. The results help us interpret nationwide evidence on decentralization's effects on government responsiveness in Bolivia.

The Public Economics Literature

Public economics is a distinct literature with a distinct style. Methodologically it relies far more on formal modeling and econometrics than the public policy literature. Rather than discussing a range of arguments for and against decentralization separately and discursively and attempting to conclude whether or not decentralization is beneficial, it builds formal models that trade off particular advantages and disadvantages directly and tries to specify *under what conditions* each regime is advantageous. This has the benefit of clarity in focusing on specific trade-offs. But it has the disadvantage of narrowing the discussion to just a few of decentralization's many claimed positive and negative effects. Hence it makes sense to treat this literature separately.

In terms of productive efficiency, central government should be naturally superior to local government so long as returns are at least slightly increasing. Any economic case for decentralization must therefore invoke a counterbalancing source of efficiency in which local government has an advantage. Different authors have approached the problem in different ways. Tiebout's (1956) seminal work focuses on heterogeneity in both individual tastes and public goods provision across different localities. He posits a world in which individuals move costlessly among localities that offer different levels of provision of a public good, which are fully financed by local taxation. The ensuing competitive equilibrium in locational choices produces an efficient allocation. Hence information about what individuals want is revealed when they "vote with their feet." The Tiebout model has been influential, spawning a large subliterature of empirical "Tiebout studies," especially in the 1960s through 1980s. Interesting examples of these include works by Oates (1972, 1985) and Elinor Ostrom and others (see, for example, Ostrom and Whitaker 1973, 1974; Ostrom, Parks, and Whitaker 1977, 1978; Ostrom, Schroeder, and Wynne 1993). Dowding and John (1994) survey over 200 such studies.

But this approach assumes a highly mobile population and fixed governments, which is at odds with anecdotal evidence from most countries and with studies of the (comparatively mobile) United States, as Bardhan (2001)[9] and others have noted. A better assumption would seem to be that government is the "mobile" element in most local democratic systems, changing with relative frequency, whereas the population is essentially fixed over typical four- or five-year electoral periods. European countries' notably low rates of internal migration support this view. Observations along these lines seem to have led to a broad shift in the literature in recent years, as Tiebout studies have declined in number and a spate of new approaches have emerged. Tiebout-style "voting with your feet" is undoubtedly a valid mechanism for preference revelation at the margins and may be more important for particular services, such as education.[10] But the principal mechanism for joining demand and supply for public goods must involve the political process. Indeed this is arguably why local government exists at all.

The most influential public economics model of decentralization over the past 40 years is due to Oates (1972), who builds on Tiebout to compare decentralized with centralized public goods provision. In both cases governments seek to maximize the welfare of their constituents. Under centralization, government chooses—crucially—a uniform level of public good for all districts, even though districts may vary in their preferences or needs. Under decentralization, heterogeneous districts can choose different levels of public good provision. But decentralized governments ignore "spillovers"—the benefits that one district's public goods may provide to residents of other districts (e.g., infectious disease control, tertiary health care), whereas centralized government takes them into account in determining the level of public goods.

The trade-off at the heart of Oates's analysis, and most of the generation of public economics models of decentralization that followed,[11] pits the extent of heterogeneity in tastes between districts against the degree of spillovers among them. In terms of the broad arguments about decentralization reviewed above, this can be thought of as "responsiveness" versus "efficiency." The resulting Oates Decentralization Theorem states that where there are no spillovers, but tastes among districts vary, decentralization is superior. Where there are spillovers but districts have identical tastes, centralization is superior. Where both spillovers and heterogeneity of tastes exist, the two effects must be compared in order to determine which regime is preferable.

As Besley and Coate note, the assumption about central government policy uniformity is neither theoretically nor empirically satisfactory. When relaxed, central government is always preferred in this "standard model" as it takes account of spillovers. When might local government be preferred? Besley and Coate's (2003) reexamination of this problem abandons the assumption of uniform provision under centralization. Instead, they place at the heart of their treatment a political economy model of elections followed by legislative bargaining. Costs of provision are shared under centralization, creating conflicts of interest between citizens in different districts, who will disagree about both the best level of goods provision and their distribution across districts. This conflict of interest plays out in the legislature, where representatives elected by each district make policy decisions.

They analyze two broad cases. In the first, a minimum winning coalition of representatives makes policy decisions in the legislature, which they call "non-cooperative policy-making." Such decision making creates two resource allocation problems: (1) *misallocation,* where spending is skewed toward those districts represented in the winning coalition, and (2) *uncertainty,* where districts cannot predict who will be in the winning coalition, and thus are unsure of the amount of public good they will receive. Besley and Coate show that both problems weaken the case for centralization. The second case involves "cooperative policy-making," in which legislators maximize the welfare of all districts. Counterintuitively, such policy-making does not maximize welfare for the economy as a whole. This is because citizens in such a regime face strong incentives to vote strategically for representatives with high demands for public spending, leading to general overprovision of public goods under centralization. For heterogeneous districts they find that decentralization continues to be welfare superior in the absence of spillovers, but centralization is no longer superior when spillovers are present. They also find that higher heterogeneity reduces the relative performance of centralization for any level of spillovers. Although these conclusions mirror those of Oates, the logic underpinning them is quite different.

Another approach that has proved influential is Bardhan and Mookherjee (1998), who develop a model of public service provision that examines the implications of decentralization for the targeting and cost effectiveness of public expenditure. In terms of the broad arguments for and against decentralization reviewed above, this can also be thought of as "responsiveness" versus "efficiency." They find that for provision of a merit good available on competitive markets to the poor, decentralization dominates with respect to intercommunity targeting and cost effectiveness, though not necessarily for intracommunity targeting. For the provision of infrastructure, decentralization dominates only if local governments are not vulnerable to capture, local government has adequate financing, interjurisdictional externalities do not exist, and local governments have all the bargaining power versus public enterprise managers.

Each of these arguments for and against decentralization, or in the case of the public economics literature each side of the trade-offs posed, is logically plausible. Although different authors may assess their strengths differently, students of decentralization cannot accept some and reject others on theoretical grounds alone. How do we move beyond statements of belief about decentralization to test competing theories? For that, evidence is required. And happily, a huge empirical literature beckons.

The Empirical Literature

The empirical literature on decentralization also spans a number of disciplines. I focus here on those fields that collectively dominate the empirical evidence available on decentralization's effects: public economics, comparative politics, development studies, and public policy. Conveniently, these are also the fields that concern themselves most with questions of government accountability and responsiveness.

The move from theory to evidence presents a number of practical problems. The first is that empirical work tends to be shaped by the data available, which often do not permit clean "tests" of one or another of the arguments laid out above. This is because the data are messy and can be ambiguous in their interpretation, but more importantly because a particular empirical outcome that follows decentralization can be associated with more than one causal pathway. Which of these is responsible may not be clear from the evidence alone. Hence specific empirical results often invoke more than one of our arguments listed above. For example, improvements in nutrition following reform could be due to local services that are better designed for local conditions, improved targeting to needy populations, greater citizen participation in service implementation, or faster economic growth. Disentangling which of these factors is primarily responsible for falling malnutrition can be difficult.

A second practical challenge is simply the size of the empirical literature in this field. Including the "gray" policy literature, this runs literally into the thousands of studies over the past 40 years. Any attempt to review results by country or region will quickly lose the forest for the trees in a confusion of particular results that are often contradictory and usually simply different. A clear organizing principle is required. Hence I organize empirical results into three themes: (1) the quality of governance and policy-making, (2) economic performance, and (3) accountability and responsiveness, where each corresponds to interrelated groupings of the arguments for and against decentralization presented above. For clarity, these arguments are flagged in the points that follow each section heading below. What follows is I hope representative of the main questions asked and methodologies employed by students of decentralization. The section ends with a number of meta-studies that summarize a great deal of additional work. Even so, I do not pretend that this brief survey can cover more than a fraction of a huge literature.

The Quality of Governance and Policy-making

policy quality per se   graft and corruption
policy stability   elite capture

This category refers to the technical quality of policy in the sense of the public decisions that local governments make, and the public goods and services they produce. Necessarily, it also refers to the quality of the policy-making processes that go into the production of the same. For example, how has decentralization affected local education and health services? How has it affected districts' ability to plan and implement investment projects? These must be considered alongside questions of capture and corruption because in empirical terms the quality of policy and governance achieved in a municipality is often determined by the level and type of capture that obtains.

Among service outputs, empirical studies have focused disproportionately on the effects of decentralization on education. This is partly due to the importance that economists and policy specialists alike assign to education as a public good, and also probably reflects the abundance of education statistics available in many developing countries. A number of good, clear contributions have permitted this particular strain of the literature to advance in recent years. One such study is by Galiani, Gertler, and Schargrodsky (2008), who investigate evidence from a natural experiment in Argentina. They find that decentralization of school control from central to provincial governments had a positive impact on student test scores; the poorest, however, did not gain, and indeed may have lost ground compared to their previous performance. Barankay and Lockwood (2007) find that greater decentralization of education to Swiss cantons led to higher educational attainment, allowing boys to close the gender gap with girls. Eskeland and Filmer (2002) also find econometric evidence that decentralization led to improvements in Argentine educational achievement scores. And Parry (1997) finds evidence that decentralization improved educational outcomes across the mountains in Chile.

Other studies cast a broader net, seeking to link reform to such outcomes as poverty, inequality, environmental protection, and broader measures of human development. In a 2002 study, Oliveira (2002) shows that decentralization boosted the creation and administration of protected areas in the Brazilian state of Bahia. Habibi et al. (2003) find that increasing devolution to the provinces in Argentina led to sustained improvements in human development. Infant mortality fell and educational retention rates (from primary to secondary school) rose as decentralization deepened. More broadly still, Shankar and Shah (2003) find that the political competition spurred by decentralization decreased levels of regional inequality in a sample of 26 countries. And Johnson, Deshingkar, and Start (2005) present evidence that India's recent decentralization empowered the rural poor in Andhra Pradesh and Madhya Pradesh through such instruments as rice subsidies and credit for women. But their enthusiasm for decentralization is nonetheless limited. The pro-poor outcomes achieved, they argue, were due to central and state governments' ability to counterbalance the elite capture that decentralization tends to spawn, which naturally favors the rich.

The notion that decentralization naturally abets elite capture is strongly disputed by Parker (1995), who argues that reform is associated not only with better substantive outcomes but with improved government processes as well. In various case studies he finds evidence that decentralization increased beneficiary participation in decision making in rural development schemes throughout Colombia, Mexico, and Brazil, leading to superior outcomes. Parker also relates the suggestive story of decentralization in

Bangladesh, where extremes of wealth and power allowed local elites to capture nascent local governments (25). Subsequent elections overcame this distortion, and over 90 percent of local councilmen were ejected from office. In a similar vein, Rowland (2001) and Blair (2000) show how decentralization improved the quality of democratic governance achieved in both large cities and small towns in Bolivia, Honduras, India, Mali, Mexico, the Philippines, and Ukraine. Reform can help fight corruption too. The econometric results of Fisman and Gatti (2000) show that fiscal decentralization is consistently associated with lower measures of corruption across a sample of countries. Fiszbein's (1997) research uses qualitative methods to help explain how. Decentralization spurred capacity building in local government in Colombia, providing authorities with the skills and tools, and citizens the transparency, to achieve better government.

Such conclusions are echoed and amplified by Huther and Shah (1998), who find positive correlations between decentralization and indices of political participation, social development, and an overall quality-of-government index in a sample of 80 countries, for all of which they infer causal relationships. Campbell's (2001) study of Latin America goes further. Highlighting the extraordinary scope of authority and resources that have been decentralized throughout the region, he argues that this "quiet revolution" has generated a new model of governance based on innovative, capable leadership, high popular participation, and a new implicit contract governing local taxation. Such results are possible, according to Petro (2001), because decentralization not only affects formal, official institutions of government but also spurs changes in the very fabric of society. In his case study of Novgorod, Russia, he finds that local government played a pivotal role in raising levels of social capital by establishing common social values and priorities for the community.

With so many positive results, can we conclude that decentralization improves the quality of governance and policy-making? Sadly things are not so clear; the evidence against decentralization is also compelling. Where public services are concerned, much evidence points to decentralization's harmful effects. For example, Akin, Hutchinson, and Strumpf (2005) analyze a detailed database of Ugandan local government health budgets. Using subjective characterizations of the degree of "publicness" of different health activities, they find evidence that local governments are allocating declining proportions of their budgets to public goods, and increasing shares to publicly financed private goods. They attribute this behavior to free riding by local officials on the health expenditures of their neighbors. Bardhan and Mookherjee (2006) test for elite capture in 89 villages in West Bengal. Although they find little evidence of elite capture in the allocation of private goods, public goods projects do exhibit capture. They theorize that this is because public goods are inherently less transparent—it is less clear than for private goods who gets how much.

On poverty and the environment as well, the news is not good. Woodhouse (2003) predicts that decentralization will fail to improve access of the poor to natural resources and will fail to reduce ecological damage. Casson and Obidzinski (2002) go further, reporting that decentralization in Indonesia actively spurs depredatory logging by creating bureaucratic actors with a stake in its proliferation.

Why do decentralized governments perform so poorly in terms of policy outputs? According to Ellis and Mdoe (2003) and Ellis and Bahiigwa (2003), the policy processes that it creates are to blame. Both find that decentralization propagated rent-seeking behavior down to the district and lower levels in Tanzania and Uganda, so becoming "part of the problem of rural poverty, not part of the solution" (Ellis and Bahiigwa 2003, 1010). Similarly, Bahiigwa, Rigby, and Woodhouse (2005) and Francis and James (2003) show that decentralization in Uganda has not led to independent, accountable local governments but rather to their capture by local elites. Decentralization has thus failed as a tool for poverty reduction in Uganda. Porter (2002) agrees for sub-Saharan Africa more generally.

Montero and Samuels (2004) explain the empirical link between decentralization and elite capture, arguing that the political motives of reformers often combine with ex post vertical imbalances to exacerbate elite capture and regional inequality. Crook and Sverrisson (1999), Smith (1985), and Solnick (1996) take the argument further. The evidence, they claim, shows that local government's lack of human, financial, and technical resources— and its greater propensity to corruption and elite capture—will prevent it from providing effective public services under decentralization, regardless of whether policies are "tailored" to local conditions or not. Using similar language, Crook and Sverrisson (1999) and Smith (1985) argue that local government's lack of human, financial, and technical resources will cripple their production of local public goods, and thus power should remain in the hands of relatively resource-rich central governments.

Thus a large set of positive results concerning decentralization's effects on the quality of governance and policy-making are more or less counterbalanced by a smaller but still compelling set of negative results, leaving it hard to conclude whether reform improves or degrades governance.

Economic Performance

economic performance   efficiency in public goods production
public spending and deficits   macroeconomic stability

This category is concerned with the level and efficiency of public expenditures, their effects on macroeconomic stability (via the fiscal deficit), and—at one or more removes—their effects on economic growth more broadly. We have discussed above how decentralization might impact public service efficiency, fiscal deficits, and macroeconomic stability. Regarding growth, it is important to note that decentralization's effect is at best indirect and long-term, via raising the efficiency of public expenditure. Despite the fact that many reform programs cite raising the growth rate as one of their primary goals (Martinez-Vazquez and McNab 2003), there is no reason to expect decentralization to raise growth in the short term or via a more direct path unless it is accompanied by a separate fiscal boost. This is because in terms relevant to economic growth, decentralization is simply a reorganization of existing public expenditure patterns. Altering who undertakes and executes such decisions may in the best case improve the quality and efficiency of government services, and hence of the economy as a whole, and so raise growth as such effects feed through to increased productivity. But such effects will take time to become noticeable. Advocating decentralization as a short-term solution for low economic growth is mistaken.

By contrast, the link between decentralization and public expenditure levels is much simpler in theory. What does the evidence say? In a study of 20 countries' spending on infrastructure over 10 years, Estache and Sinha (1995) find that decentralization increased both total and subnational spending on public infrastructure. But methodological difficulties mean that no conclusions can be drawn from this about whether decentralization made spending more or less efficient. First, there are various data problems: the absence of information on autonomous parastatals' spending; the inability to distinguish between capital and recurrent expenditures; and finally the volatility of exchange rates and multiplicity of exchange rate regimes, which made data from one of the countries unreliable. To these can be added the perils of using measures such as the share of subnational expenditure in total expenditure to define the degree of decentralization; Smoke (2001) provides a specific example (12). Zax (1989) similarly finds that electoral considerations lead to significantly higher levels of spending in those U.S. states and municipalities that permit initiatives, but interpreting these spending levels in terms of efficiency or welfare is fraught with difficulty.

Other studies, however, do report efficiency increases from decentralization. Studies of small-scale rural projects in Mexico managed by Comités de Solidaridad (community self-help groups supported by World Bank–financed projects) find cost savings of up to 50 percent relative to similar projects managed by state agencies (World Bank 1994b). And Piriou-Sall (1998) finds that decentralization boosted the overall cost effectiveness of public health services in Chile. Effects in education were mixed, however. In Brazil reform led to increased administrative costs without significant service improvements, while Chile managed to avoid this problem.

Estache (1995) finds strong evidence that even for services with high technological or coordination requirements, such as paved roads or piped water networks, where central governments have an advantage in building systems, local authorities are almost always able to operate them more cheaply. Using panel data to study the cost of road provision in eight countries over 25 years, Humplick and Moini-Araghi (1996) are able to go further. They show that concave resource costs are offset by downward-sloping "preference costs," so that initial losses in economies of scale from decentralization are outweighed by efficiency gains when the locus of roadworks is closer to the people. Hence where road maintenance was decentralized, unit costs were lower *and* roads were of better quality.

The changes so documented could in principle lead to macroeconomic management that is better, as a given level of public goods can be provided more cheaply, or worse, if increasing spending levels lead to larger aggregate public sector deficits. What does the evidence say? Huther and Shah (1998) find positive correlations between decentralization and a quality index of economic management for a sample of 80 countries, a relationship that they interpret as causal. This is explained by Shah (1998b), who argues that better clarity and transparency in the rules of the game give decentralized fiscal systems greater potential for macroeconomic management than centralized systems do.

So does decentralization improve the cost effectiveness of public expenditures? Can it lead to macroeconomic stability? Unfortunately this is only half of the empirical story. In a study of rural water supply in central India,

Asthana (2003) finds that decentralization of water provision decreased efficiency. Operating costs per unit of output were higher in decentralized utilities, and asset utilization was lower. Both differences are statistically significant. And Rodden (2003) finds that decentralization contributed to chronic macroeconomic instability and disastrous bailouts in Brazil in the 1980s and 1990s. Webb (2003) examines similar macroeconomic instability in Argentina in the 1980s, which appeared to improve in the 1990s only to end in full-scale economic collapse at the turn of the new millennium.

The news on deficits and macroeconomic stability is worse. According to Dillinger and Webb (1999), decentralization led to significant fiscal problems in Colombia both at the national level as central resources were transferred outward and at the subnational level where unsustainable deficits accumulated. Wildasin (1998) cites a number of countries where decentralization-inspired deficits have put pressure on central banks to monetize debt, placing exchange rates and price stability at risk. Worse, Mello's (2000) study of 30 countries predicts that failures of intergovernmental fiscal coordination will lead to chronic deficits and, eventually, macroeconomic instability. This scenario is supported by Tanzi (1995) and Prud'homme (1995), who set out clear examples of the dangers decentralization can pose to macroeconomic stability, and also by Montero and Samuels (2004), for whom the political dynamic mentioned above (a combination of the political motives of reformers with ex post vertical imbalances) can lead to macroeconomic instability in decentralizing countries.

Rodríguez-Posé and Gill (2004) elaborate further on the increasing regional inequality that decentralization can be expected to bring to Brazil, reducing living standards in poorer areas and increasing tensions within the federation. Most pessimistically of all, Treisman (1999) cites recent events in Yugoslavia, Russia, Argentina, and Brazil to suggest that decentralization can interact with economic liberalization to intensify fiscal, macroeconomic, and even territorial instability.

The least ambiguous strand of this empirical literature is the one examining economic growth, where studies find results that are either insignificant or negative. Among serious empirical studies, I found only one presenting credible evidence that decentralization sometimes spurs growth. Rodríguez-Posé and Bwire (2004) study links between devolution and growth in Germany, India, Italy, Mexico, Spain, and the United States. They find that devolution is for the most part irrelevant for economic growth. When it does matter—for Mexico and the United States—it is linked to lower economic efficiency and hence lower growth. Blanchard and Shleifer

(2000) distinguish the case of Russia from Weingast's (1995) account of China. In Russia, local governments' capture by existing firms, and the competition for rents by local officials, eliminated incentives to firm entry, thus strangling a nascent economy. According to the authors, such behavior was absent in China on account of the party's political centralization.

Ellis, Kutengule, and Nyasulu (2003) find evidence that in Malawi decentralization is likely to depress growth and rural livelihoods by facilitating the creation of new business licenses and taxes that stifle private enterprise. The only possibly positive voice is Loboguerrero (2008), whose evidence implies that the effects of decentralization on local economic growth in Colombia depend on the governance structure of municipalities. Where bad local governance prevails, resources will flow to less efficient sectors, facilitating corruption and waste, and ultimately leading to lower growth. Where local authorities have better information on local needs, resources will be allocated in the sectors with the highest rate of return, which should in time promote growth.

These small-N results have not proved replicable in larger studies, where insignificance dominates. Woller and Phillips (1998) test the broad claim that decentralization will increase the long-term growth rate by making the public sector more responsive and efficient. Using panel data on 23 developing countries between 1974 and 1991, they find no strong evidence of any systematic effect of decentralization on economic growth. Martinez-Vazquez and McNab's (2003) survey of over 120 empirical studies shows that we do not know empirically whether decentralization affects growth directly or indirectly; the existing empirical evidence is mixed, and methodological problems with the specific tests used make much of it unreliable. In addition, they find no clear theoretical grounds for predicting a relationship in either direction.

In summary, while decentralization does seem to increase expenditures on public services, it is unclear whether the efficiency and cost effectiveness of public resource use rise or fall. Evidence on deficits and macroeconomic stability is also mixed but on balance negative. And the effects of decentralization on economic growth appear to be either insignificant or negative.

Accountability and Responsiveness

citizen voice and participation
deepening democracy
government accountability and
   hence responsiveness

individual liberties
(reduce) bureaucracy

The separate treatment of accountability and responsiveness here is admittedly somewhat artificial. Both are part of the policy-making process in the sense that voice and participation are policy inputs, not outputs, and the degree to which officials are responsible for their decisions has more to do with the processes than substance of policy. Thus accountability and responsiveness could easily have been subsumed under the first theme above. But they are the focus of this book, and so it is useful to examine them separately here.

Accountability and responsiveness ranked among the principal concerns of empiricists a generation ago. Thus surveys like Rondinelli, Cheema, and Nellis (1983) could summarize case studies showing that decentralization seems to have made government more responsive to local needs in Papua New Guinea by improving the capacity of provincial administrators, albeit with a significantly increased cost base of public services; reform also improved the access of people in neglected rural areas to central government resources and institutions "perceptibly" in Indonesia, Morocco, Pakistan, Thailand, and Tunisia. But the theme fell from favor during the following quarter-century, perhaps in part a victim of the increasing quantification of empirical work in the field. Of the few studies that do report results, Manor (1999) finds evidence that decentralization enhanced the responsiveness of government in the Philippines, India, and Côte d'Ivoire. And a World Bank (1995) case study of Colombia shows that satisfaction with government and local services improved notably after decentralization.

Along related lines, Alderman (2002) finds that decentralization of social assistance in Albania improved poverty targeting compared to other safety net programs in similar countries. Local governments appear to be using information not available to outsiders to tailor policies to particular local needs. Similarly, Galasso and Ravallion (2005) find that decentralized targeting of an antipoverty program in Bangladesh has clear informational advantages. Village governments achieved a degree of pro-poor targeting at the household level, whereas the center was broadly neutral.

Against this, Samoff (1990) finds the evidence on responsiveness strongly negative, arguing that decentralization schemes around the world have largely failed to work. They have neither enhanced local capacities nor improved local programs, in large part because they were neutralized by elaborate mechanisms of central supervision and control. Slater (1989) supports this view with the example of Tanzania, where elected councils were eliminated and replaced by District Development Councils reporting directly to central government, leading one observer to comment that "the state was now moving its guns from Dar-es-Salaam to the villages" (514). And while Kubal (2006) finds evidence that Chile's local service administration did improve in equity and efficiency under decentralization, these changes were caused by policy changes of the center-left Concertación government that were exogenous to the decentralization process itself.

In summary, we know little about decentralization's empirical effects on government accountability and responsiveness. Some qualitative evidence from the 1970s and early 1980s has been supported with a few more recent case studies, plus a handful of quantitative works on informational aspects of responsiveness. But in sum, and especially in comparison to the evidence on policy quality or macroeconomic stability, the evidence is scant. Moreover, what there is is somewhat contradictory and, taken as a whole, uncompelling. Given that the matter in question is the single most powerful argument concerning decentralization, this is an especially unfortunate state of affairs.

The Broadest Surveys of Decentralization

Perhaps this assessment of the literature is unfair? Or perhaps it is based on a selection of studies that is skewed in some way so as to be unrepresentative? We can check for this possibility by consulting several broad surveys that, at various points over the past 25 years, have assessed the state of the field attempting to reach concrete conclusions about decentralization's empirical effects. Among the most general and most cited international surveys is Rondinelli, Cheema, and Nellis (1983), who note that decentralization seldom, if ever, lives up to expectations. Most of the developing countries they report on experienced serious administrative problems implementing decentralization. Although few comprehensive evaluations of the benefits and costs of decentralization efforts had been conducted then, those that were attempted indicated limited success in some countries but not others.

A decade and a half later, surveys by Piriou-Sall (1998), Manor (1999), and Smoke (2001) are slightly more positive, but with caveats about the strength of the evidence in decentralization's favor. Manor notes that the evidence, though extensive, is still incomplete, but ends on the positive note that "while decentralization ... is no panacea, it has many virtues and is worth pursuing"

(1999, 120). Smoke finds the evidence mixed and anecdotal, and asks whether there is empirical justification for pursuing decentralization at all. More recently, in a review of 56 studies published since the late 1990s, Shah, Thompson, and Zou (2004) find evidence that decentralization has in some cases improved, and in others worsened, service delivery, corruption, macroeconomic stability, and growth across a large range of countries.

Litvack, Ahmad, and Bird (1998) summarize the literature this way: "It is not much of an exaggeration to say that one can prove, or disprove, almost any proposition about decentralization by throwing together some set of cases or data" (30). Treisman's (2007) more recent review of the literature is bleaker still. He finds results on the effects of decentralization mixed at best, and for the most part inconclusive, weak, and contradictory. "To date," he says, "there are almost no solidly established, general empirical findings about the consequences of decentralization" (250). "Almost nothing that is robust or general has emerged" (268). The lack of progress over 25 years and hundreds of studies reviewed by these authors is striking.

The Trouble with the Literature

What are we to make of a reform that theory strongly supports, which is the subject of broad enthusiasm across all of the world's regions and most of its countries, but about which hundreds of empirical studies fail to find systematic results, either for or against? Such a deep discord between theory, evidence, and practice—both broad and sustained over time—presents us with a true paradox that no scholar has been able to resolve. Most (myself[12] included) have resorted to shaking our heads in puzzlement before renewing efforts to find empirical results that point more clearly in one direction or another.

It is important to note that while any two of the three elements of this paradox are potentially reconcilable, the coexistence of all three is extremely unlikely. For example, it is possible that theory supports decentralization but the evidence does not—the theory could simply be wrong. Or that theory supports decentralization and there is much enthusiasm among policymakers—the latter follows from the former. Or indeed that there is enthusiasm for reform but no clear evidence—decentralization is a pure fashion with no firm theoretical basis. But the persistence of all three elements simultaneously over decades is highly unlikely and demands an explanation.

Treisman's response is that the evidence is right and the theory and practitioners' enthusiasm wrong. "To those convinced that theory in this area implies almost no general effects, the weak, partial, and inconclusive flavor of the empirical literature is not puzzling at all. It is what one would expect" (2007, 296). After failing to find any effects of decentralization that are systematic across countries or political-institutional contexts despite looking in many different ways, researchers should in effect admit defeat and give up. This accords well with his position that theoretical predictions about the effects of reform are indeterminate. In theory anything is possible, and in practice everything happens.

It seems to me that this position is untenable. With respect to theory, I have laid out in detail above why decentralization should be expected to make government more responsive and accountable to the governed. With respect to practice, this position requires us to believe that a reform that has been sweeping the world for decades has no systematic effect on material and political outcomes. This implies that the politicians and policy advisers who undertake reform suffer from a sort of collective delusion that has persisted for a generation and shows no signs of abating. They expend nontrivial amounts of energy and political capital pursuing a difficult change that may well have no effects, or—when it does—effects that cannot be predicted. A look at their peers' experiences in other countries reveals no particular pattern. And yet they persist.

While such a scenario is strictly possible, it must be judged highly unlikely. Some (perhaps many) of the politicians pursuing decentralization are no doubt dishonest, hapless, or dim. But with most or all of the world's countries participating, it must be the case that at least some of the reformers are intelligent, strategic, and acting in their own self-interest or the interests of (some portion of) their constituents. They expend effort and political capital because they have reasonable expectations that beneficial outcomes will follow—not least for themselves. And after decades of reform, they must see some evidence that coincides with their expectations. Otherwise why would they act?

A New Approach

A way out of the paradox, and a way forward for the literature, is to begin with the incentive-based theory I lay out above: Decentralization produces a fundamental change in the incentives of the officials who govern locally. Accountability shifts from running upward to higher levels of the central administration, to running downward to the voters directly affected by local policies and services. This changes officials' incentives and thus their behavior. Second, we must accept that reformers' broad enthusiasm for decentralization is substantively significant. The breadth and persistence of reformers' efforts over decades and across countries are much more likely to be due to their expectations of specific material or political outcomes based on real outcomes they have observed than some sort of delusion or giant mistake.

What then of the contradictory evidence? This book argues that most attempts to evaluate decentralization reforms—both national and cross-country studies—have asked the wrong questions. Such questions along the lines of "What is decentralization's effect on economic growth/service provision/pro-poor outcomes/citizen participation/fiscal deficits?" are far too general and commit the common mistake of construing decentralization as a unidimensional policy intervention with discrete effects on outcomes of interest. This is akin to treating decentralization reform like raising expenditures on education or roads, and looking for effects on student test scores, or the efficiency of transport. In the latter cases, policy changes consist of mechanical interventions (pump more resources through the system for providing public education or roads). The main questions for evaluators concern the efficiency with which certain inputs are turned into well-defined outputs, and the quality of those outputs.

Decentralization is not like this. It is an act of letting go, in which central government devolves resources and authority to locally elected officials who are free to use them as they choose. It is not so much a discrete policy lever as a *process* in which both sets of officials, as well as citizens and other interested actors, learn and refine their behavior over time. Its outcomes are not easily predictable because the underlying relationships that are determinant are not mechanical; they are, rather, contingent on the characteristics of society, the economy, and key political actors *at the local level*, and the dynamics among them that decentralization unleashes.

Put another way, the obvious answer to the question, Does decentralization lead to local governments more corrupt than central government was before? is "Yes." Some will be more corrupt. And the answer to the question, Does decentralization lead to local governments *less* corrupt than central government was before? is also obviously "Yes." Some will be less cor-

rupt. We can substitute "corrupt" here with any of the main objects of evaluation that occur in the literature without changing either answer. This is
because what decentralization does is to set in motion local dynamics organized around the new incentives that it puts in place. The outcomes of these
dynamics will vary from district to district as their underlying characteristics vary, and they are difficult to predict in advance of reform. The "effect"
of decentralization in any dimension of interest is simply the aggregate of
these local political and institutional dynamics.

This focus on local heterogeneity places my research within a small but
growing strand of the decentralization literature that includes Putnam
(1993, 2000) and Grindle (2007), as well as the broader political science literature, such as Beer (2003), Boone (2003), and Wibbels (2005). Of these,
the most similar is Grindle's detailed study of decentralization in 30 Mexican municipalities, which explains local governments' variable performance as a function of four factors: local political competition, reformist
leaders' level of entrepreneurship, public sector modernization efforts, and
civil society activism. Putnam's (1993) classic study of Italian regional governments explains heterogeneous performance as resulting from differing
levels of civic engagement with government and social capital.

It follows that to understand decentralization we must first understand
how local government works. It is important to note that ex ante uncertainty
about decentralization's effects is not due to theoretical indeterminacy, as
some claim, but rather to empirical variation across districts. It is not that
theory cannot identify effects of decentralization when local governments
are freely elected and accountable to voters, but rather that there is so much
empirical variation around precisely these qualities. This, in turn, is because
the key variables that impinge upon political outcomes and policy-making
processes vary widely across space. Understanding local governance, by
which I mean identifying the key variables and describing how they interact
to produce local government that is effective, responsive, and accountable,
or not, is the single most important contribution of this book.

The way forward that I propose, and which this book adopts, is to abandon broad empirical questions like "Is decentralization good or bad for X?"
in favor of an approach that admits from the outset that reform will be followed by a broad array of outcomes along any dimension, and then asks
questions of the kind "Why are the good good and the bad bad?" After any
decentralization experience, why do some districts perform well and others
badly? Such questions are much better suited to the contingent, dynamic

nature of decentralization as policy process, and hence much more likely to yield analytical insight. The approach they imply takes both the parameters of a specific decentralization reform and a country's broad institutional structure and norms as given, and asks how variation in local characteristics determine key outcomes of interest. This eschews cross-country comparisons, based on either statistics or case study, in favor of an approach that can plumb more narrowly—and hence deeply—into the causes of good and bad local governance in a single country.

This book adopts a blend of quantitative and qualitative tools in the aid of a comparative methodology at the municipal level. Doing so has a number of advantages compared to the existing literature, which mostly falls into one camp or the other. Small-N work (e.g., Blanchard and Shleifer 2000; Parker 1995; Slater 1989; Grindle 2007) usually focuses on a single country, or else it develops comparisons between a small set of countries, relying primarily on descriptive and qualitative evidence. The analysis is often careful, deep, and nuanced. But the methodology employed makes it difficult to generalize beyond the cases reported. Many such studies, especially those undertaken at the national level, suffer the additional problem of an excess of variables over observations, undermining any causal inferences that may be made. When there are more explanatory factors than observations it is difficult to determine analytically which explanatory factor does what.

On the other hand, quantitative studies (e.g., Mello 2000; Fisman and Gatti 2000; Huther and Shah 1998; Zax 1989) benefit from the high degree of generality, consistency, and empirical transparency that statistical approaches provide. But they have difficulty quantifying nuanced concepts, and with data comparability across diverse countries (or regions). These problems combine into the largest single drawback such studies suffer: their difficulty controlling for institutional variation across countries with very different histories, constitutions, economies, and cultures. Because institutional factors are powerful determinants of government performance, cross-country studies that fail to control for them risk misattributing their effects to decentralization.

This book attempts to overcome such limitations by attacking its research question with a blend of qualitative and quantitative evidence[13] in the hope of combining the advantages of each while avoiding some of the pitfalls of either, and so obtain a higher level of overall methodological rigor than either independently can achieve. I focus on a single country—Bolivia. The underlying question is, Why do some local governments perform well and others badly? As we shall see below, this question transforms itself rapidly into, How does (democratic) local governance work, and what are the major ways in which it can be deformed? The empirical strategy I employ combines deep insight into the causes of government quality in nine case studies, including two that define the extremes of municipal performance, with national data on all of the country's municipalities. In this way, I can approach the elusive goal of an explanation that has both generality and deep understanding. I can avoid problems of cross-country comparison (e.g., different institutions, political regimes, idiosyncratic shocks) while still benefiting from the formal rigor of large-N studies. And I can retain a central focus on complex, nuanced explanatory factors—such as accountability, trust, and political entrepreneurialism—that are hard to treat with quantitative data alone.

A Definitional Failure

In addition to research questions and methodology, a third root cause of contradiction in empirical studies of decentralization is a conceptual confusion—in practice if not in theory—about what exactly decentralization comprises. This is especially true of the older literature, in large part due to a definitional failure at the core of the subject. Instead of articulating a clear definition of decentralization from the start, many authors allowed themselves to be led conceptually by the phenomena they encountered. The quasi-spontaneous definition that so emerged is opaque, malleable, and ultimately unstable. It ranges from the *deconcentration* of central personnel to field offices in authoritarian systems, via the *delegation* of managerial responsibilities to organizations outside the regular bureaucratic structure, and the wholesale *divestiture* of public functions to the private sector, to the *devolution* of resources to autonomous, elected subnational governments (see Ostrom, Schroeder, and Wynne 1993 and Rondinelli, Cheema, and Nellis 1983 for detailed discussions). All of these phenomena often find themselves jostling together under the rubric *decentralization*. But these are, instead, fundamentally different institutional reforms that establish systematically different incentives and thus prompt government officials to different behavior. When researchers use the same language to talk about fundamentally different things, especially when making cross-country comparisons, the literature as a whole stagnates. This multiplication of meanings is not entirely incidental, as Slater notes, paraphrasing Curbelo.

> The popularity of the concept of decentralization can be linked to a combi-nation of elements—its ambiguity, its capacity to conceal more than it re-veals, its identification with long-established sentiments, its facile justification from purely technocratic points of view and the political in-strumentality that it potentially engenders. (Slater 1989, 501)

This study employs a definition of decentralization that is clear and conceptually discrete, so facilitating analytical precision.

> *Decentralization* is the devolution by central (i.e., national) government of specific functions, with all of the administrative, political, and economic attributes that these entail, to democratic local (i.e., mu-nicipal) governments that are independent of the center within a legally delimited geographic and functional domain.

I restrict my focus to decentralization under a democratic regime. The rea-sons for choosing this usage are both compelling and fortuitous. First, its restrictiveness aids analysis by excluding a number of phenomena that, though superficially similar, are in incentive terms fundamentally different from those I study here; this greatly simplifies the identification of endoge-nous and exogenous variables, and thus the measurement of ultimate ef-fects. And second, the case of Bolivia involves precisely this form of decen-tralization, implemented vigorously.

Residual Authority

A second definitional failure, and one that compounds the first, concerns the very different degrees to which whatever forms of decentralization gov-ernments decide on are actually implemented. The importance of this be-comes obvious when we consider the incentives that officials in decentral-izing governments face. When a government passes a decentralization reform as defined above (i.e., democratic devolution), it is by definition asking its executive branch to hand over resources and authority to inde-pendent bodies and officials that it does not control. Those who man the central executive, whose effectiveness depends on the power and resources at their disposal, are not interested in doing this and often will commence a rearguard battle to undermine reform.

The key question is who holds residual authority. In the spirit of Alchian and Demsetz (1972), Hart (1995), and Williamson (1995), by *residual authority* I mean authority over all resources not explicitly allocated. In a democratic system, many public resources will be explicitly allocated to particular uses and places as a result of political negotiation. Those with power to dispose freely of all remaining resources hold residual authority. *Decentralization* can accordingly be defined as a division of the national resource pool among a country's subnational districts, and the allocation of residual authority to independent and accountable governments in each. Residual authority is spread throughout the system, even if resources are distributed unevenly. Centralization, by contrast, is where both resources and residual authority are concentrated into national aggregates.

The implication is straightforward: for a system to be decentralized, residual authority must lie at the periphery. Where this is not the case, the country in question is not decentralized and should not be studied as if it were. This is true regardless of whether the reform implemented is called deconcentration, delegation, privatization, or any of a number of other categories that fill the public management lexicon.

Thus while dozens of countries have announced decentralizing reforms, it is likely that many of these have been undermined from within. This is not to impugn the honesty of decentralization's advocates but rather to underline the obstacles they face. Even when decentralization is promulgated with genuine enthusiasm by a country's leadership, its ultimate success depends upon the substantial and sustained cooperation of politicians and bureaucrats throughout central government. But these are precisely the people with the least interest in its success. They benefit from the residual authority they hold and do not want to see it, or resources, dispersed. Decentralization requires them to undermine their own position by transferring authority to the periphery. They do not collaborate, and deploy obstructive strategies to thwart reformer's intent.

The outcomes of such dynamics produce what Devarajan, Shah, and Khemani (2009) and others have referred to as *partial decentralizations*. The implication is that we must think of decentralization in the "real world" as a continuous, not bipolar, variable where both extremes represent feasible outcomes. Thus the degree to which a country that has announced reforms is actually decentralized will depend not only on the letter of the law but also on the extent to which the bureaucracy's rearguard battle to undermine reform succeeds. Where on the centralization–decentralization continuum a country ends up depends on the equilibria that result when the impulse to reform and the backlash against reform have spent each other. This will usually result in a movement away from the previous institutional arrangement that satisfies neither reformers nor bureaucrats entirely, and that may create opportunities from which new political actors can profit. This appears to be the story of recent upheavals in Bolivia, a point to which we return in the final chapter.

Studies that characterize countries as "decentralized" based on the simple passage of laws or executive decrees miss this Hegelian dynamic entirely. Studies of countries with similar legal instruments of reform may be comparing cases where deep devolution is taking place with others where little or nothing has actually changed. It is not surprising that those results are inconclusive.

I do not pretend that this is the one-book solution for understanding decentralization. This book offers what I hope is a deep yet robust account of the effects of decentralization in one country over a generation. But it is just a beginning. To understand the effects of decentralization in the world, more country studies blending deep qualitative with broad quantitative evidence are needed. Only once many such studies are available can we stand back from the details and assess decentralization's systematic effects across nations, cultures, and histories. My hope is that this book will hasten the process along.

CHAPTER 6
Governance from Below: Theory

Chapters 2 and 3 examined in great detail how local government functions in two very different municipalities. We focused on extremes of municipal performance in order to highlight how different institutional characteristics and political dynamics affect the quality of government. The districts operated in a common constitutional and legal framework, under the same institutions of the central state. And yet in Viacha government was deplorable during the period in question, with an ineffective council, a corrupt mayor, and competing oversight committees, while in Charagua an energetic and competent mayor, hardworking council, and strong oversight committee governed well. How can we explain these differences? As we have seen, the decentralization literature provides limited help, focusing as much of it does on central reform measures and symmetric or aggregate outcomes. To understand divergent outcomes, we must take the lessons of the previous chapter and drive our analysis deeper.

Close analysis of the principal social dynamics in each municipality suggests that the quality of their government institutions, and hence of the policy outputs they provide, is the product of deeper economic, political, and civic factors that characterize each district. This chapter goes beyond a descriptive account of good and bad municipal outcomes, to a more rigorous analysis of their underlying economic and social determinants. I develop a theory of local government that integrates a variety of well-established insights on the role of elections and lobbying in democratic politics with more recent ideas about civic organizations and social linkages. The framework provides a structure in which economic interests, political actors, and civic organizations interact to make policy decisions. I derive predictions based on local characteristics and then test them in the chapter that follows with extensive quantitative evidence from the universe of Bolivian municipalities.

I argue that the "outputs" of decentralization within any given country are largely determined by local-level political and institutional dynamics. This is a significant departure from the bulk of the decentralization literature, where the analytical approach is top-down, treating reform as an essentially national phenomenon. Here we take the opposite tack, approaching decentralization as a single reform that sets into motion a substantial number of largely independent local processes. The effects of decentralization are to a great extent the sum of the effects of these local dynamics, which inevitably diverge as much as local conditions do. To understand decentralization, we must first understand how local government works, and in particular when it works well and when badly.

The economic and political theories of decentralization explored in chapter 5 are of limited help. They largely assume that local government will be more sensitive to local needs, but fail to ground this in convincing micropolitical foundations. As a result, these theories cannot adequately explain why, within a given country, some local governments are more responsive or effective than others. Empirical analyses based on such ideas are often left clutching at the straws of staff quality, resources available, and other proximate explanations. But another strand of scholarship is more helpful. Although traditionally focused on national government, a number of recent contributions in comparative politics focus instead on local government, theorizing about its origins and structure (Boone 2003), central-local fiscal and political relations (Diaz-Cayeros 2006), and subnational electoral competition and institutional development (Beer 2003), to name a few.

Following in their wake, I reverse my approach to the problem. I first contrast the empirical attributes and experiences of our two extreme cases of municipal performance as a means of generalizing about the deeper social and institutional dynamics that underpin local government. From these observations I induce a model of government that accounts for both responsiveness and accountability through simple electoral and social behavior. The model will in turn serve to explain the results of chapters 1 and 4 (and 7)—why decentralization led to broad changes in national investment flows and made government systematically more responsive to objective local needs.

The rest of this chapter is organized as follows. The second section contrasts the social and institutional characteristics of Viacha and Charagua under three headings—the local economy, local politics, and civil society—in a search for underlying patterns that explain municipal performance.

The third section describes a structural model of local government, focusing on how governments are selected and what sorts of social relationships they then enter into. The fourth derives from this a dynamic model of the determinants of local government responsiveness and accountability. The fifth section concludes.

Society and Governance

The Local Economy

The economic differences between Viacha and Charagua are huge. The former is dominated by an industrial city, home to two of Bolivia's largest businesses and with a well-developed and vibrant private sector. The latter is a rural district dominated by cattle ranching and subsistence farming, centered on a town of 2,500 inhabitants with little commerce and no industry. With respect to local government, the fundamental difference between the two is in the economic interest that dominates each, and its role in the local political system. The vast majority of Charagua's wealth is held by large landowning cattle ranchers who traditionally ran the region. But by 1997, after years of economic hardship, the *ganaderos* were dispirited and increasingly impoverished, and felt that the tide of history had turned against them. Their power was waning, and both they and the Guaraníes knew it. Viacha, by contrast, had in the CBN a firm that was in clear economic and political ascendancy, which dominated the city's political life like few others in Bolivia.

Even though the brewery's assets and income were a considerably smaller share of the local economy than those of the cattle ranchers in Charagua, the single-minded exploitation of its human and financial resources, combined with skillful political tactics, allowed it a degree of influence over local politics and government far in excess of what Charagua's ranchers managed. Unlike the CBN, the latter were not, after all, a firm, but rather a collection of independent businessmen who did not face identical business conditions and accordingly did not act politically or commercially with a single will. Although most AGACOR members sympathized with either the ADN or MNR, at least a few could be found in all of Charagua's political parties. In addition, ranchers were willing to support parties' electoral campaigns regardless of their personal sympathies, in order to remain on good terms with all of the principal parties. In business also, AGACOR helped (nonmember) Guaraní farming communities drill rural wells and provided technical and veterinary assistance. In Viacha, by contrast, the CBN behaved with fiercely partisan aggression and went to great lengths to undermine or discredit opposition political parties, including bribing their councilmen and—in the case of the MIR—mounting a campaign against the SOBOCE factory. The bottling plant made no pretense of working evenhandedly with rival political or business groups. All of its public actions formed part of a simple strategy designed to capture votes and promote the UCS-CBN brand.

The withdrawal of SOBOCE from local politics left the CBN in a dominant position, as the near-monopsonistic provider of political funds to the local party system. The brewery was only too happy to exploit this role to hobble the opposition in the interests of the political dominance of the UCS. Thus what was in political terms an economic monoculture became, at least for a time, a political monopoly as well, as the CBN-UCS stifled competition and steadily raised the price of opposition and dissent. Charagua's ranchers behaved in a very different way, eschewing monolithic political action in favor of a gentler and more diverse approach better suited to a pluralistic group of businessmen. By supporting a variety of parties, they contributed to opening the political regime in Charagua and encouraging competition among parties. And when their rivals won power, far from attempting to undermine them the ranchers of AGACOR found an accommodation and were able to work with the new municipal authorities.

Local Politics

The analysis of local politics can be usefully divided into systemic issues and the party system per se. The former refer to the ground rules of electoral competition, and its fairness and openness to both parties and voters, while the latter refers to the nature of local party organizations and how they compete. The systemic reforms noted in Charagua correspond to nationwide changes that affected municipalities throughout Bolivia. These include reforms of electoral laws to increase transparency in the vote count, ensure voting secrecy, provide for independent oversight of the voting process, and increase the number of polling stations in rural areas. But they also include nonelectoral reforms, such as a new, efficient citizen registration process (which in turn permitted voter registration) and the extension of rural literacy programs (especially among women). Their collective effects were a broad increase in voter registration and improved voter participation. But the secret to the success of these reforms lies in large part with the design of the decentralization program itself. The LPP brought rural areas into the municipal system and then devolved significant authority and political responsibility to them. Whereas before rural dwellers voted, if at all, for cantonal officials who had neither resources nor political power, now full-fledged municipal governments with real resources and legislative authority were at stake. The prospect of gaining control over these drove political parties into the countryside in search of rural votes. The prospect of benefiting from them pushed villagers and farmers into municipal politics and into the voting booth. In this way the concerns and opinions of the rural 50 percent of Bolivians were brought into the political mainstream as electoral politics penetrated deeper and deeper into the hinterland.

Charagua provides a case study of this process. Registered voters increased by 72 percent between the 1993 and 1995 elections, and total votes cast by twice that—139 percent—while absenteeism fell by one-third.[1] The reforms that opened politics to a new electorate simultaneously established the conditions for fair and open competition. The old methods of bribery and intimidation no longer worked in Charagua; the MNR's attempt to bribe Councilman Vargas failed because, given electoral transparency, the transaction would have been apparent and would have exposed Vargas to the voters' wrath.[2] And so the Guaraní majority was able to overturn a cozy duopoly that had run the town for so long. In this political aperture, the parties that underwent comparable openings benefited most, and those that attempted to carry on as before suffered. Thus the MBL, previously irrelevant in Charagua, struck a deal with the APG and captured the majority of new votes, while the MNR lost its local preeminence and was thrown out of government. But the MBL was more than tactically clever—it had deep roots in rural life through its affiliated NGOs, which had earned the trust of Guaraníes after years of patient work. The presence of such a party not only facilitated the alliance between the APG and the political establishment but was instrumental in raising the quality of government after the election. NGOs like CIPCA and Teko-Guaraní specialized in planning and carrying out rural projects. The skills they had developed, and their relationships with rural communities, were instrumental to the transformation of Charagua into an effective municipality that served its rural majority.

By contrast, decentralization contributed to a very different process in

Viacha. Although voter registration did increase, Viacha's gain of 22 percent was an order of magnitude lower than Charagua's, while absenteeism remained roughly static.[3] This reflected the fact that Viacha's politics remained a closed affair, inured to the concerns and priorities of the rural majority. This, in turn, was largely due to Viacha's status as a comparatively small city dominated politically by the imperatives and dynamics of the La Paz–El Alto conurbation. Viacha was sufficiently close to the capital, and transport links sufficiently good, that national political leaders could intervene in local affairs at relatively low cost. Because it offered a fairly easy way to score political points without the public scrutiny that they were subjected to at home, party leaders essentially ran their Viachan affiliates from La Paz. Their directives were based on strategies that responded to events in the capital or nationwide, and not on the needs and circumstances of Viacha. They allowed their subordinates in Viacha very little room for initiative, reducing them to spokesmen and messengers. In this way, more powerful actors invaded the local political stage, trampling local concerns and stifling local politics.

The lamentable consequence was that the legal-electoral reforms detailed above were insufficient to counter the CBN-UCS's capture of local government. The party exploited the resources of the CBN to suborn and intimidate the opposition until it achieved a near-monopoly on local politics. Its hand thus freed, it indulged in a spiral of corruption and misrule. Under normal conditions, political competition and openness could be expected to catalyze a cleansing of the political system. But a substantive political choice is required for this mechanism to operate. And in Viacha the choices on offer were pale simulacra of political options, marionettes whose strings jerked across the horizon. The fact that the Viachan party system was dominated from beyond implied that local party leaders did not innovate in search of new voters. They did not have the operational independence to strike a deal along the lines of the MBL's in Charagua, and any such agreement that might occur was likely to be rejected by a national leadership more concerned with avoiding embarrassment than with policy experimentation. The generally poor quality of Viachan political leaders—another by-product of political dependence—made the leadership even less likely to tolerate local originality.

Why would parties err in such an obvious way in the first place? A compelling answer lies in their own organizations. Political parties are naturally vertical organizations, structured to conquer the highest levels of power to which they can reasonably aspire (e.g., national government). The devolution of authority required for municipal politics to take on its own self-sustaining dynamic requires an internal decentralization that many party leaders will resist as an unacceptable erosion of their power. But this is, of course, precisely the point, and confirms a much larger truth about decentralization: in order to work it requires people who hold resources and authority to let go, and they will always have strong reasons not to. Thus, while decentralization created many opportunities to make political gains and win votes in Viacha by reaching out to newly incorporated communities and addressing their concerns, the local establishment's efforts were limited to mundane extensions of campaign rallies and sloganeering to the countryside. Voters offered a false choice between options devoid of local content eschewed politics altogether and dropped out of the system. And so Callisaya was able to perpetuate his misrule until popular revulsion spilled into the streets and forced him from office.

Civil Society

The conspicuous economic and political differences between Viacha and Charagua are matched by the disparate characteristics of local society in each. In Charagua the Guaraní majority formed a territorially vast network of rural villages with similar social characteristics and similar self-governing community structures. These villages had autonomously organized themselves in the 1980s into the APG, an independent civic organization that acted as ethnic advocate and regional self-government. The APG's roots in the spontaneous village traditions of the Guaraníes gave it both tremendous legitimacy and a high capacity for mobilizing the opinions and efforts of its constituents, qualities that were to prove invaluable after decentralization. Townspeople formed the other important local group, with their own organizational structures based on neighborhood councils. They were less uniform socially than the Guaraníes, and less united in their goals and policy preferences. But they proved pragmatic in the end, willing to work with the new majority when the Guaraníes took over local government.

Viachan civil society, by contrast, is a heterogeneous mix, including two groups with strong and divergent identities and a long history of mutual antagonism marked by episodic outbreaks of civil violence. The city of Viacha is dominated by an urban elite that defines itself in opposition to the indigenous countryside, and that suddenly found itself miscegenated with a large rural hinterland that greatly outnumbered it. Like Charagua, Viacha's urban organization is centered on neighborhood councils, which are quick to confirm their legitimacy in national federations headquartered in La Paz. Rural Viacha is itself divided between the Machaqas in the west and the remainder, closer to the city. The former is a distinct region where the Aymara language predominates and communities are organized into traditional, pre-Columbian *ayllus* and *mallkus*. The latter see themselves as more modern, speak a mixture of Spanish and Aymara, and base their social organization on the peasant union's general secretariats. Of these three, the Machaqas region—the furthest from the city—is the most homogeneous and boasts the most robust social organization. The other two regions are strongly affected by the status of Viacha as an urban transition zone, an important threshold in the slow urbanization process that characterized Bolivia during the latter half of the twentieth century. The difficult journey from rural *campesino* on the altiplano to urban *vecino* in La Paz–El Alto can take several generations, and for many thousands their path takes them through Viacha. The two worlds collide in the city's markets and peri-urban areas, and in adjacent rural communities, and the resulting frictions lead inevitably to social tensions.

That these differences proved crucial to the quality of governance achieved in the two municipalities should not be surprising. Even without a theory of how society relates to government, the Law of Popular Participation marked the formal incorporation of civil society into the governance process as a governing institution, via the oversight committee. The OC is charged with overseeing all municipal activities on behalf of grassroots organizations and can effectively paralyze the administration if it objects. But the law did not specify the norms or procedures by which the social groups that give rise to the OC should operate, preferring to trust in their autonomous dynamics. The innate characteristics and internal workings of civil society are thus vital to the quality of government that municipalities can achieve, as both Viacha and Charagua illustrate.

In order for civil society to provide useful oversight and a feedback mechanism for the governing process, it must be able to accomplish a limited but important set of tasks. First, it must be able to identify a specific failing of local policy at the community level. It must then formulate a coherent demand or complaint and transmit it upward through, typically, two or three of its own hierarchical levels. Finally, local civic leaders must be able to take up this complaint and communicate it convincingly to the mayor or municipal council. Such abilities are not ethnically, culturally, or organizationally specific, and thus a wide variety of societies are likely to have them. But they will all share four general traits that facilitate these tasks. The first is simply the ability to communicate, often across large areas and diverse ethnic groups—a significant challenge in many areas of Bolivia. The second is norms of trust and responsibility, both within communities and across them (including leaders in the seat of government), as well as across time. Where community leaders do not comply with their duties of leadership and advocacy, government will not reap the information it needs to right policy mistakes. Communities must then trust leaders further up the hierarchy to accurately represent their interests before government, and leaders must trust that their information is correct. And civic leaders at the municipal level must then actively pursue communities' demands if government is to be held socially accountable for its policies at the community level.

The third trait is a minimum level of human capital among civic leaders such that those at the municipal level are able to interact productively with local government. This involves both cooperating with elected officials to advance policy goals and opposing their decisions in such a way as to modify their actions. The last trait is a minimum level of resources required to carry out these activities. Even if civic officials are unpaid, there remain unavoidable and nontrivial transaction costs associated with their activities. Communities in Bolivia have for the most part long-standing traditions of reciprocal generosity that cover the transaction costs of community self-government.[4] But the extension of these social institutions to the municipal level has in many places strained such finances beyond the breaking point, making it impossible for OC presidents in districts as diverse as Viacha, Porongo, Baures, and Atocha to operate effectively.[5]

In these terms it is easy to see why civil society was a significant benefit to local government in Charagua, and a significant liability in Viacha. Charagua benefited from a highly structured and coherent civil organization dating from before decentralization, in which communication was fluid and norms of trust and responsibility were strong. That these were Guaraní norms is far less important than the fact that the norms existed and effectively constrained behavior. Through this organization, civic and municipal authorities found it easy to stay in touch with local demands at the village level, as well as mobilize support for collective efforts. By promoting local authorities up through its hierarchy, the APG developed its own leaders internally; and the covenants it signed with NGOs provided it with the modest resources it needed to operate.

In Viacha, however, civil society was functionally broken. Its constituent parts did not trust each other and in many cases could not communicate with one another. Government travesties in the countryside went unreported in the city, where civil authorities of all extractions ignored village requests. Civic leaders with proven effectiveness at the village level were overwhelmed by the pressures and scale of municipal government. With no budget of their own and depending on official generosity for their sustenance in the city, they were easily neutralized as independent actors by government authorities. In Charagua, a civil society that functioned organically essentially took over local government and made it work. In Viacha society was a bubbling cauldron of resentment and discontent, composed of people so mutually suspicious of each other as to make social oversight virtually impossible. Callisaya's installation of his own OC is an illustration of sorts. Viachan society's inability to resist this ludicrous ploy confirms that its internal divisions left it unable to act in even its most basic defense.

It is instructive to remember that Charagua, while in some ways more homogeneous than Viacha, is itself a heterogeneous society, with its minority *criollo*, Mennonite, Quechua, and Aymara populations. Even with a well-functioning APG, it would have been feasible for Guaraní politicians to assume authority and ignore or exploit rival ethnic groups. That they did not must in part be due to enlightened leadership. But it is also due to the structure of interests in the district. The fact that Guaraníes are not only the largest population group but form a majority of the population implies that there existed in Charagua, in Olson's (2000b, chap. 1) terms, an "encompassing interest"—that is, one whose incentives were consistent with the growth of the collectivity. Viacha, on the other hand, had no encompassing interest, only narrow interests that sought to exploit power for the short-term gain of narrowly defined groups. This explains why the role of history varies so much between the two districts. For centuries both had suffered from state oppression, extremes of inequality, and periodic outbursts of civil violence. But Charagua's history was if anything more repressive and more cruel than Viacha's, leaving a potentially deeper reservoir of resentment. And yet it is in Charagua that the victims of oppression were able to overcome their past sufficiently to reach an accommodation with the urban elite, whereas in Viacha lingering social tensions contributed to government breakdown. In Charagua the group that stood to benefit most from government formed the majority and therefore had an encompassing interest in its success. In Viacha, groups that lacked such interest fought for and abused municipal power to the point of disaster.

An alternative view is to infer from the comparative demographics that social homogeneity, or even a particular ethnicity, is an important determinant of the quality of local government. Casual empiricism suggests that homogeneity is positively associated with communication, trust, and social responsibility in a society. Sameness may also make it easier for civil institutions to elicit contributions for projects of collective benefit, although its effect on the formation of human capital is difficult to predict a priori. But cultural sameness is a far from sufficient condition to ensure good government, as some of my other case studies make clear. Social homogeneity in Sipe Sipe and Desaguadero is similar to that of Charagua, both among the rural population and also between town and country, yet both had poor quality governments. And the immigrant nations of North America and Australia provide a clear counterexample of the possibility of organizing heterogeneous civil societies that function cohesively. They suggest that the more subtle concepts of social organization and encompassing interest provide a fuller explanation than simple homogeneity of why some societies are more cohesive and equitable than others. Homogeneity may be helpful in launching civic organizations, but it is neither necessary nor determinant.

The Structure of Local Government: Economy, Politics, Society

Local government produces local services and policies at the crux of a complex, dynamic environment. It is necessary to understand this environment in order to explain why some municipalities respond effectively to local needs and others do not. We consider first a structural model of the relationships out of which local government emerges, followed by an analytical model of the determinants of government responsiveness and accountability.

A local government's environment is defined by three distinct institutional relationships. The first of these—voting—occurs between voters and political parties or candidates. Parties compete with promises and ideas to attract individual voters, who vote for the party or candidate they prefer. Elections select governments and thus are implicated in the responsiveness of those governments. How exactly does this work?

Elections do not establish a contract (explicit or implicit) between government and governed, nor do they set a specific policy agenda. There are two reasons for this: political contracting and cycling/informational consistency. The former, emerging from the incomplete contracts literature (e.g., Hart 1995; Hart and Moore 1990), refers to the impossibility of writing a comprehensive platform that links politicians' actions to voters' policy preferences. Specific responses to all possible contingencies cannot be contracted for the simple reason that all possible contingencies cannot be foreseen. The latter, well-known problem of cycling in multidimensional space (Condorcet 1785; Dodgson 1884; Black 1948; Mueller 1989) limits elections' ability to convey information with anywhere near enough detail to inform specific policy decisions (Verba, Brady, and Nie 1993). Additional problems like clientelism, authoritarian political cultures, and other principal-agent distortions (Cleary 2007) further limit elections' ability to convey information on voter preferences accurately. Hence elections are not about conveying what voters want in detail but rather about allocating control over governing institutions to the "team" (Downs 1957) most trusted by voters. Elections allocate power—power to make future decisions that affect society's welfare.

We assume that voters vote according to their preferences or interests. That is to say, citizens vote for the candidate whose actions, once in office, they think will benefit some combination of their own interests and the community's. Different voters may weight these two factors differently. The process by which such voting decisions are made is nonlinear and imprecise, and may vary by individual. Voters themselves may not be aware of how their own voting intentions form. Hence I do not try to model it. The variability of this process means that it can be expressed in a number of ways, such as voting for a candidate's policy proposals, party affiliation, personal history, or ethnic or other background. Each of these criteria can, and probably often does, operate as a utility proxy—"a candidate like me is more likely to choose policies good for me." This assumption does not deny that other individuals' voting decisions may be truly orthogonal to calculative (utility maximizing) voting. Rather we assume that if the vote is free and elections regular and repeated, the strongest tendency over large numbers of votes will favor candidates and parties whose future actions voters think will improve their welfare. (Some may find the negative formulation more convincing: citizens will vote against candidates whose actions they expect to decrease their welfare, or whose actions have done so in the past.)

Second, we assume that voters vote individually. Although interest groups and organizations may try to influence voters' decisions, the technology of voting—each adult casts one private vote—implies that these decisions are ultimately exercised at the most disaggregated level. Where voting is concerned, there are no intervening organizations that aggregate preferences, and hence the process of preference aggregation should be a simple, mechanical, and ex post transparent one: many secret ballots are cast, votes are tallied, and a winner is declared. The winner should represent the electoral option that most voters judge best for their collective welfare. In other words, the election winner should, in some fuzzy, nonlinear way, represent the "will of the majority."

For this to obtain, two further conditions must hold. The first is that elections must be open, free, and fair: open to registered voters and politicians/parties, based on the free participation of both, and fairly administered, counted, and reported. Where some citizens are prevented from voting, or their decisions constrained at the ballot box, or where vote counting is manipulated, we can expect the authorities elected to respond poorly to the wishes of the majority. The second condition is that, given the above, voters be presented with a range of options that substantively address the needs and challenges facing them. In other words, elections must be *substantively competitive*.

The logic is similar for both conditions. Where voters are not free to choose, or are "free" to choose among options that are externally constrained in the policy dimensions most important to them, the competitive dynamic will tend to operate in dimensions different from citizens' needs. Governments elected on such criteria have little incentive to address voter needs, especially when this is costly, because they can expect reelection without doing so. By contrast, free and fair elections that are substantively competitive support policy innovation. Innovation happens when parties actively canvass local society, identifying pockets of voters, currents of opinion, or particular interests that are underrepresented, and propose policies that respond to these and other changing voter needs. Policy innovation of this sort can be termed *political entrepreneurship*.

Substantively competitive politics is characterized by a greater diversity of ideas and policy proposals competing for public favor, and hence a broader representation of the public's needs. A direct result of this is improved responsiveness and public accountability of government officials, as opposition parties continually search for advantage over their rivals (Beer 2003; Grindle 2007). By contrast, a substantively uncompetitive politics leads to lower levels of policy innovation and entrepreneurialism, which in turn reduce the level of oversight that local government institutions are subject to. This will tend to result in a less responsive, less accountable local government.

The second relationship—lobbying—connects parties to private firms, producer associations, and other economic and issue-oriented interest groups. Following the pressure group politics work of Bentley (1907), Finer (1997), and Truman (1951), it can be thought of as a secondary, or wholesale, political "market" in which specific policies or entire policy bundles, as well as broader influence over legislators and the policy-making process, are exchanged for resources from interest groups. The rationale for this relationship is derivative but compelling: even where they are all-volunteer organizations, political parties require resources to fund election campaigns and sustain party operations. And because of the incomplete contracts problem, firms are interested in a continuing influence over government decisions and the policy environment in which they operate (Kitschelt 2000). Such wholesale exchanges, combined with gifts from the faithful, are how parties finance themselves.[6] Ben-Zion and Eytan (1974), Palda and Palda (1985), Poole and Romer (1985), and many others have tested the relationship between campaign contributions and policy-making empirically, with positive results.

The third relationship involves civil society conceived as a collectivity or set of collectivities—as opposed to atomized individuals—and their relationships with the institutions of government. Such interactions are richly discussed in the political science literature (Hirschman 1970; Putnam 1993, 2000; Verba, Schlozman, and Brady 1995). Where governance is concerned, local civil society operates as a complex of organizations. These aggregate preferences and represent community needs, mediate community participation in the production of certain services, facilitate social expression and the assertion of local identity, mobilize voters and attempt to sway their opinions, and enforce political accountability on the institutions of government. It is not useful to conceive of this interaction as a quasi market, either internally or in its dealings with government, as its dynamics are not founded on buying and selling. It is rather a set of social organizations that generate their own norms of behavior and responsibility organically and over time may develop stores of trust and credibility that enhance capacity, or may not (Putnam 1993).

Local government depends on the relationships that collectively make

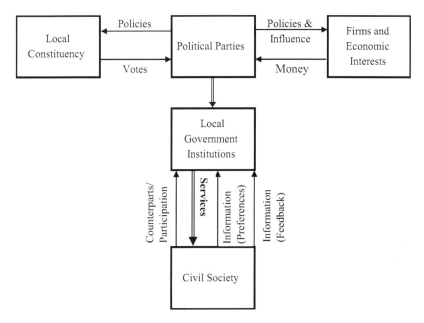

Fig. 31. A model of local government

up civil society to elicit information necessary to the policy-making process, judge the efficacy of previous interventions, and plan for the future (Bardhan 1996). Politicians also depend on these relationships to gauge public satisfaction with their performance between elections. The organizational dynamic of civil society is thus intrinsic to the process of local governance. Figure 31 illustrates how these three institutional relationships combine to give rise to local government. In this diagram, the political parties that are most successful in competing for resources and votes win control of government institutions. These institutions then enter into a separate, more complex interaction with civic organizations that features varying degrees of feedback and social participation.

A Theory of Responsiveness and Accountability

Figure 31 describes how local governments are selected and what sorts of social relationships they then enter into. But why are some governments more responsive and accountable to their voters than others? To understand why,

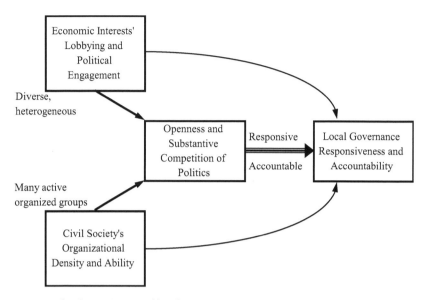

Fig. 32. The determinants of local government responsiveness and accountability

we must place our model in a dynamic context. Let us redraw the structural model of government presented above as a dynamic model that depicts how voting, lobbying, and civic organizations interact over time to produce government decision making that is responsive and accountable to voters, or not. Figure 32 depicts the key relationships involved. As opposed to figure 1, where the focus was on the actors involved, our focus here is on actors' behavior over time and how the actions of some actors change the environment in which others operate.

The quality of a municipality's politics is at the center of the model. There are two reasons for this. The first is simply that elections select governments, and hence the quality of a municipality's political competition—as explained above—is the single most important determinant of a government's responsiveness and accountability. Once governments are in office, both economic and civic organizations try to influence their decision making and hence exert second-order effects (thin arrows) as depicted in figure 32. But the principal determinant of responsiveness and accountability is the quality of a municipality's politics. The second, more subtle reason echoes Boone's (2003) argument that subnational institutions are shaped endogenously by differences in rural social structure, property relations, and other local economic interests. This is that the degrees of political openness and substantive competition emerge endogenously as the joint products of the political engagement and lobbying efforts of firms and other economic interests, and the institutional coherence and organizational ability of civil society.

To understand this, step back for a moment and consider the exogeneity or endogeneity of our three explanatory factors. Within the context and time frame of a political economy model of government decision making, it is easy to see that the characteristics of the local economy are essentially given. They are part of the superstructure within which politics and civic organizations operate, and—short of revolution or expropriation—they change too slowly to be determined in any useful sense by the other factors in the model. The institutional capacity of civil society is also exogenous. Although it will develop and change over time, internalizing the incentives generated by its environment more rapidly than economic structure can, it is ultimately dependent on characteristics such as culture, history, language, and trust—characteristics that also change slowly and so should remain exogenous in a political economy model of government.

An open, competitive political system, on the other hand, is dependent upon the constellation of economic and other interests at the local level, as well as on the institutional attributes and engagement of civil society. Consider first how lobbying interacts with voting. Figure 31 suggests a political analogue of the neoclassical argument that open and competitive markets lead to efficient resource allocations. In a diverse, heterogeneous local economy, a variety of economic actors with competing interests will tend to support a variety of political expressions. This in turn promotes competition in local politics, in which competition spurs policy innovation as parties vie to win both votes and financial backing.

Where a municipality's economic landscape is dominated by a hegemon, by contrast, that hegemon may be able to increase the efficiency of its political finance by focusing resources on the success of a single party. Competing parties will find it difficult to finance their activities, and may be actively undermined by an abusive hegemon. Monopsony in the provision of political funds thus encourages monopoly in the party system. Note that this does not refer to the simple number and size of firms, nor to broader characteristics of product or labor markets, but rather to local firms' engagement with politics. A diverse local economy where one firm is significantly engaged and other similars stand aside, such as Viacha, will tend to produce such outcomes, as will economies where the hegemon is much larger than the rest.

In fact, municipalities like Viacha may be more likely to feature distorted politics than those economically dominated by one very large firm— "one-company towns." This is because when a single firm's share of economic activity is large enough, that firm is likely to have an encompassing interest in the political and economic health of the town. In such municipalities, the well-being of the town plays a large role in the firm's prosperity, via for example its workforce, the quality of public services the firm receives, and the level of taxation. Such firms will tend not to abuse or distort local politics because it is in their own interests not to do so. Instead, they will tend to support competing political parties, to ensure that major currents of local opinion are represented and voters do not become resentful. And between elections they will seek accommodation with local government, searching out policy options that benefit both town and firm mutually. For reasons that are symmetric and obvious, the fortunes of the town also depend on those of the firm, giving local authorities a strong incentive to reciprocate. In such places, virtuous circles of cooperation and mutually beneficial investment can sometimes persist over extended periods.

Hence a diverse, heterogeneous local economy will tend to support openness and competition in politics. But so, curiously, will the presence of a single, dominant firm, when that firm has an encompassing interest in the well-being of the municipality. How do civil society dynamics interact with voting?

The insertion of civil society into the framework occurs both during elections, as organizations vie to sway the votes of their own members and others, and afterward, once a given political team has assumed control over the institutions of local government. Civic organizations' core functions include the revelation and aggregation of individual preferences into coherent collective positions, coordination among members, and information transmission upward to authority and downward to the grass roots. In so doing, they constitute a system of representation parallel to that carried out by parties within the context of political competition. The pursuit of these functions makes civic organizations natural vehicles for imposing accountability on government from the grass roots.

Civil society supports an open, substantively competitive local politics when its various, naturally occurring currents[7] form such organizations that compete with economic interests and each other to voice demands and affect policy; that is to say, when groups of citizens with similar needs and political preferences organize into groups and: (1) try to sway elections and (2) try to sway ex post policy-making. In such cases, different civic organizations can ally with different parties to refine policy platforms and mobilize voter turnout. Civic groups in effect subsidize politics by lowering the cost of political mobilization for parties and acting as interlocutors. Doing so can increase the substance of political competition, as demands are taken up from the grass roots by civic groups, transmitted to candidates and parties, and injected into a broader policy debate. This, in turn, promotes participation in policy discussions and in elections by making political competition relevant to ordinary voters in even far-flung localities.

But a homogeneous, even monolithic civil society can perform a similar function, albeit in a different way. When civil society is sufficiently homogeneous that similar groups organize vertically into an encompassing interest, as happened with the APG in Charagua, then much of the preference revelation, aggregation, and debate about policy trade-offs that would otherwise occur between competing political parties happens instead within civil society, moderated by the "peak" civic organization. Unlike a private sector encompassing interest, a civil society encompassing interest would probably see little point in supporting competing political parties, given that it carries out much of the policy discussion internally. In such municipalities the logic of political competition would be replaced by the logic of consensus and reciprocity natural to associational life, with possibly beneficial effects for policy implementation. But the levels of information and debate typical of open, competitive politics would nevertheless obtain.

The civic dynamic can fail in at least two ways. The first occurs where civil society is lacking in competent organizations and hence defined by largely atomized individuals. This echoes Hacker and Pierson (2010), who blame a decline in labor unions and other organizations that favor middle-class interests for policies that increasingly favor the rich, and a subsequent large increase in the rich's share of U.S. national wealth. The second failure occurs where competent civic organizations are so antagonistic toward each other as to be unable to work together. In both cases, collective action failures will abound, and society will lack the intermediating capability necessary to aggregate preferences, transfer information upward and downward, and enforce accountability on elected authorities.

Hence we have a theory of government responsiveness and accountability. Where local politics are nourished by a diverse, heterogeneous local economy and an active civil society rich in organized groups, political competition will tend to be open and substantive. Such politics will tend to lead, in turn, to responsive, accountable local government. Alternatively, where a single firm is sufficiently dominant in the local economy, or a single group is dominant enough in society, to constitute an encompassing interest, politics will again tend to be characterized by open debate and the substantive competition of ideas and demands. This may not be led by political parties in such cases but rather catalyzed and subsidized by the encompassing interest, which has a large interest in the well-being of the collectivity. Responsive and accountable government will once more be the result.

Conclusions

Careful consideration of a wealth of qualitative information from a very good and a very bad municipality yields a theory of local government that incorporates realistic institutional features observed in the field. This model opens the black box of local government decision making, and hence government effectiveness. Chapter 5 noted that while the fundamental argument in favor of decentralization is based on accountability and responsiveness, how these attributes come about is rarely specified. Theories lacking a convincing micropolitical foundation for presumed mechanisms of accountability ultimately fail to explain why decentralized government should be more responsive than centralized government. We can identify outcomes that decentralization should produce, but we do not know how or why they come about, and are left befuddled when they do not. This failing is mainly due to the lack of a theory of local government. Failure to understand how local government works implies ignorance of how it differs from central government.

Here we remedy the problem. The theory proposes that local government responsiveness and accountability are primarily the product of the openness and substantive competition of its politics. The quality of a municipality's politics, in turn, emerges endogenously as the joint product of the lobbying and political engagement of its firms and other economic actors, and the organizational density and ability of its civil society. Where many, diverse economic interests support a variety of political currents, and society is organized into intermediating groups that can aggregate preferences and transmit information, government will have a strong tendency toward responsiveness and accountability to citizens. The presence of an encompassing interest in either the economy or society can also sustain responsive government, although as we shall see in the next chapter this prediction is much harder to test quantitatively.

Contrast this approach with the popular counterclaim that the fundamental variable explaining government performance is the quality of political leadership. This line of reasoning focuses primarily on the character of the individuals concerned. Hence the principal difference between Viacha and Charagua is that the former suffered a corrupt mayor whereas the latter benefited from an honest and able one. A simple exchange of mayors (and other institutions of government) between the two would thus have restored probity to Viachan public life and plunged Charagua into the abyss. This study rejects such a position as simplistic and shortsighted, preferring to treat political leadership as an endogenous variable determined by the economic, political, and social processes analyzed above.

In this view, politicians can be regarded as mobile agents distributed along a quality continuum between "good" and "bad" extremes, along a common, national distribution from which all municipalities choose. That is to say, the pool of potential mayors is no better in any one place than anywhere else. The question is, What are the characteristics of municipalities where dishonest or incapable politicians gain control of public institutions (the lower tail), and where and why do honest, capable politicians prevail (the upper tail)? In addition to being more interesting, this question permits a deeper, multidimensional analysis of local government that exploits the empirical insights developed in the preceding chapters. Building on the previous analysis, the answer can be stated simply: Low-quality politicians will have far more opportunities to enrich themselves in municipalities where government oversight and accountability are crippled by a closed, uncompetitive politics. In districts where politics is open, vigorous, and devoted to substance, politicians will face strong incentives to satisfy voters' needs. Bad political agents will dedicate themselves to other pursuits or leave.

The chapter that follows tests the ideas developed here against nationwide quantitative evidence. But before doing so, it is instructive to apply the theory to our two districts. Charagua's economy consisted of heterogeneous cattle ranchers who supported competing political parties. And its civic organizations were mostly run by the majority Guaraníes through the

APG, an organization as structured and disciplined as it is legitimate in the eyes of most residents. The APG supported an open, substantive political debate with strong grassroots participation. Accountable local government responsive to both rural communities and the cattle-ranching town was the result.

In Viacha, monopsony in the market for political finance allowed the CBN/UCS to snuff out competition in the local political system. Civil society was divided along ethnic and historical lines, and riven with hostility and mistrust, rendering its organizations incapable of cooperation and unable to engage substantively with government institutions. Political debate effectively shut down as a result, with paltry competition focusing on issues extraneous to local concerns. The local government that resulted proved corrupt, unresponsive, and unaccountable.

The framework thus provides a succinct, coherent explanation of government quality in both districts. Its completeness is underlined by Viacha's dramatic dénouement, in which citizens rose up against their mayor, and the mayor resigned. In the process of entrenching itself, the CBN/UCS had so comprehensively distorted the local political system that no resolution could occur through this channel. Only a large, extrasystemic shock could break the party's hold, in this case through direct citizen action.

Can our model of local government explain not only governance in Viacha and Charagua, but also the broader results of decentralization nationwide? The following chapter tests the model directly with quantitative data from the universe of Bolivian municipalities. As we shall see, detailed large-N evidence is strongly supportive of the theory and allows us to fine-tune it further. The answer to the initial question, we shall see, is yes.

CHAPTER 7

Governance from Below: Evidence

The model laid out in the previous chapter explains outcomes in Viacha and Charagua well. But does it have more general implications? We turn now to a large-N database in search of broader support. If, as argued above, the outcomes of decentralization are largely the sum of the many local processes that it sets into motion, then a framework that models such processes should help us understand the national results of decentralization in Bolivia. Chapter 1 showed that decentralization caused important policy changes in Bolivia: public investment shifted from economic infrastructure to social services and human capital formation, and resources were distributed much more equally across space. Detailed econometric evidence in chapter 4 further suggested that local governments were more responsive than central government to objective local needs.

What are the local dynamics that drove these processes? Can our model explain such outcomes? The evidence presented below shows that it can, and surprisingly well. But first we must transform the question we initially asked of qualitative evidence from Viacha and Charagua, to one that is both informed by theory and appropriate to large-N data on the universe of Bolivian municipalities. Hence we move from Why did one municipality perform well and the other badly? to How does (democratic) local government work, and what are the major ways in which it can be deformed?

Methodology

The theory proposes that economic actors interact with civic organizations to produce open, substantive political competition, which in turn leads to responsive, accountable government. Noncompetitive political systems, by contrast, produce governments that are less accountable to voters and less responsive to their needs. Exceptions can occur where an encompassing interest supports preference revelation and policy debate outside multiparty competition in ways that also lead to responsive, accountable government. Unfortunately, the role of encompassing interests cannot be tested due to data insufficiency. No natural indicators of encompassing interests in either civil society or the private sector exist for Bolivia, nor I suspect for most developing countries. The synthetic variables I constructed from tangentially related data produced very large standard errors, implying low measurement precision. Hence the issue is left for future research.

I thus restrict myself to the main thrust of the theory. An ideal test would model the accountability of local government as a function of the interactions between the diversity of economic interests in a locality and their degree of political engagement, and the institutional coherence and ability of its civic groups. But there are no obvious measures of government accountability, economic actors' diversity and engagement, or civic groups' institutional ability for Bolivia, nor indeed for many far richer and more data-abundant countries. So instead I adopt a second-best strategy that models key policy outputs as a function of characteristics of the private sector and civil society. The policy outputs in question are local investment decisions in education, urban development, and health. We focus on these sectors because of their importance to municipal budgets—together they account for two-thirds of total local public investment—and because qualitative evidence from the case studies shows them to be consistently among ordinary citizens' top priorities. Our approach attempts to measure the extent to which private sector actors and civic organizations interact with the municipality and each other to make investment more, or less, responsive to real local needs. Using local investment as the dependent variable has three advantages: investment data are copious and reliable; investment flows are measured in noncontroversial units; and observed variation in investment levels and composition is high.

Rather than attempting to construct measures of the complex causal variables involved in the theory, I prefer to stick to raw data and simple, relatively transparent estimation techniques. Hence the main explanatory variables used include the number of firms and grassroots organizations (GROs) registered in a municipality, which I interpret below. Because the quality of local politics emerges endogenously in the model, political variables must be excluded from the right-hand side to avoid multicollinearity. I also include indicators of local need, mimicking the test in chapter 4 of whether decentralization made government more or less responsive to local conditions. Because theory stresses the importance of interactions between economic and civic actors, I include interaction terms between indicators of need, firms, and GROs as explanatory variables. If firms and GROs matter, they should matter most when both are present in a municipality (not just one), and the specific channel of their effect should be to make government more or less sensitive to local needs. The interaction terms are accordingly the most important explanatory variables in the model.

The theory's predictions are tested with an original database that marries investment data for all of Bolivia's municipalities with a rich set of indicators of local institutional and decision-making characteristics. The database includes the universe of Bolivia's more than 300 municipalities. Because need indicators are specific to each sector, I disaggregate municipal investment flows by sector, and for each sector estimate the model

$$G_m = \alpha + \beta N_m + \gamma F_m + \delta C_m + \zeta N_m F_m + \eta N_m C_m + \theta F_m C_m$$
$$+ \lambda N_m F_m C_m + \xi Z_m + \varepsilon_m \tag{1}$$

where G is investment per capita; the need variable, N, is a scalar of the existing stock of public goods of that type (variously defined, see below) at an initial period; F is a scalar of the number of private sector firms in a municipality; C is a scalar of the number of civil society organizations present in a municipality; and Z is a vector of regional, demographic, economic, and institutional controls, all subscripted by municipality. Table 14 summarizes the variables used.

My use of the F, C, and Z terms to model public investment decisions follows Bergstrom and Goodman (1973), and Rubinfeld, Shapiro, and Roberts (1987) within the context of the available data; my use of the N term follows chapter 4 and Faguet (2004); and my use of interaction terms follows Brambor, Clark, and Golder's (2006) criteria, especially with respect to the inclusion of constitutive terms. In order to compare like with like and smooth natural discontinuities, I sum municipal investment flows during the three post-decentralization periods identified in chapter 1 (1994–96, 1997–2002, and 2003–7) and run cross-sectional regressions. I assume that N, F, C, and Z are constant between censuses (the only opportunities to update such information for all Bolivian municipalities)—a necessary assumption due to the lack of time-series data. Differences in data collection between the 1992 and 2001 censuses mean that a number of the Z controls

TABLE 14. Data Summary

Variable	Obs.	Mean	Std. Dev.	Min	Max
Dependent Variables (Bs. per 1,000 pop.)					
Education investment, 1994–96	296	47,145.3	37,361.7	0	240,435.1
Education investment, 1997–2002	310	127,737.2	116,202.7	0	1,223,619.0
Education investment, 2003–7	308	419,613.8	410,860.1	25,980	3,738,896.0
Urban development investment, 1994–96	296	47,134.7	43,515.7	0	331,996.0
Urban development investment 1997–2002	310	137,141.1	133,706.8	0	1,650,702.0
Urban development investment, 2003–7	307	98,713.6	96,422.0	1,136.9	784,192.7
Health investment, 1994–96	296	9,997.0	16,830.3	0	198,589.3
Health investment, 1997–2002	310	34,077.3	42,209.4	0	361,629.3
Health investment, 2003–7	307	141,814.8	229,602.4	3,385.9	3,079,814.0
Need Variables					
Illiteracy rate (1992)	310	30.46375	15.82312	5.5	78.7
Illiteracy rate (2002)	310	16.42717	8.816236	2.1	44.058
Number of markets per capita	304	0.0014271	0.0108282	0	0.1517241
Child malnutrition rate	294	32.3682	11.76497	2.9	64.86486
Firms and GROs					
Number of firms (finance)	310	2.609677	26.72428	0	454
Number of firms (construction)	310	4.312903	37.30928	0	540
Number of firms (total)	310	337.6355	2205.563	0	26,666
Number of GROs (1997 municipal census)	305	43.85574	52.50669	0	416
Number of GROs (1992 UDAPSO)	310	46.92258	49.63505	0	339
Number of GROs (1992 SNPP)	308	34.25	41.30934	0	299
Interaction Terms					
Illiteracy (1992) × Firms	310	24.67186	187.18	0	3,165.388
Illiteracy (2002) × Firms	310	15.7132	128.5494	0	2,181.321
Illiteracy (1992) × GROs	305	1,365.108	1,650.118	0	9,018
Illiteracy (2002) × GROs	305	756.8545	942.4364	0	5,066.67
Markets × Firms	304	0.0001813	0.0019037	0	0.0316484
Markets × GRO5	304	0.0247788	0.1531316	0	1.834738
Malnutrition × Firms	294	61.53434	584.5145	0	9,727.414
Malnutrition × GROs	292	1,120.116	1,268.951	0	7,429.496
Firms (finance) × GROs (1997 municipal census)	305	537.2459	5,996.971	0	97,156
Firms (finance) × GROs (1992 SNPP)	308	310.974	3,273.774	0	48,124
Finns (construction) × GROs	310	807.2	7,934	0	105,840
Firms (total) × GROs (1992 UDAPSO)	310	59,423.35	489,629.5	0	7,039,824
Firms (total) × GROs (1992 SNPP)	308	42,836.43	431,066.4	0	7,039,824
School attendance × Firms × GROs	304	45,306.47	525,818.8	0	8,700,211
Illiteracy (2002) × Firms × GROs	305	2,835.175	28,537.18	0	46,6802.7
Markets × Firms × GROs	304	0.008533	0.0800603	0	1.105822
Malnutrition × Firms × GROs (1992 SNPP)	292	926,867.7	8,141,260	0	1.24E+08
Malnutrition × Firms × GROs (1997 municipal census)	291	1,625,553	1.26E+07	0	1.51E+08

TABLE 14.—*Continued*

Variable	Obs.	Mean	Std. Dev.	Min	Max
Control Variables					
Altiplano regional dummy	310	0.4741935	0.5001409	0	1
Eastern regional dummy	310	0.2580645	0.4382771	0	1
Rural population (%, 1992)	308	89.4978	110.0184	0	1,947.407
Rural population (%, 2000)	310	0.8147436	0.2803125	0.0037	1
Population speaking indigenous languages only (%, 1992)	310	23.18218	20.93228	0	81.40845
Population speaking indigenous languages only (%, 2001)	310	45.49752	30.71265	0.44	87.40246
High-income households, by housing category (%)	310	21.45342	20.4527	0	85.89342
Percentage of households having a kitchen	310	63.18565	14.03657	15.1	90.72581
Economically inactive population (%)	310	43.51541	10.89542	19.3	84.76659
Central government investment project (FIS) dummy	308	0.4448052	0.4977529	0	1
Local education authority	310	0.5032258	0.500798	0	1

used for the first two periods were not collected in the 2001 census. Hence I drop those Z variables for which updating information does not exist for the last period and estimate with a reduced set of controls. Although a second-best, this is preferable to retaining old information in perpetuity, given significant changes to municipal institutions and economies, as we shall see in the next chapter. Because G_m is left-censored at 0, I use Tobit estimations for equation (1).

The test proceeds as follows. I first estimate a simple base regression (1′) without interaction terms. I then add a firms*civic organizations interaction term, as in (1″). Subsequent estimations include additional interaction terms gradually until we reach the full complement of interactions in model in (1) above.

$$G_m = \alpha + \beta N_m + \gamma F_m + \delta C_m + \xi Z_m + \varepsilon_m \tag{1′}$$

$$G_m = \alpha + \beta N_m + \gamma F_m + \delta C_m + \theta F_m C_m + \xi Z_m + \varepsilon_m \tag{1″}$$

$$(\dots)$$

$$G_m = \alpha + \beta N_m + \gamma F_m + \delta C_m + \zeta N_m F_m + \eta N_m C_m$$
$$+ \theta F_m C_m + \lambda N_m F_m C_m + \xi Z_m + \varepsilon_m \tag{1}$$

Proceeding in this way allows us, first, to determine whether municipal investment was responsive to objective measures of local need in a particular sector, or not, and whether private firms and civic organizations appear to matter at all—that is, whether their presence correlates with investment levels. Gradually adding interaction terms ($1' \rightarrow 1'' \rightarrow 1$) allows us to examine whether coefficients β, γ, and δ remain significant and to compare their magnitude to those of the interaction terms. This permits a more careful exploration of the particular ways that firms and civic organizations affect the responsiveness of government investment decisions. For example, it is possible that firms and/or civic groups mediate information flows, support political competition, or otherwise influence decision makers' priorities individually. Or they may affect public decisions jointly through some mutual interaction, but not individually. We explore these possibilities empirically here. For the sake of brevity I present several specifications for the first time period (1994–96) only and then go straight to the full model for periods two and three.[1]

Coefficient β characterizes central and local investment patterns according to need, where *need* is defined as the marginal utility arising from a particular type of public service, $U'(g)$. This is based on an assumption of decreasing marginal utility of a public service as the level of provision of that service increases. Hence need falls as the stock of g rises, and vice versa. I expect β to be positive and significant when N is measured by a relevant public "bad" (e.g., illiteracy, malnutrition), and negative and significant when measured by the per capita stock of a particular type of infrastructure (e.g., markets per capita). In other words, I interpret a high illiteracy rate as evidence of a municipality's need for additional education investment, whereas relatively many markets per capita implies less need for additional investment in urban infrastructure.

Coefficients γ and δ correspond to the civic and economic factors that underpin local governance. At the simplest level we expect both to be significant, but we can also predict their signs. Our measure of economic heterogeneity and engagement, F, is the total number of private sector firms in a municipality. Ideally we would measure the *concentration* of business activity in a municipality's firms, and their political engagement, which evidence from Viacha and Charagua suggests are what matter. But information on individual firm size (sales, profits, payroll, etc.) is publicly available for very few cities in Bolivia. Hence we must rely on simpler measures that count firms.

We expect F to have two distinct effects: a sector-specific effect and a systemic effect. The term *sector-specific effects* refers to firms' preferences over investments in certain sectors. Hence construction firms, for example, will tend to prefer investment in urban development over other sectors. We expect these coefficients to be significant, with sign varying by sector and firm type. *Systemic effects* refers to the assumption that municipalities with more firms are likely to support a larger number of political parties, and hence greater competition in the local party system. This, in turn, will better allow for the transmission of voters' preferences upward to policymakers. From this effect, we expect to γ be positive.

We measure the degree of civic engagement in the policy process, C, by the number of grassroots organizations (GROs) officially registered in each municipality. Registration is with the prefecture (departmental government) and confers upon a GRO the status of formal representative of the people living in a particular geographic area. Registered GROs are invited to participate in the election of the oversight committee and help draw up a district's municipal development plan, as we saw in Charagua. Case study evidence strongly supports the view that ordinary citizens value investment in education foremost, followed by urban development and health. Hence GROs' sector-specific and systemic effects should have the same sign, and we expect δ to be positive.

The main coefficients of interest, in accordance with the theory, are those of the interaction terms—especially λ, but also ζ, η, and θ. In order of estimation, ζ captures the extent to which local investment is sensitive to need when many private sector firms are present in the local economy. If government responsiveness to local need is dependent on a strong private sector, because of its role in lobbying, funding political parties, or otherwise mediating information flows and political competition, then ζ will be significant and have the same sign as γ. This is the fundamental difference between our interpretations of γ and ζ: whereas γ provides general evidence that the *presence* of firms is a determinant of investment levels, ζ indicates that firms are engaged in the policy-making process, affecting government's response to need.

Similarly, η captures the extent to which municipalities are sensitive to local need as the density of civic organizations increases in society. If government responsiveness to need is dependent on the presence of many civic organizations, because of their role in mobilizing voters and mediating political dialogue, or otherwise facilitating political competition and information flows, then η will be significant, with the same sign as δ. Whereas δ indicates that the mere presence of civic groups affects investment levels, η is an indicator of civic organizations' involvement in the policy-making process.

It is possible that a competitive, responsive local government is dependent on the presence of both factors—many diverse firms and a highly organized civil society—and that neither alone is sufficient. The next term we add, θ, captures this by measuring the effect of interactions between civil society and private firms on per capita investment levels. The theory implies that this condition is sufficient, but it does not clarify whether it is necessary. Our model tests these propositions by adding the term sequentially. If firm-GRO interactions are necessary for responsive government, then θ should be significant and larger in magnitude than γ or δ.

Last, λ captures the extent to which interactions between firms and civic organizations affect the responsiveness of local government to objective indicators of need. This coefficient is the single clearest test of the theory laid out above. If heterogeneous firms and the organizational density of civil society matter, as in the model, their effect is to jointly make municipalities more responsive to local needs as their numbers increase. We expect λ to be significant. Its sign will vary, depending on whether the N variable is a positive or negative indicator of need (as explained above), but the sense should consistently be of increasing sensitivity to need as the numbers of firms and GROs in a municipality rise.

Results

I examine investment patterns in education, urban development, and health. Similar results, omitted for brevity, were obtained for agriculture and water & sanitation.

Education

Table 15 presents results for education investment; let us begin with the base model. The illiteracy rate is positive and significant at the 10 percent level. This implies that local governments invest more in education where the illiteracy rate is higher. I interpret this as evidence that local governments are sensitive to local needs, in line with the findings of chapter 4. The number of firms is negative and significant (1 percent), implying that investment de-

TABLE 15. Education (dependent variable: education investment [Bs.] per 1,000 population)

	Model			
	Base 1994–96	2 1994–96	3 1997–2002	4 2003–7
Need Variable				
Illiteracy rate	496.7*	319.2	2,310.8*	5,351
	(1.840)	(1.010)	(1.830)	(1.400)
Firms and GROs				
Number of firms	−258***	1,867	2,543.8	29,361.4***
	(−3.150)	(1.350)	(0.640)	(2.800)
Number of GROs (legally registered)	119.8**	−13.1	216.4	−1,718.1***
	(2.100)	(−0.100)	(0.700)	(−3.020)
Interaction Terms				
Illiteracy × Firms		−97.5	143.3	−7,748***
		(−1.010)	(0.610)	(−3.330)
Illiteracy × GROs		5.11	−8.79	42.8
		(1.280)	(−0.760)	(1.270)
Firms × GROs		12.7**	23.8*	−129.8***
		(2.320)	(1.920)	(−3.240)
# School attendance × Firms × GROs		−0.219**	−0.433*	35#***
		(−2.500)	(−1.720)	(3.650)
Control Variables				
Altiplano regional dummy	7,161.6	7,446.4	−8,675.8	−69,179.7
	(1.220)	(1.260)	(−0.630)	(−1.540)
Eastern regional dummy	1,984.4	−547.5	4,443	−166,393.2
	(0.310)	(−0.080)	(0.170)	(−1.550)
Rural population (%)	−35.7	−58.1	58,110.6	
	(−0.390)	(−0.610)	(1.520)	
Population speaking indigenous languages only (%)	−116.3	−187.7	−918.6**	−6,328***
	(−0.510)	(−0.810)	(−2.250)	(−4.150)
High-income households, by housing category (%)	−93.4	−119.8	130.3	
	(−0.700)	(−0.880)	(0.330)	
Percentage of households having a kitchen	300.3	288.3	−298.3	
	(1.590)	(1.480)	(−0.400)	
Economically inactive population (%)	−201.2	−181.6	−634.5	
	(−0.810)	(−0.730)	(−0.830)	
Central government investment project (FIS) dummy	10,868.1***	10,070.4**	12,419.5	
	(2.640)	(2.500)	(0.890)	
Local education authority dummy	7,824.2*	8,177.5*	5,527.1	
	(1.690)	(1.770)	(0.420)	
Constant	11,582.3	20,258.9	85,737	746,009***
	(0.470)	(0.720)	(1.540)	(6.170)
Pseudo R^2	−0.0367	−0.0427	−0.0699	0.1845
N	293	293	302	304

Note: Tobit estimation with robust standard errors; *t*-statistics in parentheses. *, **, *** = coefficients significant at the 10%, 5% and 1% levels. # = Illiteracy rate (2001) substitutes for school attendance in NFC interaction term during final period.

creases where firms are more numerous. The number of GROs, by contrast, is positive and significant (5 percent), implying the opposite. The two coefficients are the same order of magnitude. They imply that a one-standard-deviation increase in the number of firms reduces investment by Bs. 6,889 per thousand inhabitants, while the same increase in GROs increases education investment by Bs. 6,290 per thousand, leaving the two reasonably evenly matched.

Model 2 adds the full set of interaction terms. The illiteracy rate is no longer significant on its own, nor are firms or GROs. The NF and NC terms are also insignificant, implying that need is not communicated through the actions or voices of either set of actors independently. Of our main variables of interest, only the last two are significant. The FC term is positive, implying that the interaction of firms and GROs leads to greater education investment. The three-way interaction term (NFC) uses school attendance as the N variable in order to avoid multicollinearity with the other three interaction terms. Because attendance is a negative indicator of need, we expect λ to be negative; it is—significant at the 5 percent level—implying that investment is responsive to need where firms and GROs interact through local politics to sustain accountable government.

The full model for 1997–2002 is very similar. The interaction of firms and GROs leads to higher education investment, and their joint effect makes investment more responsive to objective measures of need. Illiteracy is once again significant on its own, implying that need affects local investment even when GROs and firms do not abound. Only the final period produces interesting variation: investment increases strongly with the number of firms but decreases (more modestly) with the number of GROs, the opposite of what we expect. The NF term, negative and significant (1 percent), seems to rebut this, implying that firms decrease investment where need is greater. The effect of firms and GROs acting together further decreases investment, in opposition to the earlier periods. But this only seems to apply to municipalities where literacy is already high. The NFC term now includes the literacy rate in place of attendance (because of data availability for 2003–7). Hence we expect it to be positive, and indeed it is positive and significant at the 1 percent level. The interaction of firms and GROs *increases* education investment in municipalities where need is high.

These results imply that since 1994 the interaction of many private firms with a dense population of civic organizations has made local government more responsive to educational needs. GROs and firms raise educational investment through their interactions with each other. Their joint effect makes investment across Bolivia more responsive to local need. Interactions between private and civic actors are the single most important determinant of municipal responsiveness and behavior. For 1994–96, a one-standard-deviation increase in firm-GRO interactions yields an increase of Bs. 76,162 per thousand inhabitants. A one-standard-deviation decrease in enrollment—given a rich context of firm-GRO interactions—yields an even larger Bs. 115,154 rise in educational investment per thousand inhabitants. These amounts rise significantly over time, resulting in huge effects on investment sums after 2003: a one-standard-deviation increase in illiteracy given dense firm-GRO interactions yields Bs. 998,795 more investment per thousand inhabitants. Where educational need is low, by contrast, a one-standard-deviation increase in firm-GRO interactions decreases investment by Bs. 779,610. All of these results are robust to different specifications, including larger and smaller sets of controls. Evidence from education thus strongly supports the theoretical model of government developed above.

Urban Development

Our measure of need in urban development is markets per capita, a negative indicator, which is positive and significant (5 percent) in all three models for 1994–96. This implies that investment was lower in places less endowed with urban infrastructure—a regressive pattern. The positive, significant (1 percent) coefficient on the high-income household control variable confirms this finding. The number of (construction) firms is associated with increasing investment, as are GROs, albeit at a lower rate and only in the base model. The *FC* term in model 2 is significant (5 percent) and positive, implying that firms and civic groups jointly increase urban investment. But this effect disappears in model 3. The regressive effect is confirmed when we add the *NF* interaction term, which is positive and significant (10 percent).

Model 3—the full test of our theory—shows that firms[2] have an independent effect on urban investment, and GROs have none. The interaction of firms, GROs, and need is notable not only for its size—more than half the size of *N* on its own—but more so because of its sign. While firms are pressing municipalities strongly to increase investments in urban infrastructure that are regressive, civic organizations mostly succeed in counter-

TABLE 16. Urban Development (dependent variable: urban development investment [Bs.] per 1,000 population)

	Model				
	Base 1994–96	2 1994–96	3 1994–96	4 1997–2002	5 2003–7
Need Variable					
Number of markets per capita	190,360.2** (2.370)	183,631.2** (2.300)	229,153.22** (2.210)	−57,771.1 (−0.160)	−47,078.8 (−0.130)
Firms and GROs					
Number of firms	220.1*** (5.420)	124.2** (2.450)	6.8** (2.390)	−1.41 (−0.310)	−179 (−0.570)
Number of GROs (legally registered)	127.7* (1.850)	105.2 (1.590)	93.3 (1.490)	137.6 (1.050)	−8.98 (−0.090)
Interaction Terms					
Markets × Firms			4,323,294* (1.690)	45,985,490*** (6.300)	−1,893,897* (−1.840)
Markets × GROs			−5,147.5 (−0.780)	−27,042.6 (−0.820)	14,681 (0.330)
Firms × GROs		0.0119** (1.980)	0.146 (0.370)	−1.34 *** (−2.810)	0.679 (0.480)
Markets × Firms × GROs			−138,560.9** (−2.190)	−148,192.6 (−1.020)	117,847*** (5.340)
Control Variables					
Altiplano regional dummy	−12,527.8** (−2.250)	−12,306.2** (−2.230)	−13,338.4** (−2.360)	7,236.3 (0.510)	−19,757 (−1.580)
Eastern regional dummy	−4,559.9 (−0.710)	−5,318 (−0.820)	−6,793 (−1.030)	982 (0.050)	−46,050.9** (−2.020)
Rural population (%)	−5.26 (−0.420)	−5.89 (−0.470)	−6.18 (−0.510)	−102,176.8*** (−3.090)	
Population speaking indigenous languages only (%)	−93.1 (−0.800)	−101.2 (−0.880)	−108.6 (−0.940)	203.7 (0.510)	−561.5** (−2.000)
High-income households, by housing category (%)	895.2*** (5.690)	847.3*** (5.370)	791.4*** (5.060)	337.7 (0.670)	
Percentage of households having a kitchen	−20.5 (−0.130)	−20 (−0.130)	−18 (−0.110)	20.1 (0.050)	
Economically inactive population (%)	−234.7 (−0.950)	−217.6 (−0.890)	−245.1 (−1.010)	111.5 (0.120)	
Central government investment project (FIS) dummy	−10,244.7** (−2.310)	−10,187.6** (−2.320)	−10,520.1** (−2.400)	−20,087.3 (−1.580)	
Constant	45,394.9*** (2.820)	46,766.8*** (2.940)	50,290.8*** (3.160)	191,975.6*** (2.900)	145,285.2*** (6.550)
Pseudo R^2	−0.1252	−0.1288	−0.1358	−0.4959	−0.0211
N	293	293	292	304	301

Note: Tobit estimation with robust standard errors; *t*-statistics in parentheses. *, **, *** = coefficients significant at the 10%, 5%, and 1% levels.

acting that through their interactions with firms. A one-standard-deviation increase in the total number of firms leads to Bs. 14,998 more of urban investment per thousand inhabitants. By comparison, a one-standard-deviation increase in the number of markets per capita, given a dense population of firms and GROs, leads to a Bs. 11,099 *decrease* per thousand.

Both need and firms lose their significance by 1997–2002, although they remain jointly significant and with a large coefficient. This implies that the presence of many firms makes urban investment regressive in terms of need. By contrast, the interaction of firms with GROs counteracts this to some extent: a one-standard-deviation increase in the *NF* term increases urban investment by Bs. 87,372 per thousand inhabitants; a one-standard-deviation increase in the *FC* term *decreases* investment by Bs. 10,631 per thousand inhabitants. The three-way interaction term is not significant for this period.

Model 5, covering 2003–7, is similar to model 4 but with an interesting change of signs. The *NF* term is significant (10 percent) but now negative, implying that the presence of firms decreases investment where urban infrastructure is abundant. This is in marked contrast to the previous effect of firms; perhaps firms have discovered more lucrative contracts in a different sector of public investment. Also, the *FC* term has lost its significance in favor of the *NFC* term (1 percent), which is now positive. This implies that the interaction of firms and GROs increases investment where urban infrastructure is abundant. This coefficient, in combination with that of the *NF* term, suggests that it is the marginal effect of GROs that is regressive, overcoming firms' tendencies toward progressivity in need.

These effects must occur through the political system, the forum where competing demands meet each other, trade-offs are made, and bargains struck. The intent of GROs in the first period, and firms in the third, is presumably to reduce budget allocations to the benefit of other sectors, such as education or sanitation. The system of public decision making, therefore, has built-in mechanisms for moderating the ability of particular actors to pursue their self-interest. All of these results are robust to different specifications, including larger and smaller sets of controls. Evidence from urban development also strongly supports the theoretical model of government developed above.

Health

Like education, health investment between 1994 and 1996 is responsive to objective indicators of need, rising as child malnutrition increases. (Malnutrition in Bolivia is associated much more with micronutrients and nutritional balance more generally, rather than caloric intake; it is thus susceptible to simple medical interventions.) The presence of GROs is associated with higher investment in the base model, though this loses significance as terms are added. Firms have no apparent effect. A one-standard-deviation increase in GROs leads to an estimated Bs. 2,410 more health investment per thousand inhabitants. The independent effect of GROs on investment disappears in favor of the FC term when the latter is added—itself positive and significant (5 percent), albeit relatively small in size. This is confirmed in model 3, which includes the three-way interaction term—also positive and significant at the 1 percent level, and also of small size. A one-standard-deviation increase in firm-GRO interactions yields an estimated Bs. 3,569 more health investment per thousand inhabitants. An increase of one standard deviation in the malnutrition rate, given a dense population of firms and GROs, leads to Bs. 5,829 more investment per thousand.

Malnutrition loses its significance during 1997–2002, although need continues to steer investment via its interaction with firms and GROs. The coefficient on the NFC term implies Bs. 127,004 additional investment per thousand inhabitants for a one-standard-deviation rise in malnutrition, in an environment dense with firms and civic groups. This effect is partially offset by a more general tendency of firms and GROs to decrease investment in health. We see in model 5 that malnutrition regains independent significance (5 percent) during the final period but this time with a negative sign, implying a regressive general pattern of investment. The independent effect of firms and GROs is to reduce investment generally, but to increase it in municipalities where malnutrition is high (NF and NC terms). Where firms and civic groups interact, investment in health increases. The NFC term is insignificant.

The evidence implies that the primary way for firms and civic organizations to affect local policy is through their interactions with each other, which result in an unambiguous collective preference for greater health investment in two of our three periods. These interaction effects are larger in resource terms than the residual impact of the need variable on investment

TABLE 17. Health (dependent variable: health investment [Bs.] per 1,000 population)

	Model				
	Base 1994–96	2 1994–96	3 1994–96	4 1997–2002	5 2003–7
Need Variable					
Child malnutrition rate (total)	289.5*	288.2*	359.3**	−183	−2,687.4**
	(1.840)	(1.850)	(1.990)	(−0.530)	(−2.070)
Firms and GROs					
Number of firms	−54.1	−260.5	833.5	4,250.9	−29.4*
	(−1.300)	(−1.000)	(0.850)	(1.140)	(−1.770)
Number of GROs (legally	45.9*	26.7	117.8	41.1	−1,337.9*
registered)	(1.720)	(0.990)	(1.520)	(0.210)	(−1.860)
Interaction Terms					
Malnutrition ✗ Firms			−34	−210.6	48.1***
			(−1.120)	(−1.180)	(3.460)
Malnutrition × GROs			−2.88	0.106	37.3*
			(−1.220)	(0.020)	(1.840)
Firms × GROs		0.00828**	−3.19	−0.28*	0.0834**
		(2.100)	(−1.320)	(−1.730)	(2.220)
Malnutrition × Firms × GROs			0.000716***	0.0156*	0.00133
			(3.490)	(1.770)	(1.020)
Control Variables					
Altiplano regional dummy	−7,368.7**	−7,504.3**	−7,278.2**	5,098.9	−56,048.3*
	(−2.266)	(−2.300)	(−2.230)	(0.890)	(−1.690)
Eastern regional dummy	−3,468.2	−4,139.1	−3,950.9	−3,589.8	−63,153.3
	(−0.870)	(−1.030)	(−0.970)	(−0.430)	(−0.820)
Rural population (%)	15	12.2	18.5	−8,207.4	
	(0.390)	(0.290)	(0.450)	(−0.440)	
Population speaking indigenous	−246.1**	−250.2**	−245.9**	−286.4**	−1,644.5*
languages only (%)	(−2.420)	(−2.470)	(−2.400)	(−2.540)	(−1.910)
High-income households, by	−37.3	−52.6	−63.9	−72.3	
housing category (%)	(−0.570)	(−0.790)	(−0.930)	(−0.380)	
Percentage of households	114.5	115.7	124.5	30.3	
having a kitchen	(1.370)	(1.380)	(1.450)	(0.180)	
Economically inactive	−156.6	−145.9	−142	262	
population (%)	(−1.610)	(−1.500)	(−1.450)	(1.080)	
Central government investment	1,011.6	1,268.5	1,063.9	2,228.9	
project (FIS) dummy	(0.520)	(0.640)	(0.540)	(0.400)	
Constant	5,981.8	6,911.6	3,382.2	42,399.4	347,283.8***
	(0.600)	(0.670)	(0.300)	(1.430)	(3.250)
Pseudo R^2	−0.0254	−0.0287	−0.0296	−0.0346	−0.6754
N	283	283	283	292	287

Note: Tobit estimation with robust standard errors; *t*-statistics in parentheses. *, **, *** = coefficients significant at the 10%, 5%, and 1% levels.

across all three periods. This implies that whatever else makes investment sensitive to health needs is somewhat less important than the interaction of economic and civic actors through the political system. All of these results are robust to different specifications, including larger and smaller sets of controls. Thus evidence from health also strongly supports the theoretical model of government developed above.

Across all three sectors our statistical models are quite similar for the first two periods but significantly different for the third. This is less surprising when placed in context. Like many primary exporters, Bolivia experienced a natural resource boom after 2002. Its effects on municipalities were exaggerated by changes in fiscal transfer rules that favored municipalities where mines, oil wells, and so forth were located. Hence the pattern of resource flows to municipalities, which changed slowly and symmetrically between 1994 and 2002, changed enormously thereafter. This underpins the periodization used here but also makes comparisons across periods more difficult.

In addition, the sustained high levels of investment in education and urban development after 1994 fundamentally changed municipalities' infrastructure endowments, and then—in all likelihood—citizens' preferences. Put simply, after a decade of building schools and fixing the town square, people's priorities shifted. Hence it is not surprising that the statistical models that seek to explain local decision making look different after 2002. These considerations, plus the lack of availability of good control variables (Z) from the 2001 census, lead me to give more weight to evidence from 1994–96 and 1997–2002, and less weight to the later years.

Conclusion

Qualitative information set out in the preceding chapters provides rich, nuanced evidence that our theory can indeed explain the quality of government in Viacha and Charagua. Quantitative evidence from the universe of Bolivian municipalities constitutes a less detailed but much more extensive and general argument that the theory can explain municipal behavior throughout the country. By weaving the two strands together, we can achieve a higher-order empirical test of the theory than either alone can achieve.

The theory proposes that local government responsiveness and accountability are primarily the product of the openness and substantive competition of its politics. The quality of a municipality's politics, in turn, emerges endogenously as the joint product of the lobbying and political engagement of its firms and other economic actors, and the organizational density and ability of its civil society. Where many, diverse economic interests support a variety of political currents, and society is organized into intermediating groups capable of solving the collective action problem, government will have a strong tendency toward responsiveness and accountability to citizens.

These predictions are supported by small-N qualitative evidence. Are they supported by large-N evidence as well? Yes—results from the universe of Bolivian municipalities mirror our qualitative findings, but on a much larger scale. Econometric evidence shows that where a large number of firms interacted through the political system with an organizationally rich civil society, local policy decisions were responsive to the objective needs and subjective preferences of voters. Firms and civic organizations proved to be important determinants of local decision making, and our empirical strategy allows us to identify how. Both firms and GROs affected how local governments prioritize local needs—via lobbying, voter mobilization, or otherwise mediating information flows and helping to sustain political competition. They not only pressed local governments for the specific policies they prefer, often at cross purposes, but also interacted directly with each other in the policy-making process.

These interactions are independently significant not only in the narrow statistical sense but substantively as well, in the sense that they resolved the competing priorities of different actors. For example, firms worked to deprioritize investment in education across Bolivia, while GROs did the opposite. The tension was resolved when firms and GROs interacted directly through the local political system, resulting in huge investment increases in those places where need was greatest. In urban development, by contrast, both firms and GROs worked to increase investment in a way that was regressive in terms of need. But the effect of their mutual interactions went in the opposite direction in 1994–96, increasing investment where infrastructure was scarce, and decreasing it where infrastructure was abundant.

In a similar vein, by 2003–7 urban investment decreased where firms and infrastructure were abundant. But the effect of many firm-and-GRO interactions was to increase investment where infrastructure was abundant. Not only was the interaction of these actors significant, it changed outcomes. This suggests a realistic picture of a healthy local democracy in which different interests compete through the political system, wielding varying amounts of influence over different issues, and voters are able to influence government through their civil institutions, providing an effective counterweight to the power of private firms and economic interests.

The data also provide significant evidence that a combination of many heterogeneous economic actors and an organizationally rich, capable civil society is not only sufficient but necessary for government to be responsive to citizens' needs. This is apparent for education, where our results imply that a municipality endowed with both factors will respond to need with large investment flows. The independent effects of GROs and firms on need responsiveness are nil for two of the three periods, and the need variable on its own becomes insignificant. The case is even stronger for urban development, where the influence of firms and GROs on investment only shows responsiveness to local need (i.e., the sign turns negative) with the addition of the three-way interaction term in model 3. The evidence shows that firms press municipalities for urban investments that are regressive. The channel through which GROs counter this—with a surprisingly large effect—is the joint channel, and no other.

The evidence is similar, although less dramatic, for health. In resource terms, the larger part of municipalities' needs-responsiveness operates through GRO-firm interactions, although there is a significant residual. Adding GRO-firm interaction terms (models 2 and 3) causes the GRO term to lose significance, implying that the coefficient is 0. We conclude that in health the combination of economic and civic actors is sufficient for responsive government but not strictly necessary, and that the evidence is weaker than for education or urban development.

These results are important beyond their face value, because they allow us to fine-tune the theory in a way that qualitative evidence alone cannot, reinforcing the value of a mixed-methods approach. Absent an encompassing interest, the theory does not provide a strong argument about whether both causal factors (economic interests and civic organizations; see chapter 6, figure 32) are required to produce responsive, accountable government, or either alone might (sometimes) be sufficient. Qualitative evidence provides too few degrees of freedom to distinguish between these possibilities. But quantitative evidence can discriminate: both are required. Our econometric models imply that firms and GROs interact through the political system to shape policy. Political competition resolves their competing priorities, producing outputs that are responsive to local needs.

Given strong results supporting the theory of a diversity of economic interests and civic organizations, and an inability to test the encompassing interest theory with large-N data, the latter must be relegated to secondary importance in this study until such time as it may be empirically validated. At this stage, it is important to acknowledge that the data come from one of the poorest countries, and one of the weakest public bureaucracies, in the Western hemisphere. In a sense, it is remarkable that such data can say anything at all about a set of nuanced, complex relationships between disparate social actors and the responsiveness of municipal policy. More abundant, higher-quality data from richer countries should produce stronger results.

The understanding of local government developed here is crucial for understanding the effects of reform more generally. Bolivian decentralization confounded the opponents of reform by empowering local governments that—not always, but more often than not—proved responsive to citizens' objective needs. Our results point to why. By creating local institutional spaces where civic and economic interests compete to influence policy, decentralization made many local authorities beholden to local voters. It put real power over public resources in the hands of ordinary citizens throughout the national territory. These citizens took advantage of the competitive dynamics between firms and civil society to hold their governments to account. The net results were large changes in national resource flows, and large changes in national policy choices.

CHAPTER 8

Return to the Extremes

Chapters 2 and 3 chronicled how the same institutional shock produced very different kinds of local governance in two extreme cases of municipal performance. Did these initial responses persist over time? Did the bad get better, or did the good degrade? This chapter returns to Viacha and Charagua in 2009 to examine how governance in each municipality evolved over the subsequent 12 years. Doing so allows us to examine the differential effects that decentralization has over time—that is, when the shock is still fresh versus later on, after the incentives and patterns of behavior it creates have become routine. It allows us to track changes over time in specific social and political dynamics that prove to be important to the quality of local government. And it allows us to test the robustness of the theory developed in chapter 6 much more rigorously, using a large quantity of deep, nuanced evidence on how municipal responsiveness and accountability change over time, based on qualitative data gathered after the theory was first proposed.

Viacha in 2009

Twelve years later the visitor's first impression of Viacha is of a central square now graced with statues, large trees, and abundant flowers and greenery, in striking contrast to its sad, gray past. Behind it stands a new, modern municipal building that is much larger, cleaner, and more functional than the one it replaced. The city center is modestly busier, with more shops, restaurants, and traffic than before, although this difference is not large. At the municipal level, the 12-year interlude saw both contraction and growth. In 2002 Districts Four, Five, and Six seceded to form two new municipalities, Jesús de Machaqa and San Andrés de Machaqa. Viacha shrank away from the Peruvian frontier and was left with four districts, only one of them rural. But the population lost was fully replaced through urban growth. Whereas before Viacha's outer neighborhoods reached tenuously toward the outskirts of El Alto, one city almost petering out before the other began, now their urban sprawls jut into one another chaotically, and only neighborhood locals can find the boundary.

Most of this growth is in District Seven, which straddles the road northward toward La Paz. In eight years it quintupled in size, from fewer than 6,000 inhabitants in 2001 to more than 30,000 in 2009.[1] With 70 civic organizations, it was, according to the president of its FEJUVE, "a little Viacha that will soon be bigger than Viacha."[2] But municipal services did not keep up with this growth. "There is no potable water or sewerage, and 20–30% of the district still has no electricity," the assistant mayor protested. "Public services are worse than in rural areas. . . . Our wells abut our septic tanks, and so we defecate in our 'potable' water."[3] Afflicted by the strains of its own rapid growth, and feeling itself abandoned by Viacha, it is not surprising that District Seven wanted to follow in the footsteps of the Machaqas and become its own municipality. "We already have the importance and size for it," the FEJUVE president insisted.[4]

Other aspects of Viachan life proved more enduring. Twelve years later the municipal coliseum was still unfinished, a brooding "cement monument" to the kickbacks of Callisaya and his ephemeral successors.[5] But under the current mayor the end, at last, was in sight. SOBOCE undertook a technical completion study, allowing the municipality to contract the specific works required before the facility could be inaugurated. And in terms of its social character too, Viacha remained "a complicated, difficult city. The people are conflictive and they like to fight."[6] Another impartial observer agreed. "People in District Seven are demanding and conflictive. Those in Districts One and Two are unhappy with everything. They've tried to overthrow the mayor each of these last five years."[7]

But in 2009 Viachan society, complicated and conflictive as ever, was enjoying local government of a very different quality from the graft and paralysis of 1997.

Local Governance in Viacha, 2009

"The electrification of Viacha's 63 rural communities is now complete," said Luis Calle Callisaya, head of the Viachan Agrarian Association, reporting a huge change in the lives of his constituents with obvious satisfaction.

With respect to potable water, most communities now have it and the rest are due to have it soon. . . . The municipality also has programs to vaccinate livestock financed 50% by the municipality, 50% by farmers, and also livestock and plant health programs. Before there were no such programs.[8]

In urban areas too, the municipality was trying to attract private investment through an industrial park and a new zoning ordinance, as well as exploit its natural gas and abundant electricity supplies.[9] Members of the Oversight Committee praised its efforts: "The municipality does a lot. It has captured resources from external sources [i.e., NGOs and donors] for hospitals, etc. Money that enters Viacha is put to work."[10] As a result of such efforts, municipal expenditures and investments nearly tripled between 2002 and 2008, from Bs. 13 million to Bs. 37 million per year (Lamas 2009). As a result, many municipal services were upgraded. For example, 70 percent of schools now had an Internet connection.[11] The contrast with previous local administrations is striking. "Under some previous mayors we saw no civil works, no projects. Now there are lots—streets, pavements, etc."[12]

It is not only the quantity of investment, but the accountability mechanisms that accompany it, that impress. In both the setting of investment priorities and the conduct of oversight, participation was broad and genuine in Viacha. "The OC meets every week to report on municipal progress and problems. . . . The municipality sits down with the OC and agrees how to proceed. The OC invites GROs to talk to municipal technical staff, and so they find out what's going on."[13] This is a stunning reversal of previous practice, and one that was confirmed by rural and urban community leaders, OC members, municipal officials, central government officials, and NGO professionals working in Viacha. In the planning of public services and investments, "everyone works well and together here," assured urban OC members Flores and Merlo.[14] According to Calle, the agrarian leader, "I call town hall meetings and invite the mayor, and the mayor goes and promises to attend to communities' problems. And then he follows through. So the municipality is responsive to community needs."[15] The results of such improved processes were visible and popular among Viachans. "Every year Annual Operating Plans (AOPs) improve in quality. Each community has resources budgeted in the AOP,"[16] said Calle. "Local authorities have all the will in the world," concurred Oscar Soto, of the Oversight Committee, even if "the money doesn't stretch" to cover all the municipality's needs.[17] *Viacheños* understood that their local government was working for them, not least because they could participate in the planning procedure, and they approved.

Independent authorities approved too. "The municipality respects all the norms and rules" that it should, assured Yajaira Barriga, local head of a prominent NGO.[18] This includes supporting education services but avoiding interference in questions of curriculum, teacher performance, and so forth in local schools.[19] The most general stamp of approval came from three successive national audits of local government performance, each of which produced positive reports for the mayor and his government,[20]—final proof, if one were needed, that Viacha had made a clean break with its past.

The Transformation of Governance

How did such a remarkable transformation of governance in Viacha come about? To understand, it is useful first to set the scene. Local government was highly unstable between 1995 and 2004, with a total of eight mayors in ten years. Politics was conflict-driven and prone to crisis. This produced deep problems of both governance and public management. "No one knew what the Law of Popular Participation was. People thought the municipal projects they received were mayoral gifts. And until 2004 there were many phantom civil works, lots of corruption, etc."[21]

The period immediately preceding the 2004 local elections is representative of the kinds of pathologies that plagued Viacha. In September 2004 Mayor Isabel Tapia was toppled for misuse of public funds involving a school lunch program. The executing agency withheld its counterpart; it provided school lunches for three months, and then closed the program and disappeared.[22] Tapia had had the support of Viacha's 63 rural communities and 9 higher-level associations. But then "the people rose up. It was a violent confrontation—there were very nearly deaths."[23] Urban residents, already upset that the contract had been awarded to small-scale rural producers from District Three, revolted. The political battle that followed pitted the city against the countryside. Tensions ran high. "In 2004 you could not walk through town wearing a poncho and *chicote* [a traditional rural whip],"[24] said the municipal council president. In the end Tapia was kicked out of office, as was the mayor who followed her.[25]

Unfortunately Viacha's problems were not limited to public scandals. According to the municipality's governance specialist, who began work under the Tapia regime,

Viacha lacked professionals capable of administering a municipality. Tapia reported to the people without exact numbers. This *does not* happen now. We had no internal regulations, norms, job descriptions, etc. The current administration had to do all of that. The current mayor is very professional. Viacha has become very transparent—there's nothing hidden here. The mayor reports every four months, as required. If he's asked for more information, he provides it. Tapia never reported anything.[26]

In other words, the local government calamity described in previous sections continued, with different mayors and different misadventures, through 2004. Under revolving-door mayors, Viachans became accustomed to crassly unresponsive, inefficient, corrupt administrations.

How was such a state of affairs put right? The story begins with a political neophyte called Arsenio Lamas. With a master's degree in engineering, Lamas is a highly educated professional, especially by Viachan standards. He had years of experience working in the SOBOCE factory, but this was his first experience of public administration. Nonetheless he led the transformation of government in Viacha. Here is the story in his own words, corroborated in all its essentials by independent observers with a variety of political and organizational affiliations.

Viacha was ungovernable. Mayors were frequently toppled, there was a lack of transparency and a lack of administration. Samuel Doria Medina [owner of SOBOCE and head of the Unidad Nacional (UN) political party] asked me to undertake a special mission: to change course and turn Viacha into a credible, honest municipality—a leader in the region. So we set about restructuring the municipality's administration and finances in 2005. Municipal staffing became competitive, based on qualifications. We implemented all of the laws, norms, and systems of administration, personnel, and finance that are required by law [but had never been done]. We chose the best local people to work with us. We instituted transparency, publishing spending plans for each of Viacha's four districts. These are disaggregated further to the community level where local priorities are determined, and the municipality then invests in those projects up to the budgeted ceilings.[27]

The entry of Lamas and the UN into town hall brought with it much greater support from SOBOCE, including technical and material support for civil works. Lamas also put great emphasis on training his competitively hired personnel, with training programs for new hires every Monday during an employee's first year and once a month thereafter.[28] A great deal of effort and attention were also given to

> transparency, communication, and participation in municipal affairs. Every year the HAM publishes the Annual Operating Plan—what it wants to do, and at the end of the year the Yearly Record—what it did. The OC reports independently on municipal performance via its Public Report. Previous mayors escaped out the back door. But not during these last 4 years—now the mayor faces the demands and complaints of the public, and responds.[29]

As a result, different observers agreed, municipal finances became much more transparent. Schools, for example, now knew how much money was assigned to them.[30] The municipality was aided in its efforts by CIPCA, the Center for the Investigation and Promotion of the Peasantry, an NGO with expertise in institution building for participation and accountability. CIPCA supported the municipality via its Pillars of Good Governance project, focusing on three areas: (1) transparency in municipal administration, (2) institutionalization of the spaces of dialogue, and (3) the efficient use of public resources.[31]

Transparency, communication, and participation—admirable goals in themselves—permitted additional, deeper changes of governance, as Lamas notes.

> We were able to gain the trust and participation of Viacheños committed to change. And we also changed the pattern of political discourse and competition in Viacha, to one that is professional and based on facts. Before there were people who specialized in toppling mayors with lies—for example, school headmasters who played dirty politics. We began responding directly to these accusations in press conferences with documents and facts that unveiled the lies. In one case, for example, a headmistress denounced me. I invited her to a public meeting, where I arrived armed with facts and documentation. She did not dare to appear.[32]

Not surprisingly, objective measures of the quality of local governance increased dramatically. A 2009 UNDP study of governance indicators ranked Viacha fifth in the department, and in the top one-sixth of municipalities nationwide (Ayala Sánchez 2009). Perhaps the most convincing evidence of a change of governance in Viacha is that Lamas was the first mayor in 20 years to complete his term. Viachan voters could see what their government was doing, much of which they themselves had decided. They had material evidence that corruption had decreased[33] and could see that public employees who continued in the bad old ways faced consequences: "One employee tried [to extract kickbacks], but he was fired and charged with corruption."[34] They saw many more public works built each year of Lamas's tenure than in the past.[35] And so when—inevitably in Viacha—his enemies tried to overthrow him, voters and civic organizations resisted. They did not follow agitators into the streets. Civic leaders worked to defuse conflict, lower tempers, and allow the municipality to govern.

This last observation raises an interesting point about social learning and governance. The story of Viacha can be told simply, as one respondent did.

> The Law of Popular Participation was traumatic for, I think, all municipalities. Money came into Viacha and the municipality didn't know what to do with all that money. The municipality lacked capacity, experience. It was a huge shock—before 1994 they had maybe 12 employees. Bad administration, malfeasance, and corruption ensued, and so the mayor was kicked out. The following one also couldn't manage and was also kicked out, and on and on. But there has been a process of maturation over the past 12 years.[36]

This maturation goes well beyond the person of the mayor, or even his employees. The more important learning that occurred in Viacha is not reflected on anyone's CV. It concerns the knowledge of municipal norms and procedures, and the *voters' own* expectations of how public officials should behave and perform. In 1994 Viacheños understood little of what a municipal government was for and had no notion of how it should operate. Now all that has changed. In the words of Calle, "The people are awake now."[37]

If the election of Lamas was the catalyst for change in Viacha, how did this nonpolitician win? What deeper factors collaborated with the wholesale transformation that ensued? To answer these questions we now probe deeper into Viacha's political economy using the same analytical categories employed above: the private sector, political parties and elections, and community and grassroots organizations.

Private Sector

In 1997 one could not have explained the performance of local government in Viacha without referring centrally to the role of the CBN bottling plant. The only other firm of comparable size and importance, SOBOCE, remained aloof from local affairs in self-imposed isolation. Other, medium-sized and smaller firms, mostly strung along the highway to La Paz, ignored the municipality and were content to be ignored by it.

Returning in 2009, the most important, and startling, change was the demise of the CBN. The founder, owner, and guiding force behind the CBN, Max Fernandez, had died in an airplane crash in 1995, beginning a period of uncertainty for the company. In 2000 Fernandez's heirs sold a controlling majority to Quilmes, an Argentine brewery, which shut down the bottling plant and severed the company's umbilical link to the UCS political party. "That ended the UCS' political presence in Viacha."[38] Its place was taken by the CBN's alter ego, SOBOCE, which emerged from seclusion around 2004 to reengage with local public life. SOBOCE executive Marcos López tells the story.

> SOBOCE has tripled its output in recent years. We ceded ground to the CBN in Viacha because we had very serious production problems around 1995. We had to import cement to cover our production deficits. Because of this, SOBOCE had neither time for nor interest in politics. Only in 2001, when production began to grow and we solved the company's financial problems, were we able to respond to the people of Viacha's demands for more cooperation. This coincided with the company's new Corporate Social Responsibility (CSR) policy. Beginning five or six years ago, the company now allocates money, structure, processes, etc. towards carrying out an orderly CSR. During that time it also happened that the CBN withdrew from politics.[39]

The cement company's withdrawal from public life in the 1990s, leaving the field clear for the CBN to dominate and distort local politics, was neither accidental nor idiosyncratic, but rather a product of serious internal technical and commercial pressures. Once these were resolved, the firm returned to the public arena to pursue its interests. And these interests were significant. As López explained, the factory has been in Viacha for 84 years and produces 70 to 80 percent of SOBOCE's national output.[40] With 309 well-paid employees, and over 1,500 more indirectly employed, the plant was important for the city as well. This mutual importance was reflected in the 10 percent of its profits that the company dedicated to CSR, half of which it spent in Viacha.[41]

The way the company organized its CSR was symptomatic of deeper differences between the cement and beer firms. SOBOCE maintained five-year covenants with Viacha for the support of street building.[42] It contributed material, funds, and technical expertise to public projects in an orderly, planned way; it did not respond to sudden requests for money, trucks, or men from city hall. Although it supported the UN political party's campaigns, it tried to demarcate a clear line between its business and the political activities of its owner.[43] It was a professionally managed firm that approached its dealings with the municipality in a professional way.

Political Parties and Elections

As is the case for most of Bolivia, the "traditional" political parties that dominated the 1990s have mostly expired. Not one survived on the 2009 Municipal Council; whereas before Viacha's seven seats were shared out between the UCS, Condepa, and the MNR, now it was the UN (4), the Association of Progressive Communities (ACP, 1), the Indigenous Pachacuti Movement (MIP, 1), and President Evo Morales's Movement Towards Socialism (MAS, 1) that held power. "The older parties—MNR, MIR, ADN, etc.—no longer exist in Viacha. . . . [They] have no support."[44] And political preferences continued to change. "The MAS now has 80% of the voting intentions in Viacha," says Marcos López, a point on which all interviewees agreed.

The appeal of the MAS was based on two overriding factors: indigenous identity politics focused on the powerful figure of Evo Morales, which echoed very loudly in both rural and urban areas, and the access to state largesse that a MAS affiliation brought. The people of the altiplano voted MAS because they saw themselves reflected in the party, and after 500 years of Spanish and *criollo* rule this was a powerful motivator. They also voted MAS because of the health and education programs instituted by the Morales government, which were quite popular with poor Bolivians.[45] But many feared that Viacha was shut out of additional national programs because of their mayor's party. "The municipality has a number of project proposals that have been rejected by the national government due to 'technical errors,'" was one much-echoed view,[46] prompting many to change their vote.

This is interesting for its own sake but also because it marked a significant shift in the basis of political competition in Viacha—away from the clientelistic purchase of votes with gifts, toward programmatic appeals based on universal benefits, and toward the politics of identity. In the 1990s, "the CBN bought votes in exchange for beer and plastic buckets. They bought the families of opposition politicians too."[47] The 2004 election marked a stopover in this transformation: the systematic undermining of the opposition had ended, but the UN still offered rural communities bags of cement alongside promises of transparency and participation. Although temporarily successful, this hybrid mix of gifts and policies proved powerless to stem the rising tide of the MAS. And with it, there was further transformation: "People have stopped responding to clientelism in Viacha. They received bags of cement but didn't vote for the UN."[48] The fundamental cleavage of Viachan politics had pivoted; people's motivations for voting had changed.

Community and Grassroots Organizations

Perhaps the single most important change in Viacha since 1997 was the broad ascendance of civil society. Previously neutralized and sidelined by the noxious alliance of politics and beer, rural and urban civic organizations now occupied center stage in politics, and local public life more broadly. In both 1997 and 2009, my interviews ended with several related questions on "Who's the boss here?" ("*Quién manda acá?*"). Whereas respondents in 1997 almost unanimously signaled Juan Carlos Blanco as the boss—the only municipality to name an individual (*con nombre y apellido*) rather than a group or sector—responses in 2009 were very different.

"There isn't any of that here," explained Flores and Merlo of the OC. "Community organizations are the boss now. Here everything is done by consensus. We hold meetings in order to arrive at agreements. We have to work with the grass-roots because we all came from there."[49] Mayta of CIPCA agreed. "Social organizations are the boss here—each in its own community."[50] The district director of education and the local head of CIPCA agreed that the mantle of power had passed to civil society, although they disagreed on which part held more. "Neighborhood councils hold power in Viacha—they define how investment funds are used," explained the DDE, and then, generalizing, said, "Civic organizations and social organizations are the boss in Viacha. They hold the municipality to account."[51] Barriga, by contrast, stressed the role of rural communities. "The Agrarian Association [is the boss]. They're well organized, with a strong organizational structure. They're better than the neighborhood councils, who fight more and are less organized."[52] The head of the Agrarian Association himself was more reserved: "Who's the boss? There's not that anymore. Everyone does what he should. No one dominates the rest."[53] Mayor Lamas agreed. "Everything is democratic here. Citizens have the same rights as their leaders."[54] Allow the last word to the authorities of District Seven, who put it best. "Before, the CBN dominated Viacha. Everyone supported the UCS because the CBN gave them everything. Then the brewer leaves and the cement-maker touches down. But today no one is the boss. Here today the boss is the people, the grass roots."[55]

To accomplish this remarkable transformation, civil society had first to overcome its chronic divisions and infighting. This was not easy, and indeed harmony did not yet reign.

> There is still tension between the city and countryside. The political elite has always been urban. They take decisions and do things for themselves. Now with the Machaqas gone the city has greater political weight, and uses it. Rural District Three has been left behind. . . . District Three residents are 50% rural indigenous, and 50% urban dwellers—traders, transport workers, etc.—a middle stratum in Viacha. That further divides civil society in Viacha.[56]

Even within urban areas, communities were still divided against one another. Unusually for Bolivia, Viacha had two Federations of Neighborhood Councils, with one for most of Viacha and the other for District Seven. And the former was unstable. "It's about to complete its 1st year," District Seven explained. "The previous leaders were very authoritarian—that's why they were thrown out. Our federation is better."[57]

But such frictions can be overcome, and in Viacha the worst of them had been. The DDE provided an example.

> The Ministry of Education approved the transfer of 20 teaching posts to District Seven, where they were needed. Rural mallkus and urban commu-

nity leaders agreed to demand that the ministry leave those posts in rural Viacha, and designate 20 new posts to District Seven [rather than fight over them]. The ministry agreed.[58]

Similarly, the mayor explained how in 2004, the Viachan Agrarian Association did not march in the city's festival—a sharp affront to the city and its authorities—because of the buildup of tensions with urban federations over the previous years. "After 2005, this was buried in the past. Everyone feels part of Viacha now. Agrarian and urban organizations carry on a constant dialogue and work together on common programs."[59]

How was social conflict overcome? The DDE explains it this way.

The idea of political parties before was the politics of division and confrontation. Also, Viacha before was 3 municipalities lumped together [Viacha plus the Machaqas]. Different organizations and regions wrested resources from the municipality by force—via loud demands and confrontation. In 2005 a *mallku* [traditional rural leader] entered the municipal council. He has informed communities about what's going on, leading to a decrease in pressures and conflict.[60]

Two things happened to quell social conflict in Viacha. The first was the departure of the chief instigator of conflict and division, Juan Carlos Blanco and his beer-politics machine. The second, which could probably only happen second, was far more subtle. The leaders of civic organizations, and many of their followers, learned the value of cooperation—or perhaps rather the opportunity costs of conflict and paralysis.

Mayor Callisaya ended his tenure in 1997 with many demands for investment and large sums of unspent funds. All over Viacha investment projects large and small were mired in controversy and chronically delayed. When Viacha's civic organizations stepped into the vacuum left by the CBN, they realized that both success and failure lay in their hands. And the cost of failure, they knew well, was high. "Social conflict? Very little with this mayor," reported Calle. "Some did want to unseat him, but I said no. Unseating the Mayor would paralyze everything."[61] A rapid process of social learning ensued, one for which the groundwork had been prepared and primed during a decade of lost opportunities. "The neighborhood federation intervenes in incipient conflicts to say 'Let them govern. What you want is to occupy the mayor's seat. Don't be a pest. Let them govern!' "[62]

This process was abetted by a broader shift in Bolivia's main political cleavage. A new politics of race and culture that united rural communities with many urban voters, especially on the altiplano, under the same political banner told them that they were all the same and should cooperate. And they did. Now there was broad agreement in Viacha that "political candidates have to emerge from the grass roots, not directed from above. That is good. That way you get good candidates."[63]

Could Viacha Revert to Bad Governance?

The transformation in Viacha—not only of government policies and outputs, but of the governance arrangements by which power is allocated, public priorities determined, and public officials held to account—was remarkable. Nothing in the underlying drivers of appalling municipal performance in 1997 could have predicted it. Certainly I did not. But the central role played by Mayor Lamas and the UN in driving the process forward cannot but put the entire project into doubt. Was it dependent upon the man? Was it a temporary confluence of factors? Could it all go wrong?

Lamas seemed to hint darkly at the fragility of change. "The only guarantee of sustaining good governance is in the hands of Viachan voters—voting for a good candidate and program, and not just a party's colors and slogan."[64] But Mayta, the organizational expert, gave those words deeper meaning. "A consciousness of voting for the person and policy proposals is being created in Viacha, not just voting for a party."[65] The best safeguard of good democratic governance is indeed the electorate. In Viacha, voters had internalized this. They had changed how they evaluate candidates and the basis on which they cast their vote. Beer and buckets no longer sufficed. Voters now evaluated the quality of government that candidates were likely to provide.

And they did so with the help of larger structures that informed them, transmitted their demands, and organized their collective action. These are the civic organizations that they voluntarily join, that operate above the level of the individual to institutionalize norms of behavior, to project voice, and to make accountability binding on politicians. Civic organizations interacted with public bodies and private firms in Viacha to operate the machinery of governance. "Spaces of information and accountability have been created in Viacha—by the municipal council, the OC, etc. The Annual Operating Plan is widely disseminated, and this is widely recognized by citizens. There's a permanent dialogue with the 4 districts," reported Mayta. "Good Government traditions are being created here," he continued. "Presenting the AOP, then the Yearly Record—the people will demand that these continue."[66] Mechanisms of social control had been created in Viacha that would be difficult to thwart.

The DDE summarized the dominant view that I found among many thoughtful *Viacheños:* "The dramatic change in government in Viacha is due to the person of the mayor, who is very good. But a bad mayor could not be elected because civic organizations keep watch and exert control, and would not permit this."[67] It could not happen, Flores and Merlo insisted. "The people now know how to administer a municipality well. If a bad mayor comes, no one will want him. There will be conflict in Viacha. GROs will fight to continue doing things correctly. The OC will vigilantly work to continue the good works of this mayor."[68]

What, then, is the future likely to hold? Once again we give the last word to District Seven. "Any entering mayor will find complete, orderly, and stable municipal accounts. Annual Operating Plans are drawn up jointly with GRO presidents who *know* what an AOP is, how much money is involved, etc. GRO presidents have been trained. Everyone works together: the municipality, neighborhood federations, OC, etc." Good governance was likely to endure in Viacha not because the figure of Mayor Lamas was so large, nor because the city's luck would hold, but for a much more credible reason. The processes, practices, and behaviors that underpin good governance were becoming progressively institutionalized in the actions and interactions of private and civic organizations, and through them were becoming embedded in the expectations of the electorate. After five good years, voters now understood that firms financed parties but did not make policy. They expected to participate in budgeting and policy-making. They expected to hold their leaders to account.

Charagua in 2009

Returning to Charagua is a very pleasant surprise. Twelve years later the sleepy town has come awake and bustles with activity. Whereas before I stayed in a room rented from my driver's acquaintance, now there are several hotels, including two on the main square. There are many restaurants and cafés where before there were almost none, frequent bus and *trufi*[69] services to Santa Cruz and Camiri (on paved roads that now reach Argentina), and a much expanded market. Mennonites, previously invisible in the town, now wander about casually and congregate in the market. Most noticeably, the central plaza—dry and dilapidated when I first visited—is now large, verdant, and frankly beautiful. The streets in the square are paved, most of the buildings have been renovated, and in the late afternoon sun central Charagua glows like a rural idyll. More important, most of Charagua's Guaraní communities now have electricity, running water, and new schools and health posts, and many have benefited from housing renovation projects cosponsored by municipal, departmental, and national governments. Charagua is still a small town in the vast Chaco that feels distant from the world. But in many significant ways it is transformed.

Much of this transformation is due to the large increases in income that Charagua has enjoyed since 1997. The national government devolved hydrocarbon royalties to municipalities, increasing Charaguan inflows notably from 2001 when local oil and gas pipelines became operational.[70] Resources from international donor debt relief programs also helped swell municipal coffers. Agricultural property taxes that used to be paid to the Cattle Ranchers' Federation in Santa Cruz are now collected by AGACOR and deposited in the municipality's account.[71] And in 2007 the Santa Cruz prefecture decentralized its natural resource royalties to municipalities. "Charagua had previously received Bs. 174,000 from the prefecture; this year it received Bs. 2,400,000," explained councilman Gustavo García. "In 1996 Lucho [ex-mayor Saucedo] managed Bs. 3–4 million in total. Now it's in excess of Bs. 20 million!"[72] Against this huge increase in resources, population had risen by a bit less than half to 27,410,[73] resulting in a substantial increase in resources per capita. Another significant change from the early days of decentralization was that other branches of the state had become accustomed to working with municipal governments. Hence the improvements to Charagua's central square, which cost Bs. 1.3 million, were a joint project with the prefecture, which contributed Bs. 1.1 million.[74] The combination of increased resources and improved opportunities for cooperation vastly expanded the range of what the municipality could do.

Alongside improvements in technical and financial resources were interesting changes to the municipality's human resources. In 1995 Guaraníes took control of the municipality behind the acceptable figure of Luis Saucedo and his technical staff; throughout the unstable decade that followed, urban "whites" continued to occupy the upper echelons of the local executive. This changed in 2004 when a Guaraní from San Francisco (rural South Charagua) was elected mayor. A change in municipal complexion followed, to the point where 90 percent of (the expanded) municipal staff are now Guaraní.[75] In Charagua the Guaraní people now represented themselves. In the words of a municipal insider, "Before Guaraníes had to request an audience in order to enter the municipal council chamber. Now they're guests of honor."[76] More than a change of style, this has changed how the municipality operates. Spokesmen for rural North Charagua put it thus: "Now the municipality *has to* listen to the people. The council isn't so closed to them. Ordinary people can enter the council chamber and propose ideas."[77] We return to this point in detail below.

The latest, and perhaps most important, event in Charagua's political evolution occurred a few days before my arrival. On 6 December 2009 Charaguans voted in favor of "indigenous autonomy," a legal status defined by the new Bolivian constitution that municipalities and regions can accede to. It allows "nations and peoples who share a cultural identity, language, historical traditions, institutions, territory, and world view"[78] to apply their own principles and institutional forms to the question of self-government, defense of their cultures, and organization of their economies. Indigenous autonomy was supported by most Guaraníes but strongly opposed by urban residents. The outcome of the plebiscite caused much anxiety in the town and led to increased tensions between urban and rural Charagua.

Local Governance in Charagua, 2009

"Our relations with the municipality are very good. I deal directly with them. My requests are always dealt with in a timely manner," reported Sr. Marleny González, administrator of Charagua's hospital.[79] Another independent observer, the local army commander, agreed: "The municipality works well here. There are many civil works—they do good work that benefits the community."[80] Interestingly, it was the head of the OC, José Núñez, who provided a more critical view. "Local government performance is not 100%. Over the past two years it has been closer to 70%. The 30% negative is due to mistakes" the municipality has made. But things are getting better these last two years because of a change of municipal council president, he reported.[81]

It is notable that the manager and director of AGACOR[82] agreed with officers of the North Charagua captaincy[83] and the South Charagua Great

Captain[84]—fully spanning Charagua's ethnic and economic divides—that projects were being administered well and, although there was room for improvement, municipal performance was good. Local governance advisers from CIPCA described an upward tendency in municipal performance, which they attributed to the involvement of the Guaraní captaincies.[85] In effect, all sectors of society that I encountered upon my return agreed that their local government was serious, inclusive, and honest. Despite variations in emphasis and differences on some specifics, they were united in the view that the projects that local government pursued were important to the municipality, and the results it obtained ranged from good to very good. The cattle ranchers' assessment was typical.

> The municipality supports the cattle fair, finances the drilling of [water] wells for communities, and also the building and maintenance of roads. The rancher's association supports and advises the municipality. We don't want that to change. The municipality works well. . . . He is an excellent mayor. There is a good environment.[86]

Objective external assessments agreed. A recent ranking of Bolivian municipalities ranked Charagua the second best administered in Santa Cruz, and third best nationwide.[87]

Strikingly, respondents' opinions were specific and contextualized. "Local government is much better than in 1990s or early 2000s—there is more commitment, more covenants. The people participate more and understand more what's happening in their municipality," reported Núñez.[88] "Before the municipality did what and served whom it wanted," explained Professor Chávez. "Local government served the municipality very little and badly. And as administrators they were miserable and arrogant. They didn't respond to popular needs. This government is more open, flexible, and responds to all the petitions that they can and that are made correctly."[89]

The physical evidence of this improvement in government was easy to identify. "Before economic management wasn't very good. Now there's more investment in communities, more inclusion. Before everything was for the town," reported two knowledgeable observers,[90] a point with which the head of the teacher-training center agreed. "Before there was no development here. There was no constant electricity or water service—only occasionally. With the Law of Popular Participation the municipality began to grow: schools in communities, health clinics, etc. Now almost all communities have both."[91] "There are now more investment projects, and of better quality, than before 1997—roads, productive projects, bridges, schools, etc.," the chief administrative officer added. "This is especially true of the last 5 years, and especially regarding forms of participation. . . . Before it took more than a day to reach the last community in the Isoso; now just hours."[92] A program to provide each rural community with a school was now complete, and the municipality was turning to other services. "Electricity arrived in San Antonio del Parapetí in May of 2009," reported an obviously delighted Sr. Dolores Quevedo, of the village's center for disabled children. "It makes our work so much easier."[93]

It was not just building works that pleased Charaguans, but the services the municipality provided as well. In education, ten rural schools in Charagua lack (national government) budget lines for staff and so are supported only by the municipality. The municipality pays them Bs. 600 per month to teach in the communities.[94] The pay is modest, "but it makes their work possible—in communities that otherwise wouldn't have a school," Charagua town[95] and Prof. Chávez[96] agreed. The municipality also pays for poor children's school supplies, such as pencils and notebooks. As a result of such programs, "Now Charagua is free of illiteracy," reported Chávez, and the district was moving to "post-literacy" training, again financed entirely by local government.[97] Other services were more integrated and creative. "We're supporting economic production in the majority of communities," reported the mayor. In the past, "many people left the communities to go to the sugar harvest in Santa Cruz. That was bad for children's education. Now the desertion rate has fallen from 10% to 2–3%."[98]

The institutional underpinnings of local government success in Charagua featured, first and foremost, a highly inclusive system of planning and budgeting. "Local government responds to the entire population," reported North Charagua. "Because resources are devolved to each district according to population, and each district draws up its own AOP."[99] On this point agreement was unanimous. "Budget ceilings are determined according to population," explained the chief administrative officer. "Charagua town has 4,000 inhabitants, the Isoso has 11,000, Charagua North has 5,800, and Charagua South has 2,500."[100] The limits these populations imply were then subdivided further into community budget ceilings. "The community receives its ceiling and *they* prioritize. The municipality administers this money without touching the prioritization. This has been the case since 2005–06."[101] Sánchez and Aramayo agreed with this description, as did councilwoman Yavita. "There are 90 indigenous communities in Charagua. Each community presents six projects and chooses one itself, and the municipality executes that one," explained Chávez. The community further defined how to divide resources between investment and expenditures.[102] To aggregate all of these community plans, the municipality announced a "municipal summit" at least one week in advance. Community assemblies were then held to determine local priorities. "Then one man and one woman come from each community to represent it at the municipal summit,"[103] where investment plans are coordinated. The municipal council and oversight committee approved the resulting budget in a second summit. Running costs could reach 25 percent of the total; the remaining 75 percent or more had to be investment.[104] "Communities decide and then the municipal council passes an ordinance to make it [the resulting budget] legal."[105]

The difference with the 1997 budgeting system, then lauded as highly participative, is that decision making had been pushed all the way down to the village level, and participation was accordingly higher. In 1997, communities made their wishes known upward through the parallel structures of the municipal council and OC, but municipal authorities made all final decisions. In 2009, it was the communities themselves who made decisions about how to spend *their* resources, reducing the mayor, municipal council, and OC to coordinating roles. It is notable that such changes could succeed in a vast municipality sparsely populated by poor indigenous people with traditionally high levels of illiteracy. Their significance was not lost on my interviewees, all of whom signaled the internal decentralization of government in Charagua as the "best thing about the municipality."

The second, closely related support on which good governance rested in Charagua was high accountability. Municipal officials gave account to lower levels of the population, and they did so more often than in 1997. "The mayor gives quarterly reports regarding physical advances [of works], expenditures and investments, etc.," testified both the OC head and CIPCA. These reports are not given behind closed doors but rather publicly, to GRO presidents and grassroots members.[106] Between 1996 and 2005, "The people didn't know how much money was being spent on individual projects," Núñez continued. "Now they do." But, in a striking change from 1997, their involvement goes much deeper than that of passive recipients of official reports. Now, very often, *"the community manages the money."*[107] Bidding processes for contracts and works had been made more transparent, facilitating local administration.[108] "If things go wrong the fault lies not with the mayor or councilors, but with the community."[109] Sánchez and Aramayo of the northern *capitanía* agreed.[110]

But not all was perfect in Charagua. The most immediate problem was a shortfall in central government disbursements. "This year the problem has been that money doesn't reach the municipality in time. The central government doesn't disburse as promised, and there's no reason given," Núñez[111] complained. At times, "money's lacking even for salaries," added Yavita. According to Charagua town, "The central government cut Charagua's budget by Bs. 4 million this year. . . . October is the only month this year in which central transfers have occurred normally. In other months Charagua has received only half its due."[112] This was compounded by rising input prices, reported the mayor, which further stretched the budget, leaving the municipality unable to finance all of the projects initially budgeted.[113]

The performance of the oversight committee also concerned most respondents. Despite new offices built for it by the municipality (in 1997 there were none), almost all interviewed accused it of performing poorly and neglecting its responsibilities. This included Charagua town,[114] CIPCA,[115] officers for the urban merchants' association,[116] the head of a rural development project,[117] and the head of teacher training.[118] APG officers from North Charagua offered the following explanation. "No OC ever worked in Charagua," and this one is no exception.

Even though it's "ours" [the OC head is an APG member from a northern village], it doesn't work. It falls short because: (i) there are serious economic interests behind the scenes; (ii) it has no independent sources of income— it receives money only from the municipality, and so cannot fight with the municipality; (iii) the APG and OC were not close enough—now they are; and (iv) the APG also made mistakes—we are learning. Poverty can make you do anything. The lack of a good salary makes you do anything.[119]

Whatever the explanation, there was firm evidence that the OC contributed little to good local governance. "The OC has its own accounts frozen because it hasn't accounted for its own expenditures for the 2nd semester of 2008 and 1st semester 2009," reported the mayor with disgust. "They are capricious and irresponsible."[120] Effective oversight, many reported, was carried out instead by communities and civic organizations, a point to which we return below.

The Deepening of Governance

Governance in Charagua was significantly deepened between 1997 and 2009. How did this change come about? The descent of decision making, and hence power, to lower and lower levels of the spatial hierarchy (municipality → district → village), with attendant increases in participation and accountability, is intimately linked to the rise of the APG and its entry into electoral politics. The APG was formed in 1986–87 after a long series of meetings at the community and captaincy levels to discuss the problems common to Guaraní villagers in the departments of Santa Cruz, Chuquisaca, and Tarija.[121] Since then it has grown steadily in organization and strength, and by 2009 included 25 zones and more than 300 communities.[122]

At the onset of decentralization Guaraní communities were unfamiliar with municipal AOPs and found it difficult to organize themselves to participate in budget planning. Hence the APG focused initially on strengthening both Guaraní communities and its own internal structure. This permitted them to enter into political accords with traditional parties, as occurred in Charagua with the MBL. If it is true that Mayor Saucedo's tenure was a revolution of municipal attention to rural communities and their needs as compared to the status quo ante, APG leaders came to feel that the participation of Guaraníes in their own government was still insufficient. "There was some relation of the municipality with communities," now growing in organizational ability, "but communities [still] did not participate in the making of the Annual Operating Plan," explained Guarupachi.[123] Other problems also originated in politics. "From 1999–2003 there was ingovernability due to party quotas that debilitated the municipality. The mayor changed four times in four years," explained CIPCA.[124] And "political jealousies were a barrier for popular participation in local government. Candidates were chosen directly by party chiefs."[125]

In 2004 the national government promulgated the Law of Citizen Associations, which opened the way for civic groups to compete in national and local elections. Sánchez and Aramayo take up the story.

> Then the door is opened for citizen associations to participate in elections. The APG studies the matter and decides to participate in 2004, directly, as the APG. The people feel they have a better guarantee this way. They can go

to town hall [to speak to their authorities]. There's a greater opening in local government for citizens.[126]

The APG won the 2004 local election, and Claudio López, previously
president of the oversight committee, became Charagua's first indigenous
mayor. The changes that ensued were significant. In the words of CIPCA,

> The maturity of the Guaraníes led them to occupy the spaces of power in
> order to increase their own development. Planning at the level of indige-
> nous districts was instituted. Assistant mayors are suggested by GROs, not
> directly by the mayor like the mayor wanted. The large increase in resources
> due to hydrocarbons royalties has led to more and better investment for the
> municipality. This is supported by the organic demand of the captaincies
> and their integration with the municipality.[127]

Numerous interviewees testified that Charagua's new Guaraní authorities
worked more fluidly together and with communities than previous authorities had. "Now it's the people themselves who govern," explained the APG.
"Before the mayor was steered by the political party. Not now. Now there's
more social control."[128] Whereas before the municipality contracted building works with firms from Santa Cruz, now it contracts projects and programs directly with communities, whose residents build the works.
Charagua also benefited from a degree of political stability unprecedented
in the era of decentralization: five continuous years with one government.

In power alone, the APG proved far more capable than when accompanied by the MBL at fomenting participation, transparency, and accountability. Nevertheless it is important to note that the seeds of later success
were sown during the former period. The election of Luis Saucedo was the
APG's first important foray into local politics. Saucedo then "opened spaces
for Guaraníes to participate in politics, and to solicit things in the AOP. The
APG and Guaraníes grew with this insertion into the AOP process."[129]
Tellingly, the then-head of AGACOR remembers this period as a positive,
productive time when cattle ranchers, the municipality, and Guaraníes
worked well together on a wide range of projects.[130] The material legacy of
the APG-MBL alliance, clearly positive, may have been modest. But by giving the APG and Guaraní communities the experience of policy-making
and public responsibility, and by demonstrating to townsfolk—and indeed
to themselves—that Guaraníes were capable of administering power and

resources responsibly, it marked the first step in the transformation of Charaguan politics and laid the groundwork for the far deeper changes yet to come.

The net effect of these developments was a shift in the balance of power from the town, cattle ranchers, and *karai* toward the poor Guaraní who formed the large majority of Charaguans. "Before the *karai* [white people] ran the show," explained Yavita. "All that has changed."[131] Now, "the Guaraní people run the show here. Before the political parties did, and behind them were the cattle ranchers. How did this come about? The Law of Citizen Associations. That's how we took power," said Sánchez and Aramayo of the APG.[132] "We've taken a big step towards social integration," added Chávez.[133] Almost all respondents agreed. Both the mayor and great captain of South Charagua described the change in far more specific terms. "Before the Gutiérrezes were the bosses—not just here but in several places where they owned lands. Miguelito Gutiérrez is of that family—owners of the gas company, La Bélgica, etc. . . . Now he's a good friend of the Guaraníes. . . . Those people have lost a lot."[134]

Private Sector

In 1997 Charagua's only cogent economic force was AGACOR, the cattle ranchers association, whose power and wealth were suffering the effects of long-term decline in agricultural prices. By 2009 there were two important changes. The first change, respondents from across the municipality agreed, was that the rural economy of eastern Bolivia was no longer in decline. During much of the first decade of the new millennium, Bolivia benefited from a worldwide natural resource boom that raised prices for its commodity exports. This helped spur sustained economic growth in Bolivia and in many of its trade partners, which in turn raised agricultural prices for Charagua's farmers. Ranching had become "much more profitable than before,"[135] and as a result the municipality was registering increases in the number of ranchers and farms instead of declines. In addition, some Charaguans reported anecdotal evidence that the labor market in Santa Cruz was oversupplied with young rural migrants looking for jobs. With grins of satisfaction, AGACOR's Arriaga and Ortiz summarized things thus.

> That tendency did exist before. But now the labor market in Santa Cruz is saturated. Now many teachers there drive taxis or have become merchants,

etc. Things have turned around and now people are returning to Charagua to follow in the footsteps of their fathers. And in the city, people from the countryside are always marginalized. The future of the people is in the country. You live much better in the country.[136]

Second, ranchers had been joined by other powerful groups. The first of these, according to all my respondents, were the Mennonites. Most interviewees also signaled indigenous farming communities, the oil and gas industry, and bus and *trufi* operators as emerging actors. Ranchers continued to be by far the most important economic force, with more than 100,000 head of cattle, 50,000 hectares devoted to agriculture,[137] and a capable organization that kept daily records of cattle sales by farmer and pushed animal vaccination rates above 90 percent.[138] With Charagua's slaughterhouse, a supply center, and a well-drilling rig under its command, AGACOR was well placed to cooperate with local government, and cooperate it did. "Our best governmental relations are with the municipality," its manager and director explained. "When there is a problem of disease or pestilence, one of our technicians speeds to the case in a municipal vehicle."[139] The municipality confirmed that it relied on AGACOR's expertise for a livestock improvement program, for which AGACOR donated part of the cost.[140]

A large part of Charagua's agricultural renaissance was driven by its growing Mennonite colonies. With 40,000 hectares mainly in the Isoso, Mennonites operated on a large scale, but with very different methods from either cattle ranchers or Guaraníes. "We keep our cattle in fields planted with grass that are fenced in," explained Pedro Martins, head of the oldest Mennonite colony in Charagua.[141] This required far more work than the traditional Guaraní approach, which allowed cattle to wander around the countryside freely in search of food and fend for themselves in the dry season. By contrast Mennonites built fences, harvested and stored corn, and drilled wells so that their cattle might be adequately fed year-round. The Guaraní approach, to them, was simple "abandonment."[142]

The results were impressive. Charagua had become a large producer of milk, cheese, guano, corn, and other crops, and a bigger producer of meat and live cattle, most of which was sold in Santa Cruz, bringing large amounts of money into Charagua. This created many year-round jobs for Guaraní villagers on Mennonite lands. Admiration for Mennonite success was widespread. "They work really hard—beautifully. . . . They make the economy grow," enthused Arriaga and Ortiz of AGACOR. "Hell, I learned to plant corn and raise cows from the Mennonites!" laughed Juan Carlos Gutiérrez, ex-president of the cattle ranchers.

> I sell 70% of the corn and the other 30% I keep for the cattle during the dry season. Also the well drilling rig—we bought it from the Mennonites. It cost us US$24,000 and can drill down to 240 meters. 15 years later it's still working! We drilled 52 wells with that rig. Fifty-one struck water.[143]

Sánchez and Aramayo of the APG and Professor Chávez agreed.

Of the other rising economic actors, oil and gas firms probably accounted for the largest financial flows into local coffers. Recent arrivals, they did not yet make themselves felt locally as interest groups; given the scale of resources and royalties involved, this situation was unlikely to last long. Bus and *trufi* operators—much smaller actors—also failed to make themselves felt in the municipality. The most interesting and promising economic actors were the Guaraníes themselves, who, according to the parish priest,

> are gaining in strength now that they begin to negotiate their production— they begin to have a surplus they can sell. Especially in North and South Charagua, they're trying to get into higher-value products like honey, milk, cheese, cattle and lesser livestock to sell and for meat. Also algarroba—the powder from grinding the husk is very nutritious.[144]

The combination of technical support from NGOs, aid agencies, and the municipality, combined with the potent demonstration effect of Mennonites who employed Guaraníes to make the "dry Chaco" bloom, was spurring rural communities to greater production. This development was still incipient, but—if sustained in time and extended across the hinterland—had the potential not just to multiply Charagua's output but to transform its social fabric.

Political Parties and Elections

The top vote-getters in 1997 were the MNR, MBL, and ADN, who shared out Charagua's five municipal council seats. Only the MNR survived into 2009, coming second in the last local elections, which were won by the APG (27 percent) with almost twice the MNR's tally. Second, third, and fourth places were essentially a tie between the MNR, MAS, and CACHA (Change for Charagua). Various observers agreed that the distribution of seats on the municipal council accurately represented political sentiment in the population. CACHA is a new political group whose strength lies in Charagua town and the community of San Antonio. The MNR is also strong in the town and among older Guaraníes in rural areas. The MAS's vote is particularly strong in Charagua Station and parts of the Isoso. By contrast the APG's electoral support, overwhelmingly Guaraní, is strong throughout rural Charagua.[145] The coalition governing Charagua in 2009 was an alliance between the APG and the MAS, which—in the telling opinion of the cattle ranchers—"generated a local stability here like never before—5 years of continuous local government. . . . This was the best feature of local government here recently: continuity."[146]

Like in Viacha, the basis of political competition in Charagua was also changing. According to some observers, many Charaguans continued to vote according to political colors and clientelistic gifts.[147] But others argued that votes were now swayed more by policy ideas and proposals.[148] CIPCA distinguish between two periods: (1) from the Law of Popular Participation until 2002, when parties competed for clients with state gifts and jobs, and people voted according to which party benefited them most; and (2) since 2002, when citizens began to reject this competition and the "party-ocracy"[149] began to collapse. "The parties also react, and become more programmatic and ideological. This gives rise to the MAS, a transformative party that is against the positions and practices of the parties of the past."[150] From 2004, citizen associations entered politics in Bolivia. The APG won the 2004 election, and traditional parties wasted away. Indeed many voters of the center-right also shifted their allegiances, from the ADN and MNR to CACHA. CACHA is another citizen association—a reaction against, and mirror of, the rise of the APG across the Chaco.

The shift away from clientelism was well under way in Charagua. But where it would take the municipality was difficult to predict. On the one hand, the purchase of voters with pencils, notebooks, and barbecues seemed destined to die out. "The vote is secret," explained the mayor. "Voters receive gifts but then vote for policy proposals for Charagua."[151] But on the other hand the rise of the APG and the MAS, with their hybrid programs of universal benefits plus the politics of identity, permitted both abstract policy discussions and the "instructed vote" (*voto consigna*) to flourish. Charagua town made blunt accusations.

Before individuals decided whom to vote for in the communities. Now it's obligatory. CIPCA runs this; GROs are its front. . . . CIPCA orders captains, who order community captains, who order the grass roots whom to vote for. If they don't vote for the right candidate, individuals and families are thrown out of their communities and barred from receiving help. Political delegates aren't allowed into some communities, and enter others with fear. Innocent peasants are told their leaders know how they all vote, and the peasants believe them.[152]

As unlikely as such charges may have sounded, their substance was confirmed by the Great Captain of South Charagua. "Now, 4 elections later, we instruct communities and they obey. The APG now has confidence in the communities that they will obey. For the referendum on the departmental statute of [opposition-run] Santa Cruz, the APG told them not to vote, *and they did not vote!*"[153] Likewise in the run-up to the recent referendum, "The departmental court gave 24 hours for 10% of the population to sign a petition in favor of the referendum on indigenous autonomy. Only Huacaya [another Guaraní-dominated municipality] and Charagua achieved this. We had to work hard to get there." Were the town's fears of a Guaraní dictatorship well founded? We return to this question below.

Community and Grassroots Organizations

The most important change in Charaguan civil society since 1997 was the growth of the Mennonite community in population, number of colonies, and hectares cultivated. The initial colony, called Pinondi, was joined during subsequent years by Durango, Casa Grande, and Pirango, all on land purchased from ranchers in the Isoso. A fifth colony was being planned in South Charagua.[154] Like Mennonites in the United States, Argentina, and elsewhere, Charagua's Mennonites are of European descent, speak a form of low German among themselves (and obviously accented Spanish with others), and seek the full autonomy of the group regardless of where they reside. They entered Bolivia under the authority of a Supreme Script negotiated with the government that frees them from military service and the obligation to vote, and leaves them free to run their own schools and churches. They are a community apart whose cohesion and distinctiveness is maintained through formal and informal norms of religion, language, gender roles, education, and dress that have the strong effect of isolating them from the rest of the population. Charagua's Mennonites came from Mexico and Canada mostly, but also Paraguay, Belize, and Argentina.[155]

All land in Mennonite communities is held centrally, "in the name of the colony, and is divided up among families internally," explained Martins, the head of Pinondi.[156] This cements not only the role of the colony as the principal unit of Mennonite society but also as a social organization that is highly patriarchal. When the Mennonite youth come of age and want to marry, they must first be assigned a plot of land to farm. That power lies in the hands of the small number of men who govern the colony. The Pinondi colony has 2,800 inhabitants on 21,000 hectares, half the Mennonite total in Charagua.[157]

Their separation gives Mennonites an experience of local government that is different from the rest of Charagua. Although they pay taxes to the Bolivian state, they do not vote and thus have no representation on the municipal council. Inevitably this lowers the priority that the municipality gives their concerns. "Three years ago we made a covenant with the municipality to build a rural road, but the mayor didn't keep his side of the agreement," complained Martins. "We spent Bs. 60,000, but now the road is messed up. . . . Beyond that there are no covenants with the municipality."[158] Although disappointed about the roads, Martins was untroubled by any broader implications. "I don't know if the municipality serves the rest of Charagua. That's their problem," Martins said. "He's not our mayor. He's the Guaraní communities' mayor."[159]

Collitas, Quechua- and Aymara-speaking (often indigenous) highlanders, form another group that has grown significantly since 1997. "There are lots of them!" exclaim the cattle ranchers. "In the market mainly. They are merchants. Some produce too. We have good relations with them. Many of them already speak Guaraní."[160] "Many people have migrated to Charagua from the 'interior' recently," explains the local army commander. "Families come to visit their soldiers and see that there is work here, so they stay."[161] Relations with the rest of Charagua are generally good. "Whoever comes here to work is a *Charagueño*," declares Charagua town. An independent observer went further: "Sometimes the *collitas* get along better with Guaraníes. . . . The *collas* take potatoes and vegetables, onions, clothes—they go through the Isoso with their merchandise. You've never seen a local do that."[162]

Guaraní society had also changed since 1997. Most dramatically, the APG/Guaraní captaincies—previously penniless—now handled proportionately almost as much money as the municipality. Many investment projects were designed by local government and executed—that is, built, managed, overseen, and operated—by a captaincy, or even a village. Their willingness to commit their own resources to public projects allowed rural Guaraní communities to benefit from the new budgeting regime to a far greater extent than urban Charagua, which did not contribute money of its own. "Guaraní communities *do* contribute—they raise money from wherever they can," the APG explained. "In 2009 Guaraní communities contributed Bs. 538,000 towards public investment projects."[163] The mayor corroborated this point. "North and South Charagua contribute 10% of the value of their works from their own pockets."[164]

The Guaraníes' ability to benefit from decentralization was a tribute to the strength and ability of their social organization—not only to raise counterparts but more importantly to prioritize community needs, plan actions in a participative manner, and manage budgets and contracts. The social bonds of trust both within and across Guaraní communities identified a decade earlier remained strong—indeed had probably grown stronger. "In my district," testified Núñez, "fifteen communities get money one year, and the other fifteen get money the next year. There are formal agreements among communities to operate this way."[165]

With so much money at stake, why did the Guaraníes not abuse their large majority? After generations of oppression, why did they not take revenge? The APG explained it thus: "The development and liberation of a people will come from those same people." They must cooperate—both among themselves and with other communities—for development to follow.

> They are often called "conformist," but the Guaraní people are, rather, reflective. They wait and plan for the future. The culture is of dialogue. Years ago local authorities did not respect individuals' rights. The Guaraní people *do* respect your rights. History makes you think differently without losing your sense of right and wrong. What happened happened—it must serve as a framework to help you advance. They want to show others that they *do* respect their rights. That's why the Guaraní people are more about dialogue than confrontation. From vengeance does not come development.[166]

I had found little social discord in 1997, and little again in 2009. Some interviewees identified particular tensions concerning indigenous autonomy, but most respondents across all of Charagua's ethnic groups agreed that these were modest. Conflict per se was nonexistent. "The process of 'inter-culturality' has cost us so much, but it's going well," reported Charagua town.[167] Located somewhere between psychology and culture, the character traits of the Guaraní had permitted a revolution—literally—in Guaraní affairs. "Thirty years ago the Guaraníes were totally 'invisible-ized,'" explained CIPCA, and the mayor agreed. "Now they lead the process" of change in Charagua.[168]

But despite vast progress, there was still work to be done, not least within Guaraní communities themselves, as Elfie Yavita, the first woman to complete a term on the municipal council, lamented.

> In North Charagua there are some communities that didn't permit the entry of urns during the last election—there was no secret ballot there. South Charagua has communities that don't permit the construction of health centers because women will learn to control their fertility and they don't want that.[169]

This comment revealed a consciousness among some Guaraní leaders of the social development their community still required. The road ahead was still long, but perhaps not as long as the road already traveled.

Could Governance Deteriorate in Charagua?

Charagua in 2009 was a model Bolivian municipality in which the promise of decentralization had quickly been met—efficient, participative local government that provided important primary services to a poor population—and then transcended, as the deeper political and social changes prompted by self-government took hold. Twelve years later, grassroots participation in prioritizing and budgeting, monitoring, and ex post reporting of municipal activities not only were maintained in Charagua but had been driven down to the level of district and community, which not only provided oversight but now also financed, managed, and often executed investment projects and programs. This deep, continuous exercise of power and responsibility had led the Guaraní majority to progress from its first, tentative foray into politics under cover of a traditional party and *karai* mayor, to the direct exercise of power by themselves as themselves—the Asamblea del Pueblo Guaraní. They had shown the rest of Charagua that they could be trusted to wield power responsibly, and in so doing had convinced themselves too.

Could local government deteriorate in the future? Strictly speaking, yes, of course. But the unspoken leitmotif throughout many hours of interviews in 2009 was the enormous increase in the standards to which local government was held in Charagua. Municipal performance was already comparatively high in 1997. But local government was new then, and many seemed unsure how to judge it. As citizens became more familiar with the processes and rituals of (a good) local government, these uncertainties vanished, and expectations for it grew. Rising standards were endogenous, driven by Charagua's own success rather than by training or external interventions. And participation in government drove rising standards deeper and deeper into the social fabric. Although not all was perfect in the municipality, the level of information in the population about local needs, what local government was doing, and what it could achieve—implying how it should behave—greatly exceeded that of 1997. Happily, and at least partly in response to this, so did performance. Charaguans had developed much higher expectations of their municipality—expectations that, to a great extent, the municipality was meeting. These expectations were firmly anchored in individual voters and expressed by their civic organizations, creating strong electoral incentives against a sustained deterioration of municipal performance.

Perhaps Guaraní culture contained dictatorial strains that could undermine open, accountable government? After generations of exclusion and discrimination, the Guaraníes were rising up and seizing control of their own destiny. They tended to vote as a bloc by community, but not—as some accused—unthinkingly. This was not the *voto consigna* of peasants who obeyed orders from above. Rather, communities discussed and debated candidates in exhaustive detail as chronicled above, reached consensus, and then took collective action in the field of politics, according to Guaraní tradition. So long as the debate continued to be open and grassroots opinions were taken into account, the positive changes seen in Charagua since the onset of decentralization were likely to continue. It is nonetheless true that the mechanism of Guaraní consensus and collective voting did open the door to the fears of the town—a tyranny of the Guaraní leadership. But in practical terms such a tyranny was much further away than townsfolk believed. The Guaraní vote was already divided between APG and MAS, which both sides insisted were distinct political forces, and to a lesser extent the MNR. Attempts to form alliances within the municipal council had proven unstable—the APG had allied with each of the other parties on the council at some point. Its behavior, far from idiosyncratically

"Guaraní," was that of a normal, successful political party acting strategically in the interests of its constituency. Fears of tyranny seemed overblown.

Last, we do well to remember that the transformation of governance in Charagua was not due to the awakening of the Guaraní and the rise of the APG alone. The *ganaderos* had dealt with more serious challenges in the past. The flowering of effective government providing services to all citizens in a context of participation and accountability can only be explained by the confluence of decentralization, the formation of the APG, and a deep crisis in the rural economy that sapped the ranchers' will. But by 2009 this crisis had reverted, and farm prices were once again good. A simple rational actor theory would predict a cattleman's revenge. Why did this not happen? The ranchers' product and assets were once again valuable; they had something to fight for and much to fight with. Their future as a group and even—in some cases at least—individuals' rights to their property were uncertain as agricultural policy was reformed and indigenous autonomy approached. And yet they did not fight. Why not? Because decentralization changed not only the performance of local government, nor merely its processes, but rather the underpinnings of politics and—ultimately—power in Charagua. In the era of transparency and participation, it was the citizen who was empowered. The time for tyrannies—Guaraní or *karai*—was past.

Transformation at the Extremes

By 2009 participation in Charagua's local government had been driven deeper and deeper down into civil society, without apparent loss of quality. And in Viacha local government had been changed beyond all recognition—from a corrupt, unresponsive municipality to one that boasted extensive participation and high-quality policy outputs. In both districts the major change is the ascendancy of civil society. But this is not enough to explain transformation in either. In both districts, the interaction of civic actors with their private sector counterparts is determinant. Hence civil society could only emerge in Viacha after the withdrawal of the CBN from public life ended systematic political and electoral distortions. Similarly, Guaraní society's organization and emergence in Charagua was greatly facilitated by the decline of the cattle-ranching economy, which weakened the previous hegemon. But here decentralization exerted its own distinct effect.

The return of the agrarian economy to rude health in the 2000s did not lead to rancher reprisals because, by placing real power in the hands of ordinary Charaguans, decentralization changed the meaning of citizenship and so changed the terms on which politics is conducted there.

A similar change occurred in Viacha, where a consciousness of voting for candidates and policy ideas, as opposed to responding to gifts or party colors, was gaining ground among voters. In both municipalities, changes in expectations about processes (participation, transparency) and outcomes (needs responsiveness) were critically intermediated by civic organizations, which organized and amplified voters' voices, facilitated their collective action, and represented their interests in holding government to account. Their actions educated (especially poorer) voters both in their political rights and in the possibilities of what local government could achieve. Initial success in Charagua raised citizen expectations and deepened participation; 10 years later, belated success in Viacha seemed to catalyze a process of institutional catch-up in which standards of transparency and participation previously unknown there quickly became the norm.

The transformation of governance in both municipalities was driven by the interaction of private sector actors with civic organizations, cleaning up politics and making it more transparent in Viacha, and driving decision making and power deeper and deeper into the social structure in Charagua. These processes, in turn, drove increasing government responsiveness and accountability in both. Thus a theory that explains the quality of local government in the years immediately following reform can also explain its transformation during the 12 years that followed.

CHAPTER 9

Conclusion

Decentralization in Bolivia

Prior to 1994 Bolivia was one of the most centralized states in Latin America, with few elected officials of any description at the subnational level and chains of authority that stretched from the lowliest nurse or schoolteacher in a distant village directly up to the president and his ministers in the Palacio Quemado in La Paz. Decentralization changed this overnight. On 1 July 1994, responsibility for a suite of local public services was transferred, along with 20 percent of all national tax revenues, to 311 municipal governments newly created or expanded to make up the entire national territory. A two-tiered system of local oversight and accountability was put into place, and Bolivia became decentralized.

The changes were immediate and dramatic. National public investment patterns shifted from economic production to human capital formation and primary social services. The spatial distribution of resources across Bolivia became far more equitable. And local governments proved far more responsive to objective indicators of local need than central government had been before in all of the sectors examined: education, agriculture, water & sanitation, health, urban development, and transport. These shifts were disproportionately driven by Bolivia's smaller, poorer districts, which benefited from a massive transfer of resources at the expense of the center and cities.

The temporal pattern of investment—very heavy in certain sectors immediately following reform, with other sectors rising in prominence in later years—is highly suggestive. What it suggests is a process of organizational learning in which local governments cut their teeth on comparatively simple, highly visible projects that enjoy broad support such as building schools and town squares. In the process they built capacity in budgeting, bidding, technical oversight, and other skills important to public management. This allowed them to progress to projects that are more complicated, expensive, and intensive in capital and technical skills, such as roads, health clinics, water & sewerage systems, and improving agricultural productivity.

These results are exactly the opposite of what many academics and policymakers predict, and what some researchers have found in the past. Why is Bolivia different? Why did Bolivia's municipalities behave in this manner? To answer, we must investigate the political mechanisms by which power is allocated locally, and the social and institutional methods by which public decisions are made. Chapters 2 and 3 did so with qualitative evidence, using thick description to provide accounts of the workings of local government in the best and worst of my case studies, which ranked easily among the best and worst municipalities in Bolivia as a whole. The extremal focus places in stark relief the systematic differences in decision making that characterize each. This, in turn, facilitated theorizing about institutional causes, effects, and necessary conditions relating to the quality of local government.

In Viacha (chapter 2) government was unresponsive, violent, and corrupt. This was largely due to the mayor's successful efforts to short-circuit public accountability by sabotaging the institutions of government, leaving them unable to carry out their role in the governance system, and him free to deform local policy in his own, and his party's, interests. By contrast governance in Charagua (chapter 3) was participative and responsive, led by strong institutions of government that produced high-quality policy outputs. Careful consideration of how policy is made, from the perspectives of all the major and intermediate players in each district, shows that the performance of public institutions was firmly grounded in the local economy, political system, civil society, and the interactions among them.

The case studies showed that local governments in Bolivia were capable of accountable, responsive, and efficient government, and also of systematic corruption, unresponsiveness and ineptitude. Which response predominated? Quantitative data on the universe of Bolivian municipalities over the period 1987–2007 provide more rigorous econometric evidence in chapter 4 confirming the shifts in investment patterns described above. Decentralization changed investment significantly in education, water management, industry & tourism, health, and agriculture after the 1994 reform, and to a lesser degree in transport and water & sanitation. These shifts are strongly and positively related to real local needs. In education, water & sanitation, health, agriculture, and at least one kind of urban development, decentralized investments are higher where illiteracy rates are higher, sewerage connection rates lower, malnutrition a greater risk, and so on respectively. These relationships are robust and insensitive to specification. Decentralization thus led to higher investment in human capital and social services as poorer, more deprived regions of the country chose the investment projects they needed most.

Why does the Bolivian experience of decentralization speak so clearly? This question has two broad answers. The first is that Bolivia decentralized sincerely. Unlike many countries, where reform is promised and even legislated, but only partially if at all implemented, in Bolivia real power and resources were devolved to local governments. This process was both rapid and surprisingly transparent. The second answer, as argued in chapter 5, is the approach employed in this book, consisting of three elements: (1) a clear, restrictive definition of decentralization; (2) combined quantitative and qualitative methods that produce empirical results characterized by high generality and deep nuance, and thus powerful insight; and (3) asking the right kind of question.

This last point is especially important. The right kind of question is not "What does decentralization do?" as if reform were a policy lever yielding discrete, well-defined outputs. Asking such questions has drawn many studies into an analytical stance that is deeply ironic given its subject matter: a centralized focus on top-down processes such as legal and regulatory changes, or fiscal transfer rules, that are national-systemic in character. Such concerns are obviously important but should not obscure the very different local dynamics that decentralization sets into motion. The right question begins, instead, with the presumption that decentralization in any context produces a range of responses that are heterogeneous and complex. The main question is not which response dominates—in a fluid social system all dominances can be transient and none in particular need last for long. The main question, rather, is What underlying factors cause such variation in response? And what are the political and societal determinants of certain responses of particular interest, for example, those that make municipalities more honest and transparent, equitable, or prosperous? In simple terms, what makes good municipalities good, and what makes bad ones bad?

Taking up such questions forces us to understand not just municipalities' static characteristics (history, geography, local structure of production), but also the microdynamics by which social, economic, and political actors relate to each other, compete for advantage, and cooperate or conflict. It is these dynamics, as we have seen in detail, that determine the effectiveness of local government, and its accountability and responsiveness to the governed. Ultimately, the success or failure of decentralization depends upon the character of such local dynamics. The overarching lesson of this book is that the outcome of decentralization is largely the aggregation of the abundance of local processes that it sets into motion. To understand decentralization, we must understand governance from the ground up. We must think less about "decentralization," and more about grassroots democracy.

Understanding Governance

Why, then, are good municipalities good and bad ones bad? Chapter 6 stepped back from the wealth of empirical data to ask this canonical question. I analyzed key factors in the local economy, politics, and society that drive government performance. Using these building blocks, I developed a model of government that integrates a variety of well-established insights on the role of elections and lobbying in democratic politics with more recent ideas about civic organizations and social linkages. The framework provides a structure in which economic interests, political actors, and civic organizations interact to make policy decisions. Placing this structural model of government in a dynamic context allows us to analyze how voting, lobbying, and civic organizations interact over time to produce public decision making that is responsive and accountable to voters, or not.

The resulting theory of government proposes that responsiveness and accountability are primarily products of the openness and substantive competition of politics. The quality of a municipality's politics, in turn, emerges endogenously as the joint product of the lobbying and political engagement of its firms and other economic actors, and the organizational density and ability of its civil society. Where economic interests are many and diverse, the chances are greater that a broad variety of political parties will find financial support and vie for votes. The ensuing competition will better represent diverse currents within society, giving voice to groups whose interests might otherwise be overlooked. And where society is organized into a dense network of intermediating organizations that can solve the collective action problem to aggregate preferences and transmit information, government will receive more and better-quality information about society's needs, as well as feedback on previous interventions. An organized society is far more likely to participate in public decision making and provide counterpart contributions, thus extending investment budgets and increasing the quality and sustainability of public goods and services. Where there is broad representation and competition in politics combined with high information and mobilizing capacity in civil society, government will have a strong tendency toward responsiveness and accountability to citizens. This model is notable for going beyond the correlation that others have found between "civicness" or "social capital" and government performance, and proposing a specific mechanism by which civic groups interact with economic and political agents to determine policy outcomes.

These predictions accord well with my case study evidence. Do large-scale statistical results concur? Yes. Econometric evidence in chapter 7, covering all municipalities over the period 1994–2007, shows that where a large number of firms interacted through the political system with an organizationally rich civil society, local policy decisions were responsive to the objective needs and subjective preferences of voters. Firms and civic organizations proved to be important determinants of local decision making, and our empirical strategy allows us to identify how. Both firms and GROs affected how local governments prioritize local needs—via lobbying, voter mobilization, or otherwise mediating information flows and helping to sustain political competition. They not only pressed local governments for the specific policies they prefer, often at cross purposes, but also interacted directly with each other in the policy-making process.

These interactions are independently significant not only in the narrow statistical sense but substantively as well, in the sense that they resolved the competing priorities of different actors. For example the independent effect of GROs was to increase, and of firms to decrease, investment in education. The tension was resolved when firms and GROs interacted directly through the local political system; these interactions led to investment *increases* that were positively related to local need and huge. In urban development, by contrast, both firms and GROs worked to increase investment in places where it was needed less. But the effect of their mutual interactions went in the opposite direction, increasing investment where infrastructure was scarce and decreasing it where infrastructure was abundant.

Why would the interaction of firms and GROs change the effects of their actions on policy outcomes? Because it revealed new information to each side? Because it permitted firms and GROs to reach a broader accommodation across different policy areas? Or perhaps the priorities of one or both actors actually changed as a result of interacting? What exactly does it mean for the private sector and civil society to interact, and by doing so to create an open, competitive politics? Such questions are beyond the scope of my evidence, and so I leave them for future empirical research. But in theoretical terms we can say more now. The prominence of social interactions in a model of governance is deeply rooted in our knowledge of human behavior and echoes some of the most important insights of other branches of the social sciences.

The benefits of trade, for example, are not limited to the economies of scale and division of labor it permits, although these are significant. Trade is also a key vector for the entry of new ideas, technologies, and ways of doing things into a society. By opening an economy to trade, a society necessarily opens itself to the ideas of those it trades with. Over time such ideas can transform not only what the society makes and how it makes these things, but how the society itself is organized. Witness the social and economic transformation of China since 1979. In this intellectual sense, trade is a form of interaction across distance. Its power lies in facilitating an exchange of ideas that is both extended across time and intimate in its intrusion into people's lives, with societies that may be very far away and very different from our own. The literature on innovation, too, shows that industries tend naturally to cluster in certain places in defiance of congestion costs and competitive disadvantages. They do so not just for the natural and human resources that may be available there, but because the intensity of interactions facilitated by being close to similar firms spurs efficiency and innovation.

And urban theorists point out that people continue flocking to cities, even mega-cities afflicted by crime, congestion, and pollution, all over the world. This is not the oddity it is sometimes made out to be but rather a continuing echo of the first humans who abandoned foraging to live together in the first proto-urban settlements some 10,000 years ago. They continue because despite the costs of city life, which are real, city dwellers are systematically healthier, smarter, and happier; lead greener lives; and are economically and culturally richer than those who live elsewhere. These advantages flow from the scale and intensity of social interactions that cities create, which speeds the circulation and mutation of ideas, encouraging invention and creativity in technology, organization, the arts—indeed all aspects of life. Two heads think better than one, the adage tells us, and ten million heads think better still.

Interactions benefit many realms of human activity, and government is no exception. The theory developed in this book shows that they are central to democracy. More than voting, it is the intensity and quality of interactions that largely determine whether governments are accountable and responsive to citizens or not. Interactions between and among citizens, civic organizations, firms, religious groups, NGOs, universities, and all of the other myriad groups that make up society are how policy-relevant information is acquired, opinions exchanged, and positions formed. For responsive governance to obtain, the political system must be capable of three things: (1) the formation and articulation of shared preferences, (2) the aggregation of shared preference into agreed-upon programs, and (3) the enforcement of accountability.

Politics does not achieve this through elections. Elections allocate power to winning teams, and in doing so anchor the system. But they are not themselves key. Rather they provide the incentive for citizens and groups to invest significant resources generating and consuming policy-relevant information, discussing, debating, lobbying, rallying, protesting, and engaging in all of the related activities that are crucial for society to analyze challenges, weigh options, and select policies. People expend these resources to engage in these interactions in order to sway elections. But it is the interactions that are crucial.

By engaging in such interactions, the citizens of a democracy do more than engage in governance. It is often said that, by conveying language, culture, history, norms and rules of behavior, and other abstract ideas that have accreted over time down through the generations, education is what perpetuates civilization and makes people fully human. In a similar vein, the interactions implicit in democracy turn individuals into citizens—citizens who ponder, investigate, express public views, debate specific solutions, and vote. In so doing, they take some measure of responsibility for the decisions and actions of the polity. Where the citizen cannot vote, she does not investigate, discuss, or expend effort on public affairs. Rather, she waits for policy to happen and then adjusts her personal life accordingly. She may gripe about government, but in the deeper sense she does not think about it because she is not responsible.

In Bolivia, decentralization turned passive residents into engaged citizens, many of whom became deeply involved in local affairs, and most of whom voted. The econometric evidence of chapter 7 suggests a healthy local democracy in which different interests competed through the political system, wielding varying amounts of influence over different issues, and voters were able to influence government through their civil institutions, providing an effective counterweight to the power of private firms and economic interests.

Put another way, the model explains that good municipalities are good because the residual authority that decentralization disperses from the center to the periphery accrues by and large to citizens. This happens as a result of civic groups and private firms competing for influence in the realm of local politics. Such interactions provide citizens with distinct pathways for influencing policy and making their voices heard. Bad municipalities, by contrast, are bad because economic interests are insufficiently diverse, or civil society insufficiently organized, leading to a local politics that is closed and uncompetitive. This in turn allows residual authority to be captured by intermediaries who exercise it in their own interests and not those of the mass of citizens.

But neither "good" nor "bad" is destiny, and indeed the theory can also explain how municipalities can be transformed over time. Chapter 8 returned to Viacha and Charagua 12 years later to examine persistence and change in governance. We found transformation in both, most dramatically in Viacha, from dismal performance to a capable administration that invited citizen participation and gave quarterly public reports. In Charagua, decision making had been driven deep down into the social fabric—small, dispersed Guaraní communities—resulting in a multiplication of participation and information among villagers, and of accountability to them. In both municipalities, transformation was driven by the emergence of dense networks of civic organizations that organized and educated citizens, amplified their voices, and represented their interests in the local government process. But this ascendancy of civil society, which occurred in both municipalities, is insufficient to explain the transformation of either. Civil society could only emerge in Viacha after the withdrawal of the CBN from public life ended systematic political and electoral distortions. And Guarani society's emergence in Charagua is tied to the decline of the cattle-ranching economy. Hence the transformation of governance in both was driven by the interaction of private sector actors with civic organizations. In each place, civic groups interacted with economic actors to support a local politics that was increasingly open, competitive, and focused on local needs.

This led, in turn, to improving responsiveness and accountability, as the theory would predict.

Now return to the larger question of what decentralization did to Bolivia. Decentralization led to major changes in national policy by making government more responsive to real local needs. It did so via the creation of hundreds of local governments throughout the country. These proved more sensitive to local conditions, and more accessible to lobbying and grassroots pressure, than a central administration that simply abandoned large expanses of territory as convenience dictated. The superior responsiveness of local government is a product of the structure of local governance, and in particular of the local dynamics that operate within it. Indeed, the effectiveness of decentralization as policy reform is largely the result of enabling these local dynamics throughout the country, where previously no policy-making took place. In so doing, decentralization engaged thousands of neighborhood councils, peasant communities, and *ayllus* and *mallkus* that predate the Spanish Conquest, as well as interest groups and business associations that previously had no voice in how their communities were run. By locating real resources and political power in municipal institutions it reached out to rich and poor strata alike offering them the means to improve their lives, and thus a concrete incentive to participate.

This changed not only the form of government in Bolivia but also its substance. Before 1994 the relatively few central officials stationed beyond national and regional capitals had almost no incentive to concern themselves with local demands. Career success was determined by ministerial fiat unrelated to local outcomes in distant districts. Policy-making did not happen in the provinces, and officials—who could afford to ignore local interest groups—fixed their gaze firmly on La Paz. In a sparsely populated country twice the size of France with a per capita income of $4.50/day, poor groups beyond the main few cities could realistically expect to wield no influence on central government policy, especially on such issues as schools and street lighting. Business interests and the rich might eventually hope to gain some favors from the center, but throughout most of the country ordinary citizens' ordinary concerns were effectively excluded. Decentralization changed this by creating local authorities dependent on local voters. Throughout the national territory it put real power over public resources in the hands of ordinary citizens. This led officials—not always but more often than not—to respond to citizens' needs. That simple fact changed the way the country is run.

Decentralization and Political Transformation

These changes were not transient, nor were they limited to local policies and local administrations. During its first decade the effects of decentralization appeared naturally limited to municipal budgets and municipal affairs. But in its second decade the deeper changes set in motion by decentralization reached up to the national level and swept away not only the ruling party but indeed the entire political-party system.

Since 1952 politics in Bolivia was centered on the MNR—the party of the revolution—accompanied by various opponents and offshoots to both left and right that alternated in power in a broadly stable equilibrium that survived both coups and dramatic economic shocks. The government that decentralized Bolivia in 1994 was a typical product of this system, a multi-party coalition led by the MNR. But in 2003 political protests against another MNR-led coalition government turned violent, leading to a sudden popular uprising centered on La Paz and El Alto that overturned not only the president (Sánchez de Lozada, serving a second term), but—as eventually became clear—the entire political system. Sánchez de Lozada had been elected with fewer votes than before and so was dependent upon a larger number of more diverse parties for his congressional majority. As his political position weakened in 2002–3, he drew more parties into the alliance.[1] Thus when protesters were killed by the security services and protest turned into revolt, not only was the president implicated, and the MNR, but most of the political system. When Sánchez de Lozada fell, all of the "traditional" parties fell with him.

The end of that story is the beginning of Bolivia's new political trajectory led by President Evo Morales and his Movimiento al Socialismo (MAS). Most of the parties that dominated Bolivia's political life for 50 years no longer exist, or—like the MNR—survive in the dying memories of the veterans of 1952. The MAS itself is a still-developing, comparatively loose political movement much less organized or institutionalized than the MNR was before, its appeal largely centered on Morales himself. How it is likely to develop, and what sort of new political equilibrium it will help shape, is as yet impossible to say. But what can be concluded already is that the advent of local government in Bolivia was crucial to the rise of the MAS, and crucial to the political transformation that has swept the country.

To see this, consider some simple stylized facts. Until the 1990s Congress was dominated by Bolivia's business, professional and landed elite. More than 90 percent of its members were from the *clase dirigente*—educated upper-middle- and upper-class people with European surnames, private educations, and residences in its largest cities' best neighborhoods. They typically developed careers in the private sector before penetrating national politics horizontally, via a party. Today over half of Bolivia's Congress, and over 80 percent of its Constitutional Convention, comes from small towns and villages. They tend to be shorter and browner than their forebears, with indigenous surnames (e.g., Callisaya, Chacalluca, Mamani, Quispe), fewer diplomas, and previous careers as truck drivers, carpenters, and farmers (as distinct from land owners). As Zuazo (2009) notes, they overwhelmingly got their political start in municipal government, as GRO leaders, municipal councillors, and mayors. This served as platform and training ground, allowing them to ascend to departmental and national politics through successive elections. In simple terms, decentralization provided a ladder up for budding politicians in Bolivia's villages and poor neighborhoods where previously none existed. Although they adhered to established parties for the first few elections, they soon turned their backs on elites and overthrew their parties in favor of their own amorphous movement.

If the future of this new political class is hard to predict, the future of decentralization is not. Bolivia's current rulers were formed in the crucible of local politics. They see it as both natural and "theirs." They want more of it, as does the electorate. Hence one of President Morales's major reforms is the expansion of the scope and types of subnational government via the 2009 Constitution and the 2010 Law of Autonomies and Decentralization. A major innovation is the integration of the concept of autonomy into the preexisting regime of municipal and departmental decentralization. Autonomy is exercised by elected subnational authorities who have powers to create and collect taxes, enact local resolutions, design and implement local policies in the judicial, administrative, economic, cultural, and social fields, and use coercive powers to compel respect for their decisions (Article 7). Four levels of autonomy are defined: departmental, regional, municipal, and indigenous and rural. The first three represent modifications of existing subnational institutions, but the fourth is new. It concerns "nations and peoples who share a cultural identity, language, historical traditions, institutions, territory, and world view" (Art. 30(1)). The law allows such communities to apply their own principles, practices, and forms of organization to the question of self-government, defense of their cultures, and organization of their economies. Within such areas, communities' traditional or preferred forms of self government supersede the legal forms of the state (e.g., elected mayors and municipal councils) and act in their place.

Charagua was one of the first municipalities to vote in favor of indigenous autonomy but has yet to implement it. How the new, expanded regime of decentralization, with more powers and resources at its disposal, will develop will not be known for years yet. But these recent developments confirm that of all of the first Sánchez de Lozada government's reforms, decentralization is the one that has become most deeply embedded in the country's legal and political infrastructure.

Lessons from Bolivia

Let us leave aside for now the probable link between decentralization and political transformation. Although interesting, this requires further research of a different type to establish empirically. Regardless, the transformations in question are too recent to assess with confidence. This leaves us nonetheless with a dramatically positive country experience of decentralization increasing government accountability and responsiveness, and ultimately deepening democracy. Could these experiences be replicated elsewhere?

Yes. Without forgetting the common, sensible cautions against importing policy advice into inappropriate contexts, and without pretending that Bolivia provides a blueprint for all countries, it is my view—on the other hand—that Bolivia is not so unique among developing countries, and the institutional challenges of designing a good decentralization reform are not so historically or geographically specific, that we cannot learn lessons to apply elsewhere. Bolivia's decentralization succeeded because it was sincere, shifting real authority and resources from the center to the periphery, and because it created elected local governments that more often than not responded to local citizens' needs. The local dynamics that it set into motion proved virtuous, not only permitting good cases of local governance to improve but spurring distorted cases to heal themselves. How can reformers elsewhere achieve similar results?

The first concrete lesson is that decentralization in Bolivia undoubtedly benefited from speed. Decentralization was announced in January 1994, promulgated in April, and implemented on 1 July of the same year.

Any reform proposing a major redistribution of residual authority will face significant opposition from those within the executive who currently exercise residual authority, and those without who benefit from the status quo. Implementing reform slowly has few benefits in terms of municipal learning, as most of this will occur through learning-by-doing, and in a slow policy rollout those who do not do do not learn. But it will incur potentially large costs, as an opposition that is in principle formidable will have time to organize and plan how best to overturn or—more frequently—undermine reform. Implementing reform quickly, by contrast, denies the opposition time to organize, or—in the Bolivian case—even fully understand the implications of reform. Residual authority can be taken from their hands before they have found a place to hide it.

Consider two possible analogies for decentralization: stabilization and liberalization. Gradualism increases the transition cost of economic stabilization and decreases its chance of success. When the currency is falling, fiscal deficits are ballooning, and hyperinflation is eroding price signals, the best response is shock therapy, which takes those who gain from instability by surprise, rapidly resets general expectations, and creates a large constituency that benefits from reform. Liberalization, by contrast, benefits from a gradualism that provides private firms more time to adjust to increased competition from imports, often by importing foreign technologies and organizational forms. In pure incentive terms decentralization is like stabilization, and unlike liberalization.

A second advantage of Bolivian reform was its simplicity and transparency. While other countries have imposed complicated transfer systems between center and periphery in the name of equity, efficiency, or a number of more specific policy goals, Bolivia initiated reform with a simple per capita criterion that held regardless of geography, poverty, distance from a major city, and so on. Although less efficient and less equitable in purely technical terms than a number of feasible alternatives, per capita allocations aided the success of reform immensely in that the financial implications of decentralization were immediately obvious to a largely poor, poorly educated population. In my travels through Bolivia, I heard numerous times, as both praise and lament, stories of villagers accosting municipal authorities and demanding their fair share. These villagers very likely did not know their Gini coefficient, nor their index of Unsatisfied Basic Needs. But they did know how many they were.

Other aspects of decentralization were also simple. The list of services devolved and infrastructure transferred to local control consisted of obviously local services that citizens could easily identify, such as education, health, local roads, and sporting and cultural facilities. This greatly facilitated ex post oversight. Municipal boundaries were drawn to respect preexisting administrative and geographic frontiers, and a straightforward procedure was implemented for communities seeking to secede from one district and join another. The procedure for registering grassroots organizations (to form oversight committees) was made simple and (to GROs) costless. And all of this information was published in newspapers, announced by radio stations, and distributed in pamphlets throughout the country.

Third, Bolivian reform built enhanced accountability measures into decentralization via municipal oversight committees, which operate alongside the formal institutions of power—municipal councils and the mayor—and complement them both functionally and in their form of representation. Their role is in effect to incorporate preexisting levels of social organization and legitimacy, via *ayllus, mallkus,* peasant union locals, neighborhood councils, tribal structures, and so on, into the process of municipal decision making, and hence into local governance more broadly. Their power resides in their ability to suspend central transfers to local authorities, which highlights another element of simplicity. When transfers are suspended the center does not impose a solution, or even a process for their resumption. It simply invites the parties to negotiate and inform the Treasury independently when they have agreed, relying on the promise of resources to provide appropriate incentives.

Fourth, the changing pattern of municipal investment over time identified in chapter 1, and the degree of municipal learning it implies, underlines that **decentralization is a policy process,** not a policy prescription or discrete intervention similar to building a road or raising a tax. It is a devolution of resources and power from one set of people to another who face different, and in practice heterogeneous, incentives, and whose actions therefore cannot be predicted in any detail. Especially at the outset, the consequences of reform will be unstable, changing as conditions change and as important actors learn and adjust to emerging local dynamics. This is not a failing. It is a necessary implication of sincere decentralization, and indeed a sign of its success.

Perhaps because of speed, simplicity, transparency, and accountability, Bolivian decentralization proved sincere, succeeding in dispersing residual authority to the periphery. This is evident in the national budgets from those years: sectoral ministries lost resources and assets, and regional development corporations—previously central agents of regional development—saw their budgets slashed. Local governments, by contrast, gained title to significant local infrastructure and saw their incomes rise, on average, by huge amounts. Why did reformers succeed in Bolivia?

This problem is akin to a black hole at the heart of the decentralization debate that policy thinkers have been slow to grasp. The question is, Why would anyone willingly do it? Appeals to the common good or Pareto efficiency may convince academic seminars but will leave politicians unmoved. Why would someone who has finally reached a position of national power willingly give up significant authority and resources to lower, independent actors that he cannot control? This is the essence of decentralization, and politicians do not do it because it sounds nice. The logic cascades across sectors of the economy and down the chain of command. How happy is a minister of education, or the governor of a state, to hand power away? She is not—she is interested in making decentralization fail. Hence when asked to decentralize, a central bureaucracy will tend to resist, while making noises to the contrary and pleading insufficient resources for the job.

In Bolivia this problem was solved by the long-term decline of the natural party of power. The MNR, the party of the Bolivian Revolution in 1952–53, which had enjoyed the support of the peasantry, labor unions, and much of the educated middle classes, was losing votes to new ethnically based, populist parties. A reforming president was able to sell decentralization to a skeptical party with the promise that reform was likely to win back the loyalty of voters living beyond the main cities for a generation or more, much as land reform had done four decades earlier. Decentralization became viable because it solved a specific political problem for the party that held power, which could then be convinced to give some of it away. This illustrates a **fifth lesson,** which is a general point about the motivation behind decentralization. Some visionaries may embark on reform based on ideas of what is good or right. But where real politics is concerned, a more reasonable assumption is that **the parties and government officials who must cooperate with reformers for decentralization to succeed will do so if and when reform solves a particular political problem for those who hold power.** Their success in implementing decentralization will in large part rely on their ability to make subordinates obey.

Democracy and Decentralization

As we reach the end of a long, complex set of theoretical and empirical arguments, it is salutary to remember what the question of decentralization is at its most basic level. Imagine a country composed of a capital, *C,* and a number of towns, *T.* The issue of decentralization can be reduced to one simple question: Who should choose the local services provided in *T*? Officials in *T* who respond directly to its residents, or officials in *C* who do not? The formulation is, of course, simplistic. But the intuition it calls forth is powerful and, in my experience, remarkably consistent across culture, class, and region of the world. The reason behind it is the axiomatic belief in the value of democracy that most of us share. If the rule by the people for the people is self-evidently good, then why should public services in *T,* which primarily affect the people of *T,* be determined by people elsewhere? External factors like corruption, capture, and macroeconomic instability are valid objections but are less powerful than would be an objection of principle that emerged from within the argument. For people who believe in the normative value of democracy, such an objection is very hard to find.

Which is why critics overwhelmingly object to decentralization based on its real-world, empirical flaws, and not as an ideal-typical form. Indeed, they cannot do the latter as this would require them to object to a variant of democracy, which almost all that I have read (and I have read many) favor. It is interesting to note that this affinity to democracy is not to the dirty empirical reality as practiced in places like Bangladesh, Nigeria, and Russia but to its ideal-typical form. Were they to evaluate democracy as they do decentralization, they would have to conclude that the empirical evidence is indeterminate.

This book has ultimately been about the possibility of change, and its message is hopeful. The reform of institutions and their associated incentives can bring about significant, nationwide changes in social and political behavior in the space of a few years. The Bolivian experiment argues against the position that policy performance and patterns of governance are determined by centuries of historical conditioning. When reform creates opportunities to improve group welfare, people can rise to the challenge and succeed. This includes the very poor and oppressed. The conditions necessary for reform to prosper are a complex of economic, political, and social characteristics, and may well be lacking as often as they are present. But under the right circumstances, which proved widely available in Bolivia, decentralizing resources and political authority can generate real accountability where none existed before and can improve the quality of government a society achieves.

The experience of decentralization in Bolivia underlines a deeper point that is denied by some of decentralization's foes but that is nonetheless true. The poor as a rule are ignorant, but they are not stupid. They know what they want, and the things they want are by and large good for them. They can ill afford otherwise. Decentralization succeeded in Bolivia because it created more Charaguas than Viachas. It put significant power and resources in the hands of ordinary people, who then made good choices. Such a conclusion is not hopelessly naive. It is the essence of democracy.

APPENDIX: CHAPTER 4 DATA AND
PRINCIPAL COMPONENT VARIABLES

The surprisingly large amount of information available for Bolivia during the period 1987–2007 demands a strategy for choosing, from among 1,200+ variables, those that are most appropriate and most closely related to the underlying concepts I wish to test. In particular, a number of measures in which I am interested are present in my data set as multiple, finely differentiated variables. I have data on, for example, 16 varieties of capacity-building exercises undertaken by municipalities and 13 different local actors who assisted in drafting municipal development plans. The challenge is to reduce such groups to at most one indicator each without loss of information.

My empirical strategy is iterative and begins by finding the best idiosyncratic model of public investment for each of the 10 sectors of interest. I fit the equation

$$G_m = \zeta S_m + \eta Z + \varepsilon_m \tag{A1}$$

separately for central public investment (pre-1994) and local public investment (post-1994) where G_m is aggregate investment per capita in the public good subscripted by municipality, S_m is a scalar or vector of the existing stock of public goods of that type (variously defined) at an initial period, and Z is a vector of socioeconomic, demographic, regional, political, institutional, administrative, and procedural variables that might affect investment decisions. The use of the Z term follows the literature on the demand for public goods exemplified by Bergstrom and Goodman (1973) and Rubinfeld, Shapiro, and Roberts (1987) within the context of the available data. In particular, no income data is available at the municipal level in Bolivia, and so I substitute several alternative indicators of income and wealth, for example, type of cooking fuel and housing size, quality, and related characteristics. But I expand the scope of the Z vector considerably compared to previous authors by including measures of the strength of local political forces as well as municipal institutional capacity. This innovation allows me to investigate the micropolitical basis of local government decision making, explored in detail by Faguet (2008b).

No constraints across sectors are allowed on the particular variables admissible in Z. I use the Huber/White estimator of variance to produce consistent standard errors in the presence of non–identically distributed residuals. This produces 10 different models of public sector investment, one for each sector. Individually these models are quite satisfactory, with high R^2 and few variables insignificant. But because of large variation in the specification of the Z vector, comparison across sectors is problematic. In addition, on a theoretical level these models would seem to assert that public investment in different sectors happens according to different processes, in which different variables intervene. This is evidently unsatisfying.

In a second iteration I reestimate equation (A1) holding the Z vector constant across all sectors. But I take advantage of the previous stage by using only those variables found significant there; in this sense the previous stage constitutes a method for reducing the 1,200+ indicators to a subset of 197. But a dimensionality problem persists even so. I then employ a method of forward and backward substitution and elimination in order to reduce this subset to 22 variables encompassing the 13 categories of Z, in specifications of 23–30 variables overall. These models benefit from being readily comparable across sectors. The ratio of significant to insignificant variables drops sharply compared to the first stage, however, and R^2 values are somewhat lower.

The insignificance of the variables chosen is not entirely separable from the issue of comparability, however. In these results none of the variables is significant in most of the sectors, and many are significant in only two or three. How do we interpret a given variable across sectors, knowing that an alternative one from the same group would produce a different pattern of significance and insignificance? For example, how do we interpret the insignificance of training & capacity-building variables in most models when we know from stage 1 that there is at least one alternative such variable that is significant in each sector? We evidently cannot assert for any sector that capacity-building does not matter; we must conclude that the comparability constraint forces us to omit from our models information that is important in explaining investment behavior.

Indeed, given that there are 197 variables, many of them quite specific, which have explanatory power over the dependent variable, *any* subset of 20, 30, or even 100 will omit valuable information. We require a solution that allows us to retain the full breadth of information, and yet produces a specification that is both comparable and parsimonious. I turn to principal component analysis, a data reduction technique in which the objective is to find the unit-length combinations of explanatory variables with the highest variance. I follow Maddala (1977) in calculating variables z_1 to z_k where z is a linear combination of the x variables,

$$z_1 = a_1 x_1 + a_2 x_2 + \cdots + a_L x_L$$
$$z_2 = b_1 x_1 + b_2 x_2 + \cdots + b_L x_L \text{ etc.}[1]$$

ranked in order of variance, with highest first. Principal component analysis regresses y on $z_1, z_2, \ldots, z_k$, where $k < L$ and z's are constructed so as to be orthogonal. So long as the z's chosen represent combinations of variables that have economic meaning and can be interpreted, this provides a method for estimating parsimonious models with limited loss of information.

I calculate a set of principal component variables (PCVs) based on the raw variables retained in stage 1. I discard all those with low eigenvalues, as per normal procedure, and then find the remaining subset that optimally estimate equation (A1), where Z is a vector of PCVs. The PCVs used in this chapter are summarized below. Detailed interpretations follow.

Interpretation of Principal Component Variables

> *Civic Organizations:* These are indicators of the number of organizations and institutions of local civil society. They rise in all the variables, especially in the more general measures. We interpret them as a proxy for the density and strength of local civic organizations.
>
> *Private Sector:* These PCVs rise in the number of private businesses registered locally. We interpret them as indicators of the dynamism of the local private sector.
>
> *Training and Capacity Building:* These variables rise in categories of training (i.e., institutional strengthening) received by the municipality and fall in those requested but not yet received. Hence we interpret them as measures of the intensity of capacity-building efforts undertaken by/for local government.

Information Technology: These PCVs rise in the IT systems—hardware and software (especially software)—at the disposal of each municipality.

Project Planning: These PCVs load positively where municipalities use information on education and health when planning projects, where sectoral regulations are followed in water & sanitation, where a Municipal Development Plan exists, and where councilmen and oversight committees identify investment projects using the MDP and urban cadaster. They load negatively where the mayor is the one who identifies investment projects and where problems arise with the Annual Operating Plan. These are thus straightforward indicators of informed project planning that follows consensual and open procedures.

Engagement with Central Government: These PCVs load positively on the frequency with which municipalities report their spending to higher levels of government, and the existence of projects financed by the central government's Social Investment Fund. They also load positively for municipalities with direct access to the central public investment information system, and on central government audits of municipal accounts. Hence I interpret these as indicators of municipal engagement with central government systems and processes.

TABLE A.1. Chapter 4 Data Summary

Variable	Obs.	Mean	Std. Dev.	Min	Max
Need Variables					
Illiteracy rate (over-6's)	310	21.47819	10.85378	4.445149	56.83009
Illiteracy rate (over-15's)	310	20.23656	10.53749	3.846984	52.70807
Illiteracy rate (adult)	310	30.46375	15.82312	5.5	78.7
School attendance rate	309	71.83447	12.01793	23.47826	92.8
Private health care, % households using mainly	310	10.33709	12.96731	0	89.82925
Other[a] health care, % households using mainly	310	4.398462	7.420584	0	65.27062
Number of health posts (lowest tier) per capita	308	0.0004648	0.000885	0	0.0076462
Number of doctor's offices (2nd tier) per capita	308	0.0000237	0.0000891	0	0.0008677
Number of health centers (3rd tier) per capita	309	0.0001043	0.0003251	0	0.0039292
% population lacking sewerage	310	76.14236	21.88933	14.65855	100
Storm drainage per capita	301	0.0000975	0.0010796	0	0.0175824
Malnutrition rate (mild) among boys	294	23.06979	7.268409	0	57.14286
Number of markets per capita	304	0.0014271	0.0108282	0	0.1517241
Number of museums per capita	307	0.0000197	0.0000834	0	0.0007096
Number of municipal greenhouses per capita	307	0.0000261	0.0001473	0	0.0018727
Number of theaters per capita	304	0.0000283	0.0000834	0	0.0007485
Storm drainage per capita	301	0.0000975	0.0010796	0	0.0175824
Civic, Private Sector, and Institutional Principal-Component Variables					
Private sector PCV1 (narrow)	302	−3.24E-09	1.529804	−0.3014942	18.07868
Private sector PCV1 (broad)	300	3.01E-09	2.218095	−0.3939436	28.14334
Civic organizations PCV1	303	2.40E-09	2.214992	−2.113017	14.53127
Civic organizations PCV2	303	−2.09E-09	1.409639	−0.7906216	19.95697
Civic organizations PCV3	303	3.74E-10	1.22872	−4.631424	12.27311
Information technology PCV1	310	1.64E-08	1.523458	−1.559143	5.086413
Information technology PCV2	310	4.94E-09	1.269668	−3.249391	2.235586
Engagement with central government PCV1	308	−4.60E-10	1.504751	−1.34103	5.628184
Engagement with central government PCV2	308	9.52E-11	1.225236	−1.770268	2.023645
Project planning PCV1 (narrow)	310	2.36E-09	1.591479	−2.717535	2.23125
Project planning PCV1 (broad)	310	1.89E-09	1.918622	−3.742305	3.183519
Training and capacity building PCV1	309	4.59E-09	2.16697	−4.098481	5.957512
Training and capacity building PCV2	309	3.46E-09	1.774462	−3.674549	4.47929
Local health authority dummy	310	0.916129	0.2776424	0	1

[a]Nonstate, nonprivate, non-NGO provided health care.

Notes

Introduction

1. The LSE site is http://personal.lse.ac.uk/faguetj/. The Press's website is http://www.press.umich.edu/titleDetailDesc.do?id=175269.

Chapter 1

1. Klein (1993), 237. Author's translation.
2. GDP in 1952 dollars.
3. See Klein (1993), chapter 9.
4. For a discussion of Santa Cruz's regionalism and central-local relations, see Rodríguez (1993) and Dunkerley (1984), chapter 3.
5. David Tuchschneider, World Bank rural development officer, interview, La Paz, 3 May 1997.
6. Detailed accounts of the story of decentralization reform can be found in Molina (1997), Gonzales-Arana (1992), and Grupo DRU (1996).
7. At the time MNR strategists gleefully predicted such a result. They were proved wrong.
8. "Injertos Tramposos en 'Participación Popular,'" *Hoy*, 19 January 1994; "La Declaratoria de Guerra del Primer Mandatario," *La Razon*, 27 January 1994; and "Arrogancia Insultante," *Presencia*, 27 February 1994 are only three of the many articles that appeared in the Bolivian press documenting popular reaction to the "Damned Law." These are documented in Unidad de Comunicación (1995).
9. Principally new presidential administrations in 1997 and 2002, the latter followed by political turmoil and the president's resignation in 2003.
10. Municipalities' legal priorities lie elsewhere, as described in section 2; energy and hydrocarbon projects are usually of regional or national scope in terms of costs and benefits, and so unsuited to individual municipalities.
11. Where possible, I use indicators of need from the first year of the period in question (e.g., from 1994 for 1994–96). For some need indicators, collected only in the 1992 census or 1997 "municipal census," this is not possible.
12. These upper values are not dropped in the sense that they are included in the calculation of the trend line.
13. This graph is not shown in order to conserve space; it is similar to figure 13.
14. These are projected illiteracy rates using point observations from the 1992 and 2001 censuses, the only data available for Bolivia's 310 municipalities.

15. These additional graphs, as well as graphs for other sectors, are available on the Press's website at http://www.press.umich.edu/titleDetailDesc.do?id=175269 as well as at http://personal.lse.ac.uk/faguetj/.

16. They may be viewed on the Press's website at http://www.press.umich.edu/titleDetailDesc.do?id=175269 as well as at http://personal.lse .ac.uk/faguetj/.

Chapter 2

1. Instituto Nacional de Estadística, *Censo Nacional de Población y Vivenda* (La Paz: INE, 1992). Viacha is the fourteenth most populous municipality in Bolivia.

2. An official poverty index calculated from census data.

3. Remigio Quispe Mendoza, Walter Patzi Paty, and Nemesio Mamani Fernández, oversight committee (1) president, federation of neighborhood councils (1) president and federation officer respectively, interview, Viacha, 18 March 1997.

4. Huber Quintela and Esteban Ticona, municipal councilmen (MNR and Condepa, respectively), interview, Viacha, 18 March 1997.

5. Dr. Reynaldo Aguilar, district director of health, interview, Viacha, 10 October 1997.

6. Luis González, departmental director, Social Investment Fund, interview, Viacha, 17 March 1997.

7. Carlos Núñez, interview, Viacha, 19 March 1997.

8. El Alto, itself a former suburb of La Paz, is largely the result of rural–urban migration on a much larger scale.

9. Councilman Esteban Ticona and Lt. Col. Adolfo Dávila Chacón, commander of the local military garrison, are two of many who recounted this commonly held view to me. In Dávila's words, "The death of Max Fernández was a big boon to the UCS. Condepa was stronger than the UCS in Viacha, but Max's death brought out the sympathy vote and the UCS won easily" (interview, 19 March 1997).

10. The structural reforms of 1993–94 extended the local electoral cycle from two to four years.

11. Oscar Magnani Meyta, interview, Viacha, 21 March 1997.

12. Alejandro Yujra, Rony Morales, and Hipólito Tovar, vice president of the Federation of Neighborhood Councils (Juntas) of Viacha (2), secretary of the neighborhood council of San José, and member and spokesman for OC2, interview, Viacha, 19 March 1997.

13. Edwin Callisaya, interview, Viacha, 18 March 1997.

14. Jorge Rada, chief financial officer, interview, Viacha, 15 October 1997.

15. María Luisa Lucuy (who had recently assumed the position of DDE), interview, Viacha, 15 October 1997.

16. Magnani, interview.

17. For example, the Education Reform Program calls for hexagonal primary school classrooms, but all of those built in Viacha during the previous few years were traditional "square boxes."

18. Magnani, interview.

19. Callisaya, interview.

20. Rada, interview.

21. Lucuy, interview.

22. Núñez, interview.

23. Quintela and Ticona, interview.

24. Luis Paz, CEO Incerpaz, interview, Viacha, 15 October 1997.

25. Aguilar, interview.

26. Gladys Lozano, subprefect for Ingavi province (MNR), interview, Viacha, 17 March 1997.

27. Bolivian prefects are appointed directly by the president. Subprefects are thus broadly viewed as representatives of the central government.

28. An unexpected occurrence given that the UCS was part of the national ruling coalition.

29. José Luis Claros, interview, Viacha, 21 March 1997.

30. Fr. Justino Limachi, parish priest, interview, Viacha, 16 October 1997.

31. Núñez, interview.

32. L. González, interview.

33. Dávila, interview.

34. Ibid.

35. José Quezo Cusi, community leader, Lorenzo Julián, teacher and electoral notary, and Olga Cusi de Julián, Plan Internacional liaison, interview, Santa Ana de Machaqa, 23 March 1997.

36. Ibid.

37. Lozano, interview.

38. Dávila, interview.

39. Callisaya, interview.

40. Paz, interview.

41. Lozano, interview.

42. Núñez, interview.

43. Esteban Ticona, municipal councilman, interview, Viacha, 9 October 1997.

44. Dávila, interview.

45. Rada, interview.

46. Hipólito Tovar, OC2 president, interview, Viacha, 19 March 1997.

47. Dávila, interview.

48. Quintela and Ticona, interview.

49. PDMs were developed through an elaborate series of participative planning seminars held in each of about 100 Bolivian municipalities in 1994. Delegates were invited from a broad spectrum of society to workshops where needs were identified and projects ranked based on individual communities' priorities. PDMs were meant to be multiyear plans, and the basis for drawing up Annual Operating Plans.

50. Quintela and Ticona, interview.

51. Ibid.

52. Ibid.

53. Quezo, Julián, and Cusi, interview.

54. Genaro Mamani Chiri, Gumercindo Vito Guarachi, Saturnino Tola Mamani, and Doroteo Callisaya Mamani, community leader, district official, representative to the Federation of Ayllus and Indigenous Communities of Ingavi Province (FA-COPI), and community official, respectively, interview, Titik'ana Takaka, 20 March 1997.

55. Gerónimo Colque, community deputy leader (District Six), Severo Guarachi, community leader (Chama), Simon Canavi, community leader (Viacha), and Alicia Rodríguez, women's leader (District Five), interviews, Viacha, 17 March 1997.

56. Callisaya, interview.

57. Quintela and Ticona, interview.

58. Paz, interview.

59. Tomás Palacios Rodríguez, Condepa local leader, interview, Viacha, 15 October 1997.

60. Lozano, interview.

61. Aguilar, interview.

62. This is only one, albeit the most radical, of the municipal council's countervailing powers.

63. A bonus chapter analyzing local governance in seven additional municipalities is available at http://personal.lse.ac.uk/faguetj/ as well as on the Press's website, http://www.press.umich.edu/titleDetailDesc.do?id=175269.

64. Dávila, interview.

65. Max Mercado, president of the Viachan Federation of Juntas, interview, 11 October 1997.

66. Remigio Quispe, president, oversight committee, interview, Viacha, 18 March 1997.

67. Of five sectors rated from "very good" to "very bad," Quispe rated only one sector "bad." Both the mayor and the municipal council rated two sectors as "bad."

68. A mathematics schoolteacher and resident of Viacha.

69. An engineering student and also resident of Viacha.

70. Yujra, Morales, and Tovar, interview.

71. Building in this manner saves on bricks but results in a weaker structure.

72. According to Morales and Tovar.

73. Rony Morales and Hipólito Tovar, secretary of the neighborhood council of San José, and member and spokesman for OC2, respectively, interview and site visits, Viacha, 21 March 1997.

74. Quezo, Julián, and Cusi, interview.

75. Paz, interview.

76. Yujra, Morales, and Tovar, interview.

77. Ticona, interview.

78. Municipalities are ranked administratively within each province, first, second, third, etc. The first municipality in each province is its capital, and residents typically take pride in this.

79. Ticona, interview.

80. Huber Quintela (a), municipal councilman (MNR), interview, Viacha, 10 October 1997.

81. Callisaya, interview.

82. Huber Quintela (b), municipal councilman (MNR), interview, Viacha, 16 October 1997.

83. The dollar sign ($) hereafter refers to U.S. dollars, the most common unit of account for large transactions in Bolivia.

84. Paz, interview.

85. Paz was evidently referring to votes for the UCS (party), and not the CBN (brewery). The failure to distinguish between them is telling.

86. Ibid.

87. Colque, interview; Guarachi, interview; Canavi, interview; and Rodríguez, interview.

88. Núñez, interview.

89. Edgar Robles, mayor, interview, Viacha, 10 October 1997.

90. Núñez, interview.

91. Dávila, interview. "But SOBOCE doesn't get involved," he added. "They're too pragmatic."

92. Paz, interview.

93. An enormous sum in Bolivia.

94. Juan Carlos Blanco, CBN bottling plant director, interview, Viacha, 16 October 1997.

95. Max Fernández, founder of both the UCS and CBN.

96. Esteban Ticona Alejo and Xavier Albó, *Jesús de Machaqa: La Marka Rebelde 3, La Lucha Por el Poder Comunal* (La Paz: CIPCA/CEDOIN, 1997), 295–96.

97. Ticona, interview.

98. Palacios, interview.

99. Ticona, interview.

100. Literally "Creole," meaning locally born descendants of European immigrants.

101. Quintela (b), interview.

102. Antonio Soto, MIR local leader, interview, Viacha, 10 October 1997.

103. Palacios, interview.

104. Villa Santiago de Chacoma, Rosapata, and Názacara, interviews, 11, 14, and 14 October 1997.

105. Cusi, Julián, and Cusi, interview.

106. Ticona and Albó, *Jesús de Machaqa,* 295–96.

107. Armando Godínez, anthropologist, numerous conversations, La Paz, February–May and September–November 1997.

108. Quispe, Patzi, and Mamani, interview; Yujra, Morales, and Tovar, interview.

109. Colque, interview; Guarachi, interview; and Rodríguez, interview.

110. Francisco Juliano Paz, Santa Ana de Machaqa community officer, interview, Viacha, 18 March 1997.

111. Mamani, Vito, Tola, and Callisaya, interview.

112. Juan Laurel Hinojosa, Dona Francisca Plata de Maldonado, Julio Choque Huanca, and Jaime Gómez, community coordinator, community leader, education officer and school director, interview, Názacara, 14 October 1997.

113. Eulogio Choque and Valentín Atahuichi Callisaya, cantonal officer and community construction officer, interview, Villa Santiago de Chacoma, 11 October 1997.

114. Cusi, Julián, and Cusi, interview.

115. Mamani, Vito, Tola, and Callisaya, interview.

116. Laurel, Plata, Choque, and Gómez, interview.

117. Colque, interview; Guarachi, interview; and Rodríguez, interview.

118. Laurel, Plata, Choque, and Gómez, interview.

119. Cusi, Julián, and Cusi, interview.

120. Mamani, Vito, Tola, and Callisaya, interview.

121. Ibid.

122. The peasants' union was, along with miners and public employees, an important component of the Confederation of Bolivian Labor, the leadership of which for many years wielded great power in the capital.

123. See Dunkerley (1984), Klein (1993), Albó et al. (1990), Ticona and Albó (1997), among others.

124. Dávila, interview.

125. Ticona and Albó (1997), 29–43.

126. Ibid., 40.

127. Ibid., 137. Author's translation.

128. Ibid., 137–39.

129. The mother earth goddess.

130. Andean holy men or priests.

131. Xavier Albó, Armando Godínez, Kitula Libermann, and Francisco Pifarré, *Para Comprender Las Culturas Rurales en Bolivia,* MEC/CIPCA/UNICEF (La Paz: 1990), 125–35.

132. Limachi, interview.

133. Samuel Doria Medina was the MIR's vice presidential candidate in the 1997 general election.

134. Blanco, interview.

135. *Presencia,* "Los vecinos viacheños marchan hoy para que se vaya su Alcalde," 22 March 1997.

136. Estimates of crowd size vary from 150 to 200 according to UCS spokesmen, to 500 according to OC2.

Chapter 3

1. Luis Saucedo Tapia (a), mayor of Charagua, interview, Santa Cruz, 31 March 1997.

2. Dr. Fernando Muñoz Franco, interview, Santa Cruz, 31 March 1997.

3. Secretaría Nacional de Participación Popular (1997), *Matriz Resumen de las*

Auditorías SAYCO Practicadas en Gobiernos Municipales Categoría "C" (Pob. Mayor a 15,000 y Menor a 50,000 Hab.): Informe SCAE/IEA.

4. Eulogio Núñez, CIPCA director (NGO) and municipal adviser, interview, Charagua, 2 April 1997.

5. I.e., based on population.

6. Saucedo (a), interview.

7. Xavier Albó, *Los Guaraní-Chiriguano: La Comunidad de Hoy,* La Paz: CIPCA, 1990, 19–22. Albó is acknowledged to be one of the premier authorities on Guaraní culture in Bolivia.

8. Fr. Gabriel Siquier (Tiano Piru), parish priest, interview, Isoso, 3 April 1997. Siquier is another Spanish priest who has dedicated his life to understanding and working with the Guaraní people.

9. Javier Medina, ed., *Arakuarenda: Un Centro Intercultural de Capacitación Para el Desarrollo Guaraní* (La Paz: Arakuarenda/FIS, 1994), 19–30.

10. Leonardo Guarupachi, Great Captain of Parapitiguasu (South Charagua), interview, rural South Charagua, 18 December 2009.

11. Corte Nacional Electoral (Dirección de Informática), Estadística de Votación Absoluta, Elecciones Municipales de 1993 y 1995. Database.

12. Pablo Diego Vaca and David Segundo, community leader and adviser, interview, Yapiroa, 3 April 1997. Local leaders held similar views in rural communities throughout Charagua, including Kapiwasuti, Taputamí, Akae, and El Espino, among others.

13. Guaraní for "white man."

14. Florencio Antuni Sánchez (a), oversight committee president, interview, Charagua, 1 April 1997.

15. Luis Saucedo Tapia (b), mayor, interview, Charagua, 1 April 1997.

16. Ibid.

17. Crispín Solano Menacho, municipal councilman (MBL) and ex-oversight committee president, interview, Charagua, 28 October 1997.

18. Antuni (a), interview.

19. Julián Segundo Chipipi, municipal councilman (MNR), interview, Charagua, 2 April 1997.

20. Abelardo Vargas Portales, municipal council president (ADN), interview, Charagua, 1 April 1997.

21. Walter García Juárez and Jorge Cortez Romero, community association president and community member, interview, Charagua, 3 April 1997.

22. Saucedo (b), interview.

23. E. Núñez, interview.

24. Antuni (a), interview.

25. Saucedo (a), interview.

26. Antuni (a), interview; Oscar Hugo Aramayo Caballero, district director of education, interview, Charagua, 4 April 1997.

27. E. Núñez, interview.

28. Saucedo (b), interview.

29. E. Núñez, interview.

30. Francisco Chávez Flores, Delcio Moreno Candia, Mario Arreaga, Andrés Chávez Flores, Vicente Moreno, and Licelio Cuéllar Martínez, community leader, aid to the *capitanía,* hospital administrator, nursing assistant, school association president and Alto Isoso district deputy, interview, La Brecha, 3 April 1997.

31. Vaca and Segundo, interview.

32. Demetrio Caurey and Florencio Altamirano, president of the community irrigation committee and infrastructure officer, interview, Kapiwasuti, 2 April 1997.

33. Pablo Carrillo and Marcial Arumbari, community leader and officer, interview, El Espino, 4 April 1997.

34. I.e., a magnet school accepting students from a large rural area.

35. Chávez, Moreno, Arreaga, Chávez, Moreno, and Cuéllar, interview.

36. García and Cortez, interview.

37. Carrillo and Arumbari, interview.

38. Israel Romero Macuendí and Florencio Altamirano, community leader and community member, interview, Akae, 2 April 1997.

39. Carrillo and Arumbari, interview.

40. Vaca and Segundo, interview.

41. Luis García and Hipólito Sirari Ena, community founder/adviser to the *capitanía,* and community leader, interview, Rancho Nuevo, 28 October 1997.

42. Carrillo and Arumbari, interview.

43. Chávez, Moreno, Arreaga, Chávez, Moreno, and Cuéllar, interview.

44. Juan Carlos Gutiérrez, interview, Charagua, 1 April 1997.

45. Aramayo, interview.

46. Siquier, interview.

47. Antuni (a), interview.

48. Julián Segundo Chipipi, municipal councilman (MNR), interview, Charagua, 2 April 1997.

49. A. Vargas, interview.

50. Saucedo (a), interview.

51. Ibid.

52. Ibid.

53. Ibid.

54. Cabi forms part of the APG, though with somewhat older traditions than most of the rest of the APG, as is explained in greater detail below.

55. Fr. Luis Roma, parish priest, interview, Charagua, 29 October 1997.

56. Abelardo Vargas Portales and Abilio Vaca, municipal council president and councilman (ADN and MBL) respectively, interview, Charagua, 28 October 1997.

57. Segundo, interview.

58. Ibid.

59. Solano, interview.

60. Segundo, interview.

61. Ibid.

62. Caurey and Altamirano, interview.

63. Vaca and Segundo, interview.

64. Chávez, Moreno, Arreaga, Chávez, Moreno, and Cuéllar, interview.

65. Hilda Ibáñez vda. de Castro and Vidal Durán Sala, community leader and adviser, interview, Isiporenda, 29 October 1997.

66. García and Cortez, interview.

67. Carrillo and Arumbari, interview.

68. J. C. Gutiérrez (a), interview.

69. Roma, interview.

70. Saucedo (b), interview.

71. Antuni (a), interview.

72. Omar Quiroga Antelo, neighborhood council president, interview, Charagua, 30 October 1997.

73. Antuni (a), interview.

74. In Spanish, "playing politics."

75. Josué Aiduare and Florencio Aiduare, community leaders, interview, Taputamí, 2 April 1997.

76. Romero and Altamirano, interview.

77. Carrillo and Arumbari, interview.

78. García and Cortez, interview.

79. Francisco Chávez, Alberto Rodríguez, and Ignacio Álvarez, community leader, adviser to the *capitanía grande,* and community member, interview, La Brecha, 28 October 1997.

80. And Guaraníes who were so openly disdainful of their party affiliations.

81. Saucedo (b), interview.

82. A. Vargas, interview.

83. Saucedo (b), interview.

84. Segundo, interview.

85. Roberto Vargas, chief financial officer, interview, Charagua, 30 October 1997.

86. James Madison, Alexander Hamilton, and John Jay, *The Federalist Papers* (New York: New American Library, 1961). See especially no. 10.

87. Departmental prefects, named directly by the president, are essentially central government authorities.

88. Dr. Wilfredo Anzoátegui Vaca, hospital director, interview, Charagua, 30 October 1997.

89. García and Sirari, interview.

90. The speaker admitted to campaigning in the past for the ADN and being a *banzerista* (a supporter of the ADN then-president).

91. Vargas and Vaca, interview.

92. Edgar Gutiérrez Hurtado (a), ADN chief, interview, Charagua, 28 October 1997.

93. Bolivian politics traditionally divided into two groups centered on the MNR, on one hand, and the ADN, on the other. At their peak the two parties despised each other.

94. Luis Saucedo Tapia (c), mayor, interview, Charagua, 27 October 1997.

95. Florencio Antuni Sánchez (b), oversight committee president, interview, Charagua, 30 October 1997.

96. Solano, interview.

97. Vargas and Vaca, interview.

98. Ibáñez and Durán, interview.

99. J. C. Gutiérrez (a), interview.

100. Prof. Pedro Fidel Ribera Caballero, member of the directorate of AGACOR, interview, Charagua, 30 October 1997.

101. Antuni (b), interview.

102. J. C. Gutiérrez (a), interview.

103. Saucedo (b), interview.

104. J. C. Gutiérrez (a), interview. The denomination of this region as the "Dry Chaco" is accepted widely throughout Bolivia.

105. Ribera, interview.

106. Chávez, Rodríguez, and Álvarez, interview.

107. Segundo, interview.

108. E. Núñez, interview.

109. Aramayo, interview.

110. E. Núñez, interview.

111. Albó, *Los Guaraní-Chiriguano,* 19–31, 332–38. See also Kevin Healey, *Caciques y Patrones: Una Experiencia de Desarrollo Rural en el Sud de Bolivia* (Cochabamba: CERES, 1987), and Francisco Pifarré, *Los Guaraní-Chiriguano: Historia de un Pueblo* (La Paz: CIPCA, 1989).

112. E. Núñez, interview.

113. Albó, *Los Guaraní-Chiriguano.*

114. Roma, interview.

115. Ibid.

116. Chávez, Rodríguez, and Álvarez, interview.

117. Paul Carrillo, Ricardo Melgar, and Marcial Arumbari, community leader, community member, and community officer, interview, El Espino, 31 October 1997.

118. Antuni (b), interview.

119. Lt. Col. Fair Eduardo Villaroel, army garrison commander, interview, Charagua, 2 April 1997.

120. J. C. Gutiérrez (a), interview.

121. The 1952–53 revolution and subsequent agrarian reform.

122. Quiroga, interview.

123. Ibid.

124. E. Núñez, interview.

125. Quiroga, interview.

126. Nelson Eguez Gutiérrez, local leader of the MNR *comando,* interview, Charagua, 30 October 1997.

127. E. Gutiérrez, interview.

128. Ibáñez and Durán, interview.

129. E. Núñez, interview. Medina (1994) explains that the social structure of the Guaraní people was decimated by the 1950s. In the altiplano and valley regions of Bolivia the Aymara and Quechua peoples were able to present landowners with a united front in the form of peasant unions and traditional community organizations, and so demand land during the revolution of 1952–53. But in the *Cordillera* landowners were able to exploit land reform to actually extend their holdings and capture Guaraní communities.

130. E. Gutiérrez, interview.

131. Literally chief magistrate, usually a departmental official. The *corregidor* in Charagua is a municipal employee.

132. *"Nosotros los blancos."*

133. E. Núñez, interview.

134. Solano, interview.

135. Saucedo (a), interview.

136. Romero and Altamirano, interview.

137. García and Cortez, interview.

138. Carrillo and Arumbari, interview.

139. Romero and Altamirano, interview.

140. Chávez, Moreno, Arreaga, Chávez, Moreno, and Cuéllar, interview.

141. Carrillo and Arumbari, interview.

142. Abelino Sánchez Ramírez, neighborhood council vice president, interview, Charagua Station, 30 October 1997.

143. Albó, *Los Guaraní-Chiriguano,* 240–50.

144. Antuni (a), interview.

145. Muñoz, interview.

146. Ibid., 302–17. Albó describes the long Guaraní process of social organization.

147. Muñoz, interview.

148. Siquier, interview.

149. Antuni (a), interview.

150. Ibid.

151. Muñoz, interview.

152. Caurey and Altamirano, interview.

153. In Spanish, *Comunidades de trabajo.*

154. Romero and Altamirano, interview.

155. Caurey and Altamirano, interview. This, of course, was the original intent of the law.

156. Ibáñez and Durán, interview.

157. Leoncio Pabaroa and Javier Yupico, interim community leader and ex-leader, interview, Copere Brecha, 29 October 1997.

158. Vaca and Segundo, interview.

159. Tupi-Guaraní more closely resembles the Guaraní spoken in Paraguay.

160. Saucedo here referred to both locally and externally raised resources.

161. Saucedo (c), interview.

162. Antuni (b), interview.

163. Isiporenda, La Brecha, Yapiroa, and Copere Brecha, among others, testified to this effect.

164. Chávez, Rodríguez, and Álvarez, interview.

165. Eguez, interview.

166. García and Cortez, interview.

167. Carrillo and Arumbari, interview.

168. Albó, *Los Guaraní-Chiriguano.*

169. Pabaroa and Yupico, interview.

170. G. W. F. Hegel, *Philosophy of Right,* trans. S. W. Dyde (Amherst, NY: Prometheus Books, 1996).

171. Vaca and Segundo, interview.

172. Villaroel, interview.

173. E. Núñez and Aramayo, among others, concurred on this point.

174. Ribera, interview.

Chapter 4

1. See, for example, Faguet (2004) and Faguet and Sánchez (2008).

2. We only consider nonnegative values of g^{l^*} and g^{c^*}. Reversing the order of play and solving for local government as the Stackelberg leader yields symmetric results in which all provision is local unless $\alpha < \tau$. We consider this order of play less realistic.

3. Now the Ministry of Rural Development and Land Use.

4. A number of new municipalities have been created since 1994, mainly by splitting larger municipalities into two or more. In order to analyze similar geographical units, I use municipalities' 1994 borders as Minimum Comparable Areas.

5. http://personal.lse.ac.uk/faguetj/.

6. Meaning I do not combine information from different sources into a single variable.

7. Of the three discarded sectors, multisectoral includes a sufficient diversity of projects as to be functionally meaningless as a category; and almost no local governments invest in hydrocarbons or mining, rendering comparison impossible.

8. The average exchange rate for the year 2000 was Bs. 6.19 per U.S. dollar.

9. Thus α^*_m takes the value 0 for all municipalities and all years before 1994, and is identical to α_m for all years from 1994 onward.

10. Note that "rate" here denotes a stock and not flow concept.

11. I use both for education and obtain the expected variation in sign in our results (see below).

12. See, for example, Wolman in Bennett (1990), or Putnam (1993).

13. Reasons for these changes are discussed in chapter 1.

14. Irrelevance results are omitted for the sake of brevity.

Chapter 5

1. Treisman (2007), 7–8.
2. Treisman (2007), 8.
3. My use of "policy literature" is sufficiently elastic to include development studies.
4. Treisman analyzes many more arguments than I focus on in the paragraphs that follow. Most of this analysis is, in my view, correct. I urge students of decentralization to read it.
5. Minkler (2010) makes the related point that rates of newspaper readership are much higher for local than national newspapers in relation to metropolitan versus national populations. This implies that citizens are more interested in, and better informed about, local issues.
6. The Census Bureau counted some 87,525 "local governments" in its *2002 Census of Governments*.
7. For simplicity assume a balanced-budget rule at both local and national levels, else median voters will rationally choose high public goods provision and no taxes.
8. One could also conjecture that local elections help break down the well-known multidimensionality problem (see Mueller 1989 for a good survey) by creating electoral contests in smaller issue spaces. This is important not for technical analysis—electoral results are still intractable in terms of revealing information in multidimensional space—but because they create forums for campaigning, petitioning, reporting, and so on, focused on local needs.
9. Bardhan cites Hanson and Hartman's (1994) finding that few poor people move among U.S. states in search of higher welfare benefits.
10. Generalizing, a more accurate view of human behavior would seem to be that people move between regions and districts for employment, family reasons, or retirement, and not in search of particular public goods. But they do choose where to locate within a specific district—i.e., at the margin—based on the local public goods on offer.
11. Besley and Coate (2003) call this approach the "standard model."
12. See, for example, Faguet (2004) and Faguet and Sánchez (2008).
13. This is the subject of a rapidly growing literature often referred to as "Q^2." See, for example, Rao and Woolcock (2003).

Chapter 6

1. Corte Nacional Electoral.
2. A. Vargas, interview. See chapter 3, second section, "Municipal Council."
3. Corte Nacional Electoral.
4. See Albó, *Los Guaraní-Chiriguano* (1990), chapters 3 and 8, and Albó et al., *Para Comprender Las Culturas Rurales en Bolivia* (1990), part I, chapters 2 and 3, and part III, chapter 4.

5. The bonus web chapter on the Press's website at http://www.press.umich .edu/titleDetailDesc.do?id=175269, as well as at http://personal.lse.ac.uk/faguetj/ provides details for Porongo, Baures, and Atocha.

6. In some countries government is a third source of campaign finance.

7. We can think of these currents as horizontal (i.e., across space) and vertical (i.e., across sectors, activities, or identities).

Chapter 7

1. The full equation (1) is my best model of municipal investment. The results of omitted equations $(1')$ and $(1'')$ are fully consistent with those presented here.

2. This time total firms—to avoid multicollinearity with the NFC term, which includes construction firms.

Chapter 8

1. Guzman Callisaya, FEJUVE President, interview, Viacha (District Seven), 11 December 2009.

2. Ibid.

3. District Seven: Mauricio Mamani, Oscar Soto, Guzman Callisaya, Hector Mayta, Franklin Merlo, Saturnino Laguna, and Nelson Murillo, assistant mayor, OC member, FEJUVE president, municipal superintendent, municipal technician, FE-JUVE transport officer, and FEJUVE education and culture secretary, interview, Viacha, 11 December 2009.

4. Guzman Callisaya, interview.

5. Marcelo Flores Tapia and Juan David Merlo Quispe, Oversight Committee members for Districts 1 and 2, interview, Viacha, 10 December 2009.

6. Marcos López, regional director of sales, SOBOCE, interview, La Paz, 10 December 2009.

7. Fabio Mayta, CIPCA organizational technician, interview, Viacha, 11 December 2009.

8. Luis Calle Callisaya, head of the Viachan Agrarian Association, interview, Viacha, 9 December 2009.

9. Arsenio Lamas, mayor of Viacha, interview, Viacha, 10 December 2009.

10. Flores and Merlo, interview.

11. Fabio Mamani, district director of education, interview, Viacha, 10 December 2009.

12. Flores and Merlo, interview.

13. Ibid.

14. Ibid.

15. Calle, interview.

16. Ibid.

17. Oscar Soto, OC member, interview, Viacha (District Seven), 11 December 2009.

18. Yajaira Barriga, head of CIPCA's Viacha office, interview, Viacha, 10 December 2009.

19. Fabio Mamami, interview.

20. Fabio Mayta, interview.

21. Mauricio Mamani, assistant mayor, interview, Viacha (District Seven), 11 December 2009.

22. Victor Hugo Jurado, Municipality of Viacha governance specialist, interview, Viacha, 10 December 2009.

23. Hernán Arroyo Vela, president of the Municipal Council, interview, Viacha, 11 December 2009.

24. Ibid.

25. Jurado, interview.

26. Ibid.

27. Lamas, interview.

28. Lamas, interview.

29. Ibid.

30. Fabio Mamani, interview.

31. Barriga, interview.

32. Lamas, interview.

33. Calle, interview.

34. Flores and Merlo, interview.

35. Calle, interview; López, interview.

36. Hector Mayta, interview.

37. Calle, interview.

38. Lamas, interview.

39. López, interview.

40. Ibid.

41. Ibid.

42. Flores and Merlo, interview.

43. López, interview.

44. Calle, interview.

45. Hector Mayta, interview.

46. Calle, interview.

47. Arroyo, interview.

48. Fabio Mamani, interview.

49. Flores and Merlo, interview.

50. Fabio Mayta, interview.

51. Fabio Mamani, interview.

52. Barriga, interview.

53. Calle, interview.

54. Lamas, interview.

55. Mamani et al., interview.

56. Fabio Mayta, interview.

57. Ibid.

58. Fabio Mamani, interview.

59. Lamas, interview.

60. Fabiano Mamani, interview.

61. Calle, interview.

62. Arroyo, interview.

63. O. Soto, interview.

64. Lamas, interview.

65. Fabio Mayta, interview.

66. Fabio Mayta, interview.

67. Fabio Mamani, interview.

68. Flores and Merlo, interview.

69. From the Bolivian acronym for Fixed Route Taxi (*Taxi de Ruta Fija*). In Charagua these are typically minivans packed to the gills with people and cargo.

70. Gustavo García Gutiérrez, municipal councilman (and founder of CACHA), interview, Charagua, 16 December 2009.

71. Rolando Arriaga and Aníbal Ortiz López, Cattle Ranchers' Association of the Cordillera operational manager and director, interview, Charagua, 16 December 2009.

72. García G., interview.

73. Instituto Nacional de Estadística (2010), "Municipal Population Projections by Sex" (La Paz: INE). Accessed 10 September 2010 at http://www.ine.gov.bo/indice/visualizador.aspx?ah=PC20407.HTM.

74. Ricardo Chávez Montenegro, district director of education, interview, Charagua, 17 December 2009.

75. Isi Gutiérrez, municipal council secretary, interview, Charagua, 15 December 2009.

76. Ibid.

77. Carlos Sánchez and Napoleón Aramayo, education and culture officer of the North Charagua captaincy and health officer and member of the political commission of the Guaraní People's Assembly, interview, Charagua, 15 December 2009.

78. Article 30(1) of Government of Bolivia (2008), *Nueva Constitución Política de Estado*. National Congress.

79. Marleny González, hospital administrator, interview, Charagua, 16 December 2009.

80. Lt. Col. José Mario Márquez Alba, army regiment commander, interview, Charagua, 16 December 2009.

81. José Núñez, oversight committee president, interview, Charagua, 15 December 2009.

82. Rolando Arriaga and Aníbal Ortiz López, Cattle Ranchers' Association of the Cordillera (AGACOR) operational manager and director, interview, Charagua, 16 December 2009.

83. Carlos Sánchez and Napoleón Aramayo, education and culture officer of the North Charagua captaincy and health officer and member of the political commission of the Guaraní People's Assembly, interview, Charagua, 15 December 2009.

84. Leonardo Guarupachi, Great Captain of Parapitiguasu (South Charagua), interview, rural South Charagua, 18 December 2009.

85. Marcelo Arandia Alarcón and Santiago Puerta, regional support officer and technician of CIPCA (NGO), interview, Charagua, 16 December 2009.

86. Arriaga and Ortiz, interview.

87. Ronald Gómez Casanova, chief administrative officer, interview, Charagua, 15 December 2009. He referred to a ranking by FAM-Bolivia [Federación de Asociaciones Municipales de Bolivia] of municipal performance in 2006–7.

88. J. Núñez, interview.

89. Ricardo Chávez Montenegro, district director of education, interview, Charagua, 17 December 2009.

90. Marco Antonio Villaroel Carrillo and Juan Carlos Arriaga, rural development project field office head and captain's adviser (Piquiranda), interview, Charagua, 16 December 2009.

91. Elsa María Díaz, teacher-training center head, interview, Charagua, 17 December 2009.

92. Ronald Gómez Casanova, chief administrative officer, interview, Charagua, 15 December 2009.

93. Dolores Quevedo, disabled children's center officer, interview, San Antonio de Parapetí, 18 December 2009.

94. Elfie Yavita, municipal councilwoman, interview, Charagua, 17 December 2009.

95. Gustavo García Gutiérrez, Ademar Flores, Esperanza Rivera Barba, Ana Barba, and William Israel Vargas, municipal councilman (and founder of CACHA), civic committee vice president, civic committee adviser, GRO leader (Charagua), and chief magistrate, interview, Charagua, 16 December 2009.

96. Chávez, interview.

97. Chávez, interview.

98. Claudio López Miguel, mayor, interview, Charagua, 18 December 2009.

99. Carlos Sánchez and Napoleón Aramayo, interview.

100. Gómez, interview.

101. Gómez, interview.

102. Gómez, interview.

103. Gómez, interview.

104. López, interview.

105. Yavita, interview.

106. J. Núñez, interview; Arandia and Puerta, interview.

107. J. Núñez, interview. Emphasis in the original.

108. Arandia and Puerta, interview.

109. J. Núñez, interview.

110. Sánchez and Aramayo, interview.

111. J. Núñez, interview.

112. Gustavo García Gutiérrez, Ademar Flores, Esperanza Rivera Barba, Ana Barba, and William Israel Vargas, municipal councilman (and founder of CACHA),

civic committee vice president, civic committee adviser, GRO leader (Charagua), and chief magistrate, interview, Charagua, 16 December 2009.

113. López, interview.

114. García G. et al., interview.

115. Arandia and Puerta, interview.

116. Ana María Armella, María Korimalla, José Aníbal Cáceres, and Marta Leoños Ardaya, treasurer, secretary for conflicts, and director of the November 10th Merchants' Association, and Cotoca neighborhood GRO, interview, Charagua, 16 December 2009.

117. Villaroel and Arriaga, interview.

118. Díaz, interview.

119. Sánchez and Aramayo, interview.

120. López, interview.

121. Interministerial Transition Plan for the Guaraní People (2010), "El resurgimiento del Pueblo Guaraní en la APG," Government of Bolivia. Webpage accessed 17 September 2010 at http://www.planguarani.com/pages/apg.php.

122. Guarupachi, interview.

123. Guarupachi, interview.

124. Arandia and Puerta, interview.

125. Sánchez and Aramayo, interview.

126. Sánchez and Aramayo, interview.

127. Arandia and Puerta, interview.

128. Sánchez and Aramayo, interview.

129. Guarupachi, interview.

130. Juan Carlos Gutiérrez, ex-president of the Cattle Ranchers' Association of the Cordillera (and ex-congressman for the department of Santa Cruz), interview, Charagua, 18 December 2009.

131. Yavita, interview.

132. Sánchez and Aramayo, interview.

133. Chávez, interview.

134. López, interview.

135. García Gutiérrez et al., interview.

136. Arriaga and Ortiz, interview.

137. García Gutiérrez et al., interview.

138. Arriaga and Ortiz, interview.

139. Arriaga and Ortiz, interview.

140. Gómez, interview.

141. Pedro Martins, head of the Pinondi Mennonite colony, interview, Pinondi, 17 December 2009.

142. Martins, interview.

143. J. C. Gutiérrez (b), interview.

144. Fr. Mauricio Bacardit Busquet, assistant parish priest, interview, Charagua, 17 December 2009. I saw 50-pound sacks of algarroba powder for sale in Charagua's main market.

145. Gómez, interview; García G. et al., interview; J. Núñez, interview; Sánchez and Aramayo, interview.

146. Arriaga and Ortiz, interview.

147. Sánchez and Aramayo, interview; Díaz, interview.

148. J. Núñez, interview; Villaroel and Arriaga, interview.

149. *Partidocracia* in Spanish. This informal term refers to a political system that primarily benefits political parties and their leaders.

150. Arandia and Puerta, interview.

151. López, interview.

152. García G. et al., interview.

153. Guarupachi, interview. Emphasis in the original.

154. Yavita, interview.

155. Martins, interview.

156. Martins, interview.

157. Martins, interview.

158. Martins, interview.

159. Martins, interview.

160. Arriaga and Ortiz, interview.

161. Márquez, interview.

162. Villaroel, interview.

163. Sánchez and Aramayo, interview.

164. López, interview.

165. J. Núñez, interview.

166. Sánchez and Aramayo, interview.

167. García G. et al., interview.

168. Arandia and Puerta, interview.

169. Yavita, interview.

Chapter 9

1. George Gray Molina, former director of UDAPE, personal communication, London, 3 December 2010.

Appendix

1. For further treatment of this topic, see also Greene (1997).

LIST OF INTERVIEWS

Atocha

Gladys Armata de Mejía, municipal council president (MNR), interview, Atocha, 23 April 1997.

Roberto Ávila Callo, municipal councilman (UCS), interview, Atocha, 22 April 1997.

Wilfredo Chiri and Fermín León, Federation of Cooperativist Miners president and secretary, interview, Atocha, 23 April 1997.

Fr. José Dessart, parish priest, interview, Atocha, 25 April 1997.

Severo García Cándia, oversight committee member, interview, Atocha, 23 April 1997.

Fernando Hernández, Social Investment Fund departmental director, interview and site visits, Atocha, 21–22 April 1997.

Raúl Mamani Villca, oversight committee president, interview, Siete Suyos, 22 April 1997.

Pablo Victorio Ayala, mayor, interview, Ánimas, 22 April 1997.

Community and Grassroots Organizations

Atocha: Severo García Cándia, neighborhood council ex-president, interview, Atocha, 23 April 1997.

Chorolque: Albino García Choque, Juan Bonifacio Onofre, Esteban Marcha Cachambre, and Ivan Marca, miners' cooperative welfare officer, oversight officer, oversight officer, and member, interview, Chorolque, 23 April 1997.

Villa Solano: Gerónimo Ayala Hernández, community officer, interview, Chorolque, 23 April 1997.

Baures

Hugo Ayllón Parada, Cattlemen's Association president, interview, Baures, 2 May 1997.

Conrad Bruckner, cattle rancher, interview, Baures, 4 May 1997.

Elwin Bruckner, prefect, interview, Baures, 1 May 1997.

Note: [AG] denotes interviews conducted by Armando Godínez, anthropologist and assistant researcher.

Grover Martínez Franco, mayor, interview, Baures, 2 May 1997.

Hugo Melgar Barbery and Erland Ayllón Parada, municipal council president (MIR) and member (independent, ex-MNR), interview, Baures, 2 May 1997.

Dimitri Ojopi, oversight committee president, interview, Baures, 2 May 1997.

Juan Oni Antelo, municipal councilman (MNR), interview, Baures, 2 May 1997.

Srs. Pilar and Teresa and Oscar Velázquez, CETHA (adult education center officers), interview, Baures, 4 May 1997.

Ginger Yapiz, Social Investment Fund departmental director, interview and site visits, Baures, 1 May 1997.

Community and Grassroots Organizations

Baures: Oscar Durán, neighborhood council president, interview, Baures, 2 May 1997.

El Cairo: Manuel Chipeno Valdivieso, community leader, interview, El Cairo, 3 May 1997.

Jasiakiri: Juan Jahnsen, community leader, interview, El Cairo, 3 May 1997.

Tujuré: Gustavo Chonono Churipui, community leader, interview, El Cairo, 3 May 1997.

Charagua

Edwin Acuña, municipal development consultant, interview, La Paz, 9 December 2009.

Florencio Antuni Sánchez (a), oversight committee president, interview, Charagua, 1 April 1997.

Florencio Antuni Sánchez (b), oversight committee president, interview, Charagua, 30 October 1997.

Wilfredo Anzoátegui Vaca, hospital director, interview, Charagua, 30 October 1997.

Oscar Hugo Aramayo Caballero, district director of education, interview, Charagua, 4 April 1997.

Marcelo Arandia Alarcón and Santiago Puerta, regional support officer and technician of CIPCA (NGO), interview, Charagua, 16 December 2009.

Rolando Arriaga and Aníbal Ortiz López, Cattle Ranchers' Association of the Cordillera (AGACOR) operational manager and director, interview, Charagua, 16 December 2009.

Fr. Mauricio Bacardit Busquet, assistant parish priest, interview, Charagua, 17 December 2009.

Ricardo Chávez Montenegro, district director of education, interview, Charagua, 17 December 2009.

Elsa María Díaz, teacher training center head, interview, Charagua, 17 December 2009.

José Durán, Social Investment Fund finance director, interview, 3 October 1997.

Nelson Egüez Gutiérrez, MNR chief, interview, Charagua, 30 October 1997.

Gustavo García Gutiérrez, municipal councilman (and founder of CACHA), interview, Charagua, 16 December 2009.

Ronald Gómez Casanova, chief administrative officer, interview, Charagua, 15 December 2009.

Marleny González, hospital administrator, interview, Charagua, 16 December 2009.

Edgar Gutiérrez Hurtado (a), ADN chief, interview, Charagua, 28 October 1997.

Edgar Gutiérrez Hurtado (b), district officer, interview, Charagua, 28 October 1997.

Isi Gutiérrez, municipal council secretary, interview, Charagua, 15 December 2009.

Juan Carlos Gutiérrez (a), Cattle Ranchers' Association of the Cordillera president, interview, Charagua, 1 April 1997.

Juan Carlos Gutiérrez (b), ex-president of the Cattle Ranchers' Association of the Cordillera (and ex-congressman for the department of Santa Cruz), interview, Charagua, 18 December 2009.

Rolando Gutiérrez, municipal councilman (MNR), interview, Charagua, 2 April 1997.

Dante Hurtado Salse, oversight committee secretary, interview, Charagua, 30 October 1997.

Claudio López Miguel, mayor, interview, Charagua, 18 December 2009.

Lt. Col. José Mario Márquez Alba, army regiment commander, interview, Charagua, 16 December 2009.

Fernando Muñoz Franco, Social Investment Fund departmental director, interview, Santa Cruz, 31 March 1997.

Eulogio Núñez, CIPCA director (NGO) and municipal adviser, interview, Charagua, 2 April 1997.

José Núñez, oversight committee president, interview, Charagua, 15 December 2009.

Rosario Pantoja de Cuéllar, education center director, interview, Charagua, 4 April 1997.

Pedro Fidel Ribera Caballero, member of the directorate of AGACOR, interview, Charagua, 30 October 1997.

Fr. Luis Roma, parish priest, interview, Charagua, 29 October 1997.

Luis Saucedo Tapia (a), mayor, interview, Santa Cruz, 31 March 1997.

Luis Saucedo Tapia (b), mayor, interview, Charagua, 1 April 1997.

Luis Saucedo Tapia (c), mayor, interview, Charagua, 27 October 1997.

Julián Segundo Chipipi, municipal councilman (MNR), interview, Charagua, 2 April 1997.

Fr. Gabriel Siquier (Tiano Piru), parish priest, interview, Isoso, 3 April 1997.

Crispín Solano Menacho, municipal councilman (MBL) and ex-oversight committee president, interview, Charagua, 28 October 1997.

Abelardo Vargas Portales, municipal council president (ADN), interview, Charagua, 1 April 1997.

Abelardo Vargas Portales and Abilio Vaca, municipal council president and councilman (ADN and MBL) respectively, interview, Charagua, 28 October 1997.

Roberto Vargas, chief financial officer, interview, Charagua, 30 October 1997.

Lt. Col. Fair Eduardo Villaroel, army garrison commander, interview, Charagua, 2 April 1997.

Marco Antonio Villaroel Carrillo and Juan Carlos Arriaga, rural development project field office head and captain's adviser (Piquiranda), interview, Charagua, 16 December 2009.

Elfie Yavita, municipal councilwoman, interview, Charagua, 17 December 2009.

Community and Grassroots Organizations

Akae: Israel Romero Macuendí and Florencio Altamirano, community leader and community member, interview, Akae, 2 April 1997.

La Brecha: Francisco Chávez Flores, Delcio Moreno Candia, Mario Arreaga, Andrés Chávez Flores, Vicente Moreno, and Licelio Cuéllar Martínez, community leader, aid to the *capitanía,* hospital administrator, nursing assistant, school association president, and Alto Isoso district deputy, interview, La Brecha, 3 April 1997.

La Brecha: Francisco Chávez, Alberto Rodríguez, and Ignacio Álvarez, community leader, adviser to the *capitanía grande,* and community member, interview, La Brecha, 28 October 1997.

Charagua: Walter García Juárez and Jorge Cortez Romero, community association president and community member, interview, Charagua, 3 April 1997.

Charagua: Omar Quiroga Antelo, neighborhood council president, interview, Charagua, 30 October 1997.

Charagua: Ana María Armella, María Korimalla, José Aníbal Cáceres, and Marta Leoños Ardaya, treasurer, secretary for conflicts, and director of the November 10th Merchants' Association, and Cotoca neghborhood GRO, interview, Charagua, 16 December 2009.

Charagua: Gustavo García Gutiérrez, Ademar Flores, Esperanza Rivera Barba, Ana Barba, and William Israel Vargas, municipal councilman (and founder of CACHA), civic committee vice president, civic committee adviser, GRO leader (Charagua), and chief magistrate, interview, Charagua, 16 December 2009.

Charagua Station: Abelino Sánchez Ramírez, neighborhood council vice president, interview, Charagua Station, 30 October 1997.

Copere Brecha: Leoncio Pabaroa and Javier Yupico, interim community leader and ex-leader, interview, Copere Brecha, 29 October 1997.

El Espino: Pablo Carrillo and Marcial Arumbari, community leader and officer, interview, El Espino, 4 April 1997.

El Espino: Paul Carrillo, Ricardo Melgar, and Marcial Arumbari, community leader, community member, and community officer, interview, El Espino, 31 October 1997.

Isiporenda: Hilda Ibáñez vda. de Castro and Vidal Durán Sala, community leader and adviser, interview, Isiporenda, 29 October 1997.

Kapiwasuti: Demetrio Caurey and Florencio Altamirano, president of the community irrigation committee and infrastructure officer, interview, Kapiwasuti, 2 April 1997.

Mennonites: Pedro Martins, head of the Pinondi Mennonite colony, interview, Pinondi, 17 December 2009.

North Charagua (rural): Carlos Sánchez and Napoleón Aramayo, education and culture officer of the North Charagua captaincy and health officer and member of the political commission of the Guaraní People's Assembly, interview, Charagua, 15 December 2009.

Parapitiguasu (rural South Charagua): Leonardo Guarupachi, Great Captain of Parapitiguasu (South Charagua), interview, rural South Charagua, 18 December 2009.

Rancho Nuevo: Luis García and Hipólito Sirari Ena, community founder/adviser to the *capitanía,* and community leader, interview, Rancho Nuevo, 28 October 1997.

San Antonio de Parapetí: Dolores Quevedo, disabled children's center officer, interview, San Antonio de Parapetí, 18 December 2009.

Taputamí: Josué Aiduare and Florencio Aiduare, community leaders, interview, Taputamí, 2 April 1997.

Yapiroa: Pablo Diego Vaca and David Segundo, community leader and adviser, interview, Yapiroa, 3 April 1997.

Desaguadero

Anonymous, primary and secondary school directors, and various members of the school association, interview, Desaguadero, 24 March 1997.

Alfredo Bravo Mujica and Mario Cerda Escalante, municipal councilmen (MNR and ADN respectively), interview, Desaguadero, 24 March 1997.

Luis González, Social Investment Fund departmental director, interview, Desaguadero, 22 March 1997.

Rosendo Mamani Quispe, mayor, interview, Desaguadero, 25 March 1997.

Juan Nina Quispe, oversight committee vice president and neighborhood council president, interview, Desaguadero, 25 March 1997.

Community and Grassroots Organizations

Azafranal: Augusto Ibáñez Ayoroc, Lucio Quispe, and Leonardo Saiga Torres, school principal, school adviser, and primary school director, interview, Azafranal, 26 March 1997.

Azafranal: Dionisio López, anonymous, and anonymous, community leader and two officers, interview, Desaguadero, 25 March 1997.

Comunidad San Pedro: Faustino Mamani Chura and Seferino Torres, water committee president and secretary, interview, Desaguadero, 25 March 1997.

Desaguadero (neighborhood council): Pastor Huaywa Nino, water committee vice president, interview, Desaguadero, 25 March 1997.

Huancollo: Constantino Aruquipa and anonymous, school association president and member, interview, Desaguadero, 25 March 1997.

San Pedro Okorani: Nicolás Condori Laura, Cresóstomo Ticona, and Felipe Apaza Callisaya, community leader, general officer, and school officer, interview, San Pedro Okorani, 26 March 1997.

Titijumi: Justo José Apaza, community leader, interview, Desaguadero, 25 March 1997.

Vitunkani: Francisco Quispe Huanca, Venturo Quispe, Juan Quispe Fernández, and Mario Quispe, community leader, justice officer, education officer, and community member, interview, Vitunkani, 26 March 1997.

Yanal: Pascual Fernández, Eulogio Limachi, and anonymous, community leader, school association president, and community education officer, interview, Desaguadero, 25 March 1997.

Guayaramerín

Alberto Albert, municipal technical adviser and ex-municipal council president, interview, Guayaramerín, 20 October 1997.

Fr. Fernando Bendoraitis, health NGO director, interview, Guayaramerín, 19 October 1997.

Zacarías Catalayud, oversight committee vice president, interview, Guayaramerín, 20 October 1997.

Fr. Julio Corredor, parish priest, interview, Guayaramerín, 19 October 1997.

Orlando del Río, oversight committee secretary, interview, Guayaramerín, 5 June 1997. [AG]

Pedro Noel Herrera Delgado, departmental forest inspector, interview, Guayaramerín, 21 October 1997.

Sr. Ana López, NGO director, interview, Guayaramerín, 22 October 1997.

Carlos Luna, chief officer, interview, Guayaramerín, 5 June 1997. [AG]

Elias Mesquita Coimbra, mayor, interview, Guayaramerín, 20 October 1997.

Iván Nincevic Landívar, municipal council president (ADN) and telephone cooperative president, interview, Guayaramerín, 20 October 1997.

Carmelo Parada Zarco, chief magistrate, interview, Guayaramerín, 21 October 1997.

Adrián "Gigi" Rivera, electricity cooperative president, moneylender and hotel owner, interview, Guayaramerín, 21 October 1997.

Erasmo Roca, municipal councilman (ADN), interview, Guayaramerín, 6 June 1997. [AG]

Manlio Roca, port (customs) manager, ex-mayor and ex-MP, interview, Guayaramerín, 21 October 1997.

Ruth Roca, Zacarías Catalayud, Orlando del Río, and José Guali, oversight committee president, vice president, secretary, and member, interview, Guayaramerín, 5 June 1997. [AG]

Elío Simoni Casangeli, Chamber of Industry and Commerce secretary, interview, Guayaramerín, 21 October 1997.

Gabriel Sosa Salvatierra, hospital director, interview, Guayaramerín, 22 October 1997.

Hernán "Cacho" Vargas Rivera, agro-industrialist, television station owner and ADN chief, interview, Guayaramerín, 21 October 1997.

Community and Grassroots Organizations

1° de Mayo: Dionisia Cuéllar Pérez, Emilse Choquere, and Santiago Méndez, community officers, interview, 1° de Mayo, 23 October 1997.

Cachuela Esperanza: Angélica Méndez de Languideiz, María Doris Soleto de Otubo, and Rodolfo Otubo Sánchez, community officer and oversight committee member, community education officer, and community member, interview, Cachuela Esperanza, 6 June 1997. [AG]

Guayaramerín: Rubén Darío Melgar Añez, neighborhood council president, interview, Guayaramerín, 21 October 1997.

Porongo

Benedicto Bonilla Rojas, oversight committee president, interview, Porongo, 7 April 1997.

Felix Domínguez Parada, district director of education, interview, Porongo, 7 April 1997.

Fernando Muñoz Franco, Social Investment Fund departmental director, interview, Santa Cruz, 5 April 1997.

Hernán Gutiérrez Viveros and Rómulo Oyola Morales, chief administrative officer and ex-mayor, and technical officer, interview, Porongo, 8 April 1997.

Martha Oyola Morales, Women's Civic Committee president, interview, Porongo, 7 April 1997.

Silvio Rojas Aguilera, Ricardo Larachi, and José Mario Bejarano Saucedo, mayor, municipal council president (MIR), and municipal councilman (ADN), interview, Porongo, 7 April 1997.

Roberto Saavedra Gutiérrez, municipal councilman (ADN), interview, Porongo, 10 April 1997.

Roberto Suárez, district doctor, interview, Porongo, 9 April 1997.

Community and Grassroots Organizations

Las Cruces: Walter Céspedes Montalván, community leader, interview, Las Cruces, 9 April 1997.

Nueva Palestina: Clemente Cerezo Vargas, community leader, interview, Nueva Palestina, 10 April 1997.

Porongo: Aida Velazco Susano, neighborhood council president, interview, Porongo, 9 April 1997.

San Simón: Agrián Amador, community leader, interview, Terebinto, 10 April 1997.

Terebinto: Vicente Roca Menacho and Alejandro García Gutiérrez, community leader and oversight committee member, and peasants' union leader, interview, Terebinto, 10 April 1997.

Villa Guadalupe: Cecilia Bonilla, school association president, interview, Villa Guadalupe, 8 April 1997.

Sipe Sipe [all AG]

Rogelio Durán, mayor and ex-municipal council president, interview, Sipe Sipe, 27 May 1997.

Justo Mercado Chávez, oversight committee president, interview, Sipe Sipe, 27 May 1997.

Alfredo Taja, municipal councilman and NGO head, interview, Quillacollo, 28 May 1997.

Community and Grassroots Organizations

Mallco Rancho: Guillermo Saavedra Crespo, César Árnez Mondragón, Eduardo Céspedes, and Fernando Montán Árnez, community president, vice president, officer, and oversight committee vice president, interview, Mallco Rancho, 28 May 1997.

Parotani: Demetrio Orellana, community leader, interview, Parotani, 27 May 1997.

Siquisiquía: Eduardo Ala, Celso Cuba, and Andrés Cuba, community leader, spokesman, and officer, interview, Siquisiquía, 29 May 1997.

Urinsaya: Amadeo Cartajira, community leader, interview, Urinsaya, 29 May 1997.

Sucre

Alejandro Arancibia and Gladys Campos, district director of health and health district manager, interview, Sucre, 15 April 1997.

Fernando Beltrán, FANCESA (cement company) general manager, interview, Sucre, 18 April 1997.

Juan José Bonifaz, general adviser to the prefect, interview, Sucre, 15 April 1997.

David Borda, Social Investment Fund departmental director, interview, Sucre, 14 April 1997.

Raimundo Candia (a), municipal general secretary (i.e., chief officer), interview, Sucre, 15 April 1997.

Raimundo Candia (b), municipal general secretary (in lieu of mayor), interview, Sucre, 17 April 1997.

Gregorio Corso, municipal education officer, interview, Sucre, 15 April 1997.

Jaime Gallo Garabinto, municipal councilman (MIR), interview, Sucre, 15 April 1997.

Samuel Montellano Aparicio, district director of education, interview, Sucre, 14 April 1997.

Sixto Rosas Venegas and Carlos Cors, oversight committee president and vice president, interview, Sucre, 16 April 1997.

Roxana Sarmiento, municipal planning and coordination officer, interview, Sucre, 15 April 1997.

René Subieta, municipal chief technical officer, interview, Sucre, 14 April 1997.

Juan Torrico, NGO director, interview, Sucre, 16 April 1997.

Alfredo Yáñez and Juan Carlos Sobut, Chamber of Commerce directors, interview, Sucre, 16 April 1997.

Community and Grassroots Organizations

Chuqui-Chuquí: Claudio Torres, community leader, interview, Chuqui-Chuquí, 18 April 1997.

Mojotoro: Juan Velabaruta, Esteban Copa, Felipe Sapana, and Sabanio Fernández Alanoca, community leader, community, ex-leader, and officer, interview, Mojotoro, 18 April 1997.

Potolo: Walter Encinas, community leader, interview, Potolo, 19 April 1997.

Sucre: Jorge Chaira Piuca and Marcial Javier Pérez, neighborhood council president and education officer, interview, Sucre, 17 April 1997.

Sucre: Javier Tango Aramayo, neighborhood council president, interview, Sucre, 16 April 1997.

Viacha

Edwin Acuña, municipal development consultant, interview, La Paz, 9 December 2009.

Reynaldo Aguilar, district director of health, interview, Viacha, 10 October 1997.

Celestino Arauz, subprefecture general secretary (disputed), interview, Viacha, 9 October 1997.

Hernán Arroyo Vela, president of the Municipal Council, interview, Viacha, 11 December 2009.

Yajaira Barriga, head of CIPCA's Viacha office, interview, Viacha, 10 December 2009.

Juan Carlos Blanco, CBN bottling plant director, interview, Viacha, 16 October 1997.

Edwin Callisaya, mayor, interview, Viacha, 18 March 1997.

José Luis Claros, CBN production supervisor, interview, Viacha, 21 March 1997.

Donato Cuéllar Cusi, Agapito Yujra, Manuel Colque, and Carmelo Quispe, municipal councilmen (all UCS), interview, Viacha, 15 October 1997.

Lt. Col. Adolfo Dávila Chacón, 1st Division, GADA 231 commander (local army garrison), interview, Viacha, 19 March 1997.

Marcelo Flores Tapia and Juan David Merlo Quispe, Oversight Committee members for Districts 1 and 2, interview, Viacha, 10 December 2009.

Luis González, Social Investment Fund departmental director, interview and site visits, Viacha, 17 March 1997.

Victor Hugo Jurado, Municipality of Viacha Governance Specialist, interview, Viacha, 10 December 2009.

Arsenio Lamas, mayor of Viacha, interview, Viacha, 10 December 2009.

Fr. Justino Limachi, parish priest, interview, Viacha, 16 October 1997.

Marcos López, regional director of sales, SOBOCE, interview, La Paz, 10 December 2009.

Gladys Lozano, subprefect, interview, Viacha, 17 March 1997.

Maria Luisa Lucuy, district director of education, interview, Viacha, 15 October 1997.

Oscar Alfonso Magnani Meyta and Franklin Carlo Megillanes, district director of education and education technician, interview, Viacha, 21 March 1997.

Fabio Mamani, district director of education, interview, Viacha, 10 December 2009.

Rolando Marín Ibáñez, chief financial officer, interview, Viacha, 17 March 1997.

Fabio Mayta, CIPCA Organizational Technician, interview, Viacha, 11 December 2009.

Max Mercado Mozo, federation of neighborhood councils (2) president, interview, Viacha, 11 October 1997.

Carlos Núñez, Sociedad Boliviana de Cementos (SOBOCE) financial director, interview, Viacha, 19 March 1997.

Tomás Palacios Rodríguez, Condepa chief, interview, Viacha, 15 October 1997.

Luis Paz, Incerpaz CEO, interview, Viacha, 15 October 1997.

Huber Quintela Alarcón (a), municipal council president, interview, Viacha, 10 October 1997.

Huber Quintela Alarcón (b), MNR chief, interview, Viacha, 16 October 1997.

Huber Quintela Alarcón and Esteban Ticona, municipal councilmen (MNR and Condepa), interview, Viacha, 18 March 1997.

Remigio Quispe Mendoza, Walter Patzi Paty, and Nemesio Mamani Fernández, oversight committee (1) president, federation of neighborhood councils (1) president, and federation officer respectively, interview, Viacha, 18 March 1997.

Jorge Rada, chief financial officer, interview, Viacha, 15 October 1997.

Edgar Robles, mayor, interview, Viacha, 10 October 1997.

Antonio Soto, MIR chief, interview, Viacha, 10 October 1997.

Esteban Ticona, municipal councilman, interview, Viacha, 9 October 1997.

Hipólito Tovar, Alejandro Yujra Laura, and Rony Morales Quispe, oversight committee (2) president, vice president, and officer, interview, Viacha, 19 May 1997.

Hipólito Tovar and Rony Morales Quispe, oversight committee (2) president and officer, interview and site visits, Viacha, 21 May 1997.

Community and Grassroots Organizations

Canton Chama: Severo Guarachi Ramos, community officer, interview, Viacha, 17 May 1997.

District Five: Alicia Rodríguez, women's leader, interview, Viacha, 17 May 1997.

District Six: Gerónimo Colque Velarde, community officer, interview, Viacha, 17 May 1997.

District Seven: Guzman Callisaya, FEJUVE president, interview, Viacha (District Seven), 11 December 2009.

District Seven: Saturnino Laguna, FEJUVE transport officer, interview, Viacha (District Seven), 11 December 2009.

District Seven: Mauricio Mamani, assistant mayor, interview, Viacha (District Seven), 11 December 2009.

District Seven: Mauricio Mamani, Oscar Soto, Guzman Callisaya, Hector Mayta, Franklin Merlo, Saturnino Laguna, and Nelson Murillo, assistant mayor, OC member, FEJUVE president, municipal superintendent, municipal technician, FEJUVE transport officer, and FEJUVE education and culture secretary, interview, Viacha, 11 December 2009.

District Seven: Hector Mayta, municipal superintendent, interview, Viacha (District Seven), 11 December 2009.

District Seven: Franklin Merlo, municipal technician, interview, Viacha (District Seven), 11 December 2009.

District Seven: Nelson Murillo, FEJUVE education and culture secretary, interview, Viacha (District Seven), 11 December 2009.

District Seven: Oscar Soto, OC member, interview, Viacha (District Seven), 11 December 2009.

Názacara: Juan Laurel Hinojosa, Dona Francisca Plata de Maldonado, Julio Choque Huanca, and Jaime Gómez, community coordinator, community leader, education officer, and school director, interview, Názacara, 14 October 1997.

Rosapata: Marcelino Chuy Quenta, Cecilio Plata Flores, Teodoro Casita Ticona, and Daniel Mamani Churra, community leader, community education officer, schoolteacher, and school teacher, interview, Rosapata, 14 October 1997.

Santa Ana de Machaqa: Francisco Juliano Paz, community officer, interview, Viacha, 18 March 1997.

Santa Ana de Machaqa: José Quezo Cusi, Lorenzo Julián, and Olga Cusi de Julián, community leader, teacher, and electoral notary, and Plan Internacional liaison, interview, Santa Ana de Machaqa, 23 March 1997.

Titik'ana Tacaca: Genaro Mamani Chiri, Gumercindo Vito Guarachi, Saturnino Tola Mamani, and Doroteo Callisaya Mamani, community leader, district officer, representative to the Federation of Ayllus and indigenous communities of Ingavi Province (FACOPI), and community officer, interview, Titik'ana Takaka, 20 March 1997.

Viacha: Simon Canavi Rojas, community officer, interview, Viacha, 17 May 1997.

Viachan Agrarian Association: Luis Calle Callisaya, Head of the Viachan Agrarian Association, interview, Viacha, 9 December 2009.

Villa Santiago de Chacoma: Eulogio Choque and Valentín Atahuichi Callisaya, cantonal officer and community construction officer, interview, Villa Santiago de Chacoma, 11 October 1997.

National

Gonzalo Aguirre, congressional representative (MBL), interview, La Paz, 30 September 1997.

Joaquín Aramburo, Social Investment Fund regional director, interview, La Paz, 25 February 1997.

Eduardo Araujo, Social Investment Fund director of project implementation, interview, La Paz, 18 February 1997.

Rodolfo Araujo, coordination secretary, Ministry of the Presidency, interview, La Paz, 25 February 1997.

Rubén Ardalla, officer, Democratic Development and Citizen's Participation, interview, La Paz, 21 February 1997.

Ivan Arias, former Vice Minister for Municipal Development and Decentralization, interview, La Paz, 10 December 2007.

Percy Bacareza, information officer, National Secretariat of Rural Development, Ministry of Human Development, interview, La Paz, 2 October 1997.

Mauricio Balcázar, director of Encuestas y Estudios (polling company) and ex-minister of communications, interview, La Paz, 13 October 1997.

Amparo Ballivian, World Bank economist, interview, La Paz, 18 February 1997.

Franz Barrios, Indigenous Autonomies project (USAID), interview, La Paz, 3 December 2007.

Erika Brockmann, senator (MIR), interview, La Paz, 6 October 1997.

Fernando Cajías, ex-prefect (La Paz), interview, La Paz, 25 February 1997.

Ricardo Calla, researcher, interview, La Paz, 7 March 1997.

Jose Carlos Campero, Municipal Strengthening Project (USAID), interview, La Paz, 3 December 2007.

Carlos Carafa, Cosude (Swiss aid agency), interview, La Paz, 7 December 2007.

Viviana Caro, UDAPE subdirector, interview, La Paz, 4 December 2007.

Manuel Contreras, Catholic University Public Policy Program director, interview, La Paz, 5 March 1997.

Jorge Dockweiler, municipal councilman (La Paz), interview, La Paz, 5 November 1997.

Adhemar Esquivel, UDAPE health officer, interview, La Paz, 4 December 2007.

José Luis Evia, Primary Education Development Project (GTZ), interview, La Paz, 6 December 2007.

Juan Carlos Franco, Social Investment Fund regional director, interview, La Paz, 28 February 1997.

Luis González, Social Investment Fund departmental director, interview, La Paz, 5 March 1997.

Armando Godínez, anthropologist, numerous conversations, La Paz, February–May and September–November 1997.

George Gray-Molina (a), UDAPSO subdirector, interview, La Paz, 17 February 1997.

George Gray-Molina (b), former director of UDAPE, interview, La Paz, 30 November 2007.

George Gray-Molina(c), former director of UDAPE, personal communication, London, 3 December 2010.

Walter Guevara, director of the Democratic Development and Governance Projects (USAID), interview, La Paz, 3 December 2007.

Paulino Guarachi, subsecretary of rural development, Ministry of Human Development, interview, La Paz, 6 March 1997.

Enrique Ipiña, ex-minister of human development and ex-secretary of education, interview, La Paz, 26 February 1997.

Mauricio Lea Plaza, director of participative planning, Ministry of Human Development, interview, La Paz, 29 September 1997.

Alberto Leytón (a), director of public investment, Ministry of Economic Development, interview, La Paz, 6 May 1997.

Alberto Leytón (b), subsecretary of public investment, Ministry of Economic Development, interview, La Paz, 23 September 1997.

Eduardo Mac Lean, municipal adviser (La Paz), interview, La Paz, 21 February 1997.

Fernando Medina(a), subsecretary of popular participation, Ministry of Human Development, interview, La Paz, 5 May 1997.

Fernando Medina (b), subsecretary of popular participation, Ministry of Human Development, interview, La Paz, 25 September 1997.

Javier Medina, officer, Secretariat of Rural Development, interview, La Paz, 6 March 1997.

Sebastián Michel, local government expert, interview, La Paz, 4 December 2007.

Carlos Hugo Molina (a), secretary of popular participation, interview, La Paz, 10 March 1997.

Carlos Hugo Molina (b), ex-secretary of popular participation, interview, La Paz, 10 December 2007.

Rodney Pereira, UDAPE researcher and university professor, interview, La Paz, 25 February 1997.

Martin Perez, ex-Vice Minister of Decentralization, interview, La Paz, 11 December 2007.

Marcelo Rangel, ex-Vice Minister of Decentralization, interview, La Paz, 11 December 2007.

Javier Reyes, director of public investment, Ministry of Economic Development, interview, La Paz, 5 November 1997.

Gonzalo Rojas, director for investment and analysis, Secretariat of Popular Participation, interview, La Paz, 27 February 1997.

Salvador Romero, president of the National Electoral Court, interview, La Paz, 6 December 2007.

Freddy Teodovitch, senator, interview, La Paz, 6 November 1997.

José Antonio Terán, GTZ local government expert, interview, La Paz, 6 December 2007.

Carlos Toranzo, economist, ILDIS (research foundation), interview, La Paz, 3 March 1997.

Enrique Toro, ADN national chief, interview, La Paz, 16 October 1997.

Javier Torres Goitia, subsecretary of health, interview, La Paz, 13 October 1997.

David Tuchschneider(a), World Bank rural development officer, interview, La Paz, 14 February 1997.

David Tuchschneider (b), World Bank rural development officer, interview, La Paz, 3 May 1997.

David Tuchschneider (c), World Bank rural development officer, interview, La Paz, 3 December 2007.

Miguel Urioste, congressional representative and MBL party leader, interview, La Paz, 3 October 1997.

Jorge Urquidi, general adviser to the prefect, interview, La Paz, 13 October 1997.

Ivan Vidaure, director general of public investment, Vice Ministry of Public Investment and External Finance, interview, La Paz, 5 December 2007.

Masami Yamamori, IDB officer, interview, La Paz, 5 December 2007.

BIBLIOGRAPHY

Ahmad, E., and G. Brosio, eds. 2009. *Does Decentralization Enhance Service Delivery and Poverty Reduction?* Cheltenham: Edward Elgar.

Akin, J., P. Hutchinson, and K. Strumpf. 2005. "Decentralisation and Government Provision of Public Goods: The Public Health Sector in Uganda." *Journal of Development Studies* 41:1417–43.

Albó, X. 1990. *Los Guaraní-Chiriguano: La Comunidad Hoy.* La Paz: CIPCA.

Albó, X., A. Godínez, K. Libermann, and F. Pifarré. 1990. *Para Comprender Las Culturas Rurales en Bolivia.* 2nd ed. La Paz: MEC/CIPCA/UNICEF.

Alchian, A., and H. Demsetz. 1972. "Production, Information Costs, and Economic Organization." *American Economic Review* 62:777–95.

Alderman, H. 2002. "Do Local Officials Know Something We Don't? Decentralization of Targeted Transfers in Albania." *Journal of Public Economics* 83:375–404.

Alesina, A., and N. Roubini. 1992. "Political Cycles in OECD Economies." *Review of Economic Studies* 59:663–88.

Alt, J. E., and K. A. Shepsle, eds. 1990. *Perspectives on Positive Political Economy.* New York: Cambridge University Press.

Andersson, A., B. Harsman, and J. Quigley, eds. 1997. "Government for the Future: Unification, Fragmentation, and Regionalism." *Contributions to Economic Analysis,* 238. Amsterdam: Elsevier.

Antezana, E. L. 1979. *Proceso y Sentencia a la Reforma Agraria en Bolivia.* La Paz: Los Amigos del Libro.

Arce, T., and P. Rossell, eds. 1995. *Hacia Una Propuesta Indígena de Descentralización del Estado.* CPIB/CIDDEBENI. La Paz: Artes Gráficas Latina.

Ardaya, R. 1996. *La Construcción Municipal de Bolivia.* La Paz: Editora Ateneo.

Aristotle. 1996 [ca. 350 BC]. *The Politics and the Constitution of Athens.* Ed. S. Everson. Cambridge: Cambridge University Press.

Asthana, A. N. 2003. "Decentralisation and Supply Efficiency: The Case of Rural Water Supply in Central India." *Journal of Development Studies* 39:148–59.

Atkinson, A. B., and J. E. Stiglitz. 1980. *Lectures on Public Economics.* London: McGraw-Hill.

Austen-Smith, D., and J. Banks. 1989. "Electoral Accountability and Incumbency." In *Models of Strategic Choice in Politics,* ed. P. Ordeshook. Ann Arbor: University of Michigan Press.

Axelrod, R. 1984. *The Evolution of Cooperation.* New York: Basic Books.

Ayala Sánchez, M. A. 2009. "Capacitación de Gobernabilidad Democrática: Indicadores de Gobernabilidad Municipal." Powerpoint presentation. La Paz: UNDP.

Bahiigwa, G., D. Rigby, and P. Woodhouse. 2005. "Right Target, Wrong Mechanism? Agricultural Modernization and Poverty Reduction in Uganda." *World Development* 33:481–96.

Barankay, I., and B. Lockwood. 2007. "Decentralization and the Productive Efficiency of Government: Evidence from Swiss Cantons." *Journal of Public Economics* 91:1197–1218.

Bardhan, P. 1996. "The Economics of Decentralisation." Manuscript, University of California, Berkeley.

Bardhan, P. 2000. "The Nature of Institutional Impediments to Economic Development." In *A Not-So-Dismal Science: A Broader View of Economies and Societies,* ed. M. Olson and S. Kahkonen. New York: Oxford University Press.

Bardhan, P. 2001. "Notes on Decentralization." Manuscript, University of California, Berkeley.

Bardhan, P., and D. Mookherjee. 1998. "Expenditure Decentralization and the Delivery of Public Services in Developing Countries." Working Paper No. C98–104. Berkeley: Center for International and Development Economics Research, University of California, Berkeley.

Bardhan, P., and D. Mookherjee. 1999. "Relative Capture of Local and Central Governments: An Essay in the Political Economy of Decentralization." Manuscript, University of California, Berkeley.

Bardhan, P., and D. Mookherjee, eds. 2006. *Decentralization and Local Governance in Developing Countries: A Comparative Perspective.* Cambridge: MIT Press.

Batina, R. G., and T. Ihori. 2005. *Public Goods: Theories and Evidence.* New York: Springer.

Becker, G. 1983. "A Theory of Competition among Pressure Groups for Political Influence." *Quarterly Journal of Economics* 98:329–47.

Beer, C. 2003. *Electoral Competition and Institutional Change in Mexico.* Notre Dame: University of Notre Dame Press.

Bennett, R. J., ed. 1990. *Decentralization, Local Governments, and Markets: Towards a Post-Welfare Agenda.* Oxford: Clarendon Press.

Bentley, A. F. 1907. *The Process of Government.* Chicago: University of Chicago Press.

Ben-Zion, U., and Z. Eytan. 1974. "On Money, Votes, and Policy in a Democratic Society." *Public Choice* 17:1–10.

Bergstrom, T., and R. Goodman. 1973. "Private Demand for Public Goods." *American Economic Review* 63:280–96.

Besley, T., and A. Case. 1995a. "Does Electoral Accountability Affect Economic Policy Choices? Evidence from Gubernatorial Term Limits." *Quarterly Journal of Economics* 110:769–98.

Besley, T., and A. Case. 1995b. "Incumbent Behavior: Vote-Seeking, Tax-Setting, and Yardstick Competition." *American Economic Review* 85:25–45.

Besley, T., and S. Coate. 1991. "Public Provision of Private Goods and the Redistribution of Income." *American Economic Review* 81:979–84.

Besley, T., and S. Coate. 1995. "Efficient Policy Choice in a Representative Democracy: A Dynamic Analysis." Working Paper No. 95/10. Philadelphia: Center for Analytic Research in Economics and Social Science (CARESS), University of Pennsylvania.

Besley, T., and S. Coate. 1997. "An Economic Model of Representative Democracy." *Quarterly Journal of Economics* 112:85–114.

Besley, T., and S. Coate. 2003. "Centralized versus Decentralized Provision of Local Public Goods: A Political Economy Approach." *Journal of Public Economics* 87:2611–37.

Bewley, T. 1981. "A Critique of Tiebout's Theory of Local Public Expenditure." *Econometrica* 49:713–39.

Bird, R. 1994. "Decentralizing Infrastructure: For Good or Ill?" Policy Research Working Paper No. 1258. Washington, DC: World Bank.

Black, D. 1948. "On the Rationale of Group Decision Making." *Journal of Political Economy* 56:23–34.

Blair, H. 2000. "Participation and Accountability at the Periphery: Democratic Local Governance in Six Countries." *World Development* 28, no. 1: 21–39.

Blanchard, O., and A. Shleifer. 2000. "Federalism with and without Political Centralization: China versus Russia." NBER Working Paper No. 7616. Cambridge, MA: National Bureau of Economic Research.

Bolton, P., and J. Farrell. 1990. "Decentralization, Duplication, and Delay." *Journal of Political Economy* 98:803–26.

Boone, C. 2003. *Political Topographies of the African State: Territorial Authority and Institutional Choice.* Cambridge: Cambridge University Press.

Brady, H. E., S. Verba, and K. L. Schlozman. 1995. "Beyond SES: A Resource Model of Political Participation." *American Political Science Review* 89:271–94.

Brambor, T., W. R. Clark, and M. Golder. 2006. "Understanding Interaction Models: Improving Empirical Analyses." *Political Analysis* 14:63–82.

Brennan, G., and J. M. Buchanan. 1980. *The Power to Tax: Analytical Foundations of a Fiscal Constitution.* New York: Cambridge University Press.

Brennan, G., and J. M. Buchanan. 1984. "Voter Choice: Evaluating Political Alternatives." *American Behavioral Scientist* 28:185–201.

Breton, A., and G. Galeotti. 1985. "Is Proportional Representation Always the Best Electoral Rule?" *Public Finance* 40:1–16.

Brett, E. A. 1993a. "Participation Why & When? The Costs and Benefits of Democratic Processes." Manuscript, London School of Economics.

Brett, E. A. 1993b. "Voluntary Agencies as Development Organizations: Theorizing the Problem of Efficiency and Accountability." *Development and Change* 24:269–303.

Brett, E. A. 1995a. "Adjustment Policy and Institutional Reform in Uganda." In *Uganda: Landmarks in Rebuilding a Nation,* ed. E. A. Brett, J. Munene, J. Katorobo, and P. Langseth. Kampala: Fountain Press.

Brett, E. A. 1995b. "Creating the Basis for Democratic Transition in Uganda: The Problem of Governance." In *Uganda: Landmarks in Rebuilding a Nation,* ed. E. A. Brett, J. Munene, J. Katorobo, and P. Langseth. Kampala: Fountain Press.

Brosio, G. 2000. "Decentralization in Africa." Unpublished manuscript, IMF.

Buchanan, J. M., and R. D. Tollison, eds. 1984. *The Theory of Public Choice—II*. Ann Arbor: University of Michigan Press.

Burns, D., R. Hambleton, and P. Hogget. 1994. *The Politics of Decentralization: Revitalizing Local Government*. London: Macmillan.

Cajías de la Vega, F. 1996. *Competencias del Ejecutivo Municipal, del Consejo Municipal y de los Comites de Vigilancia*. La Paz: ILDIS—Friedrich Ebert Steifung.

Calderón, G. F., and R. Laserna. 1995. *Paradojas de la Modernidad*. La Paz: CERES—Fundación Milenio.

Campbell, T. 2001. *The Quiet Revolution: The Rise of Political Participation and Leading Cities with Decentralization in Latin America and the Caribbean*. Pittsburgh: University of Pittsburgh Press.

Casson, A., and K. Obidzinski. 2002. "From New Order to Regional Autonomy: Shifting Dynamics of 'Illegal' Logging in Kalimantan, Indonesia." *World Development* 30:2133–51.

Cebula, R. J. 1979. *The Determinants of Human Migration*. Lexington, MA: Lexington Books.

Cebula, R. J., and M. Z. Kafoglis. 1986. "A Note on the Tiebout-Tullock Hypothesis: The Period 1975–1980." *Public Choice* 48:65–69.

Cheema, G. S., and D. A. Rondinelli, eds. 1983. *Decentralization and Development: Policy Implementation in Developing Countries*. Beverly Hills: Sage.

Clague, C. 1997a. "The New Institutional Economics and Economic Development." In *Institutions and Economic Development: Growth and Governance in Less-Developed and Post-Socialist Countries,* ed. C. Clague. Baltimore: Johns Hopkins University Press.

Clague, C. 1997b. "The New Institutional Economics and Institutional Reform." In *Institutions and Economic Development: Growth and Governance in Less-Developed and Post-Socialist Countries,* ed. C. Clague. Baltimore: Johns Hopkins University Press.

Cleary, M. R. 2007. "Electoral Competition, Participation, and Government Responsiveness in Mexico." *American Journal of Political Science* 51, no. 2: 283–99.

Coase, R. 1937. "The Nature of the Firm." *Economica* 4:386–405.

Coase, R. 1960. "The Problem of Social Cost." *Journal of Law and Economics* 3:1–44.

Coleman, J. 1990. *Foundations of Social Theory*. Cambridge: Harvard University Press.

Condorcet, M. de. 1785. *Essai sur l'Application de l'Analyse à la Probabilité des Décisions rendues à la Pluraliste des Voix*. Paris, 1785.

Conyers, D. 1984. "Decentralization and Development: A Review of the Literature." *Public Administration and Development* 4:187–97.

Cooter, R. D. 2000. "Law from Order: Economic Development and the Jurisprudence of Social Norms." In *A Not-So-Dismal Science: A Broader View of Economies and Societies,* ed. M. Olson and S. Kahkonen. New York: Oxford University Press.

Corte Nacional Electoral (Dirección de Informática). 1995. *Estadística de Votación Absoluta: Elecciones Municipales de 1993 y 1995*. Database. La Paz.

Crespo, A. 1981. *Los Aramayo de Chichas: Tres Generaciones de Mineros Bolivianos.* Barcelona: Editorial Blume.

Crook, R. C., and J. Manor. 1994. "Enhancing Participation and Institutional Performance: Democratic Decentralization in South Asia and West Africa." London: Overseas Development Administration.

Crook, R.C., and A. S. Sverrisson. 1999. "To What Extent Can Decentralized Forms of Government Enhance the Development of Pro-Poor Policies and Improve Poverty-Alleviation Outcomes?" Manuscript.

Dahl, R. 1971. *Polyarchy: Participation and Opposition.* New Haven: Yale University Press.

Dahl, R. 1989. *Democracy and Its Critics.* New Haven: Yale.

Davis, O. A., M. H. DeGroot, and M. J. Hinich. 1972. "Social Preference Orderings and Majority Rule." *Econometrica* 40:147–57.

Devarajan, S., S. Shah, and S. Khemani. 2009. "The Politics of Partial Decentralization." In *Does Decentralization Enhance Service Delivery and Poverty Reduction?* ed. E. Ahmad and G. Brosio. Cheltenham: Edward Elgar.

Diamond, J. 1998. *Guns, Germs, and Steel: A Short History of Everybody for the Last 13,000 Years.* London: Vintage.

Diaz-Cayeros, A. 2006. *Federalism, Fiscal Authority, and Centralization in Latin America.* Cambridge: Cambridge University Press.

Dillinger, W., and S. B. Webb. 1999. "Decentralization and Fiscal Management in Colombia." Policy Research Working Paper No. 2122. Washington, DC: World Bank.

Dixit, A. 1995. "Common Agency and Incentives in Government Bureaucracies." Manuscript, Princeton University.

Dodgson, C. L. 1884. *The Principles of Parliamentary Representation.* London: Harrison.

Dowding, K., and P. John. 1994. "Tiebout: A Survey of the Empirical Literature." *Urban Studies* 31, no. 4–5: 767–97.

Downs, A. 1957. *An Economic Theory of Democracy.* New York: Harper and Row.

Dreze, J., and A. Sen. 1996. *India: Economic Development and Social Opportunity.* Delhi: Oxford University Press.

Dryzek, J. S. 1996. "Political Inclusion and the Dynamics of Decentralization." *American Political Science Review* 90:475–87.

Dunkerley, J. 1984. *Rebellion in the Veins: Political Struggle in Bolivia, 1952–82.* London: Verso.

Dunkerley, J. 1990. "Political Transition and Economic Stabilization: Bolivia, 1982–1989." London: Institute of Latin American Studies.

Eaton, K. 2004. *Politics Beyond the Capital: The Design of Subnational Institutions in South America.* Stanford: Stanford University Press.

Eaton, K. 2006. "Decentralization's Nondemocratic Roots: Authoritarianism and Subnational Reform in Latin America." *Latin American Politics and Society* 48:1–26.

Eaton, K., and T. Dickovick. 2004. "The Politics of Re-centralization in Argentina and Brazil." *Latin American Research Review* 39, no. 1: 90–122.

Ellis, F., and G. Bahiigwa. 2003. "Livelihoods and Rural Poverty Reduction in Uganda." *World Development* 31:997–1013.

Ellis, F., M. Kutengule, and A. Nyasulu. 2003. "Livelihoods and Rural Poverty Reduction in Malawi." *World Development* 31:1495–1510.

Ellis, F., and N. Mdoe. 2003. "Livelihoods and Rural Poverty Reduction in Tanzania." *World Development* 31:1367–84.

Eskeland, G., and D. Filmer. 2002. "Autonomy, Participation, and Learning in Argentine Schools: Findings and Their Implications for Decentralization." Working Paper No. 2766. Washington, DC: World Bank.

Estache, A., ed. 1995. "Decentralizing Infrastructure: Advantages and Limitations." World Bank Discussion Paper No. 290. Washington, DC: World Bank.

Estache, A., and S. Sinha. 1995. "Does Decentralization Increase Spending on Public Infrastructure?" Policy Research Working Paper No. 1457. Washington, DC: World Bank.

Faguet, J. P. 2004. "Does Decentralization Increase Responsiveness to Local Needs? Evidence from Bolivia." *Journal of Public Economics* 88, no. 4: 867–94.

Faguet, J. P. 2006. "Decentralizing Bolivia: Local Government in the Jungle." Chap. 4 in P. Bardhan and D. Mookherjee, eds., *Decentralization and Local Governance in Developing Countries: A Comparative Perspective*. Cambridge: MIT Press.

Faguet, J. P. 2008a. "Decentralization's Effects on Public Investment: Evidence and Policy Lessons from Bolivia and Colombia." *Journal of Development Studies* 44:1100–1121.

Faguet, J. P. 2008b. "The Determinants of Central vs. Local Government Investment: Democracy and Development in Bolivia." Chap. 7 in S. Ghosh and S. S. Mishra, eds., *Decentralization and Development*. Hyderabad, India: Icfai University Press.

Faguet, J. P. 2009a. "Governance from Below in Bolivia: A Theory of Local Government With Two Empirical Tests." *Latin American Politics and Society* 29, no. 4: 29–68.

Faguet, J. P. 2009b. "Mejorando la educación y la salud de los pobres: Descentralización y reformas de política en Colombia." *Perspectivas* 7, no. 1: 73–88.

Faguet, J. P., and Z. Ali. 2009. "Making Reform Work: Institutions, Dispositions, and the Improving Health of Bangladesh." *World Development* 37, no. 1: 208–18.

Faguet, J. P., and F. Sánchez. 2008. "Decentralization's Effects on Educational Outcomes in Bolivia and Colombia." *World Development* 36, no. 7: 1294–1316.

Finer, S. E. 1980. *The Changing British Party System, 1945–1979*. Washington, DC: American Enterprise Institute for Public Policy Research.

Finer, S. E. 1997. *The History of Government from the Earliest Times*. Oxford: Oxford University Press.

Fisman, R., and R. Gatti. 2000 . "Decentralization and Corruption: Evidence across Countries." Working Paper No. 2290. Washington, DC: World Bank.

Fiszbein, A. 1997. "The Emergence of Local Capacity: Lessons from Colombia." *World Development* 25:1029–43.

Francis, P., and R. James. 2003. "Balancing Rural Poverty Reduction and Citizen

Participation: The Contradictions of Uganda's Decentralization Program." *World Development* 31:325–37.

Galasso, E., and M. Ravallion. 2005. "Decentralized Targeting of an Antipoverty Program." *Journal of Public Economics* 89: 705–27.

Galiani, S., P. Gertler, and E. Schargrodsky. 2008. "School Decentralization: Helping the Good Get Better, but Leaving the Poor Behind." *Journal of Public Economics* 92:2106–20.

Gibbons, R. 1992. *A Primer in Game Theory.* Hemel Hempstead: Harvester Wheatsheaf.

Giddens, A. 1971. *Capitalism and Modern Social Theory.* Cambridge: Cambridge University Press.

Girishankar, N. 1998. "Reforming Institutions for Service Delivery: A Framework for Development Assistance with an Application to the Health, Nutrition, and Population Portfolio." Working Paper No. 2039. Washington, DC: World Bank.

Glaeser, E. 2011. *Triumph of the City: How Our Greatest Invention Makes Us Richer, Smarter, Greener, Healthier, and Happier.* New York: Penguin Press.

Gonzales-Arana, G. 1992. *El Proceso de Descentralisación Administrativa en Bolivia.* La Paz: Los Amigos del Libro.

Goodin, R. E. "Institutionalizing the Public Interest: The Defense of Deadlock and Beyond." *American Political Science Review* 90:331–43.

Government of Bolivia. 2009. *Political Constitution of the State.* La Paz: Government of Bolivia.

Government of Bolivia. 2010. *Framework Law of Autonomies and Decentralization.* La Paz: Government of Bolivia.

Gray Molina, G., and C. H. Molina. 1997. "Popular Participation and Decentralization in Bolivia: Building Accountability from the Grass Roots." Manuscript, La Paz.

Greene, W. 1997. *Econometric Analysis.* Upper Saddle River, NJ: Prentice-Hall.

Grindle, M. S. 2007. *Going Local: Decentralization, Democratization, and the Promise of Good Governance.* Princeton: Princeton University Press.

Gronn, P. 2010. "Leadership: Its Genealogy, Configuration, and Trajectory." *Journal of Educational Administration and History* 42, no. 4: 405–35.

Grupo DRU, Unidad de Investigación y Analisis, Secretaría Nacional de Participación Popular. 1996. *Participación Popular: Avances y Obstáculos.* Ed. G. Rojas. La Paz: CID.

Habibi, N., C. Huang, D. Miranda, V. Murillo, G. Ranis, M. Sarkar, and F. Stewart. 2003. "Decentralization and Human Development in Argentina." *Journal of Human Development* 4:73–101.

Hacker, J. S., and P. Pierson. 2010. *Winner-Take-All Politics: How Washington Made the Rich Richer—and Turned Its Back on the Middle Class.* New York: Simon and Schuster.

Hamilton, A. 2001 [1769–1804]. *Writings.* New York: Library of America.

Hanson, R. L., and J. T. Hartman. 1994. "Do Welfare Magnets Attract?" Madison: Institute for Research on Poverty, University of Wisconsin at Madison.

Hart, O. 1995. *Firms, Contracts, and Financial Structure*. New York: Oxford University Press.

Hart, O., and J. H. Moore. 1990. "Property Rights and the Theory of the Firm." *Journal of Political Economy* 98:1119–58.

Hartmann, F. 1998. "Land Reform and Social Capital, Their Roles in Social and Economic Development: A Case Study of Rural Bolivia." M.Sc. dissertation. London School of Economics.

Hayek, F. 1948 [1939]. "The Economic Conditions of Interstate Federalism." Reprinted in F. Hayek, *Individualism and Economic Order*. Chicago: University of Chicago Press.

Healey, K. 1987. *Caciques y Patrones: Una Experiencia de Desarrollo Rural en el Sud de Bolivia*. 3rd ed. Cochabamba: CERES.

Heckman, J., and J. Snyder. 1997. "Linear Probability Models of the Demand for Attributes with an Empirical Application to Estimating the Preferences of Legislators." *RAND Journal of Economics* 28:S142–89.

Hegel, G. W. F. 1996. *Philosophy of Right*. Trans. S. W. Dyde. Amherst: Prometheus Books.

Hirschman, A. O. 1970. *Exit, Voice, and Loyalty*. Cambridge: Harvard University Press.

Hiskey, J. T., and M. A. Seligson. 2003. "Pitfalls of Power to the People: Decentralization, Local Government Performance, and System Support in Bolivia." *Studies in Comparative International Development* 37, no. 4: 64–88.

Hobbes, T. 1996. *Leviathan*. Ed. R. Tuck. Cambridge: Cambridge University Press.

Hotelling, H. 1929. "Stability in Competition." *Economic Journal* 39:41–57.

Hoy. "Injertos Tramposos en 'Participación Popular.'" 19 January 1994.

Humplick, F., and A. Moini-Araghi. 1996. "Decentralized Structures for Providing Roads: A Cross-Country Comparison." Policy Research Working Paper No. 1658. Washington, DC: World Bank.

Huther, J., and A. Shah. 1998. "Applying a Simple Measure of Good Governance to the Debate on Fiscal Decentralization." Policy Research Working Paper No. 1894. Washington, DC: World Bank.

Inman, R. P. 1979. "The Fiscal Performance of Local Governments: An Interpretative Review." In *Current Issues in Urban Economics*, ed. P. Mieszkowski and M. Straszheim. Baltimore: Johns Hopkins University Press.

Inman, R. P., and D. L. Rubinfeld. 1997. "Rethinking Federalism." *Journal of Economic Perspectives* 11:43–64.

Instituto Nacional de Estadística. 1992. *Censo Nacional de Población y Vivenda*. La Paz: INE.

Instituto Nacional de Estadística. 2001. *Censo Nacional de Población y Vivenda*. La Paz: INE.

Instituto Nacional de Estadística. 2010. "Municipal Population Projections by Sex." La Paz: INE. Accessed on 10 September at http://www.ine.gov.bo/indice/visualizador.aspx?ah=PC20407.HTM.

Interministerial Transition Plan for the Guaraní People. 2010. "El resurgimiento del

Pueblo Guaraní en la APG." Government of Bolivia. Webpage accessed 17 September at http://www.planguarani.com/pages/apg.php.

Jackson, J. E. 1991. *A User's Guide to Principal Components.* New York: John Wiley and Sons.

Jin, H., Y. Qian, and B. R. Weingast. 2005. "Regional Decentralization and Fiscal Incentives: Federalism, Chinese Style." *Journal of Public Economics* 89:1719–42.

Johnson, C., P. Deshingkar, and D. Start. 2005. "Grounding the State: Devolution and Development in India's Panchayats." *Journal of Development Studies* 41:937–70.

Jones, M. P., P. Sanguinetti, and M. Tommasi. 2000. "Politics, Institutions, and Fiscal Performance in a Federal System: An Analysis of the Argentine Provinces." *Journal of Development Economics* 61, no. 2: 305–33.

King, G., R. Keohane, and S. Verba. 1994. *Designing Social Inquiry: Scientific Inquiry in Qualitative Research.* Princeton: Princeton University Press.

Kitschelt, H. 2000. "Linkages between Citizens and Politicians in Democratic Polities." *Comparative Political Studies* 33:845–79.

Klein, H. 1982. *Bolivia—The Evolution of a Multi-ethnic Society.* Oxford: Oxford University Press.

Klein, H. 1993. *Historia de Bolivia.* La Paz: Libreria-Editorial Juventud.

Kramer, G. H. 1973. "On a Class of Equilibrium Conditions for Majority Rule." *Econometrica* 41:285–97.

Kubal, M. R. 2006. "Contradictions and Constraints in Chile's Health Care and Education Decentralization." *Latin American Politics and Society* 48:105–35.

Laffont, J. J., and W. Zantman. 2002. "Information Acquisition, Political Game, and the Delegation of Authority." *European Journal of Political Economy* 18:407–28.

Lamas, A. 2009. "La Gobernabilidad en el Municipio de Viacha." Powerpoint presentation. Viacha: Municipality of Viacha, Bolivia.

La Razon. "La Declaratoria de Guerra del Primer Mandatario." 27 January 1994.

La Razon. "Participación Popular: Se Democratiza la Corrupción?" 6 March 1994.

Lazarte, J. 1990. *Bolivia: Certeza e Incertidumbres de la Democracia.* Cochabamba: CERES.

Lichbach, M. 1994. "What Makes Rational Peasants Revolutionary? Dilemma, Paradox, and Irony in Peasant Collective Action." *World Politics* 46:383–418.

Litvack, J., J. Ahmad, and R. Bird. 1998. *Rethinking Decentralization in Developing Countries.* Washington, DC: World Bank.

Loboguerrero, A. 2008. "Decentralization in Colombia: Why Do Localities Respond to Fiscal Transfers in a Different Way?" PhD dissertation, University of California at Los Angeles.

Lowery, D., and V. Gray. 1998. "The Dominance of Institutions in Interest Representation: A Test of Seven Explanations." *American Journal of Political Science* 42:231–55.

Maddala, G. S. 1977. *Econometrics.* New York: McGraw-Hill.

Madison, J., A. Hamilton, and J. Jay. 1961 [1788]. *The Federalist Papers.* New York: New American Library.

Malloy, J. M., and R. S. Thorn, eds. 1971. *Beyond the Revolution: Bolivia since 1952.* Pittsburgh: University of Pittsburgh Press.

Manor, J. 1997. Lecture given at "Technical Consultation on Decentralization for Rural Development." Rome, 16–18 December 1997.

Manor, J. 1999. *The Political Economy of Democratic Decentralization.* Washington, DC: World Bank.

Marlow, M. 1988. "Fiscal Decentralization and Government Size." *Public Choice* 56:259–69.

Martinez-Vazquez, J., and R. McNab. 2003. "Fiscal Decentralization and Economic Growth." *World Development* 31, no. 9: 1597–1616.

Medina, J., ed. 1994. *Arakuarenda: Un Centro Intercultural de Capacitación Para el Desarrollo Guaraní.* La Paz: Arakuarenda/FIS.

Mello, L. de. 2000. "Can Fiscal Decentralization Strengthen Social Capital?" IMF Working Paper No. WP/00/129. Washington, DC: International Monetary Fund.

Migdal, J. S., A. Kohli, and V. Shue. 1994. *State Power and Social Forces.* Cambridge: Cambridge University Press.

Mill, J. S. 1993 [1895–61]. *Utilitarianism; On Liberty; Considerations on Representative Government; Remarks on Bentham's Philosophy.* Ed. G. Williams. London: Everyman.

Ministerio de la Presidencia. 1997. *Comportamiento Electoral de la Población Boliviana 1993–1997.* La Paz: W Producciones SRL.

Minkler, C. 2010. "Has Decentralization's Potential to Improve Government Responsiveness, Effectiveness, and Efficiency Been Greatly Exaggerated?" DV431 essay, London School of Economics.

Moe, T. M. 1984. "The New Economics of Organization." *American Journal of Political Science* 28:739–77.

Moe, T. M. 1989. "The Politics of Bureaucratic Structure." In *Can the Government Govern?,* ed. J. E. Chubb and P. E. Petersen. Washington, DC: Brookings Institution.

Moe, T. M. 1995. "The Politics of Structural Choice: Toward a Theory of Public Bureaucracy." In *Organizational Theory: From Chester Barnard to the Present and Beyond,* ed. O. E. Williamson. Expanded ed. New York: Oxford University Press.

Molina Monasterios, F. 1997. *Historia de la Participación Popular.* La Paz: Ministerio de Desarrollo Humano—Secretaría Nacional de Participación Popular.

Montero, A. P., and D. J. Samuels, eds. 2004. *Decentralization and Democracy in Latin America.* Notre Dame: University of Notre Dame Press.

Montesquieu, Baron de (C de Secondat). 1989 [1748]. *The Spirit of the Laws.* Trans. A. M. Cohler, B. C. Miller, and H. Stone. Cambridge: Cambridge University Press.

Mueller, D. 1989. *Public Choice II.* Cambridge: Cambridge University Press.

Musgrave, R. A. 1959. *The Theory of Public Finance.* New York: McGraw-Hill.

Narayan, D., and K. Ebbe. 1997. "Design of Social Funds—Participation, Demand Orientation, and Local Organizational Capacity." Discussion Paper No. 375. Washington, DC: World Bank.

Narayan, D., and L. Pritchett. 1997. "Cents and Sociability: Household Income and Social Capital in Rural Tanzania." Policy Research Working Paper No. 1796. Washington, DC: World Bank.

Nickson, R. A. 1995. *Local Government in Latin America*. Boulder: L. Rienner.

Niemi, R. G. 1969. "Majority Decision-Making with Partial Unidimensionality." *American Political Science Review* 63:488–97.

Niskanen, W. A., Jr. 1971. *Bureaucracy and Representative Government*. Chicago: Aldine-Atherton.

North, D. C. 1990. *Institutions, Institutional Change, and Economic Performance*. Cambridge: Cambridge University Press.

North, D. C. 1994. "Economic Performance through Time." *American Economic Review* 84:359–68.

Oates, W. 1972. *Fiscal Federalism*. New York: Harcourt Brace.

Oates, W. 1985. "Searching for Leviathan: An Empirical Study." *American Economic Review* 75:748–57.

Oliveira, J. A. P. de. 2002. "Implementing Environmental Policies in Developing Countries through Decentralization: The Case of Protected Areas in Bahia, Brazil." *World Development* 30:1713–36.

Oliver, J. E. 1999. "The Effects of Metropolitan Economic Segregation on Local Civic Participation." *American Journal of Political Science* 43:186–212.

Olson, M. 1965. *The Logic of Collective Action*. Cambridge: Harvard University Press.

Olson, M. 1982. *The Rise and Decline of Nations*. New Haven: Yale University Press.

Olson, M. 1997. "The New Institutional Economics and Economic Development." In *Institutions and Economic Development: Growth and Governance in Less-Developed and Post-Socialist Countries*, ed. C. Clague. Baltimore: Johns Hopkins University Press.

Olson, M. 2000a. "Big Bills Left on the Sidewalk: Why Some Nations Are Rich, and Others Poor." In *A Not-So-Dismal Science: A Broader View of Economies and Societies*, ed. M. Olson and S. Kahkonen. New York: Oxford University Press.

Olson, M. 2000b. *Power and Prosperity: Outgrowing Communist and Capitalist Dictatorships*. New York: Basic Books.

Olson, M., and S. Kahkonen. 2000. "Introduction: The Broader View." In *A Not-So-Dismal Science: A Broader View of Economies and Societies*, ed. M. Olson and S. Kahkonen. New York: Oxford University Press.

Ostrom, E., R. B. Parks, and G. P. Whitaker. 1977. *Policing Metropolitan America*. Washington, DC: U.S. Government Printing Office.

Ostrom, E., R. B. Parks, and G. P. Whitaker. 1978. *Patterns of Metropolitan Policing*. Cambridge, MA: Ballinger.

Ostrom, E., L. Schroeder, and S. Wynne. 1993. *Institutional Incentives and Sustainable Development: Infrastructure Policies in Perspective*. Boulder: Westview.

Ostrom, E., and G. P. Whitaker. 1973. "Does Local Community Control of Police Make a Difference? Some Preliminary Findings." *American Journal of Political Science* 17:48–76.

Ostrom, E., and G. P. Whitaker. 1974. "Community Control and Governmental Responsiveness: The Case of Police in Black Neighborhoods." In *Improving the Quality of Urban Management*, ed. D. Rogers and W. Hawley. Urban Affairs Annual Reviews vol. 8. Beverly Hills: Sage.

Pagaran, L. N. 1999. "The Social Fund, the Local Development Fund, and Decentralization: The Case of Cambodia." Manuscript, Massachusetts Institute of Technology.

Palda, K. F., and K. S. Palda. 1985. "Ceilings on Campaign Spending: Hypothesis and Partial Test with Canadian Data." *Public Choice* 45:313–31.

Pande, R. 1999. "Minority Representation and Policy Choices: The Significance of Legislator Identity." Development Economics Discussion Paper No. 16. London: STICERD, London School of Economics.

Parker, A. 1995. "Decentralization: The Way Forward for Rural Development?" Policy Research Working Paper No. 1475. Washington, DC: World Bank.

Parry, T. R. 1997. "Achieving Balance in Decentralization: A Case Study of Education Decentralization in Chile." *World Development* 25:211–25.

Persson, T., G. Roland, and G. Tabellini. 1997. "Separation of Powers and Political Accountability." Working Paper No. 136. Munich: Center for Economic Studies, University of Munich.

Persson, T., and G. Tabellini. 1996. "Federal Fiscal Constitutions: Risk Sharing and Redistribution." *Journal of Political Economy* 104:979–1009.

Persson, T., and G. Tabellini. 2002. "Political Economics and Public Finance." Chap. 24 in A. J. Auerbach and M. Feldstein, eds., *Handbook of Public Economics*, vol. 3, no. 3. Amsterdam: Elsevier.

Petro, N. N. 2001. "Creating Social Capital in Russia: The Novgorod Model." *World Development* 29:229–44.

Pifarré, F. 1989. *Los Guaraní-Chiriguano: Historia de un Pueblo.* La Paz: CIPCA.

Piketty, T. 1994. "Information Aggregation through Voting and Vote-Trading." Manuscript, Cambridge, MA.

Piketty, T. 1995. "Voting as Communicating." Manuscript, Cambridge, MA.

Piketty, T., and D. Spector. 1995. "Rational Debate Leads to One-Dimensional Conflict." Manuscript, Cambridge, MA.

Piriou-Sall, S. 1998. "Decentralization and Rural Development: A Review of Evidence." Manuscript, Washington, DC.

Pommerehne, W. W., and F. Schneider. 1978. "Fiscal Illusion, Political Institutions, and Local Public Spending." *Kyklos* 31:381–408.

Poole, K. T., and T. Romer. 1985. "Patterns of Political Action Committee Contributions to the 1980 Campaigns for the United States House of Representatives." *Public Choice* 47:63–111.

Porter, G. 2002. "Living in a Walking World: Rural Mobility and Social Equity Issues in Sub-Saharan Africa." *World Development* 30:285–300.

Presencia. "Arrogancia Insultante." 27 February 1994.

Presencia. "Los vecinos viacheños marchan hoy para que se vaya su Alcalde." 22 March 1997.

Proudhon, P. J. 1979 [1863]. *Du Principe Fédératif et de la Nécessité de Reconstituer le*

Parti de la Révolution. Trans. Richard Vernon. Toronto: University of Toronto Press.

Prud'homme, R. 1995. "On the Dangers of Decentralization." *World Bank Research Observer* 10:210–26.

Putnam, R. D. 1993. *Making Democracy Work: Civic Traditions in Modern Italy.* Princeton: Princeton University Press.

Putnam, R. D. 2000. *Bowling Alone: The Collapse and Revival of American Community.* New York: Simon and Schuster.

Rao, V., and M. Woolcock. 2003. "Integrating Qualitative and Quantitative Approaches in Program Evaluation." Chap. 8 in F. Bourguignon and L. A. Pereira da Silva, eds., *The Impact of Economic Policies on Poverty and Income Distribution: Evaluation Techniques and Tools.* New York: Oxford University Press and The World Bank.

Reflejos de la Semana. 1994. "Participación Popular: Se Cierne La Tormenta." *Reflejos de la Semana* 368 (14–21 January).

Rejas, S. J. 1992. *El Campesinado y su Insercion en el Mercado.* Cuzco: Centro de Estudios Regionales Andinos "Bartolome de las Casas."

Riker, W. H. 1964. *Federalism: Origin, Operation, Significance.* Boston: Little, Brown.

Riker, W. H., and P. C. Ordeshook. 1973. *An Introduction to Positive Political Theory.* Englewood Cliffs: Prentice-Hall.

Roca, J. L. 1990. *Fisonomía del Regionalismo Boliviano.* La Paz: Los Amigos del Libro.

Rodden, J. A. 2003. "Federalism and Bailouts in Brazil." In *Fiscal Decentralization and the Challenge of Hard Budget Constraints,* ed. J. A. Rodden, G. S. Eskeland, and J. Litvack. Cambridge: MIT Press.

Rodden, J. A. 2006. *Hamilton's Paradox: The Promise and Peril of Fiscal Federalism.* Cambridge: Cambridge University Press.

Rodden, J. A., G. S. Eskeland, and J. Litvack. 2003. *Fiscal Decentralization and the Challenge of Hard Budget Constraints.* Cambridge: MIT Press.

Rodriguez, O. G. 1993. *Poder Central y Proyecto Regional: Cochabamba y Santa Cruz en los Siglos XIX y XX.* La Paz: IDAES—ILDIS.

Rodríguez-Pose, A., and A. Bwire. 2004. "The Economic (In)efficiency of Devolution." *Environment and Planning A* 36, no. 11: 1907–28.

Rodríguez-Pose, A., and N. Gill. 2004. "Reassessing Relations between the Centre and the States: The Challenge for the Brazilian Administration." *Regional Studies* 38:833–44.

Rojas, G. 2009. *Cultura Política de las Élites en Bolivia (1982–2005).* La Paz: Fundación Friedrich Ebert and CIPCA.

Rojas, G., and L. Verdesoto. 1997. *La Participación Popular como Reforma de la Política: Evidencia de una Cultura Democrática Boliviana.* La Paz: Muela de Diablo.

Roland, G. 2000. *Transition and Economics: Politics, Markets, and Firms.* Cambridge, MA: MIT Press.

Rondinelli, D. A. 1981. "Government Decentralization in Comparative Perspective: Theory and Practice in Developing Countries." *International Review of Administrative Sciences* 47:133–45.

Rondinelli, D. A. 1990. "Decentralization, Territorial Power, and the State: A Critical Response." *Development and Change* 21:491–500.

Rondinelli, D. A., G. S. Cheema, and J. Nellis. 1983. "Decentralization in Developing Countries: A Review of Recent Experience." World Bank Staff Working Paper No. 581. Washington, DC: World Bank.

Rondinelli, D. A., J. S. McCullough, and R. W. Johnson. 1989. "Analysing Decentralization Policies in Developing Countries: A Political Economy Framework." *Development and Change* 20:57–87.

Rousseau, J. J. 1964 [1750, 1754]. *The First and Second Discourses.* Ed. R. D. Masters, trans. R. D. Masters and J. R. Masters. New York: St. Martin's Press.

Rousseau, J. J. 1978 [1762]. *On the Social Contract.* Ed. R. D. Masters, trans. J. R. Masters. New York: St. Martin's Press.

Rowland, A. M. 2001. "Population as a Determinant of Local Outcomes under Decentralization: Illustrations from Small Municipalities in Bolivia and Mexico." *World Development* 29:1373–89.

Rubinfeld, D. 1987. "The Economics of the Local Public Sector." In *Handbook of Public Economics,* ed. A. Auerbach and M. Feldstein. Oxford: North-Holland.

Rubinfeld, D., P. Shapiro, and J. Roberts. 1987. "Tiebout Bias and the Demand for Local Public Schooling." *Review of Economics and Statistics* 69:426–37.

Ruiz, F., and B. Giussani. 1997. "La Descentralización y el Financiamiento de la Provisión de Servicios de Educación y Salud en Bolivia." Manuscript, La Paz.

Samoff, J. 1990. "Decentralization: The Politics of Interventionism." *Development and Change* 21:513–30.

Schlesinger, J. A. 1984. "On the Theory of Party Organization." *Journal of Politics* 46:369–400.

Schumpeter, J. A. 1950. *Capitalism, Socialism, and Democracy.* 3rd ed. New York: Harper and Row.

Seabright, P. 1996. "Accountability and Decentralisation in Government: An Incomplete Contracts Model." *European Economic Review* 40:61–89.

Secretaría Nacional de Inversión Pública y Financiamento Externo. 1997. *Censo Municipal.* La Paz.

Secretaría Nacional de Participación Popular, Ministerio de Desarrollo Sostenible y Medio Ambiente. 1994. *Ley de Participación Popular, Reglamento de las Organizaciones Territoriales de Base.* La Paz.

Secretaría Nacional de Participación Popular, Ministerio de Desarrollo Sostenible y Medio Ambiente. 1997. *Matriz Resumen de las Auditorías SAYCO Practicadas en Gobiernos Municipales Categoría "C" (Pob. Mayor a 15,000 y Menor a 50,000 Hab.) Efectuados a la Fecha.* La Paz.

Selbin, E. 1993. *Modern Latin American Revolutions.* Boulder: Westview.

Sen, A. 1995. "Rationality and Social Choice." *American Economic Review* 85:1–24.

Shah, A. 1994. "The Reform of Inter-Governmental Fiscal Relations in Developing and Emerging Market Economies." Policy and Research Series Paper No. 23. Washington, DC: World Bank.

Shah, A. 1998a. "Balance, Accountability, and Responsiveness: Lessons about Decentralization." Policy Research Working Paper No. 2021. Washington, DC: World Bank.

Shah, A. 1998b. "Fiscal Federalism and Macroeconomic Governance: For Better or for Worse?" Policy Research Working Paper No. 2005. Washington, DC: World Bank.

Shah, A., T. Thompson, and H. F. Zou. 2004. "The Impact of Decentralization on Service Delivery, Corruption, Fiscal Management, and Growth in Developing and Emerging Market Economies: A Synthesis of Empirical Evidence." CESifo DICE Report, 1/2004: 10–14.

Shankar, R., and A. Shah. 2003. "Bridging the Economic Divide within Countries: A Scorecard on the Performance of Regional Policies in Reducing Regional Income Disparities." *World Development* 31:1421–41.

Shepsle, K. A. 1979. "Institutional Arrangements and Equilibrium in Multidimensional Voting Models." *American Journal of Political Science* 23:27–59.

Shepsle, K. A. 1986. "Institutional Equilibrium and Equilibrium Institutions." In *Political Science: The Science of Politics,* ed. H. Weisberg. New York: Agathon Press.

Simon, H. 1957. *Administrative Behavior.* 2nd ed. New York: Macmillan.

Slater, D. 1989. "Territorial Power and the Peripheral State: The Issue of Decentralization." *Development and Change* 20:501–31.

Smith, B. C. 1985. *Decentralization: The Territorial Dimension of the State.* London: George Allen and Unwin.

Smoke, P. 2001. "Fiscal Decentralization in Developing Countries: A Review of Current Concepts and Practice." Democracy, Governance, and Human Rights Programme Paper No. 2. Geneva: UNRISD.

Solnick, S. L. 1996. "The Breakdown of Hierarchies in the Soviet Union and China." *World Politics* 48:209–38.

Tanzi, V. 1995. "Fiscal Federalism and Decentralization: A Review of Some Efficiency and Macroeconomic Aspects." Annual World Bank Conference on Development Economics. Washington, DC: World Bank.

Tarrow, S. 1996. "Making Social Science Work across Space and Time: A Critical Reflection on Robert Putnam's *Making Democracy Work.*" *American Political Science Review* 90:389–97.

Tendler, J. 1997. *Good Government in the Tropics.* Baltimore: Johns Hopkins University Press.

Ticona Alejo, E., and X. Albó. 1997. *Jesús de Machaqa: La Marka Rebelde 3. La Lucha Por el Poder Comunal.* La Paz: CIPCA/CEDOIN.

Ticona Alejo, E., G. Rojas, and X. Albó. 1995. *Votos y Wiphalas: Campesinos y Pueblos Originarios en Democracia.* La Paz: Fundación Milenio-CIPCA.

Tiebout, C. M. 1956. "A Pure Theory of Local Expenditures." *Journal of Political Economy* 64:416–24.

Tocqueville, A. de. 1994 [1835–40]. *Democracy in America.* Ed. P. Bradley, trans. H. Reeve. London: Everyman's Library.

Toranzo, C. F. 1994. *Reflexiones sobre la Descentralización.* La Paz: ILDIS-PROADE.

Toranzo, C. F., and J. L. Exeni, eds. 1994. *Las IPDS (Instituciones Privadas de Des-*

arrollo Social) y la Descentralización: Una Relación Necesaria. La Paz: NOVIB-Bolivia and ILDIS.

Treisman, D. 1999. "Political Decentralization and Economic Reform: A Game-Theoretic Analysis." *American Journal of Political Science* 43:488–517.

Treisman, D. 2007. *The Architecture of Government: Rethinking Political Decentralization*. New York: Cambridge University Press.

Truman, D. 1951. *The Governmental Process: Political Interests and Public Opinion*. New York: Knopf.

Tsebelis, G. 2002. *Veto Players: How Political Institutions Work*. New York: Russell Sage Foundation; Princeton: Princeton University Press.

Tuchschneider, D. 1996. "Una Visión desde la Planificación Participativa Municipal." In Grupo DRU, UIA-SNPP, *Participación Popular: Avances y Obstáculos*, ed. G. Rojas. La Paz: CID.

Tullock, G. 1965. *The Politics of Bureaucracy*. Washington, DC: Public Affairs Press.

Unidad de Comunicación, Secretaría Nacional de Participación Popular. 1995. *Debate Nacional sobre la Ley de Participación Popular*. La Paz: Secretaría Nacional de Participación Popular.

United Nations Development Program (UNDP). 1993. *Informe Sobre Desarrollo Humano 1993*. Madrid: CIDEAL.

U.S. Census Bureau. 2002a. "Census Bureau Reports Number of Local Governments Nears 88,000." Press release. Accessed 4 October 2009 at http://www.census.gov/Press-Release/www/releases/archives/governments/000410.html.

U.S. Census Bureau. 2002b. *2002 Census of Governments*. Washington, DC: U.S. Government Printing Office.

U.S. Census Bureau. 2009. US Population Clock. Accessed 4 October at http://www.census.gov.

Van Zyl, J., T. Barbosa, A. N. Parker, and L. Sonn. 1995. "Decentralized Rural Development and Enhanced Community Participation: A Case Study from Northeast Brazil." Policy Research Working Paper No. 1498. Washington, DC: World Bank.

Varian, H. 1992. *Microeconomic Analysis*. 3rd ed. New York: W. W. Norton.

Varian, H. 1994. "Sequential Contributions to Public Goods." *Journal of Public Economics* 53:165–86.

Verba, S., K. Lehman, H. Brady, and N. H. Nie. 1993. "Citizen Activity: Who Participates? What Do They Say?" *American Political Science Review* 87:303–18.

Verba, S., K. L. Schlozman, and H. E. Brady. 1996. *Voice and Equality*. Cambridge: Harvard University Press.

Vieira, P. 1967. "Toward a Theory of Decentralization: A Comparative View of Forty-Five Countries." PhD dissertation. University of Southern California, Los Angeles. Cited in D. Rondinelli, G. S. Cheema, and J. Nellis, "Decentralization in Developing Countries: A Review of Recent Experience." World Bank Staff Working Paper No. 581. Washington, DC: World Bank, 1983.

Wade, N. 2006. *Before the Dawn: Recovering the Lost History of Our Ancestors*. New York: Penguin.

Wallis, J. J., and W. E. Oates. 1988. "Decentralization in the Public Sector: An Empirical Study of State and Local Government." In *Fiscal Federalism Quantitative Studies*, ed. H. Rosen. Chicago: University of Chicago Press.

Warren, D. M. 1991. "Using Indigenous Knowledge in Agricultural Development." Discussion Paper No. 127. Washington, DC: World Bank.

Webb, S. B. 2003. "Argentina: Hardening the Provincial Budget Constraint." In *Fiscal Decentralization and the Challenge of Hard Budget Constraints*, ed. J. A. Rodden, G. S. Eskeland, and J. Litvack. Cambridge: MIT Press.

Weingast, B. R. 1993. "Constitutions as Governance Structures." *Journal of Institutional and Theoretical Economics* 149:286–311.

Weingast, B. R. 1995. "The Economic Role of Political Institutions: Market-Preserving Federalism and Economic Development." *Journal of Law, Economics, and Organization* 11:1–31.

Wibbels, E. 2005. *Federalism and the Market: Intergovernmental Conflict and Economic Reform in the Developing World*. Cambridge: Cambridge University Press.

Wildasin, D. E. 1998. "Fiscal Aspects of Evolving Federations: Issues for Policy and Research." Policy Research Working Paper No. 1884. Washington, DC: World Bank.

Williamson, O. E. 1994. "Institutions and Economic Organization: The Governance Perspective." Annual World Bank Conference on Development Economics. Washington, DC: World Bank.

Williamson, O. E., ed. 1995. *Organizational Theory: From Chester Barnard to the Present and Beyond*. Expanded edition. New York: Oxford University Press.

Williamson, O. E. 2000. "Economic Institutions and Development: A View from the Bottom." In *A Not-So-Dismal Science: A Broader View of Economies and Societies*, ed. M. Olson and S. Kahkonen. New York: Oxford University Press.

Wilson, J. Q. 1961. "The Economy of Patronage." *Journal of Political Economy* 69:369–80.

Wilson, J. Q. 1973. *Political Organizations*. New York: Basic Books.

Woller, G. M., and K. Phillips. 1998. "Fiscal Decentralisation and LDC Economic Growth: An Empirical Investigation." *Journal of Development Studies* 34:139–48.

Wolman, H. 1990. "Decentralization: What It Is and Why We Should Care." In *Decentralization, Local Governments, and Markets: Towards a Post-Welfare Agenda*, ed. R. J. Bennett. Oxford: Clarendon Press.

Woodhouse, P. 2003. "African Enclosures: A Default Mode of Development." *World Development* 31:1705–20.

World Bank. 1987. "Bolivia: Emergency Social Fund Project." Staff Appraisal Report. Washington, DC: World Bank.

World Bank. 1991. "Bolivia: Second Structural Adjustment Credit." Staff Appraisal Report. Washington, DC: World Bank.

World Bank. 1993a. "Bolivia: Education Reform Project." Staff Appraisal Report. Washington, DC: World Bank.

World Bank. 1993b. "Bolivia: Social Investment Fund Project." Staff Appraisal Report. Washington, DC: World Bank.

World Bank. 1994a. "Bolivia: Integrated Child Development Project." Staff Appraisal Report. Washington, DC: World Bank.

World Bank. 1994b. *World Development Report: Infrastructure for Development.* New York: Oxford University Press.

World Bank. 1995. "Colombia Local Government Capacity: Beyond Technical Assistance." World Bank Report 14085-C. Washington, DC: World Bank.

World Bank. 1997. *World Development Report: The State in a Changing World.* New York: Oxford University Press.

World Bank. 1999. "Decentralization and Accountability of the Public Sector." *Proceedings of the Annual World Bank Conference on Development in Latin America and the Caribbean.* Washington, DC: World Bank.

World Bank. 2000a. *World Development Report: Entering the 21st Century.* New York: Oxford University Press.

World Bank. 2000b. "Decentralization Toolkit." Manuscript, Washington, DC.

Zax, J. S. 1989. "Initiatives and Government Expenditures." *Public Choice* 63:267–77

Zuazo, M. 2009. *¿Cómo Nació el MAS? La Ruralización de la Política en Bolivia. Entrevistas a 85 Parlamentarios del Partido.* La Paz: Fundación Friedrich Ebert.

INDEX

Note: Page numbers in italics denote tables or figures